SURVIVING
The Vietnam War & Its Aftermath

*This memoir is respectfully
dedicated to the souls of our parents
and our dearly departed friends,
whose love and sacrifices saved us
during the darkest days of our lives.*

*And to our children and
grandchildren, for whose sake we
lived to tell our tale.*

SURVIVING
THE VIETNAM WAR & ITS AFTERMATH

A MEMOIR
OF LOVE
& TERROR

by **DUONG PHUC & VU THANH THUY**
and AN DUONG
Translatation by JAMES BANERIAN

SH PUBLISHING

SURVIVING The Vietnam War & Its Aftermath
A Memoir of Love and Terror
Authors:
DUONG PHUC & VU THANH THUY
and AN DUONG
Translator:
JAMES BANERIAN
Designer:
DINH TIEN LUYEN
Publisher:
SH PUBLISHING

Photo sources: In addition to the personal source, we have used
a number of documentary photos published by the former
Republic of Vietnam and the United Nations, and some public domains.
The use was simply to confirm the authenticity of our stories.

CONTENTS

PREFACE

We began the first lines of this memoir in November 1979 on a boat heading to Thailand. Our family of four was among the 157 Vietnamese asylum seekers rescued by members of the United Nations High Commissioner for Refugees (UNHCR) from an island called Koh Kra in the Gulf of Thailand. We were on our way to a refugee camp in the province of Songkhla.

In a small school notebook given to us by Theodore Schweitzer III, a UNHCR field officer, we hastily jotted down a timeline of the events of our journey on the seas, followed by twenty-one days as captives of the Thai pirates on Koh Kra, a place that might have been a paradise but for the atrocities we experienced there.

In the days and months that followed in the refugee camp and when we reached the United States, we continued to write down all we could remember before time and the burden of surviving in a new land gradually eroded our memories of this period of intensely mixed fortunes. These have now been brought together in the book you are holding in your hands.

We are reporters, not fiction writers. We simply and honestly record the facts of what we heard and saw firsthand on the battlefront, in the communist re-education camps, and on the open sea. Sometimes the truth surpasses anything in the human imagination.

We truthfully present everything–episodes of stark, unbearable terror along with strange, unbelievable turns of fortune; the worst of human flaws as well as acts of kindness suddenly performed by the most despicable of people–to balance fairly the good and bad that can be found in human beings. We attempt to declare the mystery of life and the human heart that gives birth to hope even when fortune and misfortune become unexpectedly mixed up and change places in an instant.

While the story is a personal account of our lives, it is also representative of hundreds of thousands of South Vietnamese who faced similar ordeals after the events of April 30, 1975. These events must be told honestly and respectfully so that the world can read and hear them and thereby understand how deeply the war tore Vietnam. And, too, that the world should know how bravely the Vietnamese endured so many years of fighting, and how after the war they have continued to struggle to this day.

For this reason, we decided to complete this journal on our own, doing it our way, with our resources. Nearly forty years have passed from the day we first began writing in the notebook on the Gulf of Thailand. Our hair is gray now, but we finished the book at last.

We have lived out our lives' destiny, and our destiny is bound to that of the country and people of Vietnam. Some may consider this a misfortune. But for us, two war correspondents whose goal is to bear witness to history, it is a blessing, an opportunity to share the joys and sorrows with the fate of the nation, to experience the pleasures and sufferings of millions of people of South Vietnam.

In the transition from conducting war journalism to running a media company, we've gone through many changes. But deep inside, we are still searching for the truth, and we offer our lives to join in that search with everyone.

In finally giving a public voice to our private journey, we honor those warriors who gave their lives during the war, in communist prisons, or during their escape from Vietnam in search of freedom. For those who suffered on the seas with us, please know that this is your story, too.

We thank you, the readers, for giving us the opportunity to connect with you through these pages. We hope you share our faith in human dignity and our joy in facing the unknown to survive and thrive.

And above all, we give thanks to God for granting us the faith to face our fears, the hope to overcome adversity, and the love to accept in peace that we must in all circumstances do what is right.

Duong Phuc & Vu Thanh Thuy

ACKNOWLEDGMENTS

This memoir is in commemoration of our beloved parents and our dear friends, Vu Thi Binh Minh and Dang Tuong Vi, who shared life-and-death situations with us. Although they are no longer with us, they will never fade from our memory.

The authors wish to give thanks to Uncle Trinh Van Trac and Aunt Chi, Aunt Le thi Ri, dear friends Tran Thi Duyen and Nguyen Ta Anh, who opened up their homes to take us in and hid us during the years we lived under the communist regime after 1975.

We are grateful to our first daughter An Duong. This memoir would not have materialized without her support, her interviews, notes, research, and co-writing of the English version over 20 years. Many thanks to our other four daughters, Chau Giao (Su), Binh Minh, Trang Thu, Mai Kim, and our eight grandchildren, Audrey Thuy Duong, Elijah Song, Amorah Thuy Phuc, Ian Binh, Roen Vu, Eleanor Nam, Amelia Thanh, and Penelope Thuy.

Thanks to James Banerian, who lent a helping hand to the Vietnamese boat people from the day the Boat People SOS Committee began in 1980, and who completed the translation of this memoir into English.

Many thanks to Dr. Rubén G. Rumbaut of the University of California, Irvine, our closest family friend for 36 years, who was the first to give a name to this memoir and to jot down its "Table of Contents" on a napkin at the UC San Diego cafeteria in 1987. Thirty-one years later, Prof. Rumbaut was also the one who called on to his five brothers and sisters, Luis, Carlos, Miryam, Carmen, and Michelle, to take part in polishing this manuscript.

Thanks to Stone Phillips who lent us his literary agent, the famous Robert Bennett, to help with our book ideas in 1988.

Fond thanks to our friends Merle Worth and Lorraine Parmer, who have been good friends to our family from the first years of our lives in the U.S. throughout the last three decades.

Thank you to Lee Ann Pingel of Expert Eye Editing for asking clarifying questions and refining the prose; and to Harriet Wasserstrum for her precise review of the manuscript.

Thanks to Dinh Tien Luyen, an author/painter and a childhood friend, who designed and did the layout from the front cover to the back.

And special thanks to the author, Trung Duong Nguyen Thi Thai, who coordinated the final details to bring this memoir to life.

And, last but not least, we hold dear in our hearts the unconditional love of our families, our beloved parents, brothers and sisters, Duong Lan-Phung, Duong Hung-Thanh, Duong Bao-Nhan, Duong Cu-Lien, Duong Kien, Vu Kim Thuy-Ky, Vu Thi Ngoc Thanh-Fred, Vu Ngoc Bau-Hong, Vu Kim Thoa-Nam, and our nephews and nieces Dung, Tri, Duc, Kim Thy, and Tuyen, who have always been a source of support and strength throughout our life.

From the bottom of our hearts, THANK YOU!

With appreciation,
Duong Phuc & Vu Thanh Thuy

FOREWORD

When I began this book, it was from the perspective of a child whose parents were larger than life: mysterious and enigmatic. Growing up, I found them more mythical than parental – a living legend full of adventure, heartbreak, obstacles created by evil demigods, victories by divine intervention. They were the whole package: their story had it all. It was unbelievably real, a testament to what it means to survive all the trials and triumphs of humanity and to thrive on the choice between good and evil.

My first recorded conversations with my parents consisted of fragments of memories, which would slowly emerge to transport us from an air-conditioned office in Texas to a humid jungle or dusty battlefield in Vietnam. Sometimes, their words would stop short for unknown reasons, the memory hovering oppressively, intruding into the present and suddenly disappearing back into the recesses of their mind. They would snap to, look around for relief, and we would be abruptly done for the day.

Dad was a soldier with a keen eye that missed nothing and a sharp nose for the truth, the abilities that served him well in an elusive war where the face of an enemy could very well be no different than that of a friend. When he spoke of the Communists, his eyes narrowed, his tone hardened, and his voice broke with tension so thick it became difficult for him to breathe. He looked transformed, the way super heroes are triggered from ordinary to extraordinary, his superpower being his clarity. I could see that he found nothing more insidious than the tactics the Communists used to deceive, entice, recruit, and exploit otherwise good people under the guise of nationalism.

Mom was a genteel feminist, called to journalism by poetic happenstance. Her father was a scholar who sheltered her from the war but no amount of academic insulation could satisfy her curiosity or her budding activism. She was raised a lady, but her heart was all fierce warrior, and like Dad, she fought hard for her country with reports that brimmed idealistically of freedom and justice. Her work with Westerners furthered her love for democracy and her intolerance for Communists' empty promises.

This is my parents' story, and yet it belongs to an entire nation of people dispossessed of their native land at the hands of its rulers. A story of exiles that entered foreign countries empty-handed but with hearts fortified to rebuild the greatness of their homeland from afar on a miniature scale in the form of "Little Saigons" that sprang up all over the world, shaped by their commitment to assimilation *and* to cultural authenticity. My parents' success is but one example of the Vietnamese diaspora's strong work ethic, love of tradition, and an unwavering faith in the future, despite a tragic past.

They have worked tirelessly to transition from accomplished journalists to struggling immigrants. Having to start over from square one, they have proved themselves as fearless business people, compassionate community leaders, and now elders who answered the call to preserve their heritage and be a living connection to history.

I am deeply humbled to have worked with and learned from my parents. The thought of their survival has guided my steps. I hope their story continues as a bright torch in the hearts of my children.

As this book goes to print, I now write from the perspective of a parent. It is hard enough for me to raise my children with all the creature comforts of a safe suburban upbringing in a country where there is no war but peace with access to education, protection of equal rights, and the luxury of quality family time. I never know if I am doing enough to protect my children from harm, to provide for their security, or to nurture their talents, passions, and moral character. I cannot imagine what my parents had to face and am in awe of all that they have sacrificed and endured to bring their children to this land of freedom.

I will forever be grateful to them and people like them. It is humanity at its best -- ever ready to move forward, never shy to face a challenge, always strong in their love of others and of each other.

An Duong

Notes on Vietnamese
Names and Language

Vietnamese names consist of the family name followed by the given name. Thus, the authors of this memoir are (family name) Duong (given name) Phuc and (family) Vu (given) Thanh Thuy, the latter usually shortened to Thuy. Because there are relatively few families or surnames in Vietnamese, an individual is generally addressed by the given name, which may be one word (Phuc, Thuy), or two (Thuan An). A person addressed by a title would usually be known by the given name, hence President Thieu (or the entire name Nguyen Van Thieu), and the wife of a titled person would be known as Madame followed by her husband's name (Nguyen Thi Mai Anh was publicly referred to as Madame Nguyen Van Thieu). Similarly, a married woman might be addressed with her husband's name; thus, Kim-Phung, the wife of Phuc's older brother Lan, is referred to as "sister" Lan. Only in the case of a very well-known figure is the family name used in address; such as Communist Party Chairman Ho Chi Minh as Chairman Ho or (to his followers) Uncle Ho.

Prior to modern times, the Vietnamese language contained no personal pronouns; all relationships were, and basically still are, viewed according to age or social status. Even the contemporary *toi*, used for the first-person "I/me," has the original meaning of "servant," suggesting a humbling of oneself before another. The words used for Mr. and Mrs. are *Ong* and *Ba*, literally "grandfather" and "grandmother." Communication between parent and child involves the terms "father/mother-child," not "I-you." A married couple speaks to each other as "older brother-younger sister" (*anh-em*). In this way, Vietnam seems to be filled with brothers and sisters, aunts and uncles, grandparents and grandchildren, nephews and nieces, and so on. Understanding this will give the reader a sense of personal relationships within the story that cannot be adequately conveyed in English with its neutral and egalitarian pronouns.

Most Vietnamese parents choose names for their children that carry personal meaning, in the way that we named Thuan An after an important location. Others name their children whatever they like, but Vietnamese names all have direct meanings:

> **Phục**: Respect / Admire. But different diacritical marks change the meaning of words. For example, Phúc means Happiness / Blessing / Grace.
>
> **Thanh Thủy**: Blue/Clear Water (Thanh = Blue or Clear; Thủy = Water). Combined with the surname, we have Blue/Clear Water Rain (Vu = Rain). Thanh Thủy is also the name of a beautiful and historic river in the North which a famous Vietnamese writer, Nhat Linh, used as a background for his book, *The Thanh Thuy River*. He published this book in the 1940s, and Thuy's parents were his loyal readers.

Proper pronunciation of Vietnamese words and names can be a challenge for Americans. Unlike English, Vietnamese is tonal, so a single spelling could potentially be pronounced six different ways just from the tones. Diacritical marks not shown in the English print can also make a difference in how a spelling is pronounced. In addition, Vietnamese has a number of phonemes that have no equivalent in English. Regional and local variations in pronunciation can further mystify the uninitiated. Most Vietnamese people dealing with foreigners are content with well-intentioned approximations of their language. The reader may safely use the following pronunciations as "close enough":

Duong Phuc /*zoong* (Northern) or *yoong* (Southern) *fook*/
Vu Thanh Thuy /*voo tine twee*/
Thuan An /*twun ahn*/

Footnotes are provided for individual words or phrases found in the story. However, it would be impractical and disruptive to include pronunciations for all the names of persons and places in this book. The following examples may serve as a guide.

Duong Phuc's family:
Lan /lun/   Hung /hoong/   Bao /bow/
Kien /kyen/   Cu /kur/   Loan /lwahn/
Vu Thanh Thuy's family:
Kim Thuy /kim twee/   Ngoc Thanh /ngawp tine/
Bau /bow/   Kim Thoa /kim twah/
Thanh Thu /tine too/   Trang /chrahng/

Characters:

Binh Minh /bing ming/   Tuong Vi /toong vee/
Duyen /zwen or ywen/   Nhut /nyut/
Ta Anh /tah ine/   Cuong /coong/
Nghia /ngee-ah/   Khuong /khoong/
Vu Anh /voo ine/   Phu Nhuan /foo nywun/
Tran Minh Hoang /chrun ming hwahng/
Nguyen Khoa Nam /wen khwah nahm/
Pham Van Phu /fahm van foo/
Do Cao Tri /doh cow chree/
Le Van Hung /lay van hoong/
The /tay/   But /boot/
Tuat /dwut/   Nhan /nyahn/
Phi /fee/

Place Names:
Saigon /sigh-gahn/   Trang Lon /chahng lun/
Hanoi /hah-noy/   Phu Quoc /foo kwoke/
Vung Tau /voong tuhw/   Long Giao /long zhow/
Quang Tri /kwahng chree/
Cam My-Cam Duong /kum mee-kum doong/
Hue /hway/   An Loc /ahn lope/
Nha Trang /nyah chahng/   Lam Son /lahm sun/
Can Tho /kun tuh/   Bao Loc /bow lope/
Tan Son Nhat /tun sun nhut/ Gia Lam /zhah lahm/
Hoa Hung /hwah hoong/   Thai Binh /tigh bing/
Cholon /chuh-lun/   Ngoc Ha /ngawp hah/
Duyen Lang /zwen lahng/   Rach Gia /rake yah or zhah/

Common family names:

Bui /*booee*/

Cao /*kow*/

Dang /*dahng*/

Dinh /*ding* or *din*/

Do /*doh*/

Doan /*zwahn* or *ywahn*/

Duong /*zoong* or *yoong*/

Ha /*hah*/

Ho /*hoh*/

Hoang /*hwahng*/

Huy /*hwee* or *wee*/

Huynh /*win*/

Le /*lay*/

Luu /*loo*/

Ly /*lee*/

Ngo /*ngoh*/

Nguyen /*ngwen* or *wen*/

Pham /*fahm*/

Phan /*fahn*/

Tran /*chrun*/

Trinh /*chring*/

Truong /*choong*/

Vo /*vaw*/

Vu /*voo*/

PART I

THE VIETNAM WAR'S AFTERMATH

Chapter 1

The Fall of South Vietnam

April 1975

■ THUY

I n the spring of 1975, Phuc and I had been married for more than a year. Phuc tried to divide his time between work and home, but as a lieutenant in the Psywar Department and newsroom chief for Voice of the Armed Forces Radio, he was often caught in the hectic stream of current news and orders that kept him restricted to base, so he frequently couldn't get home. Meanwhile, I was a correspondent for Voice of Freedom (VOF) Radio, but only occasionally came to the station for work as I was expecting our first child.

I was the youngest daughter-in-law in a family of six married sons. Since all the older couples lived far from Saigon, the task of looking after my husband's mother fell to me, which included housekeeping and cooking, hardly my areas of expertise. When I was away from the radio station, I endeavored to fulfill my responsibilities, taking classes in homemaking and applying what I learned with enthusiasm and efficiency. Still, I felt emptiness in my life and missed my husband

Phuc and Thuy in Saigon, January 1975.

Phuc's mother, Mai thị Ro (center), and her six daughters-in-law, with Thuy second from right, Saigon, June 1974.

and my job.

The news updates I was hearing made it clear that the war was in its final stage. The country was exhausted by the conflict, political efforts for a settlement had reached a stalemate, and the South Vietnamese military could not sustain the fight with the drastic cuts in aid provided by our ally, the United States.

I could barely eat or sleep worrying about the future. Phuc and I had dedicated our lives and careers to speak out against the communists while promoting the spirit of freedom and democracy. What would fate have in store for us once our enemies take over the country? Would our child have to grow up without freedom under the communists?

■ PHUC

O ur emotions swung between joy in anticipation of our first child and worry about the imminent collapse of South Vietnam, whose citizens would be on the receiving end of vengeance meted out after our staunch resistance to the communists.

The North Vietnamese were in violation of the 1973 Paris Peace Accords by launching an offensive against the South after the United States failed to respond to the communists' seizure of the town of Phuoc Long, southwest of Saigon, in December 1974. Early the following year the North Vietnamese Army (NVA) struck again, capturing the mountain city of Ban Me Thuot in March, and then continuing to attack more cities. Hue, Da Nang, Kontum, Pleiku... city after city fell despite valiant attempts by the South Vietnamese army to halt the drive. By April 1, the communists had taken more than half of South Vietnam.

On April 7, Saigon and nearby Long An province were under siege. The Army of the Republic of Vietnam (ARVN) 18th Division staged a stiff resistance against two NVA divisions at Xuan Loc, the last defensive position before Saigon. Despite reinforcements and fierce air support, they could not hold on. Running out of ammunition, the soldiers abandoned the town. Meanwhile, in neighboring Cambodia, the communist forces known as the Khmer Rouge were poised to take over that country. The U.S. ambassador fled Phnom Penh, the Cambodian capital, just days before it fell, a foreshadowing of the fate that awaited South Vietnam.

The spirit of resistance displayed by some of the South Vietnamese units in holding off the communist invasion earned the respect and admiration of their American advisers, who had trained them over the years. No matter how creative or determined the fighters were, however, the situation grew ever more desperate with the severe reduction in military assistance provided by the U.S. after pressure from the American public and Congress caused Washington to pull out its troops and bring them home.

I never expected that the arrival of my first child would coincide with the collapse of the country I loved.

Our First Child

Very early on the morning of April 15, I woke to the sound of my wife crying out. I leaped out of bed and grabbed my pistol, braced for a fight. Only when I saw Thuy's face contorted and covered with sweat did I realize that she was going into labor.

The contractions became stronger and more urgent, causing Thuy to exclaim that we would not have time to make it to the hospital. The thought terrified me. I was prepared to do anything for my wife, but delivering a child wasn't something I wanted to go through by myself.

I jumped onto my Vespa motor scooter and started it up, silently saying a prayer as the motor roared. Thuy climbed on behind, holding on to me by the waist, even as she dealt with the discomfort. Every bump and pothole we ran over elicited a cry of pain from her.

We were violating the city's curfew, and I was well aware that the soldiers posted throughout the city had orders to shoot anyone who looked suspicious. As I drove, I went through in my head what I might need to say to pass the checkpoints as quickly as possible.

Adding to my disquiet was the gloom and eeriness of the late hour. Usually a scene of lively nighttime activity, on this occasion Saigon's streets were empty, and a misty rain made the city seem desolate and frightening.

We knew that time and the weather were against us. Thuy fought the labor pangs while my heart pounded in my chest. For safety, I had on my uniform with the lieutenant's insignia and carried my pistol. I made sure to stop at each checkpoint, even though it ate up valuable minutes while Thuy endured the increasing contractions.

Every time I stopped, I called out, "I'm Lt. Duong Phuc of the Psywar Department, and I'm taking my wife to have our baby!"

We didn't encounter any difficulties, but at every checkpoint, Thuy quivered in pain.

The streets were unlit and, mindful of the urgency, I drove so fast that Thuy gripped me like a vise. The lights of the government hospital remained frustratingly distant. Each time Thuy squeezed me in distress, I stepped harder on the gas.

Once in a while, we heard a gunshot. At some posts, the guards were overly cautious, and anytime they spotted a dark form approaching they fired a warning shot into the air. Other times there was no warning, and at the last moment gunfire would ring out, and civilians would be injured. This kind of thing seemed to happen every day.

A soldier called out, "Stop or I'll shoot!"

I slowed down, steering with one hand and holding onto Thuy with the other.

"I'm a lieutenant, and I'm taking my wife to have a baby!" I shouted back.

The guards raised their guns to fire a warning, but as soon as they saw Thuy's condition, they jumped aside and let us pass.

Once we reached the hospital, I dropped my Vespa on the curb and helped Thuy inside. Each pain caused her to double over, but she was relieved to be in the hospital, where she could stop trying to control the contractions, which by now seemed to be twice as painful. We were both completely drenched with rain and sweat.

While we got checked in, I couldn't help listening in on the conversations between the military patients and hospital staff. Everyone was anxious at the prospect of the country's fall. The defeat was ever closer, and despair lay heavy inside each of us. Even the doctor whom I had expected would give his full attention to Thuy appeared preoccupied with the decision of whether to flee the country or stay and accept the consequences.

The facility was crowded this week of mid-April, with many patients evacuated from places as far away as Quang Tri near the Demilitarized Zone to Long Khanh in the Mekong Delta. By this time, most of the country's professionals with any influence had already prepared to get out. The powerful had sent their wives and children first, intending to follow later.

This government hospital, which boasted the sponsorship of First Lady Madame Nguyen Van Thieu, still had a fairly good number of physicians and staff on hand. But it was clear to me that they were all prepared to drop everything and run at a moment's notice. Beyond concern for their safety, they were overwhelmed by the sheer number of patients.

It was a precarious situation, and tension spread through the hospital like a virus. I, too, was infected.

At one point I blew up at a duty nurse assigned to take care of Thuy. Every time I saw her, she was on the phone, pleading with this person or that to take her and her family out of Vietnam. I asked her many times to tend to my wife, but she just waved me off.

Thuy's small size belies her strength and courage, but the child struggling inside her was causing such intense discomfort that I couldn't bear to witness the extreme transformation that had come over the mother in this birthing process. I felt helpless, no longer recognizing my "friend for life" who always seemed so calm and in control.

"Miss," I said to the nurse, "my wife is in a lot of pain!"

"Have a seat," she answered, not even looking up. "The doctor will look in shortly."

I paused a moment, took a deep breath, then closed my eyes and began to count inside my head: *One...two...three...* But my anger did not subside. I reached out and grabbed the nurse by the arm. She cried out. I held her harder and looked her right in the eyes.

"You *have to* take my wife to the delivery room! And you have to stay there and take care of her until she has her baby!"

The nurse screamed and tried to pull away.

"What's going on here?"

A doctor approached. I released the nurse.

"Doctor, please help my wife!" I begged.

"Look, there are a lot of patients waiting for me. I can't just..."

He broke off as I advanced toward him.

"Doctor, watch out!" the nurse cried as she rubbed her arm.

The doctor raised both hands in the air.

"OK, OK!" he said. "Take it easy. Where's your wife?"

I led him to Thuy, and he quickly examined her.

"Your wife is coming along normally," he said before he left the room. "The nurse will monitor her progress, and I'll be back when she's ready to deliver. We don't have enough people on staff tonight, and a lot of patients are in critical condition."

He waited to gauge my reaction, and when I sat down quietly next to Thuy and took her hand, he slipped away. An hour later, when he had not returned, and Thuy's contractions lengthened, her face contorted in pain, my temper flared again.

"You have to do something to help my wife!" I screamed at the nurse.

"That kind of pain is normal," she said with a shrug, and then she, too, left the room.

The only thing that kept me from chasing after her and dragging her back was Thuy's hard, unyielding grip on my hand. The nurse got away and hid down the hall.

As dawn approached, Thuy's cries turned to stifled moans as she gathered her strength for the delivery. Occasionally one of the nurses would pop into the room to see how things were progressing, and then quickly leave.

Thuy's bed was separated from the others by a curtain. As I paced back and forth in that small space, my attention went back and forth between Thuy's agonized groans and the noise of explosions and gunfire that now sounded very close.

Finally, just before daylight, Thuy shouted, "It's coming!"

Since there was no one in the room just then, I raced

frantically down the hall calling for a doctor or nurse. I finally found two nurses, one of whom was on the phone, and pulled them into Thuy's room.

The baby came into the world at 4:15 AM. Its cry, too big for a newborn's little throat, caused me to rush into the room all flustered. Seeing the two nurses caring for the baby and Thuy, I went back outside to wait. An air of solemnity filled the room. Thuy fell into an exhausted stupor while I strode up and down the hall, my heart on fire. No one came to tell me when I was allowed to come inside. Finally, I ran in just as one of the nurses spoke.

"This is no time to be born, but that's exactly when she comes," she said in a flat voice.

A shell exploded somewhere not very far away, rattling the windows. Just then the infant's eyes were being cleaned and she opened them as if to catch her first glimpse of this world she was entering. And thus Duong Vu Thuan An, our first child, was born amidst chaos and desperation, uncertainty and hopelessness.

From the radio at the head of the hospital bed came the broken, agitated, and disjointed voices of broadcasters in an array of programs out of their usual order. The communists were taking one town, one district, one province after another and were poised to march on the gates of Saigon itself.

Interviews with evacuees from the areas that had been overrun indicated that officers caught behind the advancing communist army were being killed or taken away. We also heard that several top government officials had fled the country. The death toll continued to mount, and the ever-saddening news came as a painful blow to those of us in the South who opposed the communists. A number of our politicians, generals, and social leaders had fled, leaving behind a country full of suffering and despair.

I knew the turmoil within the hospital was beyond the control of those in charge. Everyone was directly influenced by the disorder of the country as a whole, with a shared sense of betrayal as South Vietnam slowly came apart with the shameless desertion of its leaders.

As the hospital swirled in confusion around me, I focused my attention on my wife and new child. Amid the conflicting emotions, I gazed in joy at my daughter and felt immense pride.

Thuy was tired, but at least the painful ordeal was over. I

looked at the infant, her tiny hands and feet clenched, bawling as if in protest against the light from the outside world, the troubled world she had just greeted with a powerful cry of pent-up strength.

I quickly murmured a prayer of thanks, and all at once my soul was transformed. I recalled what my friends had told me about their experience in becoming a parent for the first time. The sheer excitement of going through the process, from taking the wife to the hospital, then nervously waiting outside, and finally the reward, the grand feeling of joy and love at hearing the baby cry as it greeted the world. Now it was my turn.

Since the maternity ward had been taken over for the treatment of patients transferred from other places, there was no fanfare from the staff to celebrate the new arrival. But Thuy and I still felt the immense pleasure of being first-time parents. That feeling could not be taken from us, even in the midst of war. The wonderful feeling that comes from witnessing the miracle of new life temporarily halted for us the terrible military conflict and the calamity facing our country. The silent fear disappeared. Time stopped as if allowing the universe to share this moment with us.

We named our daughter after Thuan An beach, where Thuy and I used to go when our feelings for each other were beginning to blossom. It represented the bright sun, peaceful waves, and relaxed and pleasant air we had known there. Choosing a baby's name is very important for all parents in Vietnam. It was especially so for us because we knew deep in our hearts that there were dark days ahead for our country.

By naming our daughter Thuan An, we were promising to do all we could to preserve the light of harmony (*hoa thuan*) and peace (*binh an*)[1] in our family. Though shaken by stormy winds, that light would not go out, regardless of what tragedies lay in store for us. We secreted that promise in the name of the girl who opened her eyes to begin a new life on April 15, 1975.

---

[1] hoa thuan */hwah twun/*, binh an */bing ahn/*

Saigon in Turmoil

■ THUY

When I woke up, I found myself surrounded by my loving parents and siblings. Their faces expressed no joy as they peered down at me. Rather, they seemed to be trying to conceal a looming sadness. My family was preparing to flee Vietnam's new rulers. They had come to urge me to join them.

Baby An started crying, and since I was too weak to care for her myself, a nurse quickly picked her up and took her out to be fed. Papa saw the question on my face and spoke directly to the point.

"The whole family has to leave," he said. He explained that my oldest sister and her family were at the airport, scheduled to leave that day, while my second sister, who was married to a Frenchman, would be returning to Europe the following day. "Your Mama and I are on the American embassy's list to be evacuated. It could be in a few days, but it could be anytime as the situation changes. But we will wait for you."

The atmosphere in the room was not one of welcoming a new life into the world but, rather, of bidding farewell to a life that was over.

"Come with us," Mama pleaded.

Phuc and I said nothing. I nodded, looking around at all the somber visitors and feeling a profound sadness well up inside me. I knew my family would seek any way possible to get out of the country. The collapse of Saigon was imminent, and flight seemed the wisest course of action.

When the nurse brought An back in, Mama took her.

"Get some rest so you'll be strong enough to come with Papa and me," she advised.

When Phuc spoke up to answer for me, I didn't dare look at him as I knew his response would only disappoint them.

"That won't do, Mother. Thuy and the baby need to recover. Going now would be dangerous to their health."

Everyone was quiet. The situation was out of our hands now, and I comforted myself with the thought that my family was no different from thousands of others. If they were to go without me, my broken heart would be comforted by the thought that they had found safety.

I knew my family was not abandoning me. I knew they had gone out of their way to remain in Saigon long enough to visit me when the baby came and to try and persuade us to leave with them. Their decision to flee confirmed my fear of the bleak future that was in store for the country, as ever since we had left the North in 1954 my Papa had always said, "I can never live with the communists."

I was determined to contain my emotions. I hugged each of them and kissed them on the cheek, pressing my face against theirs, as I silently prayed that God would let them go in peace. But when Papa smiled goodbye, I couldn't hold back the tears any longer.

"Mama and I don't yet know exactly when we'll be leaving," he said to Phuc. "When Thuy gets well enough to travel and if we are still here, we will wait for you to come with us."

He gave Phuc the name of a person to contact as soon as we were ready.

"Mama and I will see you all," he said.

Before they left, Mama tucked a red envelope into An's blanket. It was a gift of "lucky money," a traditional way of sharing love, an offering for the future typically given by elders to children on important occasions.

Phuc turned to look at me and grew alarmed to find me pale and shaking. He leaned over and held me in his arms, allowing me to let go all the tears I had been holding inside. He cradled my head and told me that he loved me very much. In my sleep, I dreamed I saw him with little An in his arms, rocking her comfortingly.

///

A week later, on April 22, An and I were released from the hospital. Phuc's eldest brother, Lan, came to pick us up.

Phuc ran to greet him. Lan brightened to see his baby brother so happy and relaxed. Since their father had passed away when Phuc was nine years old, Lan had been especially protective of his much younger brother and had taken on the role of parent. He was worried now that, given the tragic turn of events in the country, Phuc might be depressed. Relieved to find him in good spirits, he shared in his brother's joy of fatherhood and gave him a grin and a big hug.

While the others climbed into the car after me, I turned to look at the hospital, hallways filled with doctors and nurses tending the wounded, who continued to be brought in from the city's outskirts. I felt a common bond with these professionals, sharing their idealism and faith. Even as calamity bore down upon them, they went on with their tasks. My eyes teared up as my heart overflowed with pride mixed with fear.

On the way home, I looked out in shock as we passed houses and buildings stripped of their contents in a veritable free-for-all. Police and security guards tried desperately to maintain order, but the situation had gotten out of control. The people were overcome with terror, and that terror made them reckless and irresponsible.

"Everyone's scared to death of living under the communists," said older brother Lan.

The streets were gray with rubbish and ash. Gunfire and explosions filled the air, making it difficult for us to catch the words coming through the static on the radio.

"The communist army has entered the area just outside the suburbs of Saigon. Cities continue to fall...."

An was not crying alone. My heart was on the verge of spilling out anger and bitterness when I saw military uniforms lying scattered in the streets. Though I was sitting safely in a car with no communist soldiers in sight, I thought I smelled the rank odor of the North Vietnamese *bo doi*,[2] (foot soldiers)—sweat mixed with farmer's tobacco—that I had become familiar with when I interviewed Viet Cong prisoners captured in battle. I rolled the window shut and turned my eyes away.

Baby An cried even louder.

By the time we arrived at the house on Truong Minh Giang Street, the news had gone from sad and troubling to utterly hopeless. Only Saigon, the capital of South Vietnam, and the area to the west had not yet fallen. The NVA had overrun nearly every city and town south of the 17th parallel. Saigon had become the lone bastion of freedom in the ocean of the country, and even it was soon to be swallowed up by the raging storm and thrown into darkness.

Brother Lan, formerly a prosecuting attorney in Phuoc Tuy province, had recently been appointed Presiding Judge in the city of

---

[2]bo doi /*boh doy*/

Tuy Hoa. Due to the fighting, he had been evacuated to Saigon, arriving just the week before on the last plane out. His wife and children had remained behind in Phuoc Tuy expecting to join him at his new post, but they rushed to Saigon as the communists approached and arrived shortly before us for a bittersweet reunion.

Phuc's second-oldest brother, Hung, had left Vietnam the year before, having been assigned Embassy Secretary in Teheran, Iran. It was his house near the Truong Minh Giang Bridge that now served as the temporary station for the extended family arriving from all over the country.

Also with us was the family of Phuc's fifth brother, Kien, who had arrived from Nha Trang at the end of March. Brother Kien was a military prosecutor tasked with bringing Viet Cong prisoners to trial. We were concerned about the possibility of his being trapped behind the invasion and falling into the hands of the enemy.

There was no news of Phuc's two remaining brothers. Bao was director of the military hospital in Bien Hoa, not far from Saigon, and Cu was a military prosecutor in Can Tho, the largest city in the Mekong Delta.

Even as we were concerned for the safety of Bao, Cu and their families, we didn't know what we should do for our own security. Nonetheless, no one on Phuc's side had decided to leave Vietnam at that time.

I was grateful to have a safe place where I could regain my strength. Still, I missed the Vietnamese tradition of being a pampered new mother. Normally, I would have had a month's bed rest, a cook to prepare special meals to facilitate healing from childbirth, and a nanny for An. Instead, I found myself hiding away, wondering where I would find An's next can of formula.[3]

The surrounding chaos prevented us from fully indulging in

---

[3] When my siblings were born, in the 1940s, each of them had a wet nurse, since our mother, like most women of social status, didn' breastfeed. Mothers who couldn't afford formula breastfed or fed their babies with condensed milk mixed with water. During the 1950s to the 1970s, formula became fashionable among middle to high-class mothers. But when the war intensified, forcing people to evacuate often, mothers went back to breastfeeding since it's more convenient when on the run. I tried to breastfeed but didn't have enough milk, so I had to rely on formula.

the pleasure of new parenthood. Besides the basic care for An, Phuc and I had to make time for the many things going on around us. Brother Lan made great efforts to keep up our spirits. He advised us to follow the example of most others in the city and pack our bags should we have to flee.

He also kept us entertained. He organized a small party for baby An. His wife, a talented cook, prepared a small pot of noodles believed to help new mothers produce milk. We all made a promise not to mention the war during the celebration. But no one could hide the war's heavy presence; no one could silence the din of bombs and guns that heralded the collapse of our beloved city.

Lan took a spoonful of broth and brought it to An's lips. She winced at first but then cooed for more. We all laughed.

"Baby An has good taste!" brother Lan declared. "We'll just have to eat like this every day!"

We nodded in agreement, comforted by his humor. Then came the crash of another bomb outside, this one closer than the one before. We finished our meal slowly, savoring each bite, and went to bed early.

Despite my exhaustion, I couldn't sleep. I stared at the dark ceiling and listened to the cicadas still chirping in the bushes outside my window, much like drunken merry-makers unmindful of the troubles that plagued human beings.

While Phuc and I lay awake for hours, baby An slept peacefully between us, as oblivious as the cicadas to what was hiding in the darkness.

Last Gasp

■ PHUC

On April 21, Nguyen Van Thieu hastily resigned as president of the Republic of Vietnam. The position was filled by Vice President Tran Van Huong. Gen. Cao Van Vien, chairman of the Joint Chiefs of Staff of the South Vietnamese armed forces, resigned as well. Shortly thereafter, former-president Thieu and other powerful figures, including Prime Minister Tran Thien Khiem and Gen. Cao Van Vien, left the country secretly.

The departure of these top men and that of the famous "cowboy general" and former Prime Minister Nguyen Cao Ky triggered a further exodus of high-ranking military and government officials. In a matter of days, the country lost nearly all of its top leaders.

Under orders of then-President Thieu, Gen. Ngo Quang Truong, commander of Military Region I (which included the northernmost provinces of South Vietnam), pulled his forces back to Saigon. Under similar orders, the head of Military Region II (the Central Highlands and coast), and two-star General Pham Van Phu, withdrew from his zone of command. Working his way up from the rank of private to a renowned officer, Gen. Phu adhered to the old principle that "a general would rather go down with his citadel than fall into the enemy's hands" and committed suicide upon his arrival in Saigon. Our military heroes had become the victims of ignominious defeat.

On April 27, Saigon was hit by North Vietnamese rocket fire for the first time in more than three years. The following day, only one week after taking office, Tran Van Huong resigned as president in favor of Gen. Duong Van Minh (popularly known as "Big Minh"), the only leader with whom the communists would deal. President Minh's first act as head of state was to issue a request that all Americans leave the country in twenty-four hours.

Later that afternoon, four A-37s captured from the South Vietnamese Air Force bombed Tan Son Nhut airport. The lead pilot was a South Vietnamese Air Force officer who on April 8 had bombed the presidential palace before defecting to the North.

At daybreak on April 29, Tan Son Nhut was hit by rockets and heavy artillery fire, cutting off all normal air travel and leaving helicopters as the only means of transportation out.

That same day, the U.S. launched the largest helicopter evacuation in its history. Named "Frequent Wind," the operation was set in motion by American Armed Forces Radio continuously broadcasting the Irving Berlin song "White Christmas," the signal for American personnel to move immediately to their evacuation points.

Over the next 19 hours, 81 helicopters transported more than 7,000 passengers to U.S. Navy ships waiting offshore. Ambassador Graham Martin, who had postponed his departure while trying to rescue more Vietnamese, finally stepped onto a helicopter as one of the last Americans to leave Vietnam.

The Day Saigon Fell

At ten o'clock in the morning on April 30, 1975, "two-day President" Duong Van Minh ordered the people and soldiers of South Vietnam to lay down their arms. Forty-five minutes later, a T-54 tank crashed through the gates of Independence Palace. The stronghold of the South, the home of our presidents, and the last symbol of the South Vietnamese government surrendered.

When Big Minh offered to negotiate the transfer of power to the communist army, Hanoi's representative, Col. Bui Tin, editor-in-chief of the Communist Party newspaper *Nhan Dan*[4] (The People), declined, stating that since South Vietnam no longer existed, and there was nothing to negotiate. Indeed, on this day, the people of South Vietnam, their soldiers, their government officials, all considered their country lost.

I felt a powerful urge to return to the newsroom of Armed Forces Radio and report to those still in the city exactly what was transpiring so they would not be confused by speculation and rumor. So strong was my desire to go back and do my job that I was prepared to step into the violence and mayhem outside in the streets. I went to say goodbye to Thuy. When she saw me standing in the wrinkled uniform I had slept in; she understood what I was planning to do. Baby An let out a wail.

"Please don't go right now," Thuy begged.

I could see the conflict in her face. She, too, felt the need to go out and perform the task she had trained for during this critical time in history, but the reality of her condition and her responsibility as a new parent held her back. It also occurred to her that it was too late, that by now the communists would have gained control of the radio stations and I would not be allowed in. At the same time, she knew I was determined to go, and nothing she said could dissuade me. Finally, she sighed.

"Just be careful. And come back soon."

She kissed me on the cheek and looked at me with fear in her eyes.

I knew her concern was reasonable, but I was overwhelmed with the pain and humiliation of a man who had lost his country and

---

[4]Nhan Dan /nyun zun/

a news correspondent who was not allowed to bear witness to history. This was not the typical grief of a person dealing with a sense of loss and separation. This was a pain that had been building up for days to the point that I could no longer hear the bombs and see the fire around me signaling the presence of the enemy army right inside my city. It was like a road spiraling down into hell.

Hopelessness seemed to spin around me like a whirlwind. Evidently, everyone else felt the same way.

In the past, Vietnam had been invaded by foreign powers, but it had always managed to come through. This time we were killing ourselves. I couldn't believe this was the end. The Communist Party would not only alter the face of my country; it would strip me of my own identity. My people would be changed.

///

Out in the streets, I saw a city gripped in panic. Even stray dogs were affected, barking at anything and chasing anyone who ran by.

Fear is a strange thing. In movies, characters caught in terror may simply freeze. But on this last day in April, fear was like an electric shock that struck all the citizens of Saigon, making them behave in a demented manner. People were like windup toys with their strings taut, running here and there, going around in circles with no real direction.

As a soldier, I felt immense shame at seeing army uniforms littering the ground. My comrades-in-arms had been loyal and brave, hopeful until the last minute that we might change the outcome of the war. At the same time, we knew that once the enemy came to the streets of Saigon, if we wanted to live and be with our families we had to discard the uniform of South Vietnam. Small fires marked where men were burning the evidence of their military service.

People went up to the terraces of tall buildings hoping a helicopter would fly over to rescue them. Others acted like ostriches and tried to hide. Many gathered in groups to share rumors, while still others went about concealing their cash and valuables. Some walked the streets zombie-like carrying their possessions in their arms. Others just sat staring into space, stunned, waiting for destiny to overtake them.

I didn't know what they thought they were doing or where they expected to go. The city had become an inescapable island of doom, and no one was willing to accept that reality. This was the last day of the war, the final exclamation mark on decades of conflict. This was also the primitive instinct for survival after a fight that had gone on for too long and finally reached its conclusion.

The day before, U.S. Navy ships had dotted the winding coastline of Vietnam and, even though already overcrowded, picked up more people fleeing frantically in small boats and barges. "Jacob's ladders" were thrown down to draw up shivering, frightened refugees. These were the last people to leave South Vietnam before the communists closed their grip on the shore to halt the escape of the original boat people.

The last image the South Vietnamese have of their great ally the United States is that of a helicopter taking off from the roof of the American embassy with desperate people dangling from the rope ladder amid the cries and pleading of those abandoned below.

The embassy was not the only building the frightened crowds descended upon in their hope for rescue, believing that these centers of power could save their lives. Other Western embassies faced the same reckless masses.

When I reached the Armed Forces radio station, I found the sound room deserted and silent. The red lights blinked on the sound equipment, waiting in vain for hands that would switch the machines on and turn the dials. I sank into my broadcasting chair and looked around dumbly. I felt as if I were witnessing the funeral of a very dear friend.

Then I went over to my boss's office, where I found Lt. Col. Van Quang with a few of my colleagues. Director Quang looked haggard, and his eyes were bloodshot. The group was discussing what to do in light of the president's order to surrender. Just then an NVA tank rumbled through the gate from Hong Thap Tu Street. His mouth set, Director Quang told us to go home. He patted each of us on the shoulder as he shook our hand and wished us luck. Then he turned sadly, stepped into his office, and shut the door behind him.

I stood there a while as the reality of the situation sank in. Then I left the building and headed for home.

As I wound through the streets on my scooter, a man suddenly blocked my path.

"Are you crazy?" he shouted, glaring at my clothes. "You'd better get rid of that. There's a communist tank right around the corner!"

In my haste, I had forgotten that I was in uniform and carrying a pistol. The stranger shook his head and took off. Others reacted the same way, calling out warnings.

"The communist army is going that way!"

"You'd better hide quickly, or they'll kill you!"

Taking their advice, I ducked into an alley and slipped into the backyard of an empty house. I took off my uniform and boots, and then stuffed them into a bush. As I did so, I swallowed a sob. I felt that by this action I was burying my whole life, consigning to the grave the very core of my military self, the foundation of my adult life. Whenever I wore that uniform, I felt responsible to personify the strength it symbolized, the sacrifice it demanded, the integrity it required to be a part of something sacred, something bigger than myself. Now I had removed that symbol of pride to survive under a new system. In that moment, steeped in shame, I finally knew I was defeated.

Eventually, I moved toward the street. The NVA was advancing, following the Soviet tanks that contemptuously pushed aside anything in their way. Realizing that my appearance would be suspicious, I hid behind a tree until the troops passed. Then I ran back to the abandoned house and grabbed some clothes hanging in one of the rooms. The outfit belonged to an elderly man – the shirt was thin, the trousers too short, and the rubber sandals too small for my feet. Then I pushed my scooter back onto the street and started off.

As I drove along, I thought of how I must look and laughed bitterly, wondering what Thuy would think if she saw me just then. Suddenly a thought struck me: What if something happened and I never saw my family again? How could I have left them at such a dangerous time? My family! The country might be lost, but my family was the only thing important to me then. More than anything, I wanted to be with my wife and child.

Wounded Capital

■ THUY

As dawn arrived that last day of April, baby An and I were the only ones awake in the house. I had gotten used to the broken sleep familiar to new mothers.

Unable to stop Phuc from going to the radio station, I said a prayer for him and went to the kitchen to prepare formula for the baby. While she was feeding, the boom of an explosion startled her, and she began to cry. I could feel the communist army approaching the city. In my head, I could almost hear the marching of enemy troops as clearly as I heard An's wailing.

For the past several days, the radio's volume had been turned up to keep the whole house informed of the progress of events. Now, abruptly, the radio went silent. The sudden absence of news from outside was terrifying. Everyone was at a loss.

When some time had passed, and Phuc had not returned, brother Lan and his wife decided to take their children and move in with Lan's sister-in-law, who held French citizenship. They told us to join them there once Phuc returned.

Waiting in the empty house with all the commotion in the streets, I became anxious. Finally, I picked up the baby and stepped outside to watch for my husband and perhaps get an idea of what was happening. The chaos that greeted my eyes shocked me, I couldn't breathe. Afraid I might drop the baby, I sat down beside the street. Everything became a blur.

Then I heard a cry of relief and saw two figures approaching.

"Papa! ... Mama!" I stammered and rose to embrace them.

Mama picked up An while Papa cleared his throat.

"Thuy, listen to me. I need you to pay close attention."

I took a deep breath and nodded as tears streamed down my cheeks.

"Saigon is lost," he went on, "and the communists are everywhere. The city is topsy-turvy, and it's dangerous for anyone who fought them, like our family. Especially Phuc and you. We need to go somewhere for a while until things settle down. I think the safest place, for now, is the Jesuit monastery. There are still some foreign priests there. Now, go and get ready to leave with us."

I shook my head.

"Phuc's not here. We have to wait."

When they heard that Phuc had gone to the radio station, they exchanged worried glances. Then they pulled me to my feet.

"You must go now with Papa and Mama. We'll leave a note for Phuc to join us."

What Papa said made sense. In all the confusion with people chasing here and there, how could I hope to find my husband? Besides, government and military media would be among the first areas the communists would take over, and who could say what fate awaited him and our colleagues?

"Many of the foreign priests are refusing to leave the monastery," they told me as they led me back inside. "Maybe their embassies will try to rescue them. It's the best place for us to go."

I thought quickly. Phuc had been gone for hours. Who knew how long I might have to wait? So, after writing a brief note, I packed a bag for An, took her in my arms, and got into my parents' car.

Almost at once we were confronted with crowds going every which way. I had seen many things while reporting the war, but nothing prepared me for this. From the safety and quiet of the house in which I indulged as a new mother, I emerged into a mass of people who seemed to be running away from hell. Those who still hoped to escape the country carried whatever possessions they could, minuscule remnants of their former lives. Others, who probably did not expect to get out, attacked shops and homes, shattering windows and kicking in doors to loot, vent their hysteria, or simply add to the mayhem.

One man carried a small refrigerator on his back, followed by others toting armchairs and a large mirror that cast a reflection of the madness going on. Looters helped themselves to deserted houses filled with their owners' personal belongings. One woman dragged a large basket likely filled with things she had "borrowed" in the chaos. Momentarily distracted, I scanned the items wondering if there was any baby formula. Suddenly I caught myself—my God, what was I doing? Would I have tried to buy it from her? Or would I stoop to "borrowing" too?

Bullets cut through the air, resulting in casualties among

innocent people in the streets. Bodies lay crumpled next to bundles. Victims fell where they were with no one to tend to them. No one tried to help another. Everyone just wanted to get away.

While Mama prayed, Papa told me what he had witnessed earlier in the day. Hordes of people raced to the harbor trying to get onto ships that were taking off. Some climbed into boats that didn't even have working engines, more and more pressing on in hopes of escaping. Others climbed the walls of the American and other embassies, grasping for helicopters in a vain attempt to be pulled out.

We passed an NVA tank rattling slowly forward, its giant treads clanking on the asphalt, its gun raised threateningly. Before then I had never seen communist soldiers that close, other than the prisoners I had interviewed. I didn't dare look them in the face, fearing my anger and resentment might betray me and prompt them to fire at me.

In the midst of this bizarre scene, I spotted a helicopter trying to land on top of a four-story house. Based on my experience with front-line helicopters, I could see the pilot was having difficulty coming down. He had probably stolen the chopper from the airfield as it was under attack that morning and now came to rescue his family waiting on the building's flat roof. The problem was that roofs like this were too small and usually crisscrossed with power lines, making it difficult for the pilot to maneuver.

"Do you remember Uncle Bui, whose son is a helicopter pilot?" Papa asked. "Yesterday he tried to land on the terrace of his house to pick up his family. The blades got tangled in a power line. It caught on fire and crashed into the neighbor's house."

Mama shook her head sadly.

"His poor kids watched him die right in front of them."

I became worried and frightened for this pilot and his family. As we drove past, I turned around and watched the scene behind us. Quickly making the sign of the cross, I prayed to myself, *Dear God, please help that family. Please help my family.*

When we reached the monastery, Mama helped baby An and me out while Papa took our bags. I looked up at the large wooden cross that marked the entrance turning blood-red in the setting sun. I shivered to think how soon my beloved South would be drenched in blood under the red flag of the victorious communists. The color grew hazy as my eyes misted over.

City in Chaos

■ PHUC

As I sped through the streets, the wall of people, motor scooters, and cars opened up in front of me, then closed behind. It was like a movie I once saw where the main character was going through a crowd whose motion was speeded up all around him. I sometimes had to stop and regain my mental bearings.

I reached my brother's house to find it deserted. Gripped by fear, I ran into the bedroom and discovered the note Thuy had attached to the bathroom mirror. The Jesuit monastery—of course! It was a safe move.

I quickly changed out of the borrowed clothes and into my own, making sure to add another layer for more pockets. Then I went into the kitchen and stuffed the pockets with as many containers of baby formula as I could manage, figuring that, with things as they were, the formula was more valuable than gold, whether it was for my baby or somebody else's. I also snatched some bread and rice cakes wrapped in banana leaves hanging by the stove and pushed them into one of the cloth bags Lan's wife had sewn should we have to evacuate without warning.

Knowing Thuy, I was sure she would be with her parents, who were still in the country. They were a close family, and if she lost me, the first thing she would try to do was find her parents.

I sped on my motor scooter toward their house, hoping to run into them before they left. Besides, I didn't know exactly where the monastery was. Along the way, I spotted *bo doi* seizing the larger houses and buildings. The South Vietnamese were too scared to wait around for their "liberators" to come calling. Instead, they were in the streets, probably hoping they wouldn't be identified and arrested. Although my head was clearing, I was not concerned for my own safety but simply wanted to find my wife and child.

To avoid the crowds, I turned into an alley. As I emerged on the other end, I saw a group of *bo doi* rush out of a building and head in my direction. They took two persons and escorted them across the street. I ducked out of sight, waiting nervously. As they went by, I got a powerful whiff of their unwashed clothes saturated with the odor of farmer's tobacco. I had to hold my breath to avoid inhaling the "genuine Viet Cong" scent.

When I thought it was safe, I shot out of my hiding place and nearly ran into someone. Panicking, I came to a halt and raised my arm in self-defense. I was face-to-face with a middle-aged Catholic priest in a black cassock and white collar leading a group of terrified children. He gaped at me suspiciously, his eyes falling on my pockets bulging with containers of milk. I backed up, apologizing, and drove off in another direction.

It had been a while since I had driven the streets at night. As a city in the throes of occupation, Saigon was in its twilight. However, its occupiers were unprepared for the swift victory they were enjoying after decades of warfare and were at a loss as to what to do. I thought painfully of the gains the North would achieve by this victory. The whole world knew that North Vietnam was a land of perpetual poverty and hunger. Ever since the great famine of 1945, the year I was born, the North had never prospered. In their ambition to seize the South, the Communist Party had made its citizens tighten their belts to pursue the cause, further impoverishing the land. I knew the communists would plunder the resources of the South to enrich their own families in the North.

With a start, I realized that I had missed a turnoff. The houses I passed were deathly silent, even though I could see the shadows of their inhabitants through the curtained windows. Only the terrified could remain so still in the night. It was as if they were holding their breath and waiting for morning when they would wake up and find the communists were gone and it had all been just a bad dream.

Eager to leave this menacing neighborhood, I hurried on, driving in the direction I hoped would take me to the monastery. As I reached Nguyen Dinh Chieu Street, I found traffic had come to a halt. While I considered my options, I heard voices softly chanting. The musical tones reminded me of the prayers I used to hear in a chapel. Drawn by the rhythmic notes, I turned and followed a small tree-lined path, and after a short distance, I came to a church. The cross on top shone with light to welcome me.

I walked my scooter through the gate and parked it in a courtyard. Scattered around the church were small groups of people sitting on the ground. A man approached, but before he could question me, I addressed him in a voice so firm it startled even me.

"I'm looking for my wife. She has a newborn baby with her."

The man nodded as if he'd been expecting me.

My heart began to pound. What force had guided me here? How had I managed to find this place? I followed as the man led me to the side of the church and into a large room filled with people. We had to step gingerly to avoid treading on anyone until we reached the back of the hall beside the kitchen. There I saw a middle-aged woman trying to calm a fussy baby by bouncing it in her arms and singing softly. She looked up, and our eyes met.

"Mother!" I cried.

My mother-in-law quickly made room for me and placed An in my arms. Thuy's father stood to greet me, then put a finger to his lips and pointed to a corner where Thuy sat with her back against the wall, asleep. I nodded, and my heart skipped a beat. How could I keep the tears from my eyes?

The baby squirmed and made a faint cry. My parents-in-law watched in amazement as I pulled from my clothes a baby bottle and powdered formula. I indicated that I needed water and Thuy's father went to get some.

Once An was feeding happily, my father-in-law leaned over and asked, "How did you find us here?"

By then the stress of the day was taking its toll on me, and I didn't answer at once. He repeated the question.

"God brought me here!" I said in a weak voice.

Heart-Wrenching Baptism

The next morning I awoke to the sound of Thuy sobbing, her head resting on my shoulder. I put one arm around her and took baby An in the other. We enjoyed this brief period of intimacy, despite our sitting on a cold floor amid a sea of bodies.

There was a flurry of nervous excitement as one of the priests entered the hall.

"The Voice of Saigon radio just announced that President Duong Van Minh has been arrested," he said. "Yesterday he went on air to order our army to surrender. The roads to all borders are blocked, and any day now the communists will be in control of the coast. There is nowhere to go. The Republic of Vietnam is lost!"

This was not news to me, but for those who had sought refuge in the monastery during the previous days, it came as a shock. Some in the hall cried out in horror, others wept. One middle-aged man sitting nearby held his head in his hands and tried to stifle his sobs; at times he pounded his head with his fist out of rage and disbelief.

The priest was a young and vigorous man with a soldier's bearing. He went around the room passing out bread and offering blessings to those who requested them.

I needed some fresh air, so I helped Thuy to her feet, and we carried An outside. Looking out from the monastery grounds, we watched as the sun rose over Saigon, bathing the city in cool yellow then blazing gold. We remained there, dispirited, neither saying anything for a while. Finally, Thuy turned to me.

"We have to ask Father to baptize An."

I nodded my agreement at once. I had been raised in the traditional Vietnamese beliefs, such as reverence for one's ancestors, but converted to Catholicism when I married Thuy. I didn't know much about Church rules, but I understood that our baby's spiritual health was the most important thing for Thuy. As we faced an uncertain future, it was important for me as well.

When we asked Father Superior Do Quang Chinh, he hesitated for a moment, and then consented, "Usually we do not do these things hastily," he said. "But in this circumstance, it will be good for her. And for everyone else, too."

The ceremony was held an hour later in a little chapel behind the hall. As Father Superior made the preparations, people began filing in to occupy the small pews.

Fr. Chinh asked me to read a passage from Scripture. Since marrying Thuy, I had attended Sunday Mass regularly but had never read the Bible out loud. I glanced questioningly at Thuy, but she nodded encouragingly.

I started to read the selection the priest had marked. However, before I finished the first paragraph, tears were running down my cheeks. I tried to hold them back, but my body trembled with emotion and the words stuck in my throat. Seeing that I was unable to go on, Fr. Chinh took the book from my unsteady hands. Fighting back his own emotions, he completed the reading and proceeded with the service.

Nearly everyone in the chapel was crying. We bowed, our faces in our hands, trying to suppress our sobs. These expressions of passion were like Deep Ocean waves that had been accumulating for days and now grown into a tidal wave that spilled over the breakwaters of self-control. Our tears joined with the holy water in blessing a new life that was to take its place in a world whose future no one could predict.

The priest concluded the ceremony by commending the fate of our country into the hands of the Blessed Mother:

O Mother, have mercy on Vietnam.
Under cloudy skies came ruinous war.
Raise your hands and grant us peace.
Bring Vietnam out of this time of danger...

The congregation lifted their trembling voices in song. Sunlight shone through the stained-glass window above the altar, making the tear-stained faces of the congregation sparkle. Little An's baptismal ceremony had turned into a shared rite, a ritual prayer for the soul of Vietnam, and a plea for peace, courage, and hope.

///

That afternoon we were told to vacate the monastery.

"There is no chance for evacuation," Father Chinh informed us sadly. "Please return to your homes and do the best you can. The new authorities have ordered that all groups must disperse and everyone must return to their own homes. Please don't give them an excuse to make trouble for the monastery. May the Lord watch over you and us!"

Before departing with Thuan An, Thuy asked me to offer up a prayer to St. Anne, our daughter's patron saint.

"Dear St. Anne," I said, "mother of Mary, the mother of Jesus, protect baby Thuan An. Preserve her, guide her family and the people of South Vietnam through the trials to come."

That night my brothers came looking for us at the home of Thuy's parents. No one bothered to congratulate us on An's baptism. Instead, we all sat down to discuss what to do next as the occasional sound of gunfire and explosions echoed in the distance.

Chapter 2

Double Bind

Persistent Persuasion

■ THUY

My parents tried to convince us to leave the country together, immediately. They had just returned to Saigon from Can Tho, where they owned and managed a private high school called Hau Giang.

"The Voice of America," declared Papa, "says the U.S. Seventh Fleet is patrolling international waters off the coast and is prepared to rescue anyone who makes it there by boat. We have to make our move before the communists blockade the shoreline."

He turned to Phuc.

"The work you did puts you in more danger than the rest of us. We are all anti-communists, but your voice was all over the radio, affirming your beliefs every day. You must leave!"

Papa knew well the area of Vung Tau, the nearest beach town, where he had had a vacation home for many years and had many friends. He had also managed a private bank that financed the fishing industry there. Some of his former clients owned fishing boats, so he had called one of them and asked for a boat. The communists had not yet started registering the boats, so many fishermen were selling their craft to finance their own escape.

"I've asked someone to put down a payment for a fishing boat and get it ready. We can all go together."

He looked around at Phuc's family, clearly indicating that the invitation included them as well.

Elder brother Lan shook his head.

SURVIVING
49

"It's too risky right now," he said. "We should have left earlier, but now the communist army is in control everywhere."

No one dared mention the biggest concern that lay beneath the surface of Papa's proposal: it would be no easy thing to survive on the open sea on a fragile fishing vessel.

Phuc agreed with his brother; he was going to stay. I remained silent, my heart pulled in two directions.

Papa did not give up, citing various arguments why we should leave. But when night fell, Phuc and his family remained adamant. We stayed at my parents' house that night so we could bid them farewell in the morning.

My Papa did not sleep. He seemed to be waiting for the kitchen light to go on, indicating that Phuc and I were preparing formula for baby An. As soon as we came in, he confronted us, applying a less aggressive approach and using history to make his point.

"I've already had experience living with the communists in the North," he said. "Many of my close friends became victims of the savage denunciation campaigns against landlords and the minor bourgeoisie. There were staged public trials, and many people were unfairly accused of exploiting the peasants. People were executed or sent to prison.

"They brainwash the people to go against everything they'd learned in the past. They proclaim a doctrine they call the *Three No's*: no family, no country, and no religion. Under communism, there is no family anymore, and everyone must spy on each other and report their crimes—children betray their parents, husbands, and wives turn in one another. There is no country because communism is an international ideology that demands the people revere 'Uncle Lenin,' 'Uncle Stalin' and 'Uncle Ho,' leaders who are never wrong and who guide the people in opposing the capitalist imperialists. For them, any means is justified, including violence, in their quest to destroy capitalism. They are against religion, which they call the 'opium of the people' that clouds people's minds, preventing them from listening to the leader and the Party. They wish to eradicate all religion so only communism will remain."

I heard the anguish in Papa's voice as he laid out his arguments, but I could also see the pain in Phuc's face as he listened. Finally, I spoke up.

"Papa, Phuc's brothers have already made up their minds. It would be hard for us to leave."

"I know it's hard," he said. "But with your record, don't imagine you could live in peace."

Papa outlined our careers as war correspondents and the accomplishments that would draw particular attention from the new regime. He took our silence as a signal to press his case.

"There's no way the communists will leave you alone. You have to risk it now and come with Mama and Papa. It's your only chance to stay alive!"

Phuc still did not reply. Papa turned to me, his eyes pleading. I did not return his gaze but looked down at little An feeding in my arms.

"Thuan An is only two weeks old," I said. "I'm afraid she's not strong enough to be out on the ocean."

He was prepared for that excuse.

"I've arranged to have medicine on the boat in case the baby gets sick. We'll bring extra formula, too. The VOA says there are lots of American ships waiting in international waters. It will only take us about a day to get to them. That's much safer than staying here with all the chaos and danger. If something happens to her here, there's nothing you can do. If you stay, I'm afraid she'll wind up an orphan!"

He went on patiently, declaring that staying in Vietnam was tantamount to suicide. He was determined not to live under the communists, so he had to take his family out of the country. But he and Mama could not accept leaving without us. Therefore he persisted in his pleading.

Phuc knew that my family was very close and that we could not bear to be separated. At the same time, he could not abandon his mother and brothers who had decided to stay. In the end, for Papa's sake, he agreed that we would accompany my family to Vung Tau. He emphasized that he had not made a firm decision yet, but for the time being, he would come with my family.

That was enough for Papa. He immediately began making preparations for all of us to go to Vung Tau where his boat was waiting.

Later that night, Trinh Ngoc Toan, an airborne major and close friend of Phuc's, showed up on our doorstep. He asked to join us, and Papa agreed.

Way to the Sea

The following day we bade farewell to Phuc's family. No one said much, as everyone realized that words or gestures would only add to the sorrow of the parting.

It normally takes two hours to drive from Saigon to Vung Tau, but on May 2, 1975, it took us nearly eight. The road was obstructed in many places by earthworks built during last-ditch efforts by the Southerners to resist the invasion. We had to abandon our car and continue by foot around one such barrier, then board a bus on the other side, an action we had to repeat several times.

The constant walking and changing vehicles were wearing me out. Just two weeks had passed since An was born, and I had not fully recovered my strength. Although I tried my best to hide my discomfort, Phuc could see how this was affecting me, and it reinforced his reluctance to risk a journey by sea.

Once we arrived in Vung Tau, Papa decided that we might draw attention to ourselves if we stayed in his beach house, so he led us to a guest residence connected to a small Buddhist temple. The site was also more convenient for departure, and he immediately set to work purchasing fuel and supplies for the escape.

Meanwhile, now that we were away from his family, I tried to convince Phuc that having come this far we should wait and see —if an opportunity arose, we should go with my family.

The first escape attempt was a dismal failure. Uninvited passengers came from out of nowhere so that instead of the intended thirty people, there were eighty cramming on board. Papa could not stop them and was forced to postpone the departure. The intended passengers gave up and went back to shore.

The would-be escapees who had sneaked in sat all day on the boat, cramped and hungry, under the watchful eye of the local security police. Eventually they, too, slipped away. Papa then moved the boat to another spot and passed the word to the others that they would set off that night. He also went to try to convince his sister and her family to come with us.

My uncle Trac was the head of the Vung Tau Department of Social Services and lived next door to my parents' vacation house. Uncle had responsibility for the hundreds of thousands of refugees who had streamed into the coastal city during April. He had heard countless tragic tales from the refugees. Now he and his wife were hesitant to leave, presuming it was too late. Like Phuc's family, they doubted they would make it safely on the open seas in a tiny boat.

At that point, Phuc and I took stock of our situation. When night fell, we sat gazing out at the horizon, black against the expanse of water, not knowing where the waves would take us and what the future had in store.

I loved my family and did not want to be separated from them. But I felt just as bad about Phuc having to leave his own family. I knew, too, that Phuc never wanted to leave the land of his birth, so much so that he had even declined opportunities for professional training abroad. Although our homeland was dead politically, it was still a place of beauty and as familiar to us as ever.

Moreover, the journalist in Phuc always came first. His passion for his career always filled me with a mixture of distress and admiration. He had a dream of being a witness to the events of history. So I knew that in his heart of hearts he did not want to leave, especially at this stage in Vietnam's history. If he were to go now, he would regret it for the rest of his life. Although he never expressed this thought out loud, I could see it in his face.

Phuc knew that I wanted to leave with my Papa and Mama, and he tried to please me. However, at the last moment, when Papa came to let us know the boat was waiting, Phuc announced that we were staying behind. Surprised to hear this, Major Toan tried to change his good friend's mind. Failing this, he hugged Phuc goodbye and went off with my Papa.

Then a nephew, Huy Cuong, an Air Force helicopter pilot who had evacuated from Nha Trang the week before, suddenly decided he wanted to leave the country after all. With his brand-new bride, he said farewell to his parents, grabbed a few belongings and followed his uncle, my Papa. With everything happening so fast, my emotions jostled and swirled in a mass of nerves.

The First Boat Escape

■ PHUC

I knew my decision would hurt Thuy and her family. Still, I had only promised that I would go with them as far as Vung Tau, so they respected that promise. Unable to convince me

SURVIVING

53

further, they resigned themselves to letting us stay in Vietnam.

As we watched their boat recede in the distance, I realized that I had made a mistake in letting Thuy come along to observe their departure. It would have been better for her to say goodbye in Saigon. She was silent and numb, her face pale and covered with tears. She remained sobbing on the pier even after the boat disappeared from view.

Holding little An, I waited patiently. There was nothing I could do to comfort her or alleviate the pain she felt at being separated from her family, so I gave her the freedom to wash away her grief in tears.

When evening came, there were no more buses to take us back to Saigon, so we stayed the night in Vung Tau. Thuy cried all night. She uttered not a word, not a moan of hurt or expression of reproach, but simply sobbed. All night I agonized inside. I couldn't stand to see her this way and, most of all, I regretted forcing her apart from her family. I hadn't realized she would take it this hard. And so the next morning when her father suddenly appeared, I was ready to give in.

"Yesterday we sailed beyond territorial waters," he explained to us. "We saw no communist patrols, the way out to international waters was completely open and safe. I came back to tell you that you can make it out with us."

Under the pretext of returning to purchase more fuel for the boat, Thuy's father had come to make one final appeal. I felt I had no choice but to surrender.

The surprising swiftness of victory had left the communists unprepared to deploy personnel to control the entire country. Perhaps, too, the Northern soldiers were celebrating their success and, dazzled by the prosperity of the South, which contrasted sharply with the poverty and deprivation they had endured for decades, they were not ready to go back to work. Thuy's father had even been able to bring the boat closer to the main beach of Vung Tau so he could come and get us.

I agreed to leave on one condition.

"If we aren't rescued by an American ship when we reach international waters, you have to let us turn back," I insisted. "I'm afraid Thuy and An wouldn't survive for days out there."

He readily accepted this proposition, confident that everything would be fine. I had never seen Thuy's face light up like it did then. Holding baby An tight, she stepped cautiously onto the boat, radiant with joy.

I was the last to come aboard. My heart sank, and this time it was I who felt like crying.

///

There were 38 passengers on the boat, all packed together and jockeying for space. With engine straining, the vessel heaved slowly out to sea.

Our escape vessel was similar to this refugee boat. Photo: UNHCR.

Once more I had doubts about the seaworthiness of the tiny fishing boat. I thought that Thuy's father was too sure of himself. The ocean might be clear of patrols, but the boat was too fragile to withstand days at sea.

When we reached international waters, everyone let out a cry of relief, and some broke into song. Thuy's father kept his ear glued to the radio, and now he turned up the volume so we could hear as the VOA announced that American naval ships were being ordered to the Pacific to pick up any Vietnamese boat people who made it out to them. The news further raised our spirits.

However, we did not see any American ships. We sailed far from the Vietnamese coastline for three days. Every time sunlight flashed on the surface of the water in the distance, someone shouted, "There's a ship!"

We prayed. We hoped. We waited, certain that at any time we would spot an American rescue vessel on the horizon. But our enthusiasm gradually waned as we realized we were alone in the middle of the vast and empty sea. And then there was the thirst.

Expecting to be rescued as soon as we made it far enough offshore, we had not brought adequate provisions, including water and fuel. On the third day, the trip's organizers huddled together and began whispering in urgent tones. By then the passengers were becoming restless.

Especially me. Up until then, I had stayed out of the boat's affairs, letting the others do whatever they wanted while I helped Thuy take care of the baby. But the situation was becoming precarious.

Right from the start of the voyage, a wealthy family had taken over the cabin, the only covered place on the boat. The four of them—a couple and their two grown children—sat comfortably in the shade while the rest of us roasted under the tropical sun, the heat intensifying by its reflection off the ocean. Children cried constantly and adults were soon grumbling.

Folks glared at the fortunate family, who seemed completely indifferent to our plight. A story went around that the family had joined the escape at the last minute and, waving a big wad of cash to meet the increase in the boat price, demanded the cabin for themselves, most likely to protect the possessions they had brought along. "Proof" of this assertion was how the father never let go of his briefcase and used it as a pillow when he slept. The family's snobbishness irked me, too, but I kept my thoughts to myself.

It was when An developed a fever that I had finally had enough. I made my way to the cabin and pounded on the door. When there was no response, I pushed it in.

The head of the family, tightly clutching his briefcase, turned to look at me. I glowered back. He looked away, pretending not to hear when I spoke with a quiet but firm voice.

"Please give up the shade for the women and children."

He shook his head carelessly as if I were a servant who had just offered him a cup of tea. Without thinking, I grabbed him by the arm. When he resisted, I lunged at him and threw him out of the cabin, flinging his precious briefcase after him. His wife and children immediately vacated the cabin and followed him.

I looked at the children huddled by the side of the boat and waved them into the cabin. They scrambled into the shade and sat down happily, scooting over to make room for their mothers. Two toddlers immediately stopped crying and fell asleep in their mothers' laps.

Thuy's father tried to relieve the tension on the boat by announcing that we were going to head for Malaysia. He argued that if we simply waited to be rescued, we would run out of food and water, as well as fuel, and we couldn't risk being caught in a storm.

He hailed a fishing boat passing our way and asked to buy some of their fuel and food. At first, the fishermen refused, but they changed their mind when he offered a price many times over the value of the supplies.

Meanwhile, I was getting more agitated and discontented. My child was beginning to show signs of dehydration. The water we were using for her formula was not pure enough for an infant. A four-day journey to Malaysia could be devastating for her. Furthermore, before agreeing to join them on the boat, I had told Thuy's father that if the Americans did not rescue us, we would turn back. I was determined to follow up on that demand.

So when the other boat pulled up alongside us, I shouted, "Can you give my family a lift back to Vietnam?"

Farewell at Sea

■ THUY

When Papa heard Phuc ask the fishermen to take us back with them, he became very upset. He tried to convince us to stay with the rest of the family, believing that Phuc would see the wisdom of this once we docked in a free port. But Phuc had made up his mind.

For my part, I was alarmed to see the two men I loved most in the world locking horns. While my heart was breaking, Mama and my siblings sobbed and pleaded with them to keep their voices down. I could tell that Phuc didn't want to get into a fight with Papa, but he went on gathering our things. Dismayed, I went from one to the other, begging them to stop.

Mama took hold of Phuc, hugging him tightly to keep him from moving. She pressed her tear-covered face into his shoulder. But he gently broke away, snatched little An from my arms, and jumped into the fishing boat before we could react.

Papa came and stood between my husband and me.

"I can't let you kill yourself by going back there!" he shouted. "Use your head. You'd be crazy to go back!"

He grabbed me by the shoulders and shook me hard, then looked directly into my eyes as if willing me to see reality. I was frantic and cried as I looked from Papa to my husband and child.

"Oh, Papa! Let me go! Don't force me!"

Mama realized that once Phuc and the baby were off the boat, I could not leave without them. She came and embraced me.

"Enough, dear!" she softly said to Papa. "Let your daughter go with her husband and baby."

Papa turned away and walked to the back of the boat. I hugged Mama, then my brother and sisters, all sobbing uncontrollably. Then, turning to Papa, I bowed in apology through my tears before climbing into the fishing boat to stand next to Phuc.

I took baby An from Phuc and held her tight. I felt as though my heart were in a million pieces.

The supplies transferred, the fishing boat, which now carried three passengers, prepared to set off. Before it did so, Mama reached over to hand me a plastic bag containing some jewelry and money. When I tried to refuse it, she tossed it at my feet.

"When you get back there, you'll need this more than we will," she said, her voice cracking. "Please be careful, child!"

The sound of her crying mixed with the beating of waves against the side of the boat augmented the storm inside my heart. The others in the two boats were silent, overcome by the drama playing out before them. My Papa, his shoulders stooped in futility, did not turn around to watch me go.

I had always been Papa's girl, and I always relied on my parents. I never really thought that one day I might have to choose between them and my husband and child in a matter of life and death. But all my life I was taught to be brave and do what I thought was right. And so, despite my heartache and fear at returning to live under the communists, I had to leave my Papa and Mama and follow my husband back to Vietnam. I believed it was the right thing to do. I thought that in time they would understand.

Still, years later, I am haunted by the image of my dear Papa turning away so I could not see him cry.

■ PHUC

I was hurting inside, knowing how close Thuy was to her parents, especially her father. I glanced at her out of the corner of my eye to gauge her feelings. Her face was drenched in tears as she stood up straight beside me clutching our baby, but her eyes were fixed on her father and mother.

We spoke not a single word all the way back to Vietnam. I could only guess at the agonized thoughts that filled her mind. As much as I was concerned about her mental state, I hoped she would share my feelings about turning back. Being a journalist herself, I hoped that Thuy would not be afraid to bear witness to history in the making and be able to cope with the challenges we would face under the communists. I trusted that regardless of what happened, the people of the South and North were all Vietnamese and there would be no rancor between them.

Although reason told me it was wiser to leave and seek a better future for my child, my heart belonged to my homeland. I felt that we must share our country's destiny. Moreover, we were not alone—millions of our fellow South Vietnamese shared that destiny.

I thought I had made the right decision. I did believe so.

Not-so-welcome Home

When we reached shore around noon the following day, I saw that we had arrived at Bac Lieu, nearly 250 miles west of Saigon, in the delta. We had to take a bus back to the capital. It was then that I first witnessed the awful reality of life under the communists.

In the few days we were away, they had seized the entire South, turning it from a free country into a land of repression. Soldiers patrolled the roads, monitoring even the slightest actions of the citizens. There was only one route back to Saigon by bus. Security police and *bo doi* were everywhere, stopping traffic and checking identity papers. Thuy and I had not imagined they could establish such authoritarian control so quickly.

About a third of the way out, the bus halted at a checkpoint and we were asked to produce our identification. When a soldier saw my military ID card, he pulled me off the bus and took me into the guardhouse. I tried to appear calm.

"Is there a problem, 'brothers'?" I asked.

"You're kept here," the soldier said without looking at me, "for the Revolution to send you to re-education."

A fellow who looked to be of higher rank grabbed my card and peered at it.

"You're an officer of the illegitimate army," he declared. "Why are you still here? You should have reported for rehabilitation."

"I was away from Saigon to get my wife and child," I explained. "We're on our way back so I can report."

I heard An crying behind me and became anxious that Thuy had followed me off the bus. Looking outside, I saw them sitting beside the guard post in the hot midday sun.

"My daughter is only two weeks old and has a fever," I said moving toward the door. "Please, let me go see"

The soldier pounded the table and shouted, then raised his rifle and ordered me to remain where I was.

■ THUY

When the *bo doi* escorted Phuc off the bus and into the guardhouse, I looked worriedly at little An, so frail and red with fever. I debated whether I should follow Phuc or continue to Saigon with the baby. Some of the others on the bus advised me to stay since Phuc was an "officer of the illegitimate regime" and would be taken away for re-education. An order for former soldiers to report had been implemented in the provinces, although not yet in Saigon.

However, as I had just lost my own family, I didn't want to lose my husband, too. So, without further thought, I took An and my bag and made my way to the guard hut.

The soldier standing outside would not let me enter but made me wait next to the gate. The silence in the guardhouse worried me. Had they beaten Phuc senseless?

The blazing sun bore down on us. I sat down against the hut's mud wall. Baby An gasped for breath. I poured some water onto a handkerchief and placed it on her forehead. A swarm of flies from a nearby rubbish heap flew over and settled on An's lips, stained with remnants of milk, causing her to cry. I covered her head with the flap of my long blouse to ward off the sun while shooing away flies and trying to soothe her.

I was frightened and worried but tried to remain calm. My emotions were strained to the breaking point, and I couldn't think straight, so I just sat there, uncertain what to do.

Some curious children gathered around me, followed by several old women who lived in the vicinity. They shared food and asked what the problem was. Their kindness touched me deeply, and through tears I told them my story, concluding with how I hoped they would send my husband to Saigon to report for re-education. The crowd grew, and they discussed my case in whispers. Finally, a few old women strode to the guardhouse and addressed the soldiers.

"Let the man go! His wife just had a baby, and she can't go home alone! Let him go, and he can report in Saigon!"

The soldiers seemed unsure about what to do with Phuc. Only a few of them looked like regular *bo doi*, while the rest were young and wore civilian clothes with a red armband, probably local youths recruited to help watch the post.

Through their exchanges, I learned that the government had ordered all South Vietnamese government and military personnel (whom they referred to as "illegitimate soldiers and officials") to register at once for re-education in their local areas. However, the rules said nothing about "officers of the illegitimate army" like Phuc who were simply passing through from one area to another.

As the soldiers argued among themselves, the crowd of women (whom the soldiers addressed as "foster mothers of the Revolutionary warriors") grew larger and more vocal. They stood right beside the window and shouted inside.

"Are you young fellows going to help this poor woman and her baby or not?"

"You want the baby to die out here in the heat?"

The guards were confused by this situation. For a time they discussed how they might properly display "revolutionary spirit" when the rules did not mention Phuc's particular case. As evening came, more locals had surrounded the post and, in the end, the *bo doi* decided to let Phuc go. One of them raised his voice to justify the decision.

"Today you were fortunate. Because of the intervention of these 'mothers' and because your newborn child is ill, the Revolution is showing leniency by allowing you to proceed to Saigon to register. Once you arrive there, you must report at once, got it?"

I sighed, relieved, when I heard Phuc reply, "Thank you, brothers. Once I reach Saigon, I will report right away!"

Then he hurried outside and helped me to my feet. We both

clasped our hands in gratitude to the kind-hearted people who had stepped in to help. Pleased with the result of their action, the villagers led us back to the road and helped us onto the next bus to Saigon.

Safely back at my parents' house, I went straight to the bedroom and lay down exhausted. My heart ached, and my mind was numb from the horrible real-life scene I had just faced. If the return trip at sea had drained me emotionally, then the bus trip from Bac Lieu had been a nightmare that wounded me physically.

The experience that day troubled me. The long time spent holding my baby on the roadside by the guard post begging others to pity me and save my husband made me feel both ashamed and frightened.

I feared for the dark future we faced, and at the same time, I worried about my parents and siblings out on the sea. Would they make it? As for me, would I survive in Vietnam?

All throughout my life I had enjoyed the love and care of my family, who were always there to help and comfort me. Now they were all gone. And I had gone back to live in Saigon. Had I done the right thing?

I was weary and hurt, but I couldn't sleep. I listened to Voice of America on the short-wave radio beside the bed. It said that over the past several days American ships had rescued many refugees from boats sailing from Vietnam. I prayed that my family's boat was among them.

I sat still in the darkness holding An close to me, rocking her in my arms, singing a lullaby that my Mama had sung to me when I was little. But when I sang it, my voice had no emotion or life.

You have your papa; you have your mama.
Mama loves you like a stream at its source.
From the day you were born
Mama coddled you as gently as an egg.
She takes you like a flower
And holds you close to her heart.
Mama holds you in her heart...

Chapter 3

Life under Communism

Winners...

■ PHUC

T he city of Saigon changed its face under the communists. The North Vietnamese flag, red with a yellow star, and the blue-and-red flag of the National Liberation Front flew from every street, every building, and even from people's homes.

Bo doi and security police encroached upon every segment of the city, which was red with banners extolling socialism and glorifying "Uncle Ho" and the Communist Party as gods who had brought life and happiness to humanity. The victors from the North constantly reviled the "imperialist Americans" and the soldiers and officials of the South Vietnamese government, to whom they referred as the "illegitimate army and illegitimate government that drank the blood of the people."

Along with the Communist Party members who held the critical positions in the city there emerged groups of Southerners wearing red armbands known as "April 30 cadres." Arrogant, brash, and foolish, these civilian "converts" to the Revolution popped up everywhere to assist Party authorities in running the day-to-day operations of the new regime. These would-be cadres, however, knew nothing about Marxism and the Revolution but simply parroted the slogans and admonitions they heard from their superiors.

Now, instead of cars and motor scooters, only bicycles filled the streets. The city-dwellers suddenly became subdued, skittish, and resigned to their fate. Women no longer wore the *ao dai*,[5] the light dress with flowing skirt panels over silky pants, nor modern attire, but rather the *ao ba ba*,[6] the purely functional dark shirt and pants of the working class. They put away their fine and colorful store-bought clothes and wore only coarse garb, even dying their clothes in somber hues according to the instruction of the April 30 cadres. From now on, the people of the South were to dress "properly," no longer in the manner of the "petty bourgeoisie," in keeping with the image of a "socialist" population. Women were also ordered to remove their nail polish to erase these "vestiges of the Americans and the illegitimate society" that violated the "good customs of Revolutionary beauty."

The city's customary cacophony of color suddenly disappeared as if behind the curtain of a devilish magic show. The former capital of South Vietnam now had only one bright color: the blood red of the communist flag flying everywhere, staining the whole of South Vietnam. Saigon was transformed from a vibrant, radiant metropolis once called "The Pearl of the Orient" into a drab, subdued place where people were afraid to let go a sigh lest they rankle "Mr. Revolutionary."

So frightened were the people of the South that they hastily destroyed all pictures that had any association with the old government. Neighbors insisted that we burn any photographs of family and friends that showed me in uniform or standing with government officials. All medals, awards, and citations were to share the same fate.

When Thuy and I returned home after our abortive escape attempt, we found that our relatives had burned all our photos, letters, newspapers clippings, radio cassette tapes—anything that the new regime might find incriminating. Thuy was so distressed at the loss that she searched throughout the house for anything they might have missed. She managed to find a few photos that had been left behind, including one of the two of us by the Thien Mu pagoda in Hue taken by a street photographer the day I first declared my love for her. Whoever had found it only tore off the section that showed my army uniform.

---

[5] ao dai /*ow zigh* or *ow yigh*/
[6] ao ba ba /*ow bah bah*/

**Love at Thien Mu Pagoda,
Hue, July 1972.**

The communists organized the population into a hierarchy of divisions. A "cell" comprised three families, several families made up a "neighborhood," and several neighborhoods formed a "ward." In this way, they managed to control everything from what we discussed in public to what we ate each day.

To blend in with the Revolutionary life, we suddenly became introverted, reticent, less sure of ourselves than before. And yet, beneath the superficial changes wrought by the communist takeover, one could see signs of a profound urge to survive. Though bent low, people shared glances of commiseration with their fellow subjects. And every once in a while one might catch a glimpse of the old Saigon. Amid the walls plastered with posters praising "Uncle and Party" were vines with purple flowers and fresh bougainvilleas reaching up as if challenging the new social order.

Out on the streets, we could exchange closeness and shared

sympathy by the look in our eyes, along with the determination not to let the new system gain control over our spirit. They might have won the war, but they had no claim to our hearts.

... and Losers

In mid-June, notices began appearing in public places addressed to those who had been in the South Vietnamese military or government. The announcement was broadcast from loudspeakers attached to lampposts and street signs, as well as on military vehicles, cars, motorcycles, and bikes driven by information cadres in the neighborhoods and wards.

"All former military and government personnel of the old regime must report to the Revolutionary government on June 26, 1975, for rehabilitation.

"Junior military officers and mid-grade government officials of any department must bring personal supplies and food to last ten days.

"High-ranking officers and government officials with the rank of department chief or higher must bring personal supplies and food to last thirty days.

"Registration will take place at the following high schools...."

The announcement was made matter-of-factly as if this were simply a routine procedure of no great consequence. Only a few weeks earlier, low-level officers and government workers had been required to register in this way, bringing with them enough food and supplies for three days. Everyone waited to see what would happen to them, as we were all familiar with the communists' tactics of propaganda and deception. But, as promised, the re-education "students" returned home after three days of lectures in nearby locations. As a result, we let down our guard. If three days was enough for those of minor rank and station, then it was natural that officers and officials higher up should be "enrolled" for ten or thirty days.

Hundreds of thousands of former members of the South Vietnamese military and government set off to report as ordered. In my family, two of my brothers were outside of the country. The four who remained prepared themselves for this formality, supposing that after our time was up, we would return to our families. Eldest brother Lan, a former judge, registered at Gia Long School, while brothers Cu, Kien, and I signed in at Vo Truong Toan School.

Thuy was beside herself. Though I tried to reassure her, she didn't trust the communists and couldn't believe they would let me return home. I pointed out that in ten days it would be our one-and-a-half-year anniversary, and told her to prepare a small party, at which time we could talk about the future.

■ THUY

I pleaded with Phuc not to report, afraid that once he entered the high school I would never see him again. Even though he and his brothers believed that they would be released like the lower officials before them, I wasn't so sure.

"The communists are Vietnamese, just like us," elder brother Lan said to me. "They got their victory. Now that they have taken over the South, there's no reason for them to continue persecuting us."

Phuc agreed.

"We have no choice. Now that we're back, we have to adapt to the new society if we want to survive. If I don't report for re-education, I'll have to live a life on the run, and that's too dangerous, especially when I have a family with a small child."

I listened to them, but no matter how rational their words seemed, I was still apprehensive. I didn't believe that after 30 years of slaughter the war would simply end easily and amicably. Moreover, how could the communists so quickly become friendly and respectable? During my childhood, I had listened to my parents' tales of what they had experienced of the communists after the first war when the Viet Minh defeated the French.

"Never trust the communists," Papa had told me. "They will say anything, make any promise, to get what they want. Their way is based on deception, and they won't hesitate to use any scheme, any means, to gain control over the people. Their word is utterly worthless."

From 1945 to 1954 the communists had used honeyed words to win over the people of the North and convince them to stay, luring them into the trap of "nation and people." Yet at the same time, they were secretly settling accounts with those who did not share their ideas, even loyal comrades who had been with them from the beginning in the struggle against the French. Once they suspected a seed of dissent, they struck at once to eliminate it.

Many people saw the true face of communism. In 1954, when the Geneva Accord divided Vietnam into two zones, one million Northern natives chose to give up their homes, their lands, and their ancestors' graves to evacuate to the South. When those who remained could no longer escape, the communists began their campaigns of retaliation.

In 1955, they instituted a land reform program. Motivated by promises of a share of the land, poor peasants were induced to denounce their landlords, even those who had treated them well. Many such landowners had provided material support to Ho Chi Minh and the Revolutionary army and were instrumental in bringing about the victory over the French. Nonetheless, they had to be eliminated for the advance of communism.

I could still hear Papa's assertion: "Friend or foe, if they need to, they are prepared to kill anybody."

Although I myself had no personal experience with the communists, everything I had heard from my parents along with everything I had seen and read during my years as a journalist convinced me that we couldn't trust anything they said. I was afraid for Phuc and his brothers. My gut feeling was that history would repeat itself, especially with regards to Marxist-Leninist communism.

And so, it was with a sense of foreboding that I accompanied Phuc to Vo Truong Toan high school. My heart was pounding so hard I did not hear him say goodbye. As he waved and turned to enter the school, I watched him go, my insides wrenched with grief.

■ PHUC

When I advised Thuy to have faith in our fellow countrymen, I was also trying to convince myself. I felt that despite our political differences, now that the communists ruled over the whole of Vietnam there would be no point in carrying on resentment or seeking vengeance. They were human and Vietnamese like us and had families of their own. After so many years of tiresome fighting, surely they wanted to live in peace and security. So, in offering her hope, I was also trying to make myself believe that things would turn out all right, if only because there was nothing else we could do.

But when we arrived at Vo Truong Toan School on June 26, Thuy was still skeptical. I hugged her and said goodbye, reminding her to come back and get me in ten days. The bag I brought with me contained the things I thought I would need just for that period.

I turned around once more and saw Thuy standing wordlessly by the entrance. Her face was pale and anguished, just as it had been when she'd stood watching the boat take away her family on the sea nearly two months earlier.

I felt a sudden chill.

The Brutal Reality

I turned in my papers, and then waited for what I thought would be a class about the new government with cadres singing the praises of socialism and the communist leadership.

Instead, the guards told a group of us to hurry across the schoolyard and wait there. I had a bad feeling about this. My heart began to pound, and I couldn't think clearly. For the remainder of the day, I lived in a state of serious misgiving while thousands of my fellow officers from the South Vietnamese army filed in to register.

As dusk fell, a convoy of military vehicles drove in through the rear gate. These were army trucks with canvas-covered beds, which must have been confiscated from an ARVN transport depot. The *bo doi* shouted for us to get in the vehicles. The covers were let down and tied shut from the outside, leaving the men in darkness. Then the trucks lurched forward, and we were carried off into the night.

So Thuy had been right after all. The order for officers to report was just a pretext to round us up and take us away. And we had fallen for it, bowing our heads in submission and cooperating with their demands, not suspecting that all their talk of reconciliation, respect, and honor was merely a ploy to capture men who truly believed in those ideals.

At first, the ride was smooth, and I prayed they were taking us someplace in the Saigon vicinity. Sometime later, however, the roads became rough and winding. We were jostled and fell on top of one another. No one bothered to apologize; we were too preoccupied with our collective fate. The air under the canvas top was stuffy and many men found it difficult to breathe.

At last, we came to a halt. The flap was lifted, and we climbed out and stretched, gasping for air.

In the darkness, a thick forest greeted us. Tall trees and dangling creepers swayed threateningly as if angry at being disturbed in the night.

"Here's your new home, guys!" said one of the cadres. "This is where you will live until you are properly rehabilitated and have learned all the lessons of socialism provided by Uncle Ho and the Party."

He checked names off a list and directed us to our quarters. We kept our eyes down to avoid disclosing our resentment at the deception that had brought us here. The site of the concentration camp was a former South Vietnamese army camp composed of primitive blockhouses with wooden frames and earth walls, the doors locked with chains. Barbed wire fences, patrolled by armed guards, surrounded the camp.

With all their experience in jungle living and guerrilla warfare, the communist soldiers were experts at selecting a location for a prison. They were used to the insects and the illnesses borne by mosquitoes and other pests. Even malaria seemed to be a common ailment that they took in stride.

From then on our days were shaped by routine. While the early morning mist still hung in the air, we were awakened by a guard banging on a sheet of metal, followed by barking commands and insults directed at those who failed to respond quickly enough. We breakfasted on thin soup made from moldy rice mixed with hard sorghum, and then went off to work. The younger prisoners felled trees and cleared brush using old, rusty tools. The older men gathered the branches and brush into bundles. We also cleared dry fields to plant sweet potatoes and manioc. We dug wells to get water for drinking and washing.

Some of the prisoners were forced to sweep for landmines left over from the war. The guards mocked us and hurled verbal abuse as part of their policy of "re-education."

"Do you see the results of American imperialism in our

country? And you were the ones who welcomed those barbarians here!"

If a mine exploded, wounding some of the prisoners, the guards just shook their heads and scolded us like children.

"You brought that on yourselves, guys!"

While we worked, the guards went around, pointing their rifles at us threateningly. Otherwise, they took turns resting on the wood piles and casually smoking cigarettes.

Indoctrination and Brainwashing

When darkness fell, we returned to the camp for a meal of old rice mixed with manioc or sorghum, a punishment for our stomachs since it was so little and provided no nutrition. It was after we were finished eating that the true goal of "rehabilitation" began.

We were taken into a large room, empty except for a few scattered chairs for the cadres. The prisoners were made to sit cross-legged on the floor. (I later learned that some of our number who practiced Zen meditation had learned to sit in that style from these sessions.)

A ranking military cadre, usually a secretary or commissar, went up to deliver the lesson. These political propaganda officers taught a revisionist history of Vietnam that directly contradicted what I had seen and experienced in the South.

For instance: "The American imperialists invaded Vietnam, and the government and military of the Republic of Vietnam were merely lackeys of the Americans exploiting the 'bones and blood' of the people."

And: "The tolerant policy of the Party and State toward those of the illegitimate army and government is not to kill them but to send them to 'education and practice' in the correct way."

The most twisted lesson of all was the one that said: "The Revolution must bring the people of the illegitimate army and government here for rehabilitation to protect them from the anger and resentment of the people...."

The goal of this "instruction" was to instill in us their fanaticism. The prisoners' first reaction was annoyance and indignation. Eventually, we began to find the exercise a joke, the lessons so perverse and foolish that we let them go in one ear and out the other, realizing that all we had to do was parrot the proper phrases to show we had "learned our lesson."

The protracted and repetitious lectures on communist theory often made me sleepy. In time, however, I came to see how this soporific quality of education was an effective element in brainwashing. I was led into a hypnotic trance in which the images they presented took form in my subconscious, and I often came abruptly awake feeling that someone had physically pounded on my brain and reconstructed the thoughts in my head.

A cadre would present each lesson for some hours, often repeated over several days, after which the "re-educated" prisoners were divided into small groups to practice and drill the material until we had mastered it. Then each of us made a self-criticism in which he declared everything he had done before April 30, 1975, confessing that these activities had been monumental crimes against the Revolution, and displaying deep remorse and throwing himself on the mercy of the Party and Country.

We watched film clips of actress Jane Fonda wearing Vietnamese peasant clothing and an army helmet as she sat grinning beside a North Vietnamese antiaircraft gun. Another film showed singer Joan Baez in the assembly area of Hoa Lo prison (known to American POWs as the "Hanoi Hilton"), strumming a guitar and singing songs against the war and America's involvement in the conflict in Vietnam.

The films had the same effect as the lectures. We knew the speakers had no idea what they were talking about but were simply repeating what they had been taught as part of their indoctrination.

Their efforts to influence our thinking about the United States, however, did have some result. In talking to my fellow prisoners, I noticed that they shared a sense of having been betrayed by our American allies. It seemed that the Americans had used us to wage war for their political interests. When popular and political opinion turned against the war, they abandoned us, and in so doing delivered us into the hands of our enemy. Now our wealthy friends no longer wanted to have anything to do with Vietnam.

Each prisoner, in turn, was called to "work" with the chief instructors. "Work" was a euphemism for interrogation. Every time I entered the little room to get brainwashed, I felt exhausted in spirit as well as in body. I was made to relate my life and activities over and over, while I racked my brain to consider what I should say so I could repeat it later precisely the same way. I figured that if I confessed to being a journalist who spent his whole life enthusiastically reporting news in opposition to the communists and presenting evidence of their atrocities, I doubted they would let me stay around much longer.

I couldn't hide the fact that I had worked for Armed Forces Radio. Still, I tried to downplay the extent of my role there in the hope that they wouldn't be paying too much attention and decide that my activities were not that noteworthy. But I must admit that the communists were quite adept at the art of interrogation and repeated a question multiple times, even though I had already answered it many times before, to break me down little by little.

After testifying verbally, I was asked to write down my personal history. Over and over, again and again. Then they compared each new report with the ones before, and if they discovered any inconsistencies they invited me back for more "work."

This exercise caused considerable stress and mental exhaustion, such that I could no longer remember what I had said at any time. As time passed, I personally witnessed many of my camp mates stumbling out of the interrogation room with haggard faces and glazed eyes.

One method they used to break our spirit of resistance was to frequently transfer us from one camp to another. Just as we were becoming accustomed to the strenuous labor routine and the camp's fare, when our minds were adjusted to the tactics of one interrogator and the endless educational sessions, we'd be called up in the middle of the night to gather our belongings and move somewhere else to start all over again. So it was that in my first year of re-education, I lived in three different places—Trang Lon, Phu Quoc, and Long Giao—but always inside the confines of concentration camps.

Fanaticism

The life of a prisoner in a communist "re-education" concentration camp was one of extreme hardship, entailing every physical and mental abuse. Meals consisted of either a half cup of rice mixed with tough sorghum and a few spoonfuls of salt water or dry, rotten manioc with hard corn. Even then, the portions were quite small, and I was always hungry.

The education cadres constantly preached something they called "revolutionary virtue," jabbering on and on in pat phrases about "Uncle Ho and the Party" without any true understanding of what they were talking about. Unable to answer a question or clarify a point of uncertainty, they simply repeated utterances they had memorized, such as, "You have a blood debt with the people and by rights should be killed, but because of the clemency of the Revolution you are being allowed to be re-educated. You should be grateful to Uncle and the Party, and if you study hard and advance, you'll be allowed to go home...."

What puzzled me most was how, despite a lack of formal education and limited understanding, these cadres were confident to the point of zealotry. They trusted that whatever "Uncle and the Party" told them was the absolute, incontrovertible truth that everyone must absorb thoroughly and take to heart. Consequently, if one of the prisoners asked for further explanation of some vague point, the cadre would angrily accuse the questioner of being "reactionary" or having "the gall to oppose Uncle Ho and the Party!" If a prisoner's reasoning stumped a cadre, he might fly into a rage and send the poor man into solitary confinement for "daring to harbor ideas in opposition to the Revolution!"

After a while, most of us realized that there was no use trying to reason with the cadres, who were unaware of their ignorance, so we simply put up with it and concentrated on surviving. At the same time, we resented the fact that the South had lost the war to an enemy that was clearly no match for us intellectually.

Day and night I thought about Thuy and worried about what was happening to her and the baby. It was the first time in her life that Thuy was entirely on her own, her family and friends now gone. I felt helpless knowing that my absence added to my wife's pain. I knew Thuy would do everything she could to take care of baby An, but I didn't know how she would take care of herself alone under the harsh communist system.

By day, my fellow prisoners and I focused on survival: performing hard labor, clearing minefields, enduring abuse to our bodies and souls. I was constantly on guard to conceal my past in this or that detail. All the while I had to defend myself against the brainwashing of re-education.

By night, I missed my wife and child and worried about their safety. I was bitter toward our leaders who had abandoned us. And I wrestled with the hunger that prevented me from falling asleep.

Bourgeois Compradors

■ THUY

Ten days after Phuc registered, I went back to Vo Truong Toan high school to check on him. I met many women there who were doing the same thing. About fifty of us then decided to go to the Independence Palace (formerly the presidential palace, now the South Management Center) to ask about our husbands. We took strength in numbers, thinking the group would lend us some power. At the gate, the guards refused to let us meet with anyone who knew about the prisoners and told us to go home and wait for news from the government. They said if we kept coming here, we would be labeled as "Anti-Revolution activists" and our husbands would be severely punished. Then armed guards came out and threatened to arrest us. Our nascent activism stopped there.

Months went by with no news from the government. Terrifying rumors spread that Southern registrants were being moved to Northern prisons with no hope of being released.

For the first time in my life, I was all by myself. I had always enjoyed being independent and self-reliant, but I knew that if I ever needed anything I could always fall back on my family and friends. Now there was no one I could call.

For days I just sat in a corner and cried. Sometimes I stood in the shower so I would not be heard sobbing or screaming out. I became seriously depressed and even thought about dying to escape the hurt. I had no idea whether my parents and siblings were safe or still at sea; whether my husband was suffering from torture, or whether he was even still alive. And how was I going to get by with my baby under this new system?

But once the tears dried, I knew I could not leave my child

alone in the world or give up on my husband in prison. I knew, too, that it wasn't just me in this circumstance, but hundreds of thousands of women in Saigon who had to bear this burden for their children and pray that their husbands were all right.

Before Phuc reported to the authorities, we had decided that my brother Bau's home in Hoa Hung was the safest place for me to stay, since hardly anyone there knew of our background. Because my name wasn't on the property title, Phuc's brother Kien carved a counterfeit seal on a sweet potato and forged a document stating that I was the owner. That way I was included in the required household registry which listed all the home's inhabitants.

During the initial stage of the so-called "Revolution," people in Saigon could still purchase some goods since small shops were permitted to continue doing business, as long as they transferred their company to a joint public-private enterprise. Large businesses were taken over by the government right after April 30.

On September 10, 1975, as part of a campaign to transfer control of small businesses, the Provisional Revolutionary Government of the South gave the order to "attack the bourgeois compradors." The campaign rounded up wealthy people in business, charged them with speculation and hoarding, and eliminated the market system. We heard that sixty richest men had been taken away the night before the order was even made public.

Tens of thousands of public workers and students were mobilized to carry out this campaign against the "bourgeois compradors" in Saigon and 17 other major cities. In one night nearly every private enterprise was shut down. Hundreds of thousands of workers were without jobs and empty-handed. From then on, the people of the South were no longer able to buy or sell anything outside of the state stores, where supplies were limited and not readily available.

Once they had expropriated the "overt" goods and properties of business families, the new government went after the "covert" wealth, thought to be worth many times more. An order went out to all agencies, groups, schools, and individuals to identify relatives, staff, servants, and tenants of the dispossessed business people for questioning about the location of any "covert goods," that their masters might have squirreled away. Were any of these possessions found, the heads of families were accused of "deception and concealing money and property obtained through the exploitation of the bones and blood of the people." The culprits were thrown into prison and their entire property confiscated, forcing their families to relocate to areas known as "New Economic Zones."

New Economic Zones and Changing Money

Who can say how many innocent young people and children of business families were persuaded or coerced by their schools and social groups to display their revolutionary zeal by disclosing the places where their elders had hidden the family's valuables? Regardless, after they had served the cause, they ended up sharing their family's fate in the New Economic Zones.

These "zones" were wild, uncultivated areas unfit for human habitation. There was no infrastructure, not to mention schools or healthcare facilities. There was nothing but some exposed huts thrown together to house the people sent to resettle there. The new inhabitants were expected to construct their own homes. The government did not provide the means of survival other than the cadres' slogan: "With human effort, even stones can be turned into rice."

I had a friend whose husband was an army captain who worked in the Armed Forces radio station with Phuc and was now in re-education. With six small children at home, there was no way she could support them while under constant pressure from the local security police. Finally, she was persuaded by the neighborhood group to take her children and live in a New Economic Zone. A few months later, I heard that she had killed herself because she could not endure the hardship and hunger in that wasteland. Her children, aged twelve to one, were dispersed to different places.

Just two weeks after the campaign against "bourgeois compradors," before the people of the South had a chance to recover from that operation, on September 22 the authorities abruptly announced a change in currency. Once more, thousands of students and government workers were mobilized and placed in charge of money-changing for the population.

We were given just one day to exchange our money for the

new currency. At the official rate, 500 *dongs*[7] of the Republic of Vietnam equaled one *dong* of the revolutionary currency. Each family, regardless of size, was only permitted to exchange up to 100,000 *dongs* for 200 of the new *dong*.

Thus, in a single day, virtually the entire sum I had gained by selling the jewelry given me by Mama came to nothing. That night, two days before my 25th birthday, I sat alone and silently berated myself for not giving it more thought before selling Mama's mementos for what amounted to a pile of scrap paper.

Millions of people panicked. Some committed suicide or lost their minds on that terrible day, a day the newspaper *Sai Gon Giai Phong*[8] (Liberated Saigon) called the culmination of "thirty years of sordid life and shameful death of Saigon money."

This is how the communists made an economy. They declared that they were creating equality among all the people so that no one had the means to exploit others. In actuality, all the Southern people were exploited by the Party and government down to the marrow of their bones, such that everyone was as poor as everyone else in the new society.

And so, in one day the communists achieved "social equality" by eliminating the bourgeois class and small businesses in the South. I did not see any "equality." Rather, I saw only the communist cadres who before were simple foot soldiers recruited from the countryside, wearing frayed rubber sandals and jungle helmets, smoking homemade cigarettes and acting like hillbillies, now all of a sudden, after the exchange of currency, becoming wealthy men lording it over the people of the South.

The Poor and the Wretched

I belonged to the element referred to as *My-Nguy*,[9] that is, "Americans and members of the illegitimate regime." With my background as a daughter of "traitors to the people," so-called because my parents fled the country, and the wife of a "soldier of the illegitimate army" who was now undergoing re-education, I couldn't

---

[7]dong /*dohng*/
[8]Sai Gon Giai Phong /*sigh gahn zigh fong* or *yigh fong*/
[9]My-Nguy /*mee ngwee*/

get a job anywhere, not even low-paying menial labor.

The security police warned the neighbors that I might be a CIA spy who was kept in the country to continue operations. During cell meetings, they often used me as an example of a "*My-Nguy* family" and urged neighbors to ask me, "Why did you stay behind when the rest of your family left?" I told them the truth: we loved our country and believed that now that the country was reunited, we should stay to enjoy the peace and help reconstruct the country.

Outside the cell meetings, almost no one dared talk to me for fear of drawing attention to them. The security police were always nosing around and interrogating people. They enlisted the families who lived around me to keep watch and report my activities, gestures, and words.

Next to my carport was a little shed made of palm fronds belonging to a single mother known as Sister Sau who hired herself out to do odd jobs in the neighborhood. Immediately after April 30, 1975, Sister Sau cast off her old persona and became a champion of the Revolution. She was selected to be the chief of the neighborhood cell. Her first action was to expand her home into my carport.

The local security police and Sister Sau took it upon themselves to enter my house anytime they felt like it and make themselves completely at home. They never ceased reminding me that as one whose family "owed a blood debt to the people," I should be grateful for the Revolution's clemency in allowing me to live.

Something as insignificant as a nail hole in the wall might provoke an inquiry.

"What used to hang here? It must be something bad. Otherwise, you wouldn't have taken it down and left a mark like this!"

Once I was in the kitchen cooking when a noise startled me. I turned around to find the security officer standing behind me, apparently watching to see what I was preparing. I locked the gate to keep him out, which only aggravated him further.

"What kind of plot are you hatching against the Revolution," he asked, "that you have to hide behind a locked gate?"

There were nights as I sat lulling the baby to sleep, overcome with a feeling of disquiet, I looked outside and was shocked to see someone standing by the hedge peering in at me. My house was often subjected to midnight raids by the security police checking whether I was harboring any undocumented occupants.

What with the hardship, deprivation, and isolation, thinking about my family, feeling afraid and hurt, constant harassment and threats by the police, and being spied on by everyone around me, I became increasingly frightened and depressed. Here I was, 25 years old, with a new baby and no family or friends. My husband was in prison somewhere, and I didn't know whether he was alive or dead, or if alive, whether he was being mistreated.

Thuy and An, Saigon, January 1976.

The situation got so bad that I started to become afraid of ghosts.

It was only after I took up residence in the house near Hoa Hung market that I discovered that all the houses in the area stood on top of an old cemetery. The families of the deceased had relocated most of the graves, but some tombs were made of tough laterite and couldn't be removed or razed, so the developer had simply built around them.

I discovered that the flower garden in my front yard occupied a huge grave, which the previous owner had covered with dirt and turned into a plot for flowers. By my back door was another grave marker situated one half in my yard and the other half in a neighbor's. Phuc and I had thought it was a stone bench and sat there on moonlit nights to take in the cool air as we talked.

After learning all this, I became so frightened at night that I couldn't sleep but sat besides the bed holding An and crying until I drifted off from sheer exhaustion. But when I awoke in the dark, I sat up in a panic, gaping at the grave outside.

I became so psychologically stressed that I was afraid to open my mouth and say anything lest someone use my words as an excuse to cause trouble. Silence led me deeper into depression until I began to see death as a way to free myself from my horrible predicament.

Finally, one night I just couldn't take it anymore. I felt as though

I was losing my mind. Then suddenly I recalled something Mama had said to me once when we went to visit my grandmother's grave.

"The dead are always more kind than the living. We only need to pray for their souls to rest in peace, and they will protect us and help us find peace."

With this thought in mind, I knelt beside my bed, laid my head on little An, and prayed for the souls of the unknown persons buried in my yard. I prayed, as well, for all the ghosts in the neighborhood, and in the country as a whole. I prayed until the sun rose the next day. Although I didn't feel tired, I lay down next to An and fell asleep at once.

Each night after that, I prayed for all the spirits of the dead around me. Something stirred inside my heart and carried me away from my worries and cares about the problems of others.

Gradually, my mental and emotional distress diminished. Over time I not only lost my fear but began to feel stronger in facing the trials of reality. It seemed as if the dead had noticed me and come to my aid when the living would not.

Queues

The campaign against the bourgeois compradors was a means of nationalizing the private property of the wealthy merchants, and the money change served to financially strip the citizens. Afterward, there was nothing left in Saigon of the free and prosperous life it had known before April 30, particularly in private commerce. All goods were under the control of the communist authorities. Necessities such as rice, milk, sugar, meat, fuels for cooking (including oil, charcoal, and firewood), materials for making clothes, and so on, were rationed to each family based on the household registry.

Each month an average family could purchase two kilos of rice, a half kilo of sugar, one can of condensed milk, and one liter of cooking oil. Once every two or three months, a household was allowed to buy 200 grams of meat. Usually, we chose fatty pork because it could be cooked to last longer than lean meat.

To purchase these items, people had to wait in line,

sometimes for an entire day.[10] Those who couldn't wait in line hired stand-ins. Otherwise, they lost their chance. Whatever was left over was snatched up by cadres and sold on the black market at a rate several times higher than the official price.

It was hard for me to stand for a long time with An, so I often had to give up my place in line. Eventually, I found a neighbor to stand for me on the condition that I share half my ration with her.

For years South Vietnam had been the world's second-biggest exporter of rice, and its people always had more than enough. And yet, in just half a year of communist rule, for the first time, people had to eat their food mixed with manioc, sweet potato, or sorghum provided by the Soviet Union. Russian sorghum was especially hard to swallow, needing to be soaked overnight before being cooked with rice. Even then it was tough to chew and didn't digest well.

I supposed I would never see my family again. As for Phuc, I lost track of his whereabouts and feared he might never be released. Feeling despondent, I drifted through the little house like a specter. My sole reason for continuing to live was to care for my baby.

Eventually, I realized that I needed to try harder to take care of my child. I began to think of ways to keep us going. I would have to sell some of my possessions on the street.

Thuy and Thuan An, Saigon, February 1977.

The baby formula that I had stocked up before the fall of Saigon, which was supposed to last a year, was used up in a few months, as I had to sell a can every few days in exchange for food. Next, I sold household items, such as furniture, the bed, mattress, curtains, clothing, even the metal from my carport roof. There was always someone willing to buy, so, gradually, I sold off all but the most essential items.

---

[10]The term for "socialism" in Vietnamese is *Xa Hoi Chu Nghia*. Its initials, XHCN, became a cynical joke, supposedly standing for the phrase *Xep Hang Ca Ngay*, that is, "Stand in Line All Day."

After all my colorful clothes were gone, I took a white bed sheet and dyed it brown to use as material to make outfits for myself and the baby, since now everyone in the South was wearing drab colors, a true reflection of our lives at the time. To remind An and myself of Phuc, I embroidered the words "Papa" or "Daddy" inside a big heart on An's shirts.

Often while doing a chore or sitting on the street to sell something, I was pulled down into a deep depression. Gradually I found that I could raise my spirits by using my imagination. I recalled the fairy tales I had read as a child, like the Vietnamese Cinderella story "Co Be Lo Lem," or the tale of the half-sisters "Tam and Cam," stories about good girls who were persecuted and suffered in life but later succeeded and found happiness. I imagined myself as one of those characters and longed for the day when I, too, might escape my miserable existence and live happily ever after.

At first, I laughed at myself for getting carried away with such silly imaginings. But after a while, I noticed that I wasn't as sad and sometimes felt better in my foolishness. I never thought that a game of fantasy might help me get through the dark days and give me hope for the future.

The more I thought about it, the more I realized that my Papa was right when he said, "There is no way we can live under the communists because people have no power over their own lives."

An grew day by day. Looking into her bright eyes, thinking of Phuc in prison camp, I felt a renewed energy to take care of my daughter and prepare to see him again. The baby smiled excitedly to see a bird fly overhead and laughed when I swung her up in the air. Despite being malnourished, she learned to crawl, then walk, her chubby legs carrying her about, barely able to keep up with her curiosity. I wanted to see the world through her eyes, how everything was new and exciting.

Sometimes I asked a kind-hearted old neighbor to watch An for a few hours. Then I'd jump on a bike and head for familiar spots that brought back happy memories. I biked past the old newspaper office, the Voice of Freedom radio station, and especially the Cafe La Pagode and Continental where Phuc and I went on dates.

Often I'd cry as I biked through the city, longing for the peaceful, carefree days with Papa and Mama, sisters and brother, and my husband.

Chapter 4

Re-Education and Rehabilitation

Trang Lon Prison Camp, Tay Ninh

■ PHUC

M y first prison camp was at Trang Lon in Tay Ninh province. It had formerly been a South Vietnamese infantry post located next to an airfield.

Right away we were assigned to small units the communists called "cells." In my cell, I encountered a familiar face: poet and author Nguyen Huu Nhat, the husband of writer Nguyen Thi Vinh, my brother Kien's mother-in-law. I learned from him that Kien and my brother Cu were both held in an adjoining camp.

All three of us Duong brothers had held the rank of first lieutenant, although in two different areas of military service. I was in the Psywar Department while my brothers were prosecutors in the Directory of Military Justice.

Nguyen Huu Nhat was assigned as leader of our labor cell, which consisted of seven men who worked and ate together every day. An old army base, the campsite had bunkers and blockhouses for storing arms and ammunition. Once a mine went off when a prisoner was moving it, fatally wounding a member of our labor cell, pharmacist Mai Thanh Dat. We wrapped his body and buried it in the camp. He was one of the first prisoners to die in that initial month in the prison camps.

Trang Lon may have been the first prison camp to execute an inmate, a sentence that was carried out right in the assembly yard.

Ngo Nghia was an army lieutenant. I don't know how he escaped; I only heard he was captured outside the fence. They locked him in a CONEX box (a shipping container) for several days before meting out the final punishment. The commandant officer, who issued the brief, single-page order, read it at the execution.

All the prisoners had to line up at the firing range and witness our comrade being bound to a post and shot by a firing squad of ten camp guards. The sight was gruesome.

I felt a mixture of emotions: pity for my brave comrade who was so unjustly punished, indignation at the cruelty of the communists for taking the life of a man who had been caught and brought back, and shame for having lost the war to such an inhuman enemy.

After this incident, the atmosphere in the camp was very tense. We saw this as a warning, a message from the cadres that they wouldn't hesitate to shoot anyone who resisted them or tried to escape, that they did not require an order from higher up, nor did they need a court trial, not even a "people's court." All that was required was an order written by a lowly lieutenant who ran the camp.

Mr. Nhat and I formed a supportive relationship in the camp since we had known each other previously. According to social rank, he was in effect my older brother's step-father-in-law, but he was rather young, only a few years older than me. The relationship between Nguyen Huu Nhat and his older wife, famous writer Nguyen Thi Vinh, had been a topic of considerable gossip among the South Vietnamese literary community.

Mr. Nhat was a cell leader, a position that typically invited resentment from the other prisoners. The cadres running the camp used cell leaders to keep an eye on the others in their group and to carry out discipline when ordered. Camp guards cajoled or compelled them to report on their fellows, generating suspicion and straining relations among the men. Many of these cell leaders later became victims at the hands of their cellmates.

During that early time at Trang Lon, the prisoners shared a deep sense of solidarity. We could speak freely and openly with one another, unencumbered by worry and mistrust. Some nights we gathered for extemporaneous performances, in the process forging close-knit relationships. We sang around a makeshift stove composed of three bricks and a few branches and boiled some roots to make tea which we sipped together from a can.

Many of the prisoners were good singers and performed all the popular love songs of the South. Some particularly clever men built functioning musical instruments, including the guitar, whose tones sounded so melodious that more and more men were attracted to our nighttime assemblies. The simple, unaffected songs performed in the dark by prisoners whose hearts were torn by memories of their families penetrated the hearts of the audience and left many, including the singers themselves, in tears.

Christmas that year was bone-chillingly cold. At night the icy wind seeped through cracks in the walls of the blockhouses, biting the flesh of the undernourished prisoners. Even though I put on all the clothes I had and covered myself with rags, I still shivered. We lay curled up on the beds, which consisted of random boards we had gathered and laid on the cold ground.

On Christmas Eve, Fr. Nguyen Van Thong, an army chaplain and assistant pastor at Our Lady Basilica in Saigon, secretly invited the Catholics among us to take part in a Mass at his bedside in the blockhouse next to mine. There were about ten of us kneeling around him as he offered a simple service and read from a tiny Bible.

During the exchange of peace, one from our group began to sob, which in turn got all of us weeping. Fr. Thong took a bit of burnt rice he had saved from his evening meal, blessed it and broke it into pieces that served as hosts. As he handed me a piece with the words "The Body of Christ," I answered "Amen," while thoughts of Thuy and little An sent streams of tears flowing down my cheeks.

As Tet, the lunar New Year, approached, we learned the camp was going to be split up, and the prisoners transferred to other locations, a process the cadres referred to as "reorganization." Mr. Nhat was quite worried, as he had a feeling the two of us were going to be separated.

One day as we were digging furrows to plant sweet potatoes and manioc out by the camp fence, I noticed Mr. Nhat suddenly stop and his face turn pale as he gaped at something behind me. I turned around and to my horror caught a glimpse of the yellow flag with three red stripes of the Republic of Vietnam. Three of the camp's guards had used a South Vietnamese flag to make undershorts, which they now rolled up to urinate right outside the fence as if they wanted the prisoners to see them.

Many of us did notice. We all ceased our labor and stood in

place, speechless. I pressed my lips together and struggled to stifle the insane rage building up inside me. Some of the others uttered curses that stuck in their throats, emerging as guttural noises. Then, without a word, we all turned and resumed our labor assignment.

Many of us did notice. We all ceased our labor and stood in place, speechless. I pressed my lips together and struggled to stifle the insane rage building up inside me. Some of the others uttered curses that stuck in their throats, emerging as guttural noises. Then, without a word, we all turned and resumed our labor assignment.

Mr. Nhat and I went back to work, unable to speak for the remainder of the shift. Fury and humiliation prevented me from sleeping that night. I was nearly out of my mind wondering how we had been defeated by such as these.

The Waiting Wives[11]

■ THUY

One day in late 1975, I was passing by a sidewalk stall next to the park across from Cafe La Pagode when suddenly I froze in my tracks, unable to believe my eyes.

"Well, are you going to buy something or should we charge you for staring?"

The speaker smiled at me with her hands on her hips. Two other ladies next to her laughed. I thought I had never seen anything more wonderful, and I almost cried.

The three women were Vu Thi Binh Minh, Dang Tuong Vi, and Tran Thi Duyen, reporters from the Viet Tan Xa, or Vietnam Press Agency, whom I had seen several times at news conferences. It turned out that their husbands, too, had been sent for "education-rehabilitation," so together they opened this stall serving coffee and beef noodle soup to earn a meager living.

---

[11]There are several Vietnamese legends that tell of a faithful wife who waits for her husband's return from afar. She stands on a mountain holding her child and looking out for him, remaining there until she turns to stone. The place is called the Rock of the Waiting Wife. In the most popular version, the husband is a soldier gone off to fight for his country.

"You know how these old communist bags are," said Binh Minh. "No one would hire us to even spit on their feet, so we thought: Screw them! We don't need them!"

"We pooled our resources and opened up this stand," added Duyen. "The best sidewalk Hue noodle soup in town!"

She banged her wooden spoon against the pot, winked and shook her head. I could hardly stop laughing. It was no secret that we journalists were not the most domestic women in the world. Still, I was ready to bet that theirs would be the best Hue noodle soup I had tasted in a long time.

Their stall consisted of a small, low table and three rickety chairs. There were three mismatched bowls set out with noodles, ready for hot broth whenever a customer came. It turned out that their little food stand had become an ideal gathering place for journalists still around after April 30. One need only sit there for a morning to see many of our colleagues from the former media sources and receive news about friends—who was still in the country, who had left, and who was in jail, etc.

That chance meeting changed my life. My friends could tell just by looking at me that I was in a rough situation, and they didn't hesitate to offer their assistance.

"I'll come by and cook for you," said Binh Minh. "Now that I'm a famous sidewalk chef, you'll have nothing but fine dining from now on!"

"Tomorrow it'll be my turn," said Tuong Vi. "We'll stay until curfew and fill you in on everyone's story. Put these old journalist's bones back to work!"

Their cheery chatter warmed me all over. I thought angels had just rescued me.

That afternoon Binh Minh stopped by my house with her five-year-old daughter Ti and kept me company the rest of the day. The next day Tuong Vi and her little son Viet-Anh showed up. After that, it was Duyen with her three daughters, Duc, Khanh, and Tin. Each day after that the three women took turns visiting An and me until I learned how to smile again.

A month later, the stall was cleared out as part of a state-sponsored "beautification" campaign, but by then the three women and I were inseparable. My little house became our new rendezvous spot, and we were soon closer than we had ever been with anyone.

Each day the three rode their bicycles with all their children—five in all, ages one to six—to my house, staying from seven in the morning until dark.

We were all in the same boat: our husbands were "illegitimate soldiers, illegitimate officials" who were in re-education camps. We were labeled as "living off the bones and blood of the people," and so were relegated to the fringes of society, isolated within our homeland. Because of our family backgrounds, we were unable to find work, and so our lives grew increasingly miserable. We sold off our possessions to raise the capital to engage in a little marketing, from buying dried shrimp to sell cheap at the market to selling bean pudding right in front of my house. But since we were inexperienced in calculating sales or were too embarrassed to take our friends' money, in the end, we lost both our profit and capital.

Besides worrying about our husbands, we all had other responsibilities as well. Tuong Vi had a young child, but she also helped her parents take care of eight younger siblings. Duyen had three children of her own. Binh Minh had her daughter, but they lived with her parents who could support them. Although I had only An, I was the sole member of the group who had no loved ones.

From then on, the four of us contributed whatever we had to the survival of the whole group. Though poor in material possessions, we were generous with our love for one another.

Some days when we had nothing to eat, Binh Minh went to her parents' home and took a little raw rice to cook for us. We made a game out of rolling cooked rice into balls and laughed like teenagers. Even if all we had was rice with soy sauce, it was a feast as far as we were concerned. One day I sold some window curtains in exchange for two kilos of fresh noodles that we ate with fish sauce, pepper, lemon, and sugar to ease our growling stomachs.

We supported each other spiritually as well and relied on each other to get through. Our children enjoyed playing together like sisters and brothers in one family. Although they had no fathers, four doting mothers took turns caring for them. We made a collective pledge that if anything happened to one of us, the others would take on her children. With that peace of mind and the earnest love we shared, we were able to pass through the hardest stage in a life filled with sadness and despair.

One of my fondest memories is the day I parted with the last luxury I had left, a French fine china tea set that had been a wedding present. I got a good price for it and took everyone on a special outing to Turtle Square on Duy Tan Boulevard. There the children were treated to ice cream and their mothers to fresh coconut drink. The four of us shared the leftover money.

We had an unspoken agreement that anytime one of us had some money, no matter how much or how little, we would first set aside a small amount for a little celebration before dividing up the rest for our necessities. We intended not only to help each other survive materially but to keep up our spirits and try to live well to preserve the "petit bourgeois" substance of the people of the South. That way we hoped to keep ourselves from becoming infected with the vulgar, uncivilized way of life promoted by the communists.

Binh Minh became "Ma" to little An and taught my daughter her first words. Tuong Vi was known as *ma so*,[12] that is Catholic sister or nun because she was always ready to sacrifice for the group. She took care of all the work so that the rest of us could relax, which often meant Minh, Duyen, and me singing and enjoying lighthearted conversation. Vi did everything from cooking for the four of us to watching the kids to making clothes for the young ones. Whenever we had some special treat, Vi took the smallest portion.

Each of us brought something to the table and pulled her weight, but we were also free to be ourselves, to let down our guard with the others and share moments of youthful yearning. We created a secret world that was magical, full of love and trust and devotion— qualities that no longer existed in the outside world. We were closer than sisters. Through our friendship, we not only were able to survive under the communist rule, but we also found the strength and passion for meeting challenges.

There were other groups of women in our situation who sought each other out to provide mutual support, to keep faith with their husbands and the country. They conducted business as street vendors—the only occupation available to those who couldn't find regular work.

The communists tried to purge society of people like us, labeled as having a "blood debt with the people and Revolution," and encouraged neighborhood groups to ostracize us to force us to the New Economic Zones. But by joining together, the women of the

---

[12]ma so /mah sur/

South were not only able to remain in Saigon but also had more optimism, strength, and hope. Our shared spirit reinforced our sense of importance and confidence and gave us a special kind of joy.

I felt empowered by my three dear friends. And while I didn't know it at the time, Phuc was building a network of his own with other prisoners while I was befriending their wives.

Families of Re-education Prisoners

Before Phuc left to register with the authorities, we promised each other we would write every day; even if we weren't able to mail the letters, we'd save them for our day of reunion. So while Phuc was in Trang Lon camp, I recorded everything that went on between mother and child from morning till night: how Thuan An was growing bigger every day, how she learned to crawl, then walk, how she was starting to talk. I also described my friendship with the women reporters from the Vietnam Press Agency. *Can you believe it? They are all journalists. Do you remember seeing them at press events? Isn't it a small world?* And so on. I poured everything into those letters, introducing my good friends, hoping he would come to know and love them the way I did.

Although the letters didn't go anywhere but simply piled up, the act of communicating solidified my love. With pen in hand, I entered another world, one in which I was sitting across from Phuc enjoying a cold drink, discussing our lives and plans. It felt as real as everything else in my life.

At first, I thought our separation would challenge our relationship. Instead, I came to understand what other people meant when they talked about a "soul mate." When I wrote to him or began to worry about whether he was still alive, something came along to reassure me. Like the time Tuong Vi walked in while I was finishing a letter, and the clinking of her spoon against the glass as she stirred her iced coffee reminded me of the sound Phuc made when he had that drink during our many cafe meetings. Little things like that brought peace and hope to my life and brought me out of despair.

At the close of 1975, the communist authorities allowed families of re-education prisoners to send packages to the men for the first time. We four friends became preoccupied with raising money so we could buy food and medicine to send to our husbands.

I looked around my empty house, but there was nothing of value left to sell. Except, that is, for the platinum ring with five small diamonds that Phuc's brother Bao had bought for our wedding. I'd promised myself that no matter how hard things got, I would never sell that ring. But if I didn't sell it now, how else would I have any money to make a package for Phuc?

After a sleepless night during which I drenched my pillow with tears, I decided to take my ring and sell it on the street. The amount I got for it allowed me not only to send a package to Phuc but also to help my friends do the same for their husbands.

The very next day something happened to make me regret my decision. An acquaintance suddenly appeared, bringing me the first gift of money my parents had sent from America. The money they sent was five times the amount I had gotten for the ring. I ran to the street market and searched for a half a day to find the buyer and redeem it, but the ring had already changed hands, gone for good.

It turned out that my parents' boat had been picked up by an American vessel just three hours after Phuc and I set off back to Vietnam. My Papa and Mama managed to resettle in the United States in a town called Overland Park, Kansas. Once there, they were able to send me money regularly so that I no longer had to scramble to make ends meet. Relieved of this burden, I began to pay more attention to what was happening in the communist society and how it operated.

With the help of my reporter friends, I regained my journalist's mind and investigated the locations of the re-education camps. From there I was able to track the movements of my husband and other prisoners in the South. Ironically, that separation from my family, which had been so painful for me before, turned into an asset. While my friends had others to take care of and answer to, I could come and go as I needed, with people to watch An when I had to follow a lead or make a contact.

I was overjoyed to confirm that Phuc was in prison but alive. With the help of my support group, I tracked his whereabouts when he went from one camp to another. Sometimes the guards at these camps accepted my letters and packages. I was never sure if Phuc received them, but at least I was making contact.

///

As the first Tet under the communists approached in early 1976, the word going around—supplemented by what the local security police told us—was that officers in re-education camps would be "shown clemency" and allowed to reunite with their families before the new year.

By the time New Year's Eve arrived I was waiting anxiously for Phuc's return. I had never worked so hard to prepare for a holiday. The house was cleaned and swept. I spent a week making rice cakes and dried candies, a traditional part of the holiday. I sewed new clothes for An, going so far as to buy a red thread to embroider the word "Papa" on the dress. And I prayed to God and my ancestors to watch over the family now scattered across the globe. I focused all my energies and hopes on the return of the prisoner, although deep down in my soul I felt uneasy, not certain I could trust the promise of "clemency" coming from the lips of the communists.

New Year's Eve came and went.

My hope turned to despair. I kicked myself for being tricked, just as I had been when I waited for ten days for Phuc to come back from reform study. As the new spring dawned, I locked myself in my room, and with nine-month-old An in my arms, I broke down and cried. Perhaps An sensed my pain, as she didn't cry out in hunger as often as usual, but lay beside me, satisfied with her pacifier.

On the third day of the year, there was a banging on my door.

"Thuy!" a voice called. "Open up! I have news!"

I went to the door and found brother Kien's wife holding a letter in her hand, looking excited. The message was from Nguyen Huu Nhat, Kien's step-father-in-law, who had been in the same camp with Phuc. The letter said that Phuc had been transferred to another location on the 23rd of the 12th lunar month (ten days ago).

"When they moved him," the letter read, "brother Phuc left behind a few personal belongings and the New Year magazine you'd just sent... Since he left, the vegetable garden he tended with his own hands has been flourishing...."

The message with its vaguely menacing tone threw me into a fright. My spirits sank, extinguishing what little fortitude I had retained after all the loss and separation I'd endured. I collapsed sobbing; certain Phuc was in danger.

I crawled into a cocoon and refused to speak to anyone. My friends were worried about me, but they knew how I felt. They dropped off food each day but left me to myself.

I later learned that on the day tradition said the kitchen god rode to heaven on a carp to make his annual report to the Jade Emperor, my husband had been taken to Phu Quoc Island along with some other prisoners to perform hard labor. Now there was no way I could get near him or obtain any news. However, in August the communists disbanded that island camp and relocated the prisoners to Long Giao on the mainland.

Hard Labor on Phu Quoc Island

■ PHUC

When it came time to "reorganize," my name was on the list of prisoners for transfer. It was completely dark out—the communists always moved us in the dead of night. Taking my small pack of belongings, I hobbled along with the others to a covered truck like the one that had brought us to Trang Lon.

Mr. Nhat had made a farewell present for me of brown-sugar pieces in a plastic bag. Father Thong slipped me a small crucifix. Later I learned of Mr. Nhat's transfer to the Suoi Mau camp and Fr. Thong's death in prison elsewhere.

Sitting under the military truck's canvas tarp, we had no idea about our destination. When we finally climbed out of the truck, we were at a dock on the waterfront. The prisoners embarked a barge already filled with men also being "reorganized."

Chaos ensued as newly arriving trucks unloaded their human cargo onto the already overloaded boat. The men inside were pushed further in and new ones shoved in, and this went on and on until the guards became furious and fired into the air. Then the soldiers shouted at everyone to squeeze in further to let more men inside. I was stuck in the middle, barely able to breathe or move. Still, I tried to comply.

In the end, a thousand or so men were crammed like cattle onto the filthy barge for a terrifying trip from Saigon to Phu Quoc

Island. Here and there was a metal drum with boards laid across that we used to relieve ourselves. The stench was unbearable.

We collapsed in exhaustion and lay on top of one another. The prisoner next to me slept with his head on one man's stomach and his feet on another man's shoulders. I hovered between sleep and wakefulness, my body numb from being kept immobile.

We had nothing to eat or drink the entire trip. Once the cadres sprayed water from above, and we pushed and shoved to get wet or drink a bit.

As we docked at Phu Quoc, we were all glad to escape the barge, even though we realized that by coming to this remote location, the day we might be released faded even further into uncertainty. Before 1976, I had been to Phu Quoc in my capacity as a reporter accompanying government delegations that visited this island famous for its fishing industry and the pungent condiment made from fermented fish called *nuoc mam*.[13]

Phu Quoc was also the site of South Vietnamese POW camps overseen by the military police. I'd been there to interview communist prisoners with delegates from the Department of Defense sent to inspect prisons there and on Con Son Island. Phu Quoc consisted of two areas. Most of the ordinary residents made their living by fishing off the coast, where the waters were clear and beautiful. The prisoners, meanwhile, were kept in camps constructed beside the forest and surrounded by barbed wire.

Now as I stepped inside one such wired fence, I thought bitterly how I never imagined that one day I would be an inmate in the same prison camp I had casually strolled through as a journalist.

///

That Tet on Phu Quoc Island was the first lunar New Year in the prison camps. I was inconsolable, torn up inside as my mind spun around and around thinking about Thuy and baby An at home.

The cadres let us kill pigs for the holiday, animals that prisoners before us had raised. Each of us got one piece of pork, which we relished as though we had never had such a delicacy in our lives. Since this was the first time we'd been allowed fresh meat, we

---

[13]nuoc mam /*nook mahm*/

savored each small bite.

From then on, day after day I worked to utter exhaustion, wracked by hunger as well as a yearning for my family. But compared to my time at Trang Lon, here at Phu Quoc, my mind was relatively at ease. Here I was one of a band of brothers who were ready to do anything for one another.

The prisoners stayed in barracks made of wooden walls and leafy roofs. Within each barrack, there were some cells with rows of beds the prisoners built themselves from scavenged pieces of wood or branches bound together, no two alike.

In my barrack, three of us formed a close bond: Ta Anh, Tan, and I. We were the same age, all strong-willed officers, yet we got along well in the day-to-day life of the camp. When we went to work, we sought each other out, sharing water and food during our lunch in the field.

Unlike at Trang Lon where we planted sweet potatoes and manioc, on Phu Quoc we went up in the mountains to fell trees. We then cut the logs to take back to the camp to build or improve the barracks or to construct residences for the cadres. If climbing the mountains left us out of breath, going back down was even harder since we had to carry back the big logs we had just chopped.

Surviving Prison Life

One day while chopping wood, I slipped and fell. My foot hurt so much I couldn't continue working, so I limped back to camp, barely making it down the mountain. I reported to the guard that I had no contribution for the day. He looked down at the roster and silently recorded my name.

"Tomorrow you must bring two trees," he said as he dismissed me.

The next day the pain in my foot was absolute agony, but I went up the mountain just the same. My friends Ta Anh and Tan helped me cut a second tree and plane it; then they took turns carrying it downhill for me, hefting my log on one side while carrying theirs on the other.

Every day was the same: climb the mountain and chop down trees. To my surprise, we got used to the routine. What with the hard labor and missing our families, we thought at first that we wouldn't be able to stand it. But as the days and months went by, the majority of the prisoners did bear it, both physically and mentally, and some even became tougher, perhaps due to the camaraderie.

Once Ta Anh found me with a long face gazing at a photograph of Thuy and An.

"I don't know why," he said, "but I have a very strong feeling that one day you and the missus will have a warm reunion, you'll have more kids and be successful somewhere far away."

Ta Anh was short and compact. He always finished cutting his logs before everyone else, after which he headed into the forest to search among the leaves or in the rocks by the stream for animals or plants to supplement our diet.

At Trang Lon, we ate manioc mixed with sorghum, but on Phu Quoc we also had fish. In the beginning, we were happy with this, figuring we were finally getting something with nutritional value. However, it was only piles of crushed fish, more bone than meat. Every man received a small portion of tiny fish, each the size of a finger. After a few days of this, the bad fish seemed to stick in our throats, but since that's all there was we had to eat them. We were famished. When we had some wild plants from the forest to add to the meal, our stomachs were quiet that night, and we slept better.

Digging up extra items for food eventually turned into a "movement." We worked faster to complete our wood-cutting so that we'd have time to forage.

Once, a prisoner from another barrack named Hung dug up a beautiful tuber that looked like a huge potato. He sneaked it back to camp, and that evening he cooked it in a can and gobbled it down. A few minutes later, he couldn't speak and started gasping for air.

His friends surrounded him, panicked. Someone ran to get another prisoner who'd been an army doctor. Doctor Man looked him over but couldn't figure out what was wrong. He tried to get Hung breathing properly and had him drink a lot of water. Hung continued to choke and had to be watched all night. A few days later he returned to normal. From that time on, no one went rooting for tubers and strange fruits in the forest.

Our time in the Phu Quoc prison camp rolled on. We cut down a large swath of the forest using tools we made ourselves. Our hands and feet grew calloused, but carrying logs on our shoulders made us resilient. And the logs and branches we brought back every day contributed to the barracks, beds, and fences around the camp.

The cadres made us clear the mountain slopes to plant manioc. The forest on the island was gradually transformed, turned into furrows, then sprouting plants, which produced leaves, and finally, there were tubers. We looked at all this and couldn't believe it had come about by our own hands.

Maybe I appreciated it more because it was the prisoners' labor that had cleared the land and planted the crop. When the manioc was ready, we were mobilized to harvest it and submit it to the cadres. Many of us, driven by hunger, took advantage of the guards' inattentiveness to dig up the plants, brush off the dirt and stuff the manioc into our mouths, consuming it raw. Some men ate too many and wound up rolling on the ground, "intoxicated" by the plant.[14] All this had to be done on the sly. If the cadres had caught us, we would have been harshly disciplined, possibly sent to solitary confinement without rations.

The camp on Phu Quoc was in a remote place that rarely saw any civilians, which made us feel more isolated from the outside world and more uncertain whether or not we'd ever be released and sent home. To combat hopelessness and hunger, we re-education prisoners clung to the memories of our family even as we created circles of friends among our fellow inmates for comfort and support.

As for me, my sole purpose for staying alive was so that I could see Thuy and An again.

Desperate Letters

■ THUY

The authorities at Phu Quoc re-education camp allowed their captives to receive only one letter a month. Meanwhile, I'd been writing Phuc a letter almost every day, so the stack accumulated.

One day in the midst of my numbing sadness, I decided that from then on, whenever I wrote a letter, I'd send it to his camp right away. I understood that each prisoner received only

---

[14] Uncooked manioc (also called cassava, tapioca, or yuca) contains a group of compounds that turn into hydrogen cyanide in your body, which interfereds with your body's use of oxygen.

one letter on a fixed date, but sending one every day kept me motivated to think of Phuc, like having a whispered conversation with him. And so, every time I finished a letter, I went to the post office and mailed it, maybe three or four times a week.

Of course, the mail was censored at the camp, and most likely the cadres wouldn't give him anything I sent, but that thought didn't deter me. The need to write and send the letters was very important to me at the time, so I continued the practice.

My notes never mentioned politics or what was going on in the country at the time. Neither, however, did I encourage my husband to "study and devote yourself well so that the Revolution will show clemency and allow you to come home," as camp cadres and local security police suggested prisoners' wives to write. I wasn't about to let the communists dictate what I could or couldn't say to my husband.

I only wrote him about An and me and our daily life. I told him how I'd gradually sold off everything in the house; how my friends brought their kids to visit each day; how we'd tried to sell dried shrimp and lost our entire investment; and how even selling bean pudding and "jelly worm" dessert had failed.

I also told him how I'd traveled to Phu Quoc Island to see him after Tet:

One morning after receiving a letter from the camp, Duyen and I asked Vi to watch our children so the two of us could visit you and Duyen's husband there. We spent a whole week gathering food and medicine with the money we'd saved.

We traveled for several days, changing buses many times before we reached Ha Tien. Then we carried our packages onto a crowded ferry that took us to Phu Quoc. We were exhausted, but we didn't dare sleep and sat up all night keeping watch over our goods so they wouldn't be stolen.

When we reached the island, it was getting dark, and we didn't know where to go. Fortunately, a young seamstress who worked near the ferry dock took pity on us and let us spend the night at her house. After days of trouble, we made our way to the camp, but no amount of begging and pleading would sway the cadres to let us visit our husbands or leave our packages. They chased us away like we were a couple of beggars.

We gathered our things and cried from grief and shame all the way back, feeling sorry for our husbands and ourselves as well. Only the kids were happy since they got to eat all the food we had scrimped and saved for.

That is how I wrote a letter a day and mailed it to Phuc, an exercise like writing a daily journal.

After more than a month of desperate hoping, one day I received a letter from Phuc through the post office. It was just a few lines hastily written to let me know that the cadre who censored the mail had let Phuc read my letters and offered to bring any letters to me on his next visit to Saigon. I was stunned to realize that my mail had gotten into Phuc's hands.

Now I waited anxiously for the surprise gift delivered by a kind-hearted cadre.

///

A few weeks later, my friends and I were coming back to my house when we saw a uniformed man standing in front of my gate. He looked to be about thirty, small, with the sallow complexion common to soldiers from the North who suffered from chronic malaria. He greeted us awkwardly and identified himself as Lt. Tran Minh Hoang.

I soon learned that he was, as Phuc had told me in his note, the camp cadre charged with censoring the prisoners' mail. Since the inmates could only send and receive one letter a month, any mail that arrived on other than the designated day would go in the trash. However, seeing so many letters coming from me—nearly one a day—Lt. Hoang grew curious. Finally, he opened one, and then he started reading them all.

From that time on he became familiar with the relationship between Phuc and me, as well as my life with baby Thuan An in Saigon and my friends who shared our plight. After weeks of reading my letters, Lt. Hoang began to feel sorry for us, so every once in a while he sneaked a letter in to Phuc. In time, his sympathy for Phuc, coupled with his curiosity, encouraged him to get to know Phuc better. Since he was about to go on leave and had a chance to visit Saigon, he agreed to bring letters from Phuc to Thuan An and me.

Now he handed me some letters and two gifts Phuc had made

for us. For An, there was a khaki-colored hat he had sewn from a sandbag with clumsy stitches. My present was a little hair comb painstakingly cut, filed, and polished from a mortar shell. Phuc had asked a talented friend to make it for me; the artist had carved on it a pair of birds flying side-by-side with their wings linked.

Phuc also sent along a photograph of me that he'd kept in his wallet when he reported for re-education. The picture was taken when we went swimming at the beach in Vung Tau. In the prison camp, Phuc had drawn graph marks over the picture so he could trace it, then he sent the original to me with a note written on the back:

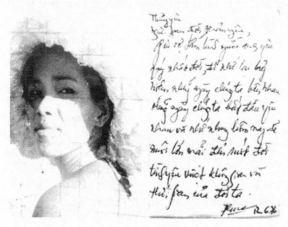

Beloved Thuy,
Dear life companion,
Sending you a picture of the one I love most in my life, to remember the days we were together, the days our love began. Today's fond remembrance will help grow our love for a lifetime, beyond time and space.
Phuc 6/12/76.

Picture Phuc sent from prison with his love note, June 1976.

These surprise letters and gifts brought tears to my eyes. I never thought that in these difficult times we'd have a chance to express our feelings for each other in such a concrete and romantic way.

From then on Hoang was the messenger bird of love notes passed between Phuc and me. My friends Binh Minh, Tuong Vi, and Duyen, became acquainted with him and in time they, too, cherished the big heart he dared to show even though he was from the opposite side of the battle line.

Hoang told us of the young wife he had just married after the country was reunited and their new child, who lived in a village in the Thai Binh province. Being poor, he could not afford to bring them to the South with him when assigned to his current post.

As he told us of the war years, we learned more about the way the Hanoi government treated their people. It had used lies and subterfuge to convince soldiers to fight on, to take pride in the slogan "Born in the North to die in the South" to "liberate the South from the clutches of Americans and the illegitimate government and army."

After the South was "liberated," the high-ranking cadres liberated the property of the Southerners to enrich themselves. However, for ordinary *bo doi* like Lt. Hoang, who sacrificed daily for Party and Country, life had not gotten any better. Over time, they grew bitter and believed the Party and Country had taken advantage of their youth and patriotism for all those years. Transferred to work in the South, these soldiers encountered a prosperous and culturally sophisticated region. Southerners had enjoyed a standard of living many times greater than that of their Northern counterparts, completely at odds with the propaganda they had heard during two decades of war about an impoverished South under the so-called oppression of the Americans and their puppet government. These soldiers began to lose faith in the authorities in Hanoi. One consequence was that they felt more and more sympathy for the people of the South.

In August 1976, the communists closed the camp on Phu Quoc and transferred all the prisoners to other areas in the South. Phuc and some of his campmates went to Long Giao camp in Long Khanh province. Lt. Hoang was transferred elsewhere, ending our mail connection, but that was not the last we would hear of Lt. Hoang.

Long Giao Re-education Camp

■ PHUC

In August 1976, I was once again "reorganized." I grabbed my meager belongings and got on a truck that took us to a boat, on which, stacked like sardines, we endured another rough crossing. We reached the dock at Saigon at night, where a covered truck took us to our next destination. It was the camp at Long Giao in the highlands of Long Khanh province. This camp, too, had once been a South Vietnamese army camp.

It was my third concentration camp after twice being

"reorganized." By then I had become used to the communist authorities' method of separating and mixing the prisoners, like reshuffling the deck, to better control us.

It was like the last time. The curtain was raised for an assembly as an administrative cadre swaggered in and launched into his blustering speech. Here was the "merciful policy of the Revolution" and advice to "learn and study well to be pardoned of the blood debt so you can go home soon..."—all the pat phrases recited mechanically by the cadres. Many of the guards were illiterate but knew how to repeat the smooth, confident talk from rote learning.

Then we were assigned to barracks and cells. It was the communists' method of keeping the prisoners divided so we couldn't form cliques or develop close relationships. This seemed to be part of an essential policy of overall suspicion by "Uncle and Party" as the cadres applied it even among themselves. They, too, were frequently reorganized by being sent from one camp to another.

At Long Giao, however, I got lucky.

When we left Phu Quoc, Ta Anh, Tan, and I bade each other farewell, assuming we would never meet again, but somehow we three ended up at Long Giao.

When we saw each other on the assembly field filled with newly transferred prisoners, we bunched together so that in the end we were not only assigned to the same barrack, but also to the same labor cell.

During the time I spent at Long Giao, camp activities were always the same: early morning assembly, division of labor assignments, then out to the fields to break ground and plant sweet potatoes and manioc. (These two types of tuber were easy to cultivate and served as staples in the prison system when mixed with rice and sorghum.)

The work site at Long Giao consisted of vast fields surrounding the camp by the crossroads leading to Cam Duong and Cam My, right by the bus route running from Long Khanh city to Ba Ria and Vung Tau. As we worked in the fields, we could see buses driving past, and this gave us a feeling of being close to the outside world, unlike at Phu Quoc where we rarely saw anybody who was not connected one way or another to the prison. Every time I watched a bus overloaded with passengers, some of them hanging onto the outside of the vehicle and some thrown off alongside the road, I grew anxious, picturing the day I would return to a normal life and be reunited with my wife and daughter.

The prisoners were required to perform every type of work, so eventually, we all became skilled at farming and lumberjacking. Those who went to the forest for wood found ways to chop faster and cleaner. Long Giao had many bamboo forests whose wood was used to make fine furniture and straighter beds than those we had fashioned from rough boards on Phu Quoc.

We made up several cells. Unskilled laborers, like me, went to teams that learned to plant vegetables or cut trees. Those with more skills made up specialty cells. Carpenters had it relatively easy since they did not have to leave the camp to work in the fields but stayed inside to make fences or furniture for the cadres.

Some of the men were accomplished craftsmen. They made guitars out of leftover wood and made strings from electrical wire; the sound was as fine as that of a conventional instrument. Others fashioned flutes out of bamboo that gave off plaintive tones. One prisoner made beautiful smoking pipes with intricate carvings.

As for me, I am clumsy with handiwork, but by learning from friends I eventually made another comb out of a mortar shell, cutting and smoothing it every day to present to my wife. It did not look as good as the one my friend had made for me last year, but I poured into it all my love for and thoughts of Thuy during the long days and nights.

Re-education, Old Songs, and Hunger

When night came, the cadres withdrew from the prisoners' area, locking the gate behind them, and returned to their section that lay outside the main gate beside the road. It was at that time that the prisoners began their activities. Some turned in early, while others got together in small groups to chat, drink tea brewed from roots, or smoke farmer's tobacco[15]. Some of the men sang forbidden music and old love songs.

There were even cultural contests, with prizes like a piece of

---

[15] An ersatz tobacco made from pulverized leaves of sweet potato and manioc, rolled into pills, and pressed into the bowl of a water pipe, which when smoked produces a mild high.

sugar or a pinch of tobacco. The performances grew larger, no longer a single group of men but a collection of groups. The programs generated more and more singers, poets, musicians, filling the air with love ballads and prison songs. A great many poems and songs were written during this time by inspired amateur artists.

During these private nighttime shows, the reform prisoners never sang revolutionary songs. We had enough of those during assemblies when we were made to listen or join in. We used to call those songs "red music," "forest music" or "farmer's tobacco music."

After a while, we realized there were informers in our midst. Once the authorities got wind of our "old music movement," the shows were shut down. We called the snitches "antennas." These were guys ready to denounce their fellow inmates for special favors from the guards.

No one was ignorant enough to believe that "anyone who studies hard will be allowed home first," so perhaps the men who agreed to act as "antennas" only did so in the hope of getting a little more to eat, exemption from labor, or a promise of special treatment. Every group has at least one such person who will sell out for personal reasons, but nothing will drive men to betray their fellow prisoners for just a little material reward or an empty promise like the hunger and hardship of a communist prison camp.

Only someone who has experienced a communist prison camp can fully comprehend that the cruelest, most troubling aspect of the communists' relationship to their prisoners is the "policy of deliberate abandonment and privation." They didn't need to commit a bloodbath, to slaughter large numbers of people in a series of executions that would make them subject to the world's condemnation or spark popular resistance. Rather, they applied a more subtle brutality, destroying the prisoners' spirit by prolonged hunger.

The desire for food obsessed us day and night—there was never a moment when we didn't crave something to eat. The thought of even a piece of sweet potato or manioc or some charred rice was enough to torment us and give us no rest. Hunger caused many to lose their willpower, their feelings for others, their very humanity. And it was hunger that brought forth the scourge of the informer in the prison camps.

Amid utter wretchedness, hunger, and exhausting labor, while being mocked and tormented physically and mentally by camp guards, we felt so degraded that at times we thought we could no longer bear it. We often confessed to one another that we wanted to scream and curse the name of Ho Chi Minh and the damned Communist Party, smash the commandant in the face, come what may. But these plans remained imaginary.

Hunger had weakened and demoralized us, topped by the subtle brainwashing. Otherwise, how could one explain a situation in which hundreds of prisoners, mainly former officers who had fought fiercely, risking their lives on the battlefield, were under the firm control of a handful of prison guards? When we went to work in the fields or forests, only a handful of armed soldiers kept watch over a hundred men wielding hoes and bladed implements; still, no one dared to rebel.

In fact, we thought about this issue a great deal and quietly argued among ourselves. It would take only a few men working together to strip the guards of their weapons and render them helpless. Some of us worked in the forest; when we finished chopping wood, we could wander about looking for edible plants. If any of us wanted to escape it wouldn't have been difficult, and yet hardly anyone tried.

The thing is, once we got out of the camp, where would we go with our starved, haggard bodies? And after that, what would we do when we had no papers to justify our presence legally? Would anyone on the outside dare to risk helping an escaped prisoner?

The mental state of the re-education prisoner was like that of millions of South Vietnamese who were repressed by the communists but rarely fought back. The entire country had become a giant prison, and escape would only bring repercussions on one's families.

Besides hunger and having no place to go, there was the example of Ngo Nghia, who had tried to flee Trang Lon and was executed right in front of our eyes. We knew that if we escaped and failed, we would be shot immediately, leaving no hope of ever seeing our loved ones again.

Looking back, I have to admit that the communists were exceptionally clever in psychological warfare, from torture and abuse of the individual's spirit to threatening and harassing his family.

We were like fish caught in a net, forced to accept our fate. Even then, the communists used the schemes of constantly moving us around from camp to camp and employing "antennas" to keep us divided and suspicious of one another. It was because of these antennas that our music programs were forbidden. This caused considerable resentment among the prisoners and led to informers frequently being beaten up by their campmates.

Each time some of the inmates got together for a clandestine songfest or activities considered violations of camp regulations, the following day the cadres singled out the culprits by name for punishment, such as solitary confinement; and that night the informant would be snatched and seriously worked over. Although the antenna was covered with a blanket so that he could not identify his assailants, he knew why he was receiving this treatment, and he would never report the beating to the authorities. Furthermore, other inmates never gave away the names of the attackers during interrogation. After a while, the problem of "antennas" became less worrisome.

Knights of the Lost Swords

Despite all this, beautiful friendships were born in the concentration camps.

I was already close to Ta Anh and Tan since our stay on Phu Quoc. When we transferred to Long Giao, we had the good fortune to be in the same cell. There we were joined by four new friends: Cuong, Ky, Nghia, and Luu Khuong, all of whom had been in different combat units. Cuong was the biggest and strongest of the lot. Luu Khuong was a Navy SEAL.

We jokingly dubbed ourselves the "Seven Knights of the Lost Swords." We were about the same age, and while we did not officially describe ourselves as brothers, I was viewed as the oldest and enjoyed the warm regard as well as the responsibility of such a role.

In the early stage of our time at Long Giao, our cell was assigned to dig a well. Wells were the sole source of the camp's clean water, and every camp had teams of diggers. At the end of each workday, hundreds of prisoners rushed to the wells, taking a quick wash before making way for others, so there was always a demand for more water.

The cadre in charge of the well teams was a little guy named Can. He was a head shorter than Cuong and a royal pain, so behind his back, we called him "Can Can Ngo," that is, "Can the Dopey Cadre." One day he led us around the camp, finally stopping at an apparently random spot beside the fence. Then, using a short stick of bamboo, he drew a circle in the dirt and ordered us to dig a well as wide as the mark he'd just made. Before leaving, he gave notice that he would visit us each day to check on our progress.

We stood there looking dumbfounded, first at each other then at the circle. How were we supposed to dig a well? All we had for tools were a few crude handmade hoes. These might be good enough to break the earth to plant sweet potatoes, but as for scratching the ground all the way down to a water source, that was a job the seven of us working all month couldn't finish. Still, we had to give it a try. After all, as they kept telling us, "From human effort, the rocky ground will become a well!"

Several days later Cadre Dopey came by and saw that the hole we had dug was only big enough to catch crickets, so he had to find us some real tools. We were, however, only permitted a few minutes of rest every hour.

The task was backbreaking, but we were glad to be working side-by-side, sharing the effort as friends. Cuong and Khuong were the ablest of the group and volunteered to do the first heavy digging, making it easier for Ky, our "little brother."

The farther down we went, the harder it was to dig, and the more dangerous. There was only enough room at the bottom of the hole for one person at a time. Since it was too tight to swing a hoe, we used a shovel, scooping the dirt into a bucket that the others pulled up, emptied, and then returned for the next load. Working this way meant progress was slow. Through the course of the day, the seven of us took turns going down in the hole to avoid anyone's straining his back.

The rope we used for hauling up the dirt was the same one we used to lower and raise the digger. We'd made it ourselves using tree bark, and it was secure enough to hold a man's weight.

One day, it was my turn to shovel when we struck water. The liquid poured in up to my ankles. The wet earth was easier to dig but heavier to drop into the bucket. As I was filling the bucket, a sudden pain shot through my lower back, which locked in place, and I crumpled to the floor. I could barely move, and then only in agony, so I called up to the others. I got down on my hands and knees in the water and held myself still to ease the pain. My cellmates panicked and heaved on the rope to pull me up. But I couldn't stand up straight, let alone wrap a cord around me, so I could be raised.

In the end, little Ky went down the well. With great effort, he wound the rope around me several times and secured it. Then he held me with one arm while grabbing onto the rope with the other as the rest of the team hauled us up.

After the accident, I was laid up for a week, without the benefit of a medicine or medical treatment, but at least exempt from laboring on the well detail. When my recovery seemed to be taking too long, my friends took me to the camp clinic. There aid was provided by a Viet Cong nurse who practiced acupuncture using needles he'd fashioned by filing pieces of metal to make what he referred to as his "treatment kit." The communist army had only medical assistants who might eventually get promoted to "doctor," and their only method of dealing with illness was with therapeutic tools. I took one look at the rusty "needles" and begged to be sent back to my barrack for a few more days of rest.

Over time the backache eased, but I got around only with difficulty. Cuong made me a cane. Ever since then I have suffered chronic back pain, aggravated when I lift something heavy or bend the wrong way. Years later, when I'm not paying attention, I might throw out my back and wind up in bed for days; this happens several times a year.

After we finished digging the well to provide fresh water for the camp, the very next day we went back to planting sweet potatoes at the road crossing. Afterward, we were all sent across to the Cam Duong rubber plantation and deep into the forest to cut bamboo and chop firewood.

This was around the beginning of 1977. I celebrated a second lunar new year in a communist prison camp.

On New Year's Day, we were relieved from labor. The prisoners went from barracks to barracks wishing each other a happy new year. We treated our guests to hot tea made from plant roots and "holiday sweets," which were just pieces of sugar, and farmer's tobacco.

By that time, we former soldiers of the South Vietnamese army had been prisoners for nearly two years. The guards who took us out for labor were now accustomed to the routine and getting lax. Our wives were becoming adept at sneaking by, secretly meeting us on the road to the work sites and passing us food or medicine. The locals pitied the prisoners and the wives who went to great lengths to see their husbands, so they helped out as much as they could. Sometimes when the locals encountered prisoners on the road, they offered us something quick to eat along with looks of encouragement and comfort.

It was at Long Giao that I saw Thuy for the first time after two years of separation.

Presents for the Prisoners

■ THUY

The evening of the 27th of the last month before the lunar new year, I arrived at the gate of Long Giao re-education camp with gifts for Phuc. The guards didn't allow relatives to visit prisoners, but they could deliver gifts as long as these conformed to certain restrictions. The cadres were given a free hand to nit-pick just to harass the families.

"Sausages are not allowed."

"Only one packet of tea permitted."

"Coffee is forbidden."

"Next time, slice the ham, so we don't have to do it ourselves to look for contraband."

Frustrated, we had no choice but to do what the cadres demanded in the hope that our loved ones would be a little less hungry and miserable for the New Year. We all knew our men were ill-fed in the camp, and we wanted to give them at least a little solid food for strength. I bit my tongue when the guard told me that Phuc could only get half the rice cake I'd made for him. The woman next to me was also having a hard time.

"How did you manage to get the money to buy all this? Exploiting the bones and blood of the people, heh?"

I shared the humiliation of those wives who had come to take care of their husbands in the camp as we were scolded and eyed suspiciously by the cadres. And I pitied the mothers who had come all the way to this remote place, their hearts breaking, their heads bowed before the haughty prison guards.

After turning in my package, I hurried over to help a friend. The guard ripped apart her bag, searching the articles inside.

"Who knows if, once the package gets inside, they go through it again," she said in a low voice. "Do the men get anything?"

I shared her concern. The mother of five small children, my friend had sold most of what she owned to make up a package for her husband. She gently held each pack of sweets, each can of milk, each container of dried meat that her children craved.

Her ten-year-old son said to me proudly, "We never touch anything in Papa's package. I have to watch my little sister because her eyes get real big when she sees Mama packing things for Papa."

I looked down at the skinny little girl, maybe five years old, standing next to her big brother. She was staring hungrily at the assortment of food in front of them. Her brother went on.

"I don't know what Papa did that he has to be in prison...."

My friend and I looked at each other, our hearts aching because we couldn't tell him the truth, that his Papa had done nothing wrong. The avenging communists had taken so many good and talented men and locked them up without the benefit of trial, offering no promise of when they might come home.

The packages were separated by barracks for each area's cadre to accept. Phuc belonged to barrack T3. The process for delivering the goods was completed, but the relatives of the T3 prisoners didn't want to leave. Along with the others standing outside the barbed-wire fence, I waited to see that the packages reached their intended destination.

Four o'clock came, and we were all anxious, afraid we might miss the last bus heading back to Saigon. I was particularly worried about my little girl, whom I had left with a neighbor. Some of the women gave up and started walking up the road to meet the bus.

Just then a commotion went through the group waiting by the fence.

"There they are! They're coming to get the packages!"

Everyone ran back and pressed up against the fence to peer inside.

On a narrow path leading far back inside the camp, several teams of men advanced toward the gate bearing shoulder poles and cloth sacks. They were dressed every which way: old military uniforms, civilian clothes, or black peasant shirts. Some wore only shorts and tank tops. Their gray and faded garments hung on bodies that were gaunt, weathered, and exhausted.

I searched their faces, trying to identify my husband. Even from a distance, I saw the mixed emotions on the men's faces: bitterness, hurt pride, indifference, shame, all overshadowed by a deep sorrow. There was, as well, defiance in their eyes, a sign of their strength and inner will that contrasted sharply with the submissive posture of their bodies. Though lean and darkened by the sun, their faces exhibited courage and dignity, unlike the guards who strutted about with their rifles, shouting orders and upbraiding the prisoners. The captives trudged steadily behind the guards as they approached the piles of gifts set on the ground.

Suddenly my heart stopped.

Phuc! There was no doubt. There he was, passing through the gate. I squeezed my friend's arm to keep from fainting.

He was in the final group being led out. Bony, his flesh browned by the sun, he wore an old uniform but no shoes or hat. Ah, the uniform we used to keep neatly cleaned and pressed that made him look so sharp and imposing. Now it was as bleak and pitiful as the man wearing it. Noticing my reaction, my neighbor spoke.

"Your husband, sister? Ask them to let you see him! If you insist, surely they'll let you talk to him."

I didn't reply but stood gripping the wire fence, ignoring the barbs that pricked my hands. I stared at him, my life's companion, the war correspondent who was always prepared to place him in the line of fire to get the story, now a beaten, wretched prisoner in the hands of the enemy jailers.

Phuc looked up and saw me. He paused a moment, then walked on. But his eyes never left mine.

The men came to the spot where the packages had been arranged on the ground. Each team collected its load and piled the items into sacks, which they hung on poles held by a man on each end. Phuc joined in but did not look down. His eyes were on me, standing outside the fence, standing outside the life of prisoners like him.

The other visitors urged me on, "You've got nothing to lose. Ask them to let you talk to him...."

Thuy and Thuan An at home, Saigon, April 1977.

Some of the women wanted me to pass on a message to their husbands. I couldn't hear them. I just stood looking at Phuc. One of his friends recognized me and poked him, gesturing. He only shook his head. We understood each other. We didn't have to speak. We would not give the camp guards the satisfaction of using their power over us, even granting us the favor of speaking to one another.

And what could we say that would express all the longing and love that had accumulated over the past months and years?

What words would put an end to the pain and indignity he endured in prison or that I felt, his wife, lost and alone, helpless beneath the ever-watchful gaze of the local security police?

We called to each other with our eyes—one inside a prison fence surrounded by soldiers with guns, the other outside the barbed wire but no less a prisoner—sending out all the love and support we felt.

I stared at my husband, my heart tightening to the point my eyes brimmed with tears. Only after Phuc had turned his back to follow his mates as they shuffled down the path far into the camp did the tears finally escape.

PART II

THE MAKING OF WAR CORRESPONDENTS

DUONG PHUC - VU THANH THUY

Chapter 5

Pathway to a Profession

Growing Up

■ PHUC

I am the only child in my family who wasn't born in the city of Hue. At that time, Hue was the royal capital of Vietnam, with its citadel of palaces, the site of a dreamy, romantic culture situated on the Perfume River.

A few months before my birth, my family moved to Thanh Hoa, a city that lies between the Northern and Central Regions of Vietnam.[16] My father, Duong Van Long, an official in the Ministry of Education under the royal court, was transferred to Thanh Hoa to serve as Superintendent of

Phuc's father, Duong Van Long (1900-1954)

[16]The Vietnamese distinguish three regions in the country, referred to simply as the North, Center, and South. The North comprises the Red River Delta and the area extending toward China, the South is the territory of the Mekong Delta, and the Center is the long stretch of coastline and mountains in between. The regions of North and South should not be confused with the entities known as North Vietnam and South Vietnam after 1954, which were first political zones, then disputed nations until 1976, when Vietnam was formally reunified by the Communist government.

Education. By the time I "greeted life" on September 9, 1945, at Truc Nhu Hospital, my family was at home in their new surroundings, and the residents of the city no longer viewed them as foreign because of their Hue accent.

There was a bridge just outside the city known as Ham Rong, or Dragon's Jaw, so-called because its truss structure resembled the teeth of a gigantic dragon. The local people used to say that the bridge was once the mouth of a great dragon that embraced and protected the city.

During the war, Thanh Hoa became famous for lying on the principal route from North Vietnam to South Vietnam. For the communists, the bridge was a critical component of its troop and supply line during the war to "liberate" the South. The Pentagon ordered the bridge destroyed to cut that supply line. Back when my family moved to Thanh Hoa, however, the Dragon's Jaw was still intact and considered one of the city's main attractions. My father enjoyed crossing the bridge to view the whole city from both ends.

As the youngest of six sons, I was the baby of the family, pampered and taken care of in every way. Since my father worked long hours, I rarely saw him. Even when he was home, he was busy with paperwork or entertaining guests with whom he shared tea or wine.

Because of my father's high position, we boys had everything we needed and lived comfortably. I was only a baby and had no idea that the year 1945 would be seen as one of the darkest times in Vietnam's history, the At Dau famine epidemic.

Early in 1940, Japan had begun pressuring the French colonial administrators in Vietnam, demanding that Japanese soldiers be allowed into the country to secure the Chinese border. In May of that year, the Nazis invaded France, which left the French colonial government in Vietnam with no option but to concede to Japanese demands. An agreement signed in June allowed Japanese troops to control the northern border between Vietnam and China and acknowledged Japan's rights and interests, giving the Japanese access to Haiphong harbor and allowing the placement of up to 6,000 troops in northern Vietnam.

But the Japanese, dissatisfied with this agreement, eventually broke it. By midnight on September 22nd, a Japanese invasion of Vietnam was underway. Japanese forces took just a week to secure control of Vietnam. For most of their occupation between 1941 and 1945, the Japanese left the French colonial government in place, with Bao Dai leading a puppet government, and developed Vietnam as a client state with unrestricted access to Vietnam's roads, rail network, and ports.

In Northern Vietnam, they seized the storehouses of rice and the peasants' seed grain to feed the occupying army. They took over each region, stole anything that was of use, and destroyed everything that was left, leaving nothing for the native people.

Moreover, the Japanese army brought in agricultural consultants who forced the Vietnamese farmers to plant trees to serve the needs of the invaders, such as hemp for rope. Fields of flowers that were not torn up for strategic planting died off as a result of the Japanese manner of cultivation, which used up the plants down to the roots.

Famine spread throughout the northern region of the country, taking the lives of countless citizens, perhaps as many as two million people. Those who survived were mere skin and bones. The poor perished first. Each day some 400 people fell, so many they couldn't be buried fast enough. My older brothers have told me that corpses lay right outside the gate of our home.

Every day my mother went out to the garden in back to look for wild herbs to supplement the family's diet. She used all her

Victims of the At Dau Famine Epidemic in 1945. Photo: *Vo An Ninh*

SURVIVING
119

cooking skill to prepare these plants using nothing but salt and garlic. But no one thought twice about this, since, except the little ones, everyone understood that they were lucky to have anything to eat at all.

I was too young to comprehend the suffering of my people. Only in looking back now do I realize the full extent of the grief and pain they endured.

Hanoi on My Mind

When I was four, my family moved to Hanoi, where my father served as Director of the Ministry of Education.

I attended Quang Trung Elementary School. Our house was located across from the courthouse, next to which was the Hoa Lo Jail. During the summers I went with my older brothers to catch cicadas clinging to the tall trees in the courthouse yard.

My most vivid childhood memories concern our house in Hanoi. Located at number 3 Ly Thuong Kiet Lane, it faced the city court

Phuc, age 5, Hanoi, 1950.

across the street. On the other side of the court was a park where my brothers Cu and Kien often took me to play. They carried me piggyback, and we chased each other around the park.

Sometimes they brought me there just to get away from the crowded household. At such times my brothers would sit on a bench reading. Meanwhile, I played by myself, but often I just sat next to

Phuc, in grade school.

In home, Hanoi, 1953.

them and watched the people coming and going from the courthouse.

The sight of the men being transferred from the court to the jail next door attracted my attention, I wondered who they were and what they had done to go back and forth between the buildings. And I secretly wished that someday I might get a look inside those places.

Since 1945, the Viet Minh seized power in North Vietnam. At first, a lot of patriotic intellectuals supported Ho Chi Minh's fight against the French. But as the communists' anti-intellectual rhetoric increased, men like my father were turned off. Ho's brutal tactics in the battle of Dien Bien Phu further alienated many potential followers.

For me, however, life went on uneventfully until 1954, when the Geneva Accord ended the war between France and its colonies. My father stopped working and told us to pack everything we could carry and prepare to move to the South. I was nine years old and thought we were going on a pleasure trip, but this was no vacation; we were joining one million others evacuating the zone that was falling under the control of the North Vietnamese Communists.

My oldest sister, Duong Thi Loan, one of the beauties of Hanoi, chose to remain in the city. She and her husband, a government employee, did not want to abandon their home and position in the North. My father could do nothing to persuade them to change their minds. In the end, he respected their decision.

The evacuees from the North were resettled throughout the Southern zone. One provision of the Geneva Accords required the government in the South to assist the refugees in finding housing and

Refugees' belongings included these symbols of their faith, Haiphong Port, 1954.

assimilating into their new lives.

The refugees, with a majority being Catholics, came in entire villages, hamlets, and groups; they could choose where they wanted to live. Those from a farming background went to places where they could put their skills to work. Likewise, fishermen settled in coastal areas. As for the people from cities such as Hanoi and Hai Phong, the Southern government let them settle in Saigon and its suburbs. Many families shared a house. Those dislocated with not enough money or having no one to help them went to temporary settlement camps.

The Vietnamese family does not consist of just the nuclear unit of parents and children, but usually included more generations and relatives in an extended clan. Such was the Duong family at this time. Besides my parents and siblings, several aunts had lived with us for years, plus a nanny who we children loved like our own mother. With so many people it was hard to find suitable housing, so we had to remain in the temporary camp while we looked for a place big enough to accommodate us all.

Every day my father went out with my brothers Lan and Hung to search for a house. Eventually, they found a place on Yen Do Street near the city's center, and we were all happy to leave the camp.

However, we had barely moved when my father suddenly took sick and was admitted to Grall Hospital for treatment. He never returned. He passed away on the 4th day of the 9th month of the lunar year Giap Ngo, that is, September 30, 1954.

The Family Duong

After Father died, I began to pay more attention to family affairs. I helped my older brothers with the funeral. I watched as the adults argued about how to bury my father according to his wishes when we lived in the North. However, because of the political situation and our displacement from our native area, and because of space scarcity in Saigon, we ended up burying our father in a cemetery for Northern Vietnamese near the Tan Son Nhat airport.

Now that my father was gone, we were uncertain about how to manage the family's affairs. Up until then, he had been the one who made all the decisions and took care of the entire household.

According to custom, mourning for one's parent lasts 49 days. At the end of that time, my eldest brother Lan called his siblings together for a family meeting. Traditionally, when a father dies, the eldest son takes over responsibility for the family. My brother Lan announced that he was going to work full-time for us. He had been attending law school and was a part-time translator on American troop transport ships bringing refugees from the North, but now he was putting aside his studies so he could work more hours.

Ever since he was a high school student at the Lycee Albert Sarraut, brother Lan had shown a real gift for languages. While other students studied French or Classical Chinese, he selected English as his second language, noting that more Americans were coming to our country now. He taught English at Tran Luc, a public high school, where his salary was sufficient to provide for the extended family at the time, allowing the rest of us to adjust to our new lives in Saigon.

I did not know why we had left the North, but I was excited to see the different cities we passed and the changing scenery between the North and the South. This was the first time that I got a taste of the itinerant lifestyle. The delight of a life filled with variety and the freedom of having no ties to a single place attracted me, unlike the cultural traditions of my country that bound a person to his or her natal place.

That period of my life planted the seed of a desire to see and experience every part of Vietnam. I began to break away from ancient cultural ways, as the pull of a nomadic existence left a deep impression in my still-developing brain. From that point on, I seized every opportunity to travel and seek out adventure.

A new house bursting at the seams with family members gave me an excuse to roam the streets at will. With my older brothers, I threw myself into the pleasure of exploring the city of Saigon.

Most of the French functionaries had already returned to their home country, but they left behind vestiges of their influence on Saigon and South Vietnamese culture. Vietnamese women still wore the traditional *ao dai*, but many, especially the younger generation, wore Western dresses which exposed arms and legs and had belts that accentuated the women's figures. Not a few men wore suits and felt hats, seemingly oblivious to the hot tropical weather.

After completing elementary school, I attended Tran Luc High School until my senior year, when I transferred to Chu Van An school in Cholon, the Chinese quarter of Saigon. I never encountered any interference with my enjoyment of life in the Southern capital.

Still, I missed Hanoi, even though for me that was merely the name of a famous city I vaguely remembered from my early childhood. While I was growing up in South Vietnam, artistic circles were inundated with the art and literature of the exiled North, and this made me crave to learn more about Hanoi. The writings of authors like Mai Thao and Thanh Tam Tuyen, the poetry of Vu Hoang Chuong and Dinh Hung, the music of Pham Duy and Vu Thanh, offered fleeting glimpses of a Northern locale, a corner of Hanoi, an odyssey at once romantic, lyrical, and mysterious, which piqued my curiosity.

Phuc, age 17, Saigon.

Brother Lan tried hard to maintain the standard of living the family had been accustomed to, but our expenses increased as we grew older. Compared to most people of that time we were rather well off, but the price of goods rose with the escalation of hostilities between the North and South. By 1956 my second oldest brother, Hung, joined Lan in providing for the extended family. He was studying law but had to end his courses to work as a hospital nurse. After that, each of us upon reaching adulthood began to take care of himself and shouldered some of the responsibility for the household's finances.

When I completed my high school education, I went to live with my third brother, Bao, the only one of us to pick medicine over law school. Brother Bao was hoping to influence me to follow in his footsteps. After a time, however, he went to work in Bien Hoa, so I returned to the house with my other brothers, my mother, and those who had migrated to the South with the family.

Each time my older brothers engaged in some discussion, I listened with fascination. They would passionately hold forth on matters of political equality and social justice, or debate the thorny points of constitutional law. Such talk motivated me to apply for law school so I could take part in their conversations.

My youngest brother was Kien, but he was still six years

older than me, and he had the most influence on me regarding a career, how to live, and the obsession with Hanoi. Talented, Kien was my idol when I was growing up. I admired how he could be so skilled in the arts and hang out with his friends all year long, yet still perform brilliantly in his studies, always passing the law school exams at the top of the class.

While an intern in a local law firm and although not yet a licensed attorney, brother Kien authored a set of texts on family law. He also composed prose and poetry, translated *The Stranger* by Albert Camus, and wrote a play that earned him the national literary award in 1969. During that time he served as editor of *Van Hoc* (Literature), one of the earliest art publications of South Vietnam.

It was while working at *Van Hoc* that he became the son-in-law of Madame Nguyen Thi Vinh, a member of the Self-Reliant Literary Group, one of the most important teams of writers and artists of the emerging modern cultural movement in Vietnam. From that point on, having to deal with an unfortunate marriage, mu brother Kien stopped writing.

///

The 1968 Tet Offensive decimated the National Liberation Front's forces, so Hanoi was forced to send its soldiers to infiltrate the South. In response to the North Vietnamese communists' escalation of the war and for its survival, the Republic of Vietnam instituted a general draft of all military-aged youth.

As the Duong family responsibilities increased, eldest brother Lan had to take on a second job to supplement his full-time teaching position. He became an editor on nights and weekends at Radio Saigon, where brother Hung was the full-time news bureau chief. The task of editor involved translating reports from international news services from English and French into Vietnamese for announcers to read on the hour.

When I visited my brothers at the station, I was immediately caught up in the dynamic atmosphere of the newsroom. The lively commotion of reporters racing into the station to deliver their news reports and features then running back out on their next assignments fascinated me. It seemed to me that this type of work would satisfy my desire to seek the news and report it to the listeners, and would also suit my restless nature.

I applied to work at the station and got a job as a reporter.

The station's director was Lieutenant Colonel Vu Duc Vinh, a writer who went by the pen name Huy Quang. A small, taciturn fellow, he was rather sentimental and particularly fond of the young news staff, which was seen as the point men for the station. I was the latest of this band of 20 reporters, but I quickly found myself fitting in and becoming close to the others.

Radio Saigon was only a small part of the government apparatus.

Phuc reporting from the field,
Khe Sanh, 1968.

But as the voice of the Republic of Vietnam and the site first seized each time there was a coup, its directorship was reserved for someone who was close to whatever individual held power at that time. Vu Duc Vinh was Gen. Nguyen Cao Ky's chief of staff, therefore he was assigned to be director of Radio Saigon.

When I came on board the station, Air Force General Nguyen Cao Ky, chairman of the Central Executive Committee, had established a War Cabinet composed of young men with the brash declaration "Anyone over 35 is garbage."

Airborne Correspondent

I can't actually recall what possessed me, along with my fellow reporters Vu Anh and Le Phu Nhuan, to apply for paratrooper training. As civilians, we needed to get special permission, but our boss campaigned hard on our behalf. In the end, we became the first civilian journalists to earn airborne certification.

Training took place at camp Hoang Hoa Tham, headquarters of the Airborne Corps. Trainees were divided into teams of seven. The officer in charge was Lt. Vuong Dinh Thuyet, who later rose to lieutenant colonel, commander of Airborne Artillery. He assigned my group to a Sgt. Ly, a tough-looking man with a boxer's build. As civilians, we three journalists were teamed up with several high-ranking officers from different branches of service, including Col. Tran Van Hai, a Ranger commander, Navy Lt. Col. Nguyen Van Anh, and a couple of other Rangers.

Broadcast journalists of Radio Saigon who joined airborne training Class 105, Saigon, 1967. From left: Le Phu Nhuan, Duong Phuc, and Vu Anh.

In the initial contact, Sgt. Ly addressed the officers by their rank, and then requested that they remove their insignia to make it easier for him to conduct their training. They all readily agreed. My colleagues and I from the Voice of Saigon radio were assigned military uniforms.

The week of training wore us out, Sgt. Ly never let us catch our breath. In one drill, each team member had to carry another on his back and run down a long course. Col. Hai chose me as his partner, probably because I weighed the least. He grabbed me, bent down, then hefted me sideways, half on his shoulders, half on his back, and huffed and puffed around the drill field. Later when we encountered each other on the front, he brought up that story and laughed about how I'd offered my body for him to run laps in paratrooper training.

The grueling physical training was not as intimidating as jumping from the "pigeon coop." This exercise involved climbing a tall tower that resembled a dovecote, then throwing ourselves off with a bungee cord attached to our shoulders and midsection to catch us just before we hit the ground. Many soldiers dropped out when they reached this part of the training.

Finally, the students were put on a plane and flown to Hoc Mon, the paratrooper exercise field, where we had to make our first real jump to complete our training.

Airborne journalist trainees after a jump at the training center, Saigon,

Col. Tran Van Hai was a member of the Rangers, a unit renowned for gallantry,[17] so I assumed his pursuit of paratrooper training was simply for his amusement and to earn the airborne badge, or maybe just to find out what it felt like to fall through the air. In that sense I was the same—a journalist doesn't need a paratrooper license.

Nearly all of the military commanders I came to know or whom I interviewed were alike in being hot-headed and prone to chewing out officers of lower rank. Perhaps this was because the Army of Republic of Vietnam (ARVN) generals were professional soldiers who had worked their way up the ranks and were more than familiar with the process of giving commands and carrying them out; consequently, they could not accept others' opinions that encroached on their domain of responsibility.

As they say in the army: "Carry out orders first, gripe about it later."

---

[17] Later on, Col. Hai left the Rangers to become a police commander, then gained promotion to commander of the 7th Infantry Division, where he earned a general's star. On April 30, 1975, he committed suicide by poison at division headquarters to avoid falling into the hands of the communists.

Radio Saigon was home to some literary and artistic figures exiled from the North. I thus had the opportunity to become close with writers of the "older brother" generation, such as Vu Duc Vinh, Thai Thuy, Pham Hau, and Nguyen Dinh Toan.

Pham Hau, also known as the poet Nhat Tuan, was not only a boss in the broadcasting section but also a childhood friend of my brother Kien. He used to say that when I was little he carried me on his back around the Lake of the Restored Sword in Hanoi.

To that generation of "older brothers," Hanoi had a very sacred quality. The North had become a subject for restless reminiscence in poetry and prose, even in vaguely defined tales told during the day. Sometimes I thought that maybe they had just fabricated the whole thing, invented this wistful longing so they'd have a motivation to write or to sound artistic. And yet, as I read or listened to them, Hanoi gradually became a place about which I felt a need to learn more.

Phuc in the military, 1969.

In June 1969, I was called up to report to the Thu Duc military academy. Since I was already an experienced reporter, Major Pham Hau, then the director of the Voice of the Armed Forces Radio, requested I be assigned to that station after my basic training. That was the year the war intensified. From then on, I was given assignments all over the country to seek out news on the war.

War Correspondent

I moved easily into the role of war reporter and eventually created my own style of presentation. Most radio reporters of that time made tape recordings of background sounds, took the tapes back to the station, did a cut-and-paste, wrote their stories and recorded a voice-over. The resulting composition was broadcast to the public.

I liked to report directly from the scene, speaking into a tape recorder as I described what I saw and heard as it happened, accompanied by the sounds of gunfire and explosions. Then I returned to the station and sent the story onto the airwaves with little or no change. I wanted listeners to know what was actually going on during the fighting as if they were right at the front. Rather than write a story or relate the impressions of those interviewed, I often asked questions and let the soldiers speak for themselves. I believed those behind the lines must hear those doing the fighting, so I did everything I could to bring the authentic voices of the soldiers onto the airwaves.

After my promotion to lieutenant, I was made chief of the newsgroup. That position allowed me to create a team that reflected my personality and work style in pursuit of the news at the war's hottest spots.

Reporting from the Central region was difficult and fraught with danger. This region lay between the more populated areas of the North and South and composed the frontier that divided the country, so both the nationalists and the communists aimed to control it. The communists attacked remote areas and hard-to-defend towns seemingly every day. The Viet Cong (underground communist forces in South Vietnam), using their guerrilla style of warfare, often struck at villages and hamlets during the night to seize control of the people.

However, the next morning the ARVN would retake the sites. The war news could change over-night, and often it was hard to tell what was true and what was not, as the news agencies—especially the international news sources—reported different things depending on when they investigated, what unit they were following, and what side of the conflict their interviewees leaned toward.

The communists took maximum advantage of the forests and mountains, which suited their style of warfare. In this way they exercised control over the Central region's front in the manner of ghosts, here one minute, gone the next. They frequently retreated during the day, only to appear at night to launch an attack or exact justice on peasants who had given assistance to the Southern army. Having accomplished their mission, they would "shape shift" into ordinary peasants when dawn arrived. Meanwhile, as both the ARVN and the American military were primarily fighting a defensive war, they followed a conventional style of warfare, where the remote forests and mountains posed a challenge. The South Vietnamese soldiers always had to be vigilant to contend with the communist methods, which were unpredictable and difficult to gauge.

The Central region was also frequently subject to air strikes. The Southern army was determined to retake any towns that fell into the hands of the communists, so they regularly needed support from the Air Force. Meanwhile, the communists struck quickly, and then retreated into tunnels and bunkers, skillfully utilizing the complex terrain to protect them from air attack and launch their assault against the ARVN.

With my paratrooper certification, I often accompanied the airborne troops flown to the Central region and dropped into areas seized by the communists. The Airborne forces comprised the military's finest troops; consequently, I made many stirring reports on their valor and fearless determination on the battlefield.

Upon my return to the city, I often received suggestions from my colleagues and listeners. Their interest fortified my passion for this career and pushed other aspects of my life more and more to the side so that journalism became my main priority. There were times tension filled my job, but I never stopped hunting for the story. Even when an explosion jolted the microphone or camera from my hands, I did not stop working. I continued to silently record the events in my head and arrange the information so that I could resume the story as soon as possible. Back at the station, the recordings went online as made, with little editing or correction.

When I was in the city on leave, strangers, on finding out who I was, came up to tell me how much they were moved to hear the voices of young soldiers on the front facing life-and-death situations every day. The news stories and vivid reports strengthened their hope in the ultimate victory of nationalism and the ideals of the people.

I constantly struggled to contain my emotions and report the news from the front dispassionately, but there were times the stories affected me profoundly. Unlike my foreign colleagues who appeared cool and objective almost to the point of indifference, I infused my reports with my personal feelings as a South Vietnamese, which made the stories biting and more relevant to the listeners.

Traversing
the Four Military Zones

I earnestly followed the war wherever it went. There was not a town or city I didn't want to visit, even while I was on leave. The journalistic profession ran through my blood with such intensity that I felt my life dull and meaningless when I was not on assignment. Being stuck in a city, safe and secure, was depressing, especially when my elders were encouraging me to "follow my bliss."

I set foot in all 44 provinces and major townships of South Vietnam. While other reporters had a preference for certain locations,

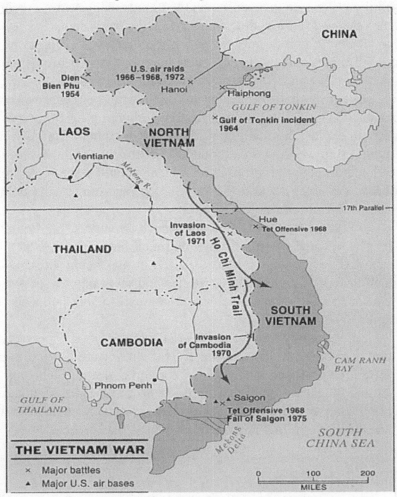

The Vietnam War – Source: amstrong.edu

my goal was to explore every area and region of the country. It was more of a mission than a job, like responding to a passionate calling.

The memories carved deepest in my mind are from the Central region, especially the area around Hue, the former imperial capital, and Quang Tri, further to the north. It was a hotly contested spot because of its location just below the Demilitarized Zone as determined by the 1954 Geneva Accords. I was particularly interested in Quang Tri and the Ho Chi Minh Trail, the communist infiltration and supply route that wound through the mountain forests from North Vietnam across southern Laos and Cambodia and into South Vietnam. The route was a crucial part in the communist scheme to invade the South, and the intricate web of trails was believed lined with anonymous graves of countless soldiers who lost their lives building or defending it.

I went there determined to learn the truth about those who died in the campaign *Sinh Bac Tu Nam*, or Born in the North, Die in the South. I never suspected that in this same area some of my colleagues and friends would also perish. I accompanied an airborne battalion into the middle of the DMZ. Soldiers were forbidden from entering the zone, but the North Vietnamese regularly violated the treaty. I could see traces of recent military activity there, evidence that the communists' promises and agreements were just for public consumption.

In Quang Tri, there was a famous site that drew me both as a journalist and personally: the Hien Luong Bridge, which divided Vietnam into two. Half the bridge belonged to the South, the other half to the North. In the middle there was a line that marked the border, indicating the 17th parallel. I had heard a lot about this bridge that spanned the Ben Hai River. The first time I saw Hien Luong bridge, I was reporting on a special prisoner release. The South Vietnamese allowed a small group of Viet Cong to cross to the other side. This scene particularly moved me.

This was several years before the official prisoner exchange called for by the Paris Peace Accords of 1973. As a correspondent for Da Nang Radio, I had flown out to Quang Tri to cover the release of prisoners of war, presided over by Major General Nguyen Chanh Thi, commander of I Corps.

Quang Tri city was divided, and this motivated me to stay and search out the story about this area. There was something especially strange about a bridge keeping two sides apart, a symbol of the war that pulled me toward it. Perhaps, too, it called up memories of my father standing on the Ham Rong Bridge when my family enjoyed a peaceful life in Thanh Hoa. I would return to Hien Luong Bridge many times just to gaze at it, my heart stirred.

My itinerant life produced many strange and marvelous experiences in every part of South Vietnam. The Central region had its beautiful beaches, like Thuan An beach near Hue, for which Thuy and I would name our first child. In the dense forest of the Central Highlands was the dreamlike little town of Pleiku. In the Mekong Delta lay sunlit rice fields with crisscrossing rivers and canals and gentle, unassuming people. I lived a vagabond's existence—by day gathering the news and writing reports, by night sleeping in the homes of strangers. I considered myself fortunate to visit so many places, to know and then take leave of people I had come to know so quickly in both the countryside and the cities.

I grew fond of these distant places and different people. In my war reporting in the field, I talked to everyone from the soldiers on the front lines to the generals who commanded them. I was lucky to have met many renowned officers of the Army of the Republic of Vietnam some of whom I felt quite close to, whose names went down in history when they sacrificed their lives on April 30, 1975, rather than give themselves up to the enemy.

As the saying goes: "In life a general; in death a deity." When they were alive, they served as military leaders, and when they died in the service of their country, their souls joined the rivers and mountains to live forever in the hearts of the people.

Chapter 6

Stepping Into the Fire

General Nguyen Khoa Nam (1927–1975)

■ PHUC

I often went on assignment with the Airborne troops, soldiers who wore the red beret and colorful camouflage uniform. These were the warriors dropped into a battle area to rescue or reinforce ground troops. At first, they were parachuted in, but later helicopters were used to transport them directly to the scene.

The last operation in which men were dropped in by parachute occurred in 1969. Then-Lt. Col. Nguyen Khoa Nam, the head of the 3rd airborne battle group, led his men into communist territory in Chuong Thien province. Knowing that this would be our last opportunity to report on such an operation, Vu Anh, Le Phu Nhuan and I went along for Radio Saigon.

Radio broadcasting in Vietnam was still in its early stages. Each of us carried a heavy UHER[18]

Gen. Nguyen Khoa Nam.

---

[18] Portable open-reel magnetic-tape audio recorders, introduced by UHER in Munich (Germany) in 1961. It was one of the first truly portable, fully transistorized recorders that dominated the professional (broadcast) market for many years.

in a pack strapped to our front and the parachute on our back. That's how we made this final *"saut do,"* or red jump, a true parachute drop into battle. The landing zone, a large clearing beside a forest, had already been shelled to discourage resistance. The descent was uneventful and we waved at each other as we watched the ground rise toward us. As in training, I pulled in my feet and bent my legs as I hit the ground to avoid injury. Meanwhile, I held on tight to my tape recorder.

By the time I'd gathered in my chute, Lt. Col. Nam had assembled his troops and was giving orders for reconnaissance and mopping up from Chuong Thien to Can Tho. In coordination with infantry and local forces, the ten-day operation aimed at cleaning out areas controlled by the guerrillas. Vu Anh and I were to accompany Capt. La Qui Trang, head of division operations and a personal friend of mine.

Lt. Col. Nguyen Khoa Nam belonged to the well-known Nguyen Khoa family of Hue. He was a serious man of few words but easygoing with his subordinates. Most commanders were fierce and hot-tempered, but Lt. Col. Nam always maintained self-control. I never saw him become upset or tense, regardless of the battle situation.

We made our way through rural villages of the southwest, past rice fields' green or deep gold. The peasants were warm, simple, hardworking folk. Had it not been for the Viet Cong, this would have been a pleasant place to live.

We encountered little resistance; perhaps the guerrillas had advance knowledge of our operation. They followed their familiar strategy of burying their weapons, disguising themselves as peasants, and mingling with the local population, expecting that once we moved on, they could reappear as soldiers. The units that preceded us discovered and wiped out several commando-sapper cells and captured some prisoners.

I interviewed some of the captives. All were native Southerners, not regular Northern troops, fighting on behalf of the National Liberation Front. Most were young, naïve, extremist in their views, and dissatisfied with the village government, which made them easy marks for Viet Cong propaganda. They were all related to one or another family in the village and used that relationship to work for the communists. The guerrillas were expert at sniping from a hidden position, which did not cause serious troop losses but did have a strong psychological effect. Sufficiently provoked, the ARVN might respond with excessive force, thereby generating local resentment against the government troops.

The prisoners were taken to Lt. Col. Nam, who asked them a few perfunctory questions then handed them over to the intelligence unit for interrogation. After that, they accompanied us on the rest of the mission to Can Tho, where they were placed in custody. During the entire time, I did not see a single prisoner tortured or abused. They were treated like anyone else and fed like the rest of us. Along the way to Can Tho, they were not bound, chained, or beaten.

The assignment proved to be the most leisurely one of my career as a war correspondent. Despite being dropped into enemy territory, I found myself enjoying the rural setting and peaceful villages that otherwise I would not have been able to visit. There were nights Vu Anh and I used our packs as pillows and slept beneath the stars beside the golden fields fragrant with the scent of ripening rice, the moon hanging over us like a lamp on high. I would fall asleep in the cool breeze, and then wake with a start in the middle of the night to the rustling of field mice scurrying about and nibbling on the rice. The villagers taught us to appreciate barbecued field mice, a popular treat since the rodents, feeding only on rice plants, were clean, fat, and easy to catch. They also went quite well with homemade rice wine.

Lt. Col. Nam did not drink, but he allowed his men to enjoy such diversions whenever they stopped at a welcoming village. He only ordered his men to remain alert at all times and take turns standing watch. When the villagers offered us chicken or fish, we laid it out and invited the commander to join us. He did not refuse, but only sampled a little for formality's sake, and he never drank.

I once asked him why he didn't marry. He laughed amiably.

"I don't want my wife to be waiting all year round while her husband's sent from one mission to another."

The officers usually set up a tent near a river or stream where it was convenient to fetch water for bathing. The troops simply bathed naked in the river. Lt. Col. Nam, however, went off by himself and bathed in seclusion, all the while whistling the "Col. Bogey March" from the Movie *Bridge on the River Kwai.*

The operation ended when we reached Can Tho. I had a chance to interview the commander later, after he had been promoted to colonel with the 7th Division, then once more when he was brigadier general in command of IV Corps. Each time he was as courteous to me as he had been as a lieutenant colonel and addressed me by my first name.

I still recall the last day of that operation in 1969. Vu Anh, Nhuan, and I went to say goodbye to Lt. Col. Nam and thank him for allowing us to accompany him. When we added that we hoped to see him again on another mission, he laughed.

"Do you plan on being war correspondents all your lives?"

We never suspected that our lives would change and the war would reach a tragic conclusion. Or that this heroic general, a modest and unassuming man who never drank, would take his own life when the NVA seized IV Corps on May 1, 1975.

He remained a bachelor to the end.

Gen. Pham Van Phu (1929-1975)

Gen. Pham Van Phu, commander of II Corps, was so small you'd probably miss him in a crowd of soldiers. However, he had a powerful voice and did not require the use of a microphone in an assembly hall. He worked his way up from soldier to general, and his military career included fighting at Dien Bien Phu. He was a Special Forces commander but gained a reputation after he took the leadership in the defense of the Central region, where he proved to be a highly talented officer.

Gen. Pham Van Phu.

My first interview with Gen. Phu was at the headquarters of the 1st Infantry Division near Hue. He had recently been assigned division commander, replacing

Gen. Ngo Quang Truong, who was promoted to head IV Corps. The ARVN 1st Infantry Division had just faced off against regular NVA divisions on Hill Bastow where the North Vietnamese used human wave attacks. In my hour-long interview, I asked the general some questions regarding the tense situation at the time.

I then changed the subject to ask about something that was currently in the press, namely, corruption in the military, specifically bribery and the buying of positions. He looked surprised.

"You want to ask me if I'm corrupt, don't you?" he laughed.

"No, sir," I stammered, embarrassed. "I only wanted to ask if there might be some corruption in the 1st Division that you didn't know about."

He laughed even harder.

"If I don't know...I don't know! Why even ask?"

After the session, Major Pham Huan, Press Officer from the Psywar Department, muttered, "Fat chance he'll let you interview him anymore!"

Major Pham Huan was very close to the general and later served as his press attache when Gen. Phu was assigned to II Corps. He remained at the general's side up to the tragic withdrawal from the highlands at the end of the war.[19]

Contrary to the major's prediction, however, I returned to interview Gen. Phu many times. His various aides and bodyguards knew the general had a special fondness for me, so they went out of their way to make my job easier.

Once I returned to Saigon after an assignment in the Central region to discover that a portion of the tape with Gen. Phu's voice was ruined. I called the base and explained the problem to the chief aide, asking if I could redo the interview. A few minutes later the general called and agreed to go over the questions again.

All this time I flew back and forth between Saigon and the Central region several times a week. I went by helicopter to the front lines to see small units in action. For all intents and purposes, I was just like one of the soldiers, except that instead of a weapon I was

---

[19] Under the March 14, 1975 order of then-President Nguyen Van Thieu, Gen. Pham Van Phu, then Commander of Military Region II (the Central Highlands and coast) pulled his forces back to Saigon and withdrew from his zone of command. When Saigon was about to fall into Communist hands, Gen. Phu committed suicide on April 29, 1975.

armed with a tape recorder and occasionally accompanied by a cameraman from military TV.

Once I got a story, I flew back to Saigon where I put the tape together, added opening and closing segments for broadcast, turned in the transcript to a newspaper, and was ready the next day to do it all over. I often slept in the sound room of Armed Forces Radio and caught naps on the plane heading back to the front.

Lam Son 719:
The Operation in Southern Laos

One battle I remember in great detail is the operation launched from Khe Sanh to Southern Laos, known as Lam Son 719. It was a significant turning point in the conflict, the beginning of what the Americans referred to as the "Vietnamization" of the war. I believe the results of that operation led to the war's outcome in 1975.

Lam Son 719 was a decisive battle in which both sides, the Republic of Vietnam and the Communist North, hurled their strongest forces at each other. The NVA moved several divisions along the Ho Chi Minh Trail, and it was the first time we saw Russian T-54 tanks in action. The enemy used human wave attacks against an airborne unit on a hill near the border between Laos and Vietnam, and, also for the first time, South Vietnamese Airborne brigade commanders were captured and taken prisoner.

A close friend of mine from high school, Lt. Dinh Duc Chinh, was captured with Col. Nguyen Van Tho, the airborne brigade commander, and taken to a prison camp inside North Vietnam where he was held and made to perform hard labor for the next 15 years. Meanwhile, countless exemplary heroes fought until their ammunition ran out, such as artillery Capt. Nguyen Van Duong, inspiring others with their patriotic fervor.

I flew up to Khe Sanh, the "brains" of the operation. From above, Khe Sanh looks like a giant wok surrounded by thick mountain forest. All day long it was obscured by the red dust kicked up by helicopters constantly coming and going. The wok's handle was a runway just long enough for the C-130 transport planes bearing men and supplies for the growing front. This was a joint military operation whose main element was the infantry from I Corps under Gen. Hoang Xuan Lam, especially the 1st Infantry Division under Gen. Phu. The initial strike force was made up of Marines and Airborne troops.

Command headquarters was a massive underground bunker safe from the incessant shelling of NVA artillery. The officers lived and worked in an interlinking web of tunnels and communications trenches. I traveled those tunnels regularly, seeking out stories and interviewing the officers as I followed the progress of the operation. At night I slept underground with my friends from Airborne.

It was at Khe Sanh that I also encountered many of my media colleagues from print, radio, and television, as well as the international news services. America's AP and UPI, Britain's Reuters, French's Agence France Press, and TV news networks from the U.S., Europe, Australia, Canada, Japan, and elsewhere all had correspondents looking for the story.

The Vietnamese media corps lacked the technology and resources to report directly from the scene like their foreign counterparts, so every day or two we would have to return to the capital to file our report. We were a small coterie of journalists who ran into each other all the time and shared news and information as friends. Vu Anh and I, who were both from the Saigon radio station and wrote for the newspaper *Song Than*, were always a pair, sharing the hardships in all four military regions.

Another of my comrades was Nguyen The Tuat Hai (nicknamed "Midget Hai" due to his small size) who worked for Voice of Freedom, the radio station funded by the U.S. that broadcast into North Vietnam. Midget Hai was sharp as a whip. His reports were lively, and he threw himself into risky situations in the front. Although a civilian, he wore a Marine uniform and always went around with a huge camera. He took one famous photograph of a wounded soldier clinging to a helicopter as it was taking off. The photo won an award, but he didn't know about it until he saw it published in *Stars and Stripes*, the American military magazine. Like other Vietnamese photographers working under verbal contract with foreign news media, he did not receive public credit for his work.

I always wore an airborne uniform and carried a backpack. Although I was a first lieutenant, I never wore the lieutenant's bar, only my airborne insignia. Besides my recording equipment, my pack held only cigarettes and dry rations.

The 1st Infantry Division was sent to secure strategic hills and cut off the road being used by the communists' Yellow Star Division to infiltrate men and supplies from North Vietnam through Southern Laos into South Vietnam. I asked Gen. Phu for permission to accompany them to the Laotian front in one of the helicopters. He turned away without replying. I thought perhaps he hadn't heard me, but after taking a few steps, he spun around, looked at me and nodded.

In all, three journalists were taken by Col. Nguyen Van Diem, Gen. Phu's assistant in command, to a casualty helicopter assigned to evacuate the wounded from the village of Tchepone. Also aboard were Midget Hai and a military film journalist known as "Elephant My," a famed cameraman from the Psywar Film Department who was big as an elephant and always gave his all for his colleagues.

The Tchepone River valley was a vast area in Southern Laos. A hill there, called Sophia, defended by the 1st Infantry, was experiencing day-and-night bombardment, and many casualties were waiting to be airlifted out. The pilots advised us that once they brought the helicopter close to the ground, we had to jump out and seek immediate cover. If the chopper were fired on, they would take off and wait for the situation to die down before coming back to pick up the wounded.

In fact, as soon as we leaped out, we heard the whistling of incoming rounds and then the loud boom of impact. We ran for our lives and threw ourselves into craters, pressing our faces to the ground to avoid the shrapnel.

The hill was barren, full of craters made by our air strikes during its capture, each hole big enough for one person to hide. But the holes were not deep, so we had to curl up and bury our heads to evade the flying metal fragments, of which even a tiny piece could kill a man. During a pause in the firing, Midget Hai, Elephant My and I ran for one of the trenches dug by the defenders.

We interviewed soldiers and shot film around Sophia. The hill had been taken to cut the communist supply line, and while the infantry was not involved in direct fighting, it suffered heavy casualties from the shelling. The communists used bombardment to maximum effect, and as the occupation dragged on, our side's ranks were attrited, and our force weakened. We required continual reinforcement; even the airborne troops, training for swift attack and fierce fighting, were called on now to take up fixed positions and hold the hills like the infantry.

Another site, designated Hill 31, held by the 3rd Airborne Battalion and serving as the headquarters of the 3rd Paratrooper brigade under Col. Nguyen Van Tho, found itself suddenly attacked by waves of NVA soldiers supported by artillery barrages and armored units, including T-54 tanks. Thousands of rounds converged on the tiny hill like a giant net, cutting off reinforcements for the defenders, who included one battalion of the 3rd Airborne with about 300 soldiers and the 3rd Brigade general staff. Despite their efforts to hold on, Hill 31 was finally overtaken on February 5, 1971.

The NVA captured Col. Tho and the general staff. The remainder of the troops were scattered in the forests surrounding the hill, but the enemy blocked their escape routes, and no one got away. Among those who fought to the death was airborne artillery Captain Nguyen Van Duong, who was immortalized in a song by Tran Thien Thanh, titled "You Did Not Die, Brother!"

Enemy Tactics

■ PHUC

O ne of the important issues we war journalists debated was the painful fact that we were fighting our own people, something the Vietnamese communists exploited to their advantage.

Both the South Vietnamese soldiers and their American allies often found themselves in gray areas when seeking out the enemy. It was hard to distinguish between Viet Cong (VC) and ordinary peasants in a country where half the people were on the government's side, and half were with the VC. By day, a fellow might be just one of the farmers, carrying his hoe on the way to the rice paddy. At night, the same man might be plotting an attack or transporting food or ammunition through the village. No longer simple, peace-loving people of the soil, they would turn into killers, setting traps, planting mines, or firing mortar rounds into crowds of innocent civilians. Then, they would blend in with the villagers so that even the ARVN soldiers found it hard to distinguish friend from foe.

Another tactic was to draw the government soldiers into an area by firing at them from nearby. I once accompanied an ARVN unit as it passed by a village on routine reconnaissance. As they walked in single file, a sudden burst of gunfire flared from behind a bush, striking two of the soldiers in the back. The ARVN returned fire in the direction from which the attack came. The VC then claimed the government soldiers had fired into the village. On another occasion, an ARVN unit was sniped at by an unseen guerrilla outside a village; all they could do was to restrain their rage and keep from storming into every house looking for the shooter.

Even though in most cases the ARVN were able to control themselves and keep from exacting revenge after being attacked, the VC in their midst used every incident as a basis for propaganda against the "transgressors" and prevent the villagers from supporting the government.

Once reporters had the chance to get close to the soldiers, we came to understand their situation and sympathized with the difficulties they faced and the sacrifices they made. They risked their lives to protect the people, yet sometimes those very people betrayed them to the enemy.

As the war intensified, the VC became more coward. They attacked haphazardly then ran away to let the villagers bear the consequences of Allied reaction. The VC units were not strong enough to defeat the government troops, so they increased tension by placing the South Vietnamese soldiers in constant danger.

Nor did the communists hesitate to use the lives of their soldiers to lure government forces into an ambush, especially the Americans, who lacked a thorough understanding of the situation and tactics of the VC. While the South Vietnamese gladly accepted the help of the American soldiers, they were unable to make their foreign comrades understand the complexities of fighting the communists or just how the Vietnamese think.

To the Americans, all Vietnamese looked alike. The Americans could not tell friendly Vietnamese from foes, the only differences being uniforms—if they wore them—or their accents. These young soldiers, trained in conventional warfare, had a hard time adjusting to the guerrilla strategies and tactics employed by the communists.

Meanwhile, the VC, like all terrorist organizations around the world, operated in small groups, maybe even a single individual working as a sniper or secret messenger. At the same time, they would surprise Allied forces by launching a major uprising, striking unexpectedly just like their guerrilla attacks.

The Tet Offensive

This is what happened in the 1968 Tet Offensive. As the lunar New Year began, the communists attacked major cities and towns throughout South Vietnam, a blatant violation of the Tet ceasefire they had agreed to so the people across the country could celebrate in peace this most sacred holiday. Using the element of surprise, the communists struck quickly, seizing some towns and other targets and throwing the Allies temporarily off guard.

In most cases, these sites were back in friendly hands in a matter of hours or days, but in a few places the fighting went on for

Map of Tet Offensive in 1968 – Source: Mountain View Mirror.

weeks or months, with considerable casualties on both sides. Among the targets that had a psychological impact on the general population were Radio Saigon and the U.S. Embassy. Besides capturing some critical military and government points, the enemy briefly paralyzed the South and stunted the Allied response.

The South Vietnamese were shocked by the cruelty of the communists. Their actions exhibited a policy of revenge against their fellow countrymen and a disregard for the virtues and traditions of our people, especially at this time of year. By this general uprising, the communists showed the world that they would take advantage of the morality and trust of the people of the South and seek to conquer the whole country at any price, even in the face of worldwide condemnation. The communists notably displayed their barbarity in seizing, exterminating, and burying alive thousands of citizens of Hue during their occupation of that city.

ARVN: American Media's Biased Treatment

Like the other South Vietnamese, I was outraged and ashamed by the savagery of the Tet attacks. I was also upset by the irrationally biased presentation of the Offensive given in the American media. American news reporters paid little attention to the communists' violations of the ceasefire or the mass murders of Southerners but dug deep into the weaknesses and failures of the American and South Vietnamese military.

Because they did not follow the ARVN soldiers, they knew nothing of the valiant spirit of the South Vietnamese army. Instead of reporting on the brave efforts of the people of South Vietnam, they depicted scenes that drew condemnation, such as burning villages, wounded women and children, or their own young men—sons, brothers, husbands— struggling and vulnerable in a faraway jungle.

No reporter can cover every aspect of a war, but the American media chose the easiest way of getting attention. They were unable to convey the savagery of the Communists because they didn't fully understand the fanaticism of the North Vietnamese commanders and their insane willingness to sacrifice their soldiers, whose corpses were found chained to their tanks or artillery.

While such devotion might be regarded as heroic and

patriotic, the truth was that the ordinary Northern soldier had only two choices: fight or die. In North Vietnam, under the tight control of the communists, there was nowhere a soldier could run without causing severe consequences to his or her family.

Only the Vietnamese reporters who accompanied the ARVN soldiers and directly interviewed communist prisoners knew about the campaign of "Born in the North, Die in the South" implemented by "Uncle Ho" and the Communist Party to sacrifice Northern soldiers in the South.

The communists' policy of concealing or distorting the news turned the people of the North into tools serving the Party like a team of horses wearing blinders who only see the path they are shown and plod forward under the driver's whip.

For my part, I just did my best to report what I saw every day, in every battle I witnessed. Based on my perspective as a war correspondent, the images shown to the world by American television revealed only a small portion of the war, and sadly, that portion was advantageous to the communist side. Everyone knows

Phuc during a live broadcast on the Tet Offensive, Cho Lon District, Saigon, 1968.

that a story has at least two sides, but unfortunately the other side—
that of the South Vietnamese army—was largely neglected and went
unreported.

The biased reporting caused problems for some Western
reporters I knew who really cared and took time to try to understand
the war. They befriended the Vietnamese and had a chance to learn
about the communists. They wanted to report the war faithfully to
justify the struggle of the South Vietnamese and describe the fighting
spirit of the Vietnamese armed forces. But their stories were often
not used or were shortened and relegated to the inside pages by
editors who had their set ideas of what the war were about.

My Lai Massacre Effects

One incident, which troubled even supporters of the war, was
the massacre of civilians at the My Lai hamlet in Son My village,
Quang Ngai province. What the American news media did not make
clear was that this tragic happening was a result of the VC's baiting
by firing on the American soldiers then slipping away, leaving the
villagers to bear the consequences of the soldiers' revenge. When
their plan succeeded and the Americans overreacted with murderous
anger, the communist propaganda machine took over, repeating the
story and showing pictures of dead and wounded civilians. This
tactic of the fleeing sniper was used all over the South, especially in
places where the VC faced resistance from the villagers.

As a reporter, I was frustrated witnessing the enemy's
cunning and the naiveté of the American press, and I asked myself
why these journalists did not understand that death and destruction
are the prices one must pay in any war. How could the American
media, thousands of miles from Vietnam, consider this an American
war when the South Vietnamese military had a million men risking
their lives every day on the front line?

It seemed to me the innocence and insincerity of the
American media influenced public opinion against the war and the
American soldiers, their own people, who fought with the
Vietnamese. Like my Vietnamese media colleagues, while I hurt
inside as I witnessed the consequences of Communist aggression day
in and day out, American reporters made our pain even greater. I felt

compelled to stand up for our cause.

Besides the My Lai massacre, there was the rough justice meted out to a VC prisoner by Gen. Nguyen Ngoc Loan, commander of the national police, on the street in Cholon during the Tet Offensive. The American media played up this story, but without stressing that Gen. Loan had just seen how the entire family of a close friend had been murdered by the Viet Cong.

Many people thought Gen. Loan was merely foolish, who did not seriously consider all the reporters around him when he walked right up to a bound prisoner, raised his gun to the man's head, and fired. The killing shocked everyone. The Americans treated it as a war crime. To me, the general was a "cowboy" out of his time, a defiant sheriff from the old West who let his rage get the better of him and ended up destroying his reputation with one gunshot fired in front of journalists.

But how many times did the Viet Cong administer "instant justice" to their prisoners with no one raising a fuss? During that same Tet Offensive, the communists murdered thousands of people, many buried alive in mass graves outside Hue, but what did the American media say about that? The images of the death and loss still stick in my brain and continue to haunt me, appearing out of nowhere to trouble me now and then. I realize that this is the price I must pay for being a war correspondent and having been witness to so much ugliness and brutality.

Vietnamization of the War

Lam Son 719 was considered the first experiment of what the Americans referred to as "Vietnamization," the plan to shift responsibility for carrying out the war from the American military to the Vietnamese. In Southern Laos, the army of South Vietnam directly faced main units of the North Vietnamese Army without the support of the U.S.

Ultimately, Operation Lam Son 719 would prove to be a heavy loss for the South Vietnamese forces. But in the early stages, ARVN succeeded in stopping the flow of men and materiel from North Vietnam down the Ho Chi Minh Trail. Because of this, the South's military spokesman, Lt. Col. Le Trung Hien, described it as a great success. There was a huge celebration in Hue, including a military parade. Medals were awarded, officers were promoted. Radio Saigon sent its top reporters to broadcast the event nationwide.

President Thieu offered a special reward of 11 days R&R in Taiwan to 25 outstanding soldiers selected from each of the units that had taken part in the operation. The delegation, led by Gen. Pham Van Phu, was warmly welcomed by South Vietnam's ambassador to Taiwan, Nguyen Van Kieu, President Thieu's older brother. The group went on a tour of the island state and enjoyed daily feasts.

I was surprised to be among the 25 chosen for this honor, as this delegation was composed of those who acted bravely in battle, whereas I was only a war correspondent from the Political Warfare Department and never carried a weapon.

General Pham Van Phu, left, and Duong Phuc, Taiwan, 1972.

We were escorted to Independence Palace to meet the president. I recall Mr. Thieu as being in good spirit and considerate, chatting and having his picture taken with each of us. At a banquet held in our honor were Brig. Gen. Pham Van Phu, Major Gen. Tran Van Trung, Director-General of the Political Warfare Department, and Hoang Duc Nha, President Thieu's press secretary, later the head of the Information and Communication Ministry.

Gen. Trung informed me that it was he who had nominated me to represent his department in the delegation. He and Hoang Duc Nha, the president's nephew, were the "big shots" in charge of information and communication, responsible for mobilizing the population for the war effort. Their job at the time was to emphasize the positive aspects of the Laos operation to counter negative press in Vietnam and the U.S. regarding Vietnamization.

Lam Son 719 was seen as a response to those skeptics who did not believe the   S. Vietnamese Army could succeed without American support. A film showing the capture of Tchepone, including the scene of reporters jumping from the helicopter and running across the hill, interviews with soldiers, and a direct report from me, was repeatedly shown on Saigon television. It was the first time the people in the capital saw the desolate mountains of southern Laos and witnessed the lonely, harsh life of the brave soldiers on the front.

Phuc and colleagues interviewing Gen. Pham Van Phu, Tchephone, Laos, 1971. Photo: Tuat Hai.

The *Hawk* and Vice President Tran Van Huong

Later, President Thieu went personally to inspect Khe Sanh and held a news conference right next to the command post for the Laos operation. It was a significant event, with many reporters from both international news agencies and Vietnam being flown in from

Saigon especially to hear the president announce the success of Vietnamization as proved by the results of Lam Son 719.

Mr. Thieu wore a khaki safari uniform as he sat on a wooden ammunition case set atop a pile of sandbags. Behind him stood the operation's commanding officers. The president gave a very long speech and detailed speech, so long and detailed that when the time came for questions, there was nothing left to ask, as he had already covered every angle.

Among the 30 or so reporters who stood around him, a few from American TV news stations asked a few trivia questions to get their camera shots. Near the end of the press conference, I stepped up to the microphone held by Press Secretary Hoang Duc Nha. Mr. Nha patted me on the shoulder as he usually did and handed me the microphone.

"Mr. President," I spoke up, "what do you think of the statement by Vice President Tran Van Huong in the *Hawk* newspaper that Vietnamization of the war is a cover for America's plan to withdraw its forces and abandon Vietnam?"

My question took everyone by surprise, and they fell silent. Even the photographers and cameramen stopped what they were doing and waited for the president's response.

Up until then, the South Vietnamese vice president had not spoken up about the war. Thus, the public was stunned when he sharply criticized America's plan to "Vietnamize the war." The newspaper *Dieu Hau* (Hawk) dropped this bombshell with a front-page picture and story of Tran Van Huong forcefully declaring that Vietnamization was simply a pretext for the withdrawal of U.S. troops in the face of pressure by Congress to reduce military spending, but especially in response to violent anti-war protests in Washington, DC. He said it was clear the United States was going to end all support for the war, pull out of Vietnam, and leave South Vietnam on its own to try to stave off the North Vietnamese, who enjoyed military support from the Soviet Union and China.

In an earlier issue, *Dieu Hau* had published a list of corrupt officers, including generals close to President Thieu. The vice president had been in charge of the campaign to eliminate corruption around the country, and rumor had it he protected this newspaper and permitted it to print bold critiques of people on high. It was also commonly believed that "Teacher" Tran Van Huong—known for his good character but thought to be politically naïve—had been selected as a running mate by Mr. Thieu when the latter decided he had had enough of his former vice president, the "cowboy" Nguyen Cao Ky.

And so, that day at Khe Sanh, everyone waited to hear President Thieu's response to my question. Gen. Cao Van Vien, head of South Vietnam's Joint Chiefs, stood expressionless as always in his neatly pressed airborne uniform. Gen. Du Quoc Dong, an airborne commander who had been speaking to an aide, paused to listen. Behind him, Gen. Pham Van Phu took one step forward in surprise. Next to him, Gen. Hoang Xuan Lam looked straight at me and nodded.

President Thieu answered the question swiftly and intelligently. He thanked the vice president for his remarks, and then explained that Vietnamization had been carefully planned and now the war had reached the stage when it could be implemented. The United States had its problems, he went on, with Congress wanting to end the conflict and a growing anti-war movement, but the American military was not running away, was not abandoning its ally, but was simply turning responsibility for the war over to the South Vietnamese. He affirmed the country's ability to defend itself and expressed confidence in America's promise to provide military assistance until the war's conclusion.

With that, the press conference ended.

A Fateful Encounter

The reporters were invited to view the base, visit the command post and interview soldiers. As I moved out with the others, I noticed a young woman standing beside a tall foreign lady. I was surprised that a Vietnamese woman would have come all the way out from Saigon to participate in a press conference on the front lines. She was small, sprightly, and wore the beige safari outfit of a journalist. I had no idea who she was or for what agency she worked. I just caught a glimpse of her beautiful eyes as she was heading off with the others. I wanted to catch up and find out her name, but for some reason, I held back.

After asking around, I learned that she was Vu Thanh Thuy who worked for Radio Voice of Freedom. Her friend was Marie

Joannidis, a Greek correspondent for the Agence France Press. The incident was over before it began and the journalists boarded the plane to return to Saigon. I supposed Miss Thuy had not noticed me, or if she had, she would not have any interest in me.

Thuy, Khe Sanh, 1971.

As for myself, I remained at Khe Sanh for another week. Having nothing to do, my mind went round and round thinking about the girl with the unusual eyes. I made up my mind to look her up the next time I was in Saigon.

All that week I often went to Dong Ha and strolled about this romantic town whose streets were filled with young soldiers on their way to and from the battlefield. I might sit at a cafe on a high street and look out at the string of mist-covered forested mountains on one side and the red-dust road on the other, a strange yearning in my heart. And I tried to push away the image of those eyes I had glimpsed in Khe Sanh.

Chapter 7

Growing Up Self-Reliant

Idyllic Upbringing

■ THUY

I was the only child in my family born in Hanoi. All of my older siblings were born south of Hanoi in the city of Thai Binh, from where both sides of my family came.

At the time, my Papa taught high school English and Latin. The education profession appealed to young, progressive intellectuals who did not want to work for the French and hoped to avoid being noticed by the colonial authorities. In those years, education followed one of two paths: a Western curriculum that immersed students in French culture, or a nationalist course that

Thuy's father,
Vu Ngoc Ban,
(1921-1993).

Thuy's mother,
Hoang Thi
Thinh,
(1923-1993).

stressed Vietnamese language and culture. Since there were few bilingual teachers, my father was assigned as needed to various schools in the region, close enough that he could travel easily from one to another. Primarily, he worked at Ho Ngoc Can High School, a religious institution that promoted ideas of human rights and social equality.

Papa was the youngest of three children. His family lived in Thai Binh, but his parents sent all of their children to school in Hanoi. While my uncle Vu Ngoc Bich attended the Vietnamese Pomelo High School and my aunt Vu Kim Chi went to a Marianist school, Papa studied at the Lycee Albert Sarraut, a French public school known for preparing the next generation of Vietnamese for administration and social reform.

As a Roman Catholic, Papa was a natural enemy of the communists, who believed that organized religion was a threat to their quest for power. The Vietnamese Catholic parishes were strongly unified and refused to support the communist movement. Whenever the Marxist revolutionaries came into an area, they dealt harshly with the Catholics, being especially hard on the priests, who were quite influential in the lives of their congregations.

When my parents met in 1940, they fell madly in love, but both their families firmly opposed the union. The reason behind their opposition was quite typical of the times and could have come out of a romance novel of the 1930s.

Papa's family owned considerable farmlands around Thai Binh, so they wanted a daughter-in-law who was strong and hardy, a good worker, quick, and submissive, to help manage the farm and house servants. Mama, on the other hand, was a pampered daughter of a bourgeois house, a delicate lady, modern and progressive.

Then, town girls wound their long hair in a braid around their head or wrapped it in a turban, and dressed in black trousers only and smiled proudly to show off their jet-black lacquered teeth. Mama did the opposite, by combing her hair with a part to the side and left it uncovered, preferring white trousers, and sporting shiny white teeth. She was also an independent woman who thought for herself. The result was that my parents' relationship met with the families' disapproval, put a lot of pressure on everyone involved, and caused a stir among the people in the city until the two finally married in 1941.

Their union only became a reality with the intervention of my father's uncle, Vu Ngoc Oanh, who was the province chief of Bac Ninh and had great influence over the affairs of the extended family. Once he agreed to it, there was nothing the two sides could do but yield to his decision.

Thuy's parents, center, at their wedding, with groomsmen and bridemaids, Thai Binh, October 30, 1941.

One consequence of this affair was that Papa chose to stay far away from the big cities and their political and social conflicts. While he was away for work, Mama remained in Thai Binh, and so my older sisters and brother were born there. In early 1949 the family moved to Hanoi but frequently had to evacuate to the countryside due to the battles between the French and the Viet Minh.

For many months, they lived in remote villages, where food and medicine were scarce. During one of these evacuations, when my mother was pregnant with me, her fourth child, my sister Trang, caught pneumonia and died at the age of 20 months. Perhaps that's why my parents pampered me and were easier with me than with their other children as if making up for the loss of my sister. I was born on September 24, 1950, at Bach Mai Hospital in Hanoi.

In 1954, when the communists took power in North Vietnam, Papa took us all to Saigon. As it happened, the Ho Ngoc Can School also transferred to the South, so Papa still had a job, unlike many other evacuees who were now unemployed. He found us a small house, and we were able to leave the crowded and uncomfortable temporary camp. Also, Papa immediately began taking part in social and political activities through various Southern associations he joined, and he even took his children to many of the meetings.

I had a lively and happy childhood and was sufficiently

Thuy, age 4, (second from left), with parents and siblings in the backyard of their home, Hanoi, 1954.

provided for materially, emotionally, intellectually, and with regards to my spiritual development. For even though Papa indulged his children and allowed us to develop our personalities, there was one thing he would not yield on, and that was our religion. To him, that was the one priceless gift he could hand down to us, a vital possession that could help us cope with all of life's challenges.

Early every morning we rose at six to accompany our parents to attend Mass at Mai Khoi chapel run by the Dominicans, which was also the boarding place for college students. And every night at nine, we had to finish our studies and say our nighttime prayers with the rest of the family, including both my paternal and maternal grandparents.

I remember how my older brother Bau used to hide in the latrine to get a little extra sleep, but Papa would always come and get him to go to church. At night I would fall asleep during prayers, and Papa would carry me upstairs with the others. That was about the only thing on which my father insisted. As for everything else, even our personal lives and who we married, he let us form our own opinions and decide for ourselves.

My older sisters Kim Thuy and Ngoc Thanh went to Trung Vuong School, and brother Bau boarded at La San in Thu Duc. When it was my turn to go to school, my parents placed me and my little sister Kim Thoa in Queen of Peace, a French school run by nuns located next to the Mai Khoi chapel.

When I was eight, Papa was sent to teach in the mountain town of Ban Me Thuot. After a few months away from his family, though, he decided to give up teaching. He took a position with the United States Office of Information, working in the Abraham Lincoln Library run by the American government. Because the Americans employed him, his salary was higher than that paid by Vietnamese employers, so he was able to provide us with a high quality of life.

I grew up thinking that Papa loved me more than my siblings, that I was his special girl and the luckiest one in the family. Many years later, when talking about our family with my brother and sisters, I learned that my parents had a way of treating each of us individually so that each thought she or he was special and the most loved.

But as a child, I enjoyed living under the illusion that for some mysterious personal reason, Papa reserved that treatment just for me.

Brush Strokes of Death

Something else occurred during my childhood that made my parents more attentive to me. When I was nine, my little sister Thanh Thu died from what was only much later identified as dengue fever.

My sister Thu was three years younger than me, and her death left me devastated. The two of us were very close, we played together every day. She was the cutest in the family, as well as the smartest and most sweet-tempered. I enjoyed the responsibility of watching over her and thought of her as my best friend.

The family in Saigon, 1958. Clockwise from left: Mama, sister Ngoc Thanh, brother Bau, sister Kim Thuy, Papa, Thuy, and sister Thanh Thu.

On a field trip, 1958. First row, from right, Thuy, age 8, Thanh Thu, age 5, and their friends.

While Thu's death was a great blow to me, my Mama was so hurt she fell ill and was regularly in and out of the hospital. The family doctor, Vu Ngoc Hoan—a cousin who called my father "young uncle" even though they were the same age and had been classmates in school—suggested that my mother needed a change of climate and proposed the town of Bao Loc in the Central Highlands with its cool, refreshing air.

My father purchased a tea plantation of more than seven acres a few miles from the center of Bao Loc at a place the locals called Ferme District. Besides the broad fields of tea, the area had various types of fruit Mama loved. Papa hoped that the rows of pomelo, orange, jackfruit, and avocado trees that grew all down the slope from the tea field would help Mama regain her spirit. They called the plantation "Trang Thu Estate" to commemorate the two children they had lost.

The town of Bao Loc, which the native people still called by its former highland name B'lao, was five hours' drive from Saigon and about three hours from Dalat. Although perhaps not as lovely as Dalat, in a tropical country like Vietnam where the climate was hot and humid, a place like B'lao with its cool mountain air all year round was considered a good place to go to restore one's strength.

Mama brought along her three youngest children. Her mother came to take care of her and help the children. Brother Bau, little Kim Thoa, and I were delighted to move to Bao Loc, while Papa and older sisters Kim Thuy and Ngoc Thanh remained in Saigon to continue their schooling.

Papa had a house built in the middle of the plantation overlooking the highway and hired a local man to manage the farm during the day. When we moved in, the house still had the scent of fresh, unpainted wood. We were about half a kilometer from our neighbors to either side, the space in between planted with tea shrubs in straight rows. Between the shrubs and the highway, there was a tall, thick row of hibiscus always flourishing with red flowers. Dividing our land and the neighbor's tea farm was a straight row of manioc that stretched from the highway a whole kilometer deep into the valley behind the house.

I rarely walked all the way down the slope behind the tea farm. A few times I went with one of the older folks, holding onto them to keep from losing my footing and tumbling down, and when I reached the bottom, I was worn out. More often I would sit beside a jackfruit tree and look for a fruit that had fallen and cracked open, then dig out a section of the fruit to eat while waiting for the others to come back.

I spent warm early afternoons walking among the fruit trees with their thick leaves. Then I'd spread out a plastic mat and lie on the ground eating fruit and gazing up to where the sky might peep through the lush canopy. Lying there among the tall trees and hearing only the singing of birds and rustling of leaves, I felt like a primitive girl living in the wild jungle.

Every two weeks dozens of workers came to pick the tea. They were mostly highland girls with rosy cheeks who plucked the tea leaves with brisk hands and tossed them into rattan baskets they wore on their backs. One of them made me my basket so I could go out with them to pick tea. I was excited to follow along and copied their actions. By the end of the day, however, my basket held only wildflowers and fruit!

Mama

The year we moved to B'Lao, Mama was 36 years old, although she looked much younger. By getting away from the house in Saigon with its constant reminders of my dead sister, she began to recover her strength, aided by the cool year-long climate and physical activity of managing the farm.

I always admired Mama's adroit and resourceful nature. Although she was quiet and appeared beside my father like a dim shadow, in reality, she was the one who directed all the affairs inside and outside the family. Anytime Papa or the children encountered some difficulty, it was she who resolved it, from financial matters to social interactions.

Mama was taciturn, and at first glance, one might think she was cold and haughty. I heard that long before, in Thai Binh, she was considered quite attractive. When I looked at her, I wished that when I got to be her age, I would still have a young face, silky skin, and long black hair like her. I also hoped to have her unparalleled energy and courage.

She was always gentle, and I rarely saw her get angry despite her being stricter than Papa in raising her children. I watched her deal with various problems with confidence and fortitude. Unlike Papa, who enjoyed socializing and involvement in outside activities, Mama's pleasure came from her family. Moreover, she set aside her own needs and followed Papa in all matters, ready to sacrifice everything for her family.

When we first moved from the crowded city of Saigon to the secluded house in the middle of a tea farm near a mountain town, I was frightened, especially at night. In the highlands, by five in the evening, the mist has already set in. Standing in the kitchen door and looking down to the fog-bound valley, I might tremble, thinking about scenes from movies like *Frankenstein* and *Dracula* that I'd seen with my parents in Saigon theaters.

I'm sure Mama was just as scared living in such an isolated spot with an old grandmother and three children, her son barely entering his teens. Nevertheless, I never saw her display any fear in front of us. Each evening, she calmly checked all the doors and windows and made sure they were properly secured. We had dinner before dark because, in the beginning, we didn't have electricity. Since our neighbors lived far away, Mama bought four big dogs to guard the property. My brother and I were responsible for calling the dogs at night and chaining them to posts at the corners of the house.

Every morning at five, Mama woke me up to walk with her three kilometers down the road to the Bao Loc church. Still troubled by the death of little Thu, she found some comfort in these morning masses. I didn't really like getting up early, but I felt sorry for her having to walk alone in the morning mist and forced myself out of bed to go with her.

Pleasures at the Manor Farm

Our time in B'Lao taught us children a great deal about living on a farm. We earned revenue from selling tea and fruit from our gardens. Once we had settled into our new house, Mama had a small shed built in the back for chickens and geese. I was responsible for feeding the chickens each morning, collecting the eggs, letting the squawking birds out in the morning and, with brother Bau, chasing them back at night.

We were each given our own flock of chickens to take care of, and we were allowed to sell some of the eggs so we could buy sweets. I loved to sit and watch the hens hatch their eggs and see the baby chicks break through the shells cheeping. Then I tended them carefully to help my little chickens grow.

Bau tended the geese. After I was done feeding the chickens I used to run over and tease the big birds, provoking them to chase me around, honking and carrying on. It caused such a fuss that Bau yelled at me to stop. I had a great time but had to put up with all the bruises on my legs where the geese had nipped me.

These games on the farm marked the beginning of my life as a tomboy. To avoid thinking about my sister Thu, I would find an escape by playing all day. Little Thoa was only three, so she stayed in the house with Mama and Grandma. I was left to play with my brother Bau. We made so much fun out of our chores with the animals that by day's end we were more exhausted from playing than working.

Most of the children who came around were boys. At first they only played with Bau, but eventually, they let me join them. After a while, I could play soccer, shoot marbles, spin tops, and climb as well as any of the boys.

When the neighbor children were busy working in their family gardens, Bau and I went exploring. We made toys out of items we salvaged, like a milk jar for a push car, or bottle caps we flattened and strung together for wind chimes. We made a sort of sled to transport fruit from the garden. It was just a wooden crate with a piece of wood nailed onto it for a handle, but little Thoa had a great time when we put her inside and slid her around the yard.

The neighbor boys were born and raised in B'Lao and had never been out of the highlands. They listened with rapt attention when we told them about the city. At the same time, my brother and I admired our friends' skill in farming, and we were eager students as they explained what was the best season for planting different types of crops, how to raise good pigs and cows, and the way to train dogs. They also showed us how to have fun in ways we had never imagined.

Blossoming Youth

On Friday nights every other week, my brother and I would stay up to wait for Papa to come in on the last bus, which usually arrived in B'Lao around 11 o'clock. If my older sisters were coming during a break from school, Papa would drive them in the office's Land Rover.

Oftentimes when Kim Thuy and Ngoc Thanh arrived for a holiday in the mountains, they brought along some of their friends. One was Kim Thuy's boyfriend Ky, who in turn had his younger sisters in tow. The estate came alive with the raucous noise of young people. The older ones led the younger children to explore the surroundings and enjoy the scenery.

There was the beautiful Dai Binh (Great Peace) forest with a high suspension bridge only as wide as a tree trunk that extended across the river with nothing but ropes for handholds. By now I was used to climbing and being up in high places, so I went first over the bridge, then stood and taunted my sisters as they followed, groping their way, slowly advancing step by trembling step.

Thuy's family in Bao Loc, South Vietnam, 1961. From left: Thuy, age 11, Grandma, sister Thanh, brother Bau, sister Kim Thuy, Mama, and Papa. Sister Kim Thoa in front.

Myrtle bushes grew lush with rich, juicy purple berries, the pale violet flowers spotting the whole forest. The berries were delicious, but under the leaves lurked scores and scores of hungry leeches. Even if we took the most stringent precautions, covering ourselves tightly from head to toes with hats, scarves, gloves, boots, and such, still we could be sure at least one of the worms would wiggle its way inside and under our protective gears. My sisters were terrified of the leeches, and once stricken, vowed never again to go and pick myrtle berries. But the next time we went out, they would come along, especially if there were guests from Saigon.

When we had electricity, the wooden house on Trang Thu Estate became a great entertainment center. Papa let us use the generator so we could play records and a few times even a movie on a 16mm projector he borrowed from work. My older sisters preferred listening to pre-war Vietnamese songs, such as *The Lilac on the Old Veranda* or *The Blue Dress*. I had the vinyl records that I'd brought up from the city but never had a chance to hear. So before my sisters had a chance to change records, I put on foreign performers like Pat Boone or Petula Clark. I had fallen in love with Pat Boone's voice after hearing him sing in the movie *Mardi Gras*, which Papa had taken me to see a few years before.

Back in Saigon, my parents used to take us to the movies every weekend. There was no movie theater in B'Lao, so I missed my favorite actors as much as I missed my family. Influenced by the movies, I began to notice how my parents' behavior looked just like the love expressed by characters on the silver screen. Mama wrote letters every day to Papa, and I often saw her press the letter to her chest just before dropping it in the mailbox. When she received a letter in return, she read us the parts about what he and my sisters were doing in Saigon; her voice flooded with emotion.

I was touched every Sunday afternoon when Papa and Mama walked away from the children to say their reluctant goodbyes before Papa returned to the city. Vietnamese custom teaches us to restrain our feelings and not display affection, but my parents broke all conventions and embraced in parting, kissing each other on the cheeks in front of their children.

The time in Bao Loc was a period in my childhood full of joy and beautiful memories. The carefree life on the farm with its small adventures was ideally suited to my love of nature and drive for independence. I felt as if I were living in a fantasy world and was no longer consumed by sadness at the loss of my sister. Mama, too, was happier. She put on weight and her health returned. After two years she decided to go back to Saigon so Papa would no longer have to make the long trip to see us every two weeks.

Meanwhile, Papa had sold the little house in the city and bought a new one near the Cho Dui market, so when we arrived in Saigon, we were making a fresh start.

A Nonconformist

Back in the city, I passed the grade-level exam and was accepted into Marie Curie School, a prestigious all-girl French high school. Since the building was under construction and there was not enough space for all the students, those in the lower grades temporarily attended class at Nguyen Ngoc Linh School, an English-language academy at the end of the block near my home.

After I completed two grades there, Marie Curie transferred me to the Fraternité School in Cholon. There I wore a school uniform consisting of a white blouse and blue skirt, with my hair in braids, not hanging loose as I preferred. I hated the style, and I hated being teased by the neighborhood kids who called us *axam*, a derogatory term for the Chinese girls of Cholon. I begged and begged my parents to send me to another school. Eventually, my parents saw how stressed I had become and finally gave in.

This time I went to a private French school near my home called Pasteur. It was a small school, and I took to it at once. My studies improved, and I made friends easily. The coeducational environment along with men and women teachers who were open and tried hard to establish a dialogue with the students agreed with my liberated personality and also encouraged me to be more independent.

In just a short time I was invited to join a group of classmates who called themselves the "Hanoi Tiger Girls," so named because we had all been born in Hanoi in the year of the tiger, according to the Chinese lunar calendar cycle. The Tiger Girls met every day, wore the same outfits and hung out together. The girls in the group shared a distinct personality: self-confident, strong, outstanding in one class or another, and excessively proud of themselves.

In just one month I seemed to be suffocated. I felt confined by the group's rules, and after a while realized that I was being fashioned in their mold. Rejecting their attempts to pull me in, I decided to quit the Tigers. I was able to focus more on my studies and made different friends. Learning from this experience, I never became too close to any group to avoid being trapped by their boundaries. I discovered that my time in B'Lao had made me independent, individualistic, and comfortable with myself.

During my teens, I unconsciously escaped the social pressures that most of my peers had to deal with to be accepted. I liked being on my own, free to study and observe the world around me, free to associate with whomever I wished, and most of all, free to do what I wanted without depending on anyone.

///

When I turned 13, my oldest sister, Kim Thuy, got married and left home. My mother, who worked full-time running a pharmacy in addition to handling household duties, didn't have enough time to look after all her children. According to culture, watching over the younger children fell to the eldest sister. My next

The wedding of sister Kim Thuy and Dinh Dang Ky at the Saigon Cathedral, 1963.
Thuy is second from left in second row.

oldest sister, Ngoc Thanh, was not used to managing her younger siblings, especially since she had always teamed up with us to help each other get out from under from Kim Thuy's strict eye. Without Kim Thuy at home, I now could stay after school and be with my friends more. We would go out for ice cream or to Tao Dan Park to gossip and peruse the newspapers, looking for photographs of young soldiers.

At that time, the front page of all the newspapers reported the escalating war and printed pictures of the fighting along with the number of casualties.[20] On the back page, one would find death notices right next to wedding and engagement announcements. My friends used to make a game of comparing the number of deaths to the number of weddings. Watching them count how many soldiers died in battle, I sometimes wondered if I were the only one who thought this was a little repugnant. A few weeks later, when tragedy struck my own neighborhood, I quit this game.

The family across the street had two sons in the Air Force. The younger one was a bomber pilot idolized by all the girls. The day he came home with a new wife, it broke countless hearts in the neighborhood. To me, the two beautiful people looked like a couple of movie stars. The bride was gorgeous and chic. She wore short skirts that showed off her long, slender legs. But she wore only gray or black, which got the neighbors whispering that she was fated to have a sad life. She was 19 or 20 and very much in love with her husband. Every afternoon I saw her sitting at the window waiting for his return. They seemed like an ideal couple: sophisticated, mod, and full of life. They paid no attention to me, a curious little girl who lived across the street and spied on their house, silently worshiping them but not brave enough to come and make their acquaintance.

Sometime later, we heard that the young pilot had been killed on a bombing mission. The neighbors gathered to discuss it and then went over to express their condolences to the family of

---

[20] The military forces of South Vietnam suffered an estimated 254,256 killed between 1960 and 1974 and other estimates point to higher figures of 313,000 casualties. *(The Pentagon Papers.* Gravel, ed. vol. 1, pp. 391–404.) The official US Department of Defense figure was 950,765 North Vietnam Army/South Vietnam National Liberation Front forces killed in Vietnam from 1965 to 1974.

the unfortunate young man. That evening, when the young wife left the house, she was no longer wearing a fashionable dress but white mourning clothes with a gauze sash, her pretty face covered by a mourning hood. I watched the grieving widow from my window and wept for her. The next day, without telling my parents, I skipped school and went to the funeral. As I walked behind the coffin with the other mourners, I glanced at the young woman sobbing from under the hood. It occurred to me then how fragile and fleeting life and happiness had become.

From then on I stopped joining my friends in counting death notices in the newspapers. Furthermore, I told them I was never going to marry a soldier so I couldn't be made a widow while still in the spring of my years. They laughed at me, just 16 years old and already worried about things so far off in time.

That year my second oldest sister, Ngoc Thanh, went to France for her studies. Brother Bau was outgrowing playing with little sisters and started spending more time with his buddies. I had only my little sister Thoa, but she was just ten while I was well into adolescence. So I began exploring the neighborhood, as I had done in B'Lao. Although during wartime the city had little to offer in the way of entertainment, I was still able to find ways to amuse myself.

In those days' families in Saigon often organized private dance parties because dancing halls and music clubs were closed due to the war. My teenage friends' parents allowed them to have such parties and invite their friends into their homes.

My best friend at Pasteur School was Le Thi Phung, whose family had a shop in downtown Saigon that made lacquer souvenirs. My friends and I used to go to dancing parties at her place that her younger brother Le Duy Hoang organized seemingly every weekend on an outdoor stage on the upstairs terrace.

Right next door to Phung's family shop was a cafe and ice cream parlor called Brodard. We loved to go there and place tokens in the only jukebox in Saigon to listen to contemporary French songs performed by Sylvie Vartan, Francoise Hardy, Sheila, or Christophe.

That was when the "hippy" craze reached South Vietnam with its "op-art" styles and clothing. For the first time, I became interested in fashion. Mama rarely took me out to buy clothes. When a special occasion came up, such as Lunar New Year or a wedding, she would make my clothes herself—when I was small it was a dress, when I was older the *ao dai* regardless, she always chose the style.

Now I asked Mama if I could make my own clothes. I had already made doll clothes, first out of paper, then later from cloth, for dolls as large as an actual child. Mama was pleased with my new interest and spent all day showing me how to measure the material and use a sewing machine. I buried my head in fashion books to pick the style I wanted and spent days at the machine before I came up with something I liked.

I was also taken with the large sunglasses worn by First Lady Jacqueline Kennedy. Not only did I wear glasses with black frames, but I purchased some sets of white frames and colored them to match my outfits, especially swimsuits that I made myself.

Except for Phung, my friends were boys, and this caused my parents no little concern. I tended to be straightforward like the boys and had been since I was little. But now I was a young woman, my parents wanted me to stop acting like a tomboy and be more feminine and reserved.

I tried to do as they said, but it was very hard. As a young girl, I had played with my brother and his friends and liked that more than being with girls. I was used to being direct and speaking my mind. When I was with girls, I often made them angry because I was overly judgmental, plus, I didn't like talking about clothes, fashion, going out and shopping, or gossiping about boys. For their part, my girlfriends didn't feel comfortable with the way I acted or talked about the meaning of life or social problems that they thought had nothing to do with them.

An Open-minded Father

My parents' goal was to give their children a balanced outlook on life. Papa did not want us to simply copy what everyone else said, holding onto our opinions out of fear of being criticized or ridiculed. Instead, he encouraged us to be "unlike anyone else." He made us see life as a never-ending challenge and understand that each choice we made entailed a price that had to be paid. When things went well, we should be prepared to deal with any untoward circumstance that might be lurking around the corner. As well, we should not give up during the darkest of times but always remain confident that things would turn out for the better.

This became a maxim for me. Later, when I encountered difficulties in life, I relied on the strength of this belief. Not only did Papa instill in us an absolute faith in God, but he also gave us an unwavering confidence in ourselves. From the time we were just babies, he taught us to rely on ourselves to survive.

I loved my Papa and thought he was "unlike anyone else" in the entire world. He never failed to find a way to deal with any difficulty that arose. When I was little, I dreamed of writing a book about him. Everything he did was etched in my mind and served as a source of strength to help me carry on whenever I needed to cling to something, to maintain my faith when everything seemed hopeless.

In a society in which it was easy for people to scorn or suspect someone who was not like them, Papa was different. While he had great faith in nationalism, he also believed that each individual made the nation and that each citizen had to know precisely why he or she believed in that ideal. He opposed popular conventions and attacked the practice of blindly following the crowd. We were to find out for ourselves what was right and follow our own conscience.

Papa also emphasized that life is not just about survival and that being human entails a responsibility that goes beyond caring about oneself, which he described as being nothing more than "a coat rack and sack of rice." He had us take part in activities with other children and young people so we would learn how to get along with people and accept others' differences as a marvelous display of life's variety.

Papa often discussed with me books he had read and theories he had studied. He was clever in elucidating a point, after which he asked for my opinion. It was not enough to merely go along with him or answer carelessly. Instead, I had to express my own ideas, which he forced me to think through.

Among other things, Papa warned me about the difficulties I would face in Vietnam's male-oriented society, where people were brought up to "honor the male, despise the female." I grew up knowing that I might have to decide whether I would rather be liked or respected. He explained there would come a time when I would have to choose between family and career, as between my emotions and my rational thinking.

On my 15th birthday, Papa gave me a little book with illustrations depicting how a well-behaved young woman should walk, stand, speak, laugh and behave. Then the whole family got a good laugh as I tried to imitate those models.

Thanks to my parents' liberal upbringing, my adolescence was warm and largely uneventful. Mama and Papa took care of my needs; I was loved and respected, so I never developed any complexes or found a need to rebel like others of my age. I didn't see myself as any better than those who were less fortunate. Papa always reminded me that one person is no better or worse than another because of what's outside or what they own, but only in their character and their determination to see things to their conclusion. Nor did I grow up with an inferiority complex or lack confidence in myself because my father paid so much attention to me and corrected me, and there was no lack of praise when I did something right.

The Extended Family

I came face-to-face with the war when my brother Bau was drafted into the army. Stunned by the news, I realized that the war was taking away someone close to me.

At the time my parents were investing in starting a private bank with a friend of theirs. When the Countryside Bank of Vung Tau had its grand opening, my family moved to that seaside town 70 kilometers south of Saigon. I remained in the capital with Papa's mother and Aunty Chi's family so I could complete my studies at the Pasteur School.

Busy with their own families, my grandmother and aunt did not keep as close an eye on me as had my parents, so I could pretty much do as I pleased. I didn't take advantage of them, but it was a chance for me to be even more independent. Before long I was taking part in activities common in a wartime country, such as visiting coffee shops frequented by soldiers on leave. I ended up spending a lot of money on coffee that I didn't drink just so I could watch the soldiers and listen to them talk about their experiences.

After two years I went to live with Papa's older brother,

Uncle Bich. Papa had only one older brother and one older sister, and both of them welcomed me and took care of me while I went to school in Saigon.

I enjoyed my freedom, and as long as my schoolwork had priority and my grades were high, no one complained. My brothers and sisters were not so fortunate. Though liberal-minded, my parents were teachers by character and strict with the rest of the children, keeping them disciplined and behaving properly. Since I was far away, I was less restricted.

Vietnam's educational system at the time was modeled after the French system, in which one had to pass exams to advance. Those sophomore students in French schools who were skilled in Vietnamese language and literature often took the first Vietnamese baccalaureate exam. If they passed, they could skip their junior class and advance to their senior year. The baccalaureate exams were very crucial for the boys because if they failed, they would be automatically taken out of school and sent into the army.

Some friends and I signed up for a three-month exam preparatory session where we concentrated on Vietnamese literature. The first novel I read was *River of Destiny* by Doan Quoc Sy. I was so taken with the book that I read the author's set entitled *Forest of Reeds*. I began to admire those who cared for others, were intelligent yet modest, and who pursued noble ideals and were faithful to their country and family.

After passing the first baccalaureate, some of my friends and I left the French educational system and entered the senior year of the Vietnamese program at Nguyen Ba Tong High School. There we prepared for the second baccalaureate, which qualified us for higher education.

Chapter 8

The Press in Wartime

Stumbling into a Career

■ THUY

One muggy day in November 1969, I had just left the library where I'd been studying for my college entrance exams and was headed for home when there came a sudden downpour. I slipped into the doorway of a nearby storefront to wait out the shower.

As I stood there idly, I peered through the window of what turned out to be the office of *Tin Dien* (The Chronicle), one of Saigon's many daily newspapers. I noticed a help-wanted sign posted on the door and saw that the paper was looking for someone to work part-time translating its astrology column from French into Vietnamese.

I hesitated, debating whether I should pretend to apply for the job so I could come inside out of the rain. Never had I given any thought to looking for work. None of my older siblings worked for a living. They just went to school until they got married or drafted.

Half out of curiosity

Thuy, age 18, Saigon 1968.

and half just wanting to get dry, I opened the door and stepped inside. After telling the receptionist that I wished to apply for the job, I reminded myself that I was just going through the motions to get the experience. I discovered that the job paid quite well, 5,000 *dongs* a month for just two hours a day. Then I realized that the required hours, from five to seven in the evening, would not interfere with my studies. No one at my uncle's house knew what my hours at school were to see if I was coming home on time. As long as I made it back by 7:30, when the family had dinner, I was all right. Best of all, my mother would no longer have to send me 500 *dongs* a month for transportation and expenses. To my surprise, I had just convinced myself to take the job.

Someone handed me a sample astrology report, which I translated in just a few minutes. They hired me on the spot, and I was to begin the very next day.

And on that day my name appeared in a newspaper for the first time.

I enjoyed working under pressure in a dynamic environment where I had to finish my article in time for it to be typeset before going to press. I liked the noise and excitement generated by a hot news item and being among the first to know the details of a story when the reporters returned to the office to write it up. The job's challenges filled me with vitality and enthusiasm.

During my second week with the newspaper, the big story everyone was interested in was a scandal regarding a movie star who also happened to be a well-known singer of popular Vietnamese opera. Her family problems had led to depression, and she had taken sleeping pills in a failed attempt at suicide. She was rescued in time and was about to give a news conference from the hospital.

At the last minute, the reporter responsible for attending the press conference called in sick. The editor looked around and, seeing no one else available, asked me to go to the hospital and pick up the news release the singer was to present at the briefing.

Once I arrived, I felt I could not simply take the press release and leave. I was absorbed in the troubling questions about the singer's story posed at the press conference. I had forgotten that I was only a translator who had been sent to fetch a pre-printed news item and not a real reporter. When I got back to the office, I handed the editor the press release along with my notes on the questions and my impressions about the performer. My boss was pleasantly surprised by my initiative and interest, so he asked me to write the story myself.

After my composition was printed, the newspaper offered me a full-time job as a reporter. I wrestled with myself about this offer. I was going to school, but newspaper work was proving an attractive career for me. Moreover, the vast majority of male South Vietnamese students had to quit school to join the army, so ending my education was not that unusual. I spent a sleepless night thinking about it, then the next morning—while wondering how I was going to explain this to my parents—I went to the newspaper office and accepted the job.

My parents didn't know about this until weeks later when they came home on their routine visit to my grandma and check on me. I just told them the truth: since so many young men, including their only son, my brother Bau, had to give up their studies for the army, why couldn't I do the same to find out what the war really was? My mother took it very hard, but my father understood. He has always told me not to let my gender limit my aspirations. After a long heated debate, they realized I was committed to journalism and they couldn't change my mind.

The Press and Censorship

During the late 1960s and early '70s, there were about 50 daily newspapers in Saigon with print circulation ranging from a few thousand to hundreds of thousands. The provinces did not have local papers and relied on the news published daily in the capital. The papers came in all kinds, from those that printed straight news for organs of the government to those that criticized the government. Besides the opposition papers that were open and genuinely concerned about public affairs, there were many neutral papers known as the "Third Force" that called for "cooperation and reconciliation" with the communists.

Of course, there were the tabloids and scandal sheets that specialized in murder, love affairs, crime, or bizarre news, such as superstition and fortunetelling. These papers tended to have quite a large readership.

Advertising was rare in those days, especially for the smaller papers, and publishers relied on sales to stay in business. If income from sales was insufficient to cover costs, the papers sought support from the government or political sponsors. With the war going on, some political factions competed for influence and used the press as a forum to garner support or attack their opponents.

Sponsorship was a popular method of subsidizing newspapers. There were, however, many papers that held to high professional standards and could be compared favorably to publications in the West. Foremost among these was the paper *Chinh Luan* (Political Commentary) run by Senator Dang Van Sung, which focused on current news and politics. Other papers like *Song* (Life) and *Song Than* (Tidal Wave) brought excitement to the profession. And one should not forget the efforts of the brothers Nguyen Ngoc Linh and Nguyen Ngoc Bich. After obtaining an education abroad, they returned to Vietnam and held key posts in communications for the government in Radio Saigon and the Vietnam Press Agency. The Nguyen Ngoc brothers trained a corps of exceptional young reporters every bit as skilled as their foreign counterparts. These journalists went out on assignment with private newspapers, brazenly seeking the news in the political arena and the war zones across South Vietnam.

Besides Senator Dang Van Sung, other politicians also started newspapers, ostensibly to present current events but actually to sway readers to their political opinions. These included the opposition papers *Dai Dan Toc* (Great National People) of Representative Vo Long Trieu, *Tin Sang* (Bright News) of Representatives Ngo Cong Duc, Ly Chanh Trung, Ho Ngoc Nhuan and Ly Quy Chung, and *Dien Tin* (The Telegraph) of Hong Son Dong.

Then there were the papers sponsored by the government to promote programs or legislation, such as the army paper *Tien Tuyen* (Front Line) of the Political Warfare Department and *Dan Chu* (The Democrat), later named *Tin Song* (Living News) published by Phung Thi Hanh, a close friend of Hoang Duc Nha, the president's press secretary and later minister of propaganda.

The South Vietnamese Central Intelligence Agency also had a paper, *Quat Cuong* (Resolute), to indirectly control the media. The news services were fertile ground for communists and international agents who portrayed themselves as journalists to operate in Vietnam, especially radical leftists who took advantage of freedom of the press. After April 30, 1975, many reporters and newspaper staff came out as communist moles or collaborators.

The paper *Tin Sang*, for example, harbored some members who claimed to be part of the Third Force, a disguised communist sympathizer group. When all the other newspapers in the South were shut down by the communists after April 1975, *Tin Sang* was the only paper allowed to keep publishing. It continued for the next six years until it "voluntarily closed its doors," citing that it had completed its mission.

Whether private or government-run, all the newspapers in South Vietnam fell under the intense scrutiny of the Information Department. In Saigon, the government had the authority to order a newspaper confiscated before or while it was out on the streets. There were instances when a paper's entire circulation was seized, resulting in significant financial losses to the publisher.

Every afternoon, a sample copy of each paper was printed and passed to the Information Department's Censorship Board to determine whether it included anything that could be considered detrimental to national security or likely to "stir up public opinion." Anything found in violation of this standard was blocked out. By then there was insufficient time to reset the page and send it for a second review. This resulted in many newspapers going to print with white blocks of space where a story had been deleted, often on the front page.

Some days there was hot political or war news that the government did not want to be published, and most of the major papers went out with up to half the front page blank. The irony was that over the blank space the papers had to print the caption "Voluntarily Deleted," which drew cynical laughs from the readers.

On August 4, 1972, the government issued a decree requiring all newspapers to pay a fee to the General Office of the Treasury of 20 million *dongs,* equal to about 500 ounces of gold. Faced with this financial burden, nearly half the dailies closed, leaving a great many reporters and newspaper staff out of work.

The Tet Offensive and Mass Graves

During my third week on the job, I heard that a major news

conference was about to take place. It was the end of 1969, approaching the second anniversary of the Tet Offensive and the communist seizure of Hue. The last imperial capital and site of historic palaces and tombs, Hue was hit harder than any other spot in South Vietnam during the 1968 attack, with thousands of citizens taken away and murdered by the communists and many essential buildings destroyed in the four-week battle to retake the city from the invaders. The most tragic event in Hue was the desperate search for thousands of missing people. Shortly after the city was recaptured in March 1968, a mass grave was found with 1,173 bodies, but thousands of ordinary civilians were still unaccounted for. A year later, a communist soldier who had come over to our side revealed that all those who had been taken away by the communists were murdered. Two more mass graves were then uncovered containing a total of 1,237 bodies.

Now it was November 1969, and another mass grave had been found, this one holding more than 300 victims. The upcoming press conference was to publicize new details about the Tet massacre.

I asked my paper to send me to the conference as I wanted to learn more about what had happened during the Tet Offensive. I anxiously anticipated my first experience as a real reporter dealing with a story I considered to be of great significance. However, once I climbed out of the airplane at Phu Bai airport, I began to feel uneasy.

There I saw a crowd of journalists, Vietnamese and foreign, fully equipped with all the instruments of the trade for television, radio, and newspaper. I became anxious and self-conscious, supposing that everyone would quickly realize that I was a novice and had no business being there. Adding to my discomfort was the fact that of the nearly one hundred correspondents present, only a handful were women, all of them actual professionals. I sat quietly during the conference, mutely recording the proceedings.

As it turned out, the formal government presentation was only a prelude. I was not prepared for the harsh reality of the mass graves themselves.

I stood in the back of the crowd and looked at the piles of human remains laid out before us. Many of the hundreds of victims were not soldiers but ordinary citizens. Some were dressed in modern style, suggesting they were professionals or students. Others wore poorer clothes with hand-dyed scarves indicating they were of the

The remains of victims, many buried alive by the communists during the Tet Offensive in Hue, 1968. Photo: Republic of Vietnam archive.

artisan and laboring class. The image of these men and women, some with their hands still bound behind their backs, cut me to the heart. On my return to Saigon, I immediately sat down to write my report. It was a personal story filled with emotion.

Aside from my brother was drafted and the death of my pilot-neighbor, I had no direct connection to war and knew little of its horrible consequences. But what I saw at the mass graves in Hue made me frightened of war and appalled at the cruelty of the communists. My story overflowed with things I had seen mixed with the swirl of emotions inside me.

As far as the newspaper and its readers were concerned, my story was only one of the countless reports about the war and the Tet Offensive. No one had any idea what impact it had on my heart; how for months I remained deeply troubled by the scenes I'd seen. Besides, it was the first time I was overwhelmed by intense passion as I wrote as if my pen was a button that when pushed flooded my heart with the relentless power of what I was writing. I knew that after that assignment, my life would never be the same.

Flying in an F-5 Fighter

After two months working as a translator and going out on reporting assignments, and following careful consideration, I decided to leave *Tin Dien*. One of the publishers was investing in a daily paper that focused more on hard events. When he invited me to be part of the new editorial board for *Su That* (Truth), I accepted.

It just so happened that during the newspaper's grand opening, my family was visited by a friend, Captain Nguyen Van Con, who had recently returned from the United States where he had undergone flight training for the F-5 fighter, the new supersonic jet the Americans were supplying to the South Vietnamese Air Force.

As I listened to Capt. Con's description of the aircraft, it occurred to me that now, as the war was escalating across the country, it would be good for the morale of the South Vietnamese military if the public were aware of the latest weaponry being employed by our side. I asked him to help me contact Major Nguyen Quoc Hung, leader of the F-5 squadron, for an interview. As the idea had just come off the top of my head, the request was not made through proper channels. Nevertheless, the major accepted and we made an appointment to meet at the squadron headquarters at Bien Hoa Air Base.

After a typical interview in which we discussed the effectiveness of the famous aircraft in the context of the Vietnam War, I asked if I could see one of the planes and take some pictures for the article. During our conversation, I learned that the pilots routinely honed their skills by flying in a two-seat training jet. I asked if I could sit inside to get a feel for the plane. Once inside the plane, I suddenly had the rash idea to ask how I could get permission to fly on an actual mission.

South Vietnam's F-5 pilots had been to the U.S. for training and were more broadminded than most Vietnamese men. Thus, they were used to treating women on an equal basis. The young pilots were amused by my brashness and went out of their way to help me with my proposal. With the approval of Major Hung, they prepared me to fly on a combat and bombing mission.

On the day of my flight, the smallest man in the squadron lent me his gray flight jumpsuit and helmet. Then they strapped me in tight to stabilize me against the change in air pressure that would occur when we achieved high altitude.

They taught me how to control my breathing and keep from tensing up when the jet rolled and pitched as the payloads were ejected. They also showed me how to take pictures when the bombs were released and when they struck. More than that, they warned me of the psychological factors I would have to deal with as I participated in a bombing event and witnessed its effects for the first time.

If my visit to Hue to witness the mass graves of those citizens massacred by the communists had fixed my opinion about the war's purpose, this flight in an F-5 fighter turned my feelings in another direction. My story on the flight combined factual information with personal feelings. I tried to present honestly and faithfully everything I went through during the trip from the moment I entered the squadron's base to the conclusion of the mission.

The pilots treated me like an inquisitive little sister and teased me when I had trouble walking around in the oversized jumpsuit. They expected me to chicken out, even asking if I wanted to change my mind while they were strapping me into my seat, and were apparently surprised when I said I was going to see it through to the end.

The nonchalant and carefree attitude of these professional pilots just before they set off on a bombing raid in which people might be killed alarmed me. It was all I could do to hide my reaction and appear unaffected. I watched as the bombs dropped into a forested area and exploded in murky red flames. Despite how high above the ground we were flying, I could still make out signs of villages and human activity down below.

And I could not remain impassive.

It wasn't that I was afraid, but my heart was horrified and my insides twisted in pain. I thought of the people below, the lives being wiped out when the bombs exploded. I thought of their families, the children who would become orphans, the parents who would lose their children, and wives who would become widows.

I thought about the young pilots, not yet 30 years old, their faces still bearing the sweet and innocent look of schoolboys. And I asked myself just what it was, what ideology had such terrifying power that it could make one Vietnamese kill another. I clearly understood—indeed was convinced—that the Vietnamese communists were the enemy of the Vietnamese nationalists and that Marxist-Leninism was something one should rather die than accept. But how many people among the Viet Cong down there had relatives in the South and were our compatriots?

If my family still lived in the North, would we too be the enemy of the people of the South? And would we be killed or would we kill to survive?

SURVIVING

183

I brooded over these questions long and hard and found myself overcome with deep sadness. Was the war simply a difference in geography and borders? For a few moments, I imagined myself down there, fleeing in terror each time a bomber flew past.

I concluded my report with doubts and a question: We are all Vietnamese. Why have we been pushed to the point of killing each other?

Pondering My Career

Upon my return to the capital, I was shaken and haunted by my reflections on the senselessness of war. The communists killed their own people with the goal of opposing the "Americans and illegitimate government" in order to unify the country and impose communism. Meanwhile, South Vietnamese soldiers bombed their fellow countrymen to defend the South and preserve its peace. I felt these two goals were greatly unbalanced, and I resolved to find out more about the war even if it proved too complicated for my limited ability to understand.

I was still young and didn't know much about war, but my heart was profoundly disturbed by its consequences. I recorded all my feelings in my articles so that readers could share the intense emotions I was experiencing. I believed that many ordinary people in both South and North Vietnam were troubled by the same vexing questions.

My story came to the attention of the Air Force journal *Ly Tuong* (Ideal), which reprinted it. After the article received praise from some established newspapers, some daily papers got in touch and asked me to write for them. I was now officially recognized as a professional correspondent and could make a living by my pen.

Aside from the really large newspapers, most Vietnamese dailies could not afford to hire a writer to work exclusively for them. Therefore, most writers were free to contribute articles to as many papers as they wished. A single-space typed story generated four or five carbon copies and could be submitted to many newspapers at the same time. That way, the reporter got paid several times for one piece of work. A lot of Saigon reporters at that time acted as though they were their own news agency and did not work for any single paper.

After a few months, my income was several times what a college graduate was making working for the government. From then on I did not need to look for work. I could pick and choose from any of the newspapers that wanted me.

However, I was still a timid female reporter. Every time I was present at a press conference, I simply recorded the questions and answers, not daring to raise my voice above my colleagues to pose a question of my own. It was especially the case at a large conference with hundreds of other journalists, including foreign reporters who went straight to the question and were not afraid to seize on someone else's comment.

As the days went on, the world more and more saw the "Vietnam problem" as a violent patch of earth engaged in a civil war between freedom and communism and the people of the North against the people of the South. The fighting increased, and neighboring countries were concerned that Vietnam was becoming a political fuse that would cause an explosion all over Southeast Asia.

Veteran reporters from around the world wanted to pursue stories in Vietnam. Some journalists who were refused permission by their editors to come to Vietnam quit their jobs to freelance so they could go after the big story. The war satisfied their occupational passion and gave them many opportunities to display their talents and help them rise in their profession.

The standards for an international correspondent were high. Most reporters received thorough training before going out on the job. Their editors provided them with all manner of support, both material and moral, to help them overcome any obstacles they might encounter while working in the midst of war.

They did not have to worry that their stories or photos would be censored, and more, they did not have to worry about upsetting the Vietnamese leaders. Nor were they constrained by the consideration of being nationalist or communist, so they were free to act according to their profession. They often asked the most direct questions, cutting to the chase, determined to get an answer, and sometimes causing tension.

I found their earnest professionalism compelling, even though my nature was to observe silently. I enjoyed watching them work, liked their self-confidence and fearlessness in the presence of powerful officials. And I dreamed of being motivated by that kind of zeal, searching for the truth, regardless of the consequences to myself.

I wanted to someday stand in the middle of a crowd of reporters in an important press conference, raise my hand and ask those questions about the Vietnam War that continued to bother me. But I was too shy. I seemed to be stuck in my chair, unable to get to my feet and speak up.

Many times I had a question in mind but was afraid to ask it, then one of my colleagues would ask that very thing, and I would upbraid myself for my cowardice. In the end, all I could do was put my head down and faithfully record what the others said while steaming inside.

I usually had to wait until a conference was over to approach someone and ask them to elaborate on some matter that I felt wasn't clear. I knew I would have to wrestle further with my timidity if I really wanted to become a professional reporter.

Besides that, I hadn't found out where I could learn the craft thoroughly or receive a formal training in journalism.

I knew that journalism demanded skills that I had not had the opportunity to learn. I also realized that I needed to get experience before I could feel confident and overcome my shyness. But expertise required time and practical training.

PART III

CAREER AND CALLING

Chapter 9

On The Battlefront

Operation Total Victory 42

■ THUY

I n 1970, after I had been working as a reporter for six months, I was sent by one of the newspapers to a major press conference in Tay Ninh regarding Operation Total Victory 42. This mission was one arm of the joint ARVN-U.S. incursion into Cambodia. President Thieu had sent the generals in charge of III Corps and IV Corps to initiate the operation to clean out Viet Cong sanctuaries in the area known as the Parrot's Beak (Mo Vet), a section of Cambodian territory that juts into the Mekong Delta.[21] Lieutenant Gen. Do Cao Tri, the commander of III Corps, was in charge of the attacks along the border and Major Gen. Nguyen Viet Thanh of IV Corps commanded Special Forces that would move north and meet him.

The press conference took place at the end of April 1970, after the ARVN had already crossed the border into Cambodia. All the media groups and many foreign reporters working in South Vietnam were present. The meeting was presided over by three-star Gen. Do Cao Tri, one of the most well-known and influential men in the country.

---

[21]South Vietnam was divided into four corps tactical zones. I Corps consisted of the five northern provinces plus the cities of Hue and Da Nang and covered territory along the Ho Chi Minh Trail. II Corps were 12 provinces along the coast and in the Central Highlands. III Corps consisted of ten provinces extending from the Cambodian border to the sea and surrounding, but not including, the Saigon area; most of the fighting in this zone occurred near the Cambodian border. IV Corps covered the Mekong Delta. Saigon and its immediate environs made up a special tactical zone.

General Do Cao Tri (1929-1971)

General Do Cao Tri (1929 -1971).

As the head of III Corps, Gen. Do Cao Tri's responsibilities were not limited to military command but included political affairs and administration as well. Since this region was the area that surrounded the capital, the man in charge had to be loyal to the president, as he held in his hands all the power necessary to overthrow the government at any time, should he be of a mind to.

Gen. Tri came from an established wealthy family that owned plantations near Bien Hoa. He was well-educated, a graduate of officer training and the airborne academy in France, and had received military training in Hanoi in the early 1950s. He was known for being determined and fearless in battle, and he did not curry favor with the country's leaders.

Rumors about Gen. Tri were legion and of every type. He was said to be corrupt, although there was no evidence. Rumored as a lady's man, stories about him were often contradictory, but that didn't deter many people from believing them. *Time* magazine called him one of Vietnam's outstanding generals, willing to take risks and quite accomplished on the battlefield.

I only knew about the general from articles in the newspapers, especially a recently published front-page story in which a member of the Assembly accused him of corruption and abuse of authority. Normally the general paid no attention to criticism in the press, but this time he felt his honor had been impugned. He challenged the politician to a duel.

My colleagues and I laughed when we read this story, which made Gen. Tri look like a medieval knight fighting to defend his honor rather than using the media to respond, the way most powerful men did.

The briefing on this occasion generated a slew of questions regarding the incursion into Cambodia from representatives of various news outlets, mostly foreign. The general responded to each question, speaking in English, French and Vietnamese. His voice was loud and clear, his responses unequivocal, and he often ended with an off-color joke that brought ripples of laughter from the audience. At the close of the conference, Gen. Tri invited reporters to come along with him on this operation named Total Victory, assuring them that they would be the first to witness a glorious victory by the Vietnamese army in Cambodia.

As the general approached the spot where I was standing, he was stopped by a reporter who asked how one might obtain a media pass. Before he could move on, I got up the courage to address him.

"General, would it be all right for a woman reporter to come with you to the front?"

Gen. Tri burst out laughing.

"Of course it would! I'd like that even more!"

All the men there found this amusing, as they were well aware of Gen. Tri's reputation with women.

My face grew hot. I hadn't yet learned how to confront a man's reckless flirtation. While I didn't know exactly what was so funny, I knew they were laughing at me. Blushing, I repeated my request.

"Please, General. I really want to report from the front."

He must have realized that I was serious and also embarrassed. He stopped laughing and his smile faded. Then he asked me for which newspaper I worked.

A few days later I received a call from the general's office inviting me to accompany him on a military action. From then on I had a reserved seat on the command helicopter to the Cambodian front.

Vicious Tiger of the Front

At 4:30 in the morning, a Jeep arrived from III Corps to take me to Bien Hoa, more than 30 kilometers from Saigon. From there I flew by helicopter with Gen. Tri and his staff to general headquarters in Tay Ninh on the Cambodia-Vietnam border.

Upon landing, we all retired to a command tent where a briefing took place before the day's operation. The military terminology that I heard for the first time in that briefing would eventually become familiar to me and help me understand about the war and battle operations.

I accompanied Gen. Tri to the headquarters of the armored battle group under Col. Tran Quang Khoi. The M113 armored personnel carriers there looked like giant crabs awaiting the order to crawl forward. I was led to one of the armored personnel carriers (APCs) that would take me to the front line. Gen. Tri was in another one directly in front of mine. Along the way, a U.S. Army Jeep pulled up beside the carriers and a one-star general with the name-tag "Abrams" got out and joined Gen. Tri.

After that, I followed Gen. Tri all over the Cambodian front, from Neak Luong to Svay Rieng, across Kompong Cham to Chup plantation, and everything I saw filled me with astonishment and admiration.

Contrary to what the newspapers said about Gen. Tri being hot-tempered and haughty, he often showed great self-restraint and knew how to listen to others. Once he spoke, he was firm and decisive. He made up his mind quickly, and everyone knew that once he had chosen a course of action, he would follow it to its conclusion.

No one charged into battle right beside his men as did Gen. Tri. It was then that I understood why the American press called him the "tiger of the battlefield" and "the Vietnamese Patton." I could see how his officers and men revered him. He seemed utterly tireless, was always right up at the front line, greeting each announcement of military action with enthusiasm, and planning every detail of his unit's advance or retreat. His bravery and character had a powerful impact on the morale of those who served under him.

Unlike other officers, including the American advisers and Gen. Creighton Abrams, who usually went to battle wearing a helmet and flak jacket, Gen. Tri would typically be seen wearing his bright camouflage airborne uniform, a cap with three silver stars, and his trademark sunglasses. For personal protection, he carried a pistol in a shoulder holster and a riding crop, which he said he would use to "whip some VC ass!"

A Day on the Front Line[22]

Saturday, May 2, 1970, day 5 of
Operation Total Victory 42 in Cambodia.

Thuy, on top of an APC (armored personnel carrier), at a Cambodian frontline, 1970.

At 9:00 a.m., Gen. Cao Van Vien, chief of the Joint General Staff for the Army of the Republic of Vietnam, arrived at the headquarters of Battle Group 318 under Col. Tran Quang Khoi at Chipou. It was Gen. Vien's second visit to an operations center for III Corps since the ARVN crossed the border into Cambodia in April. After the briefing, Lieutenant General Do Cao Tri resumed his

---

[22]This account, originally written in 1971 and won third prize for war reporting that year from the Department of Psychological Warfare, was published in the military's monthly review *Tien Phong* (Vanguard) August 15, 1972. A copy of the story was recently sent to the author by a former South Vietnamese officer currently living in New Zealand after reading the Vietnamese version of this memoir published in 2016.

assessment of the situation on the front. I accompanied him to the 5th Armored Group of Battle Group 333. The 5th Armored consisted primarily of Rangers who were engaged in a fierce battle in the village of Tadei, 6 miles south of Route 1 and 8 miles from the border.

When we arrived at 10:30, the fighting was at its worst. The rattle of AK-47s, AK-50s and AR-15s firing from nearby mixed with the ear-splitting noise of artillery and mortar fire. It was about 300 feet from the helicopter landing zone to our objective. On the way, I encountered corpses lined up, some of them blown apart by B-40 rockets, and wounded men awaiting "dust off," that is, evacuation to the rear.

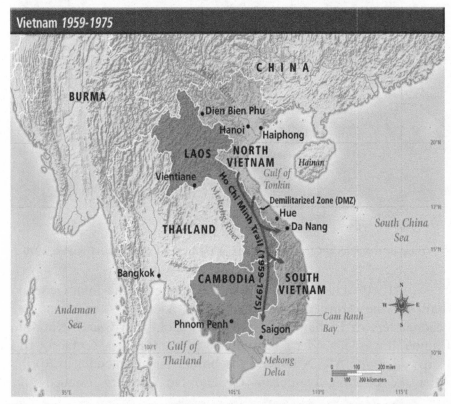

Map of the route, known as Ho Chi Minh Trail, located inside Laos and Cambodia, via which the communist North sent troops to infiltrate South Vietnam – Source: thinglink

As I ran by the casualties, one gravely injured man grabbed onto a leg of my pants. I almost tripped, and my Nikon camera spilled to the ground. I turned to look at him. His young face was covered with mud, his Ranger uniform in tatters, his left leg was soaked with blood. I can't describe my emotions just then—I was terrified out of my wits and yet overwhelmed with pity. I picked up my camera and approached. He was looking at me, eyes glazed over. He spoke slowly.

"Is...the...chopper...here...?"

I pursed my lips and fought the tightness in my chest.

"It's almost here, brother," I lied.

At that point, he seemed to recognize that I was not one of his fellow Rangers, despite the uniform I had on. He squinted up at me, his lips barely moved.

"News...paper...heh?"

I nodded, too choked up to speak.

The soldier suddenly squirmed; I saw his throat tighten in a spasm of pain. Then a cry broke out of him.

"Hurts so bad! Take off my boot! My foot...hurts...!"

I couldn't contain myself and started to cry. Looking at the soldier's writhing body and bloody feet, I realized I could not do as told. His eyes grew dimmer, pleading as they glued to me. Gathering all my strength, I knelt down and began to remove his boots full of mud and the odor of days.

Just then a hand grabbed my arm, and I heard a startled voice.

"Miss Thuy! What are you doing?"

I turned to see Capt. Tuan, Gen. Tri's aide, standing over me. Tears were running down my cheeks. The captain brought me to my feet. Then he called a medic nearby who was busy bandaging another soldier.

"Sergeant! Tend to this man. He needs help."

Gripping my arm tightly, the captain pulled me toward a group of soldiers bending over a radio behind an M113.

"From now on you stay with me, miss," he ordered. "With all the shooting going on it's dangerous for you to go wandering off by yourself. Just now, I thought you were right behind me. It was only when the general asked that I realized you'd disappeared. If you act like that every time you see someone on the front, how are you going to survive?"

Haunted by the image of the soldier covered in blood, squirming in pain and begging me to remove his boot, I was too overwhelmed to speak.

The Cambodian Battlefields

The target for engagement was a Cambodian Buddhist temple about 300 feet ahead of us. The enemy had only a platoon inside the temple, but they were receiving cover from a battalion surrounding the area. A Ranger company sent in for the first strike half an hour earlier was pinned down by enemy fire and in a tight spot. They called in that 10 of their "boys" had been hit but couldn't be extracted due to heavy fire. Gen. Tri spoke to them.

"Inside the temple are there any monks or civilians? If not, I'll order air strikes."

A second lieutenant responded, "There are about 40 civilians taking cover inside, General. They're right by our men."

Gen. Tri raised his voice and spoke deliberately.

"Call the Civil Affairs team. Have them find a way to get all the civilians out of the temple."

Then he turned to Major Son, the armored commander.

"As soon as the people are out of there, move in. If we're too late, we'll lose some of our boys."

Shortly after that, a voice coming over a bullhorn shouting a string of words in Khmer forced its way through the clamor of vicious gunfire from the fields.

Despite being shielded by the APC a little distance from the objective, I could still see the gunfire from the trees surrounding the temple. Now and then shots came in our direction.

A half-hour later, the civilians began to stagger out of the temple with their hands raised above their heads. They were all dark and looked miserable in their filthy sarongs as they walked silently towards us.

Once he was confident there were no more civilians inside the temple, Gen. Tri climbed into the M113 and took the radio to personally direct artillery fire onto the target. Black smoke rose from the trees every time a shell exploded. Capt. Tuan helped me up to sit precariously beside the general. When Gen. Tri paused from his command to light his pipe, I turned to him.

"Sir," I said quietly, "there are many wounded men, and I haven't seen anyone come to take them out."

With that, he adjusted the radio frequency and contacted air support, requesting medical evacuation helicopters. At the same time, he asked for two air squadrons to bomb the objective still doggedly held by the enemy.

When he failed to see a measurable result, the general ordered the APCs, including his own, to advance with guns blazing until they came to within 100 feet of the forest. Just then two Thunderchief jets roared in firing rockets. Cheers rang out from the APCs around me. Gen. Tri ordered the planes to unload their bombs in conjunction with rocket fire.

By 11:30, the evacuation team finally arrived. Colored smoke was laid down to mark the landing zones. Still, the helicopters continued to circle for another 10 minutes. Enraged, Gen. Tri shouted into the radio for them to land, to no avail. The choppers rose up into the sky and disappeared. Furious, the general ordered his pilot to evacuate the wounded on his personal helicopter, then return to get the men who remained.

Twenty minutes later, we received a report that the Rangers who had been pinned down before were now on their way back with a captured 81mm machine gun. The news heartened the men, while several gunships fired more rockets onto the target and the enemy base behind us.

By noon, Gen. Tri ordered the jets to cease firing. The APCs and infantrymen beside them blasted the target.

"Move in fast!" the general shouted. "Don't give them a chance to fire back!"

There was a powerful explosion right beside us. It stunned me and would have knocked me off the carrier if Capt. Tuan had not caught me in time. I gasped as the fire flared up from the M113 only about 10 meters away, making my face burning hot. The hapless vehicle had been hit dead-on by a B-40 rocket. I turned to avoid looking at the horrible scene. My heart stopped, I couldn't breathe, my chest feeling as if I had just been struck by a heavyweight.

The young soldiers, who only a short time before had been waving and smiling at me, were now trapped inside the burning personnel carrier. Sadness welled up inside, but I couldn't cry. It was beyond my imagination.

Gen. Tri turned to me, then pulled a handkerchief from his pocket and held it out.

"Are you alright, Miss Thuy?" he asked softly.

I shook my head but didn't speak. Only then could the tears

escape, trailing down my cheeks. Everyone else was probably used to such horrific scenes, so, without another word, the squadron continued on, a little more motivated by the desire for revenge.

When the APCs reached the trees, they stopped but continued firing. The soldiers climbed down from their vehicles and made their way into the trees under support fire. Major Son called on the radio.

"Hiep, this is Son Ca! Hiep, this is Son Ca! What is the enemy's situation? Can we move in? Over."

A moment later there came a reply.

"Son Ca, this is Hiep. They've withdrawn into tunnels, leaving many dead and wounded. Our boys are following close behind. There are many tunnels. We're still searching. The Sun can advance!"

An L-19 observation plane circling overhead identified some VCs emerging from underground and heading west. Gen. Tri sent men to block their escape route, then ordered the M113s to move in further.

The armored carrier I was on advanced past corpses of VC huddled in foxholes or sprawled on the ground. Many of the bodies were ripped apart; their open eyes seemed filled with indignation.

There was a radio report that the advance party had uncovered a cache of all kinds of weapons camouflaged with sacks of rice. A little further off they found a storage trench with about 300 bags of rice. Gen. Tri allowed the APC units to confiscate what they needed.

By 1:00 p.m., when we left the area, the number of VC who had "rallied" (surrendered) plus those captured came to nearly 100. Most wore the green uniform of the North Vietnamese infantry, and their faces were sallow and frightened.

On the helicopter ride back to base, Gen. Tri showed me a stack of seized documents, photos, and letters. There were letters to parents, wives, children, and friends that hadn't yet been sent off. There were diaries filled with personal sentiments, sadness, longing. Who said the Vietnamese Communists had no feelings, no families? At that very moment, how many fathers and mothers, how many wives were waiting for the letters I held in my hands? How could they know their sons, husbands, or fathers had died on the foreign ground in fire and smoke because of the ambitions of the "Uncle and Party," because of the plots hatched by the leaders in the North?

The Death of a Young General

We had a quick lunch at the base for the 18th Armored unit of the 318th Battle Group, during which we listened as Col. Khoi related the story of the previous night's battle that had left 48 VC dead, where this morning I had seen more than a dozen bodies still unburied.

The field radio reported continuously about the military situation in Bathu, a town located in the Parrot's Beak. We now made our way directly to that battle.

While we circled above waiting for the smoke to mark our landing zone, I heard the awful roar of three Cobra helicopters and two Skyraider AD-6 attack planes swooping down to strafe the communist base with rockets and beehive antipersonnel rounds. The advance party informed us that this time the communists had spread their forces thin rather than concentrating them in one place as they had at Tadei earlier in the day.

As our helicopter descended, behind us APCs were lined up facing the enemy even as evacuation choppers were landing and rising to take the wounded. There were already 38 injured men, needing evacuation. The manner in which the injured were extracted looked strange to me. Each helicopter came down like a falling leaf, loaded the men, then spun around and took off straight up into the air. All this took place in the midst of direct enemy gunfire.

After the request by Lt. Col. Quang, which he almost screamed into the radio, more evac and AD-6 squadrons flew in, as APCs and artillery blasted the enemy.

At 4:00, the APCs moved forward, their guns firing. I was sitting in an M113 with Capt. Tuan and Major Chau, commander of the 30th Communications Battalion, as we joined the others entering deep into a Cambodian village identified on the maps as No. 105.

Ten minutes later, three F-5 fighters flew in and dropped a volley of napalm bombs on the enemy, the tremendous blasts of fire followed by terrifying mushroom clouds.

Once the front quieted, Gen. Tri told me that at 5:00 p.m. we would be going to Bavet, a provincial town near the border, to meet a two-star general sent by Cambodian Prime Minister Lon Nol. This marked the first time a Cambodian general would be talking to a general from South Vietnam, even though the South Vietnamese had deployed troops in Cambodian territory for an entire month.

An hour later, while I was helping army medics load wounded soldiers onto helicopters, we received news that Major Gen. Nguyen Viet Thanh, commander of IV Corps and co-director of Operation Total Victory 42 with Gen. Tri, had died in an air collision involving his UH-1 and an American Cobra. Gen. Thanh was just 39 years old.

When the news arrived, Gen. Tri was supervising the mopping up of communist troops. Major Chau, communications chief, heard the news first, but he offered me the sad task of informing Gen. Tri.

Ignoring my bloody hands and clothes, I walked over to the general's APC. Trying to maintain my composure, I searched in my head for the most precise and softest way to break the news. Gen. Tri looked at me and laughed.

"Come up and see, Miss Thuy. They're running away like frightened ducks!"

With a steady voice, I told him the news. His reaction left me in shock. I had become used to the image of the general as stalwart and self-possessed, even in the most perilous circumstances. Now he stood in silence, his jaw dropping as if he were about to speak, his eyes gaping but seeing nothing. In an instant, his face changed as he struggled to conceal his emotion. He leaped down from the vehicle and stood staring at me as if looking for a confirmation of my message.

I nodded, unable to say another word. Then he half-ran to the communications radio and barked into it, demanding to know the fate of Gen. Thanh. The imprecise answer from the other end of the line enraged him, and he shouted even louder.

The officers behind him grew tense as they waited anxiously for his response. All of a sudden, he was silent. Then he walked off a good distance and sat down next to a dry field.

The others exchanged glances, not daring to speak. It was like we were suspended in time. The explosions were louder, closer, right on top of us. The staff officers sat on the ground and listened to the latest news about the renowned and incorruptible general who had defended IV Corps, the man who shared the heavy responsibility for this cross-border operation.

I came up beside Gen. Tri. He looked at me, his eyes

bloodshot, and his face sad beyond belief. Then he motioned for me to sit next to him.

"One never imagines it, isn't that right, Miss Thuy?" he said in a low voice. "They say when you get to be a general like us you can't die on the front. And yet people die. This time it's Gen. Thanh. Someday it'll be my turn, heh, Miss Thuy?"

His words, delivered with such pathos, sent a chill through me. I wanted to say something to comfort him, but he spoke first.

"Surely you knew Gen. Thanh, Miss Thuy?"

"Yes, once I met him in IV Corps. He didn't like the media."

Gen. Tri laughed sadly.

"Huh, Gen. Thanh didn't like the media. He never had any use for the media."

He was silent for a moment, and then suddenly his tone changed.

"Let's go, Miss Thuy. It's almost time for our meeting with the Cambodian general."

His face took on its usual hard appearance. I had just witnessed a rare expression of emotion by a man the Americans called the "vicious tiger of the battlefield."

I had always seen my role as reporter to be merely an impartial witness to history. The openness with which Gen. Tri expressed his feelings suddenly gave my job a human character.

Valor on the Battlefield

6:00 p.m. After meeting with Cambodian Gen. Mosung Fan at a small fort on the border, Gen. Tri decided to return to the front instead of to operation headquarters in Tay Ninh as he usually did. He chose to visit the 15th Armored Squadron of the 226th Task Force led by Lt. Col. Nguyen Van Dong, at the scene of the fiercest battle since Day 1 of Operation Total Victory 42.

By the time we arrived the sun was just a bright red disc on the horizon. Two Ranger battalions led by Col. Nguyen Thanh Chuan had already reinforced the raging battle since noon. From the map, Capt. Tuan explained that the target was near the village of Don Noy, 12 kilometers from Bathu, that is 42 kilometers from Route 1 as the crow flies.

Our landing zone was a broad plain beside a thick forest thought to conceal the communists' base. All the villages around were from in ruins by the fighting over the past several days.

Lt. Col. Dong told us the situation had gotten worse since noon when the communists ceased shelling and retreated into the forest, firing all types of weapons. He also said that besides the two Ranger battalions already there, another unit of 30 Rangers was on the way.

Ten minutes after our arrival, the wounded began to arrive. Out of the night they came, shadowy figures staggering, leaning on one another as they hobbled towards us then collapsed to the ground. Seen against the backdrop of the twilit sky, it made a nightmarish scene. The fields all around resounded in gunfire. During those shocking moments, I felt as if I were watching a scene from the movie *The Longest Day*.

After one M113 was hit, bursting into flames, and mortar fire killed soldiers in another APC, some of our vehicles hesitated to advance. As they started turning back, others stopped as if everyone had suddenly lost their nerve.

This infuriated Gen. Tri. To regain morale, he immediately leaped on the lead APC and ordered the unit to move forward. Meanwhile, he shouted into the radio requesting priority in obtaining maximum reinforcements. The general yelled, until his voice became hoarse, for all armored vehicles and soldiers to keep advancing while awaiting help. Beside him, Lt. Col. Dong tried to control his anger as he aggressively ordered the soldiers and M113s to proceed together.

An American adviser grabbed a flak vest and handed it to me, telling me to put it on. I nodded my thanks, took the heavy jacket and set it down. The entire general's staff put on body armor. Col. Dong took one for Gen. Tri, who refused it and told me to wear it. Capt. Tuan also insisted, but I shook my head, offering it instead to a cavalry gunner next to me whose vest had already been ripped to shreds.

The sky was dark over the vast battlefield. I could no longer even see the APCs on either side of me. I could only hear guns firing everywhere, and the armored cars rumbling as fire split the sky. It was getting cold and misty. Huddled in my mud-covered uniform, I felt a strange trance-like state, perhaps from the smell of gunpowder in the air.

Our APC reached the front line across from the enemy, just

another 20 meters from the forest. Our adversary showering us with gunfire was now just a dark block in front of us from which specks of light poured out. Flares dropped from the sky to cast a red glow over the battlefield. The men's faces were set off in crimson, grimy, sweaty, their mouths tight, their eyes fixed ahead of them. His eyes hardened, Gen. Tri spoke into the radio.

"This is the Sun. Orders are to reserve all priority for fighter planes, artillery, and soldiers to reinforce at once!"

At 7:15 p.m., fires flared all over the front. The explosion from APCs that had been hit, fires from bushes where the communists launched their mortars, and small fires all over the dry fields.

Suddenly, the gunner sitting next to me and in front of Gen. Tri—the one I had given the flak vest to—was cut down right beside me. A bullet had gone through his forehead, his face covered with blood. He died right there, wearing my present, his lips still bearing a trace of the smile he'd given me two minutes before. I felt my heart squeezed. I felt cold and numb inside. I was too young and innocent to accept the cruelties of war. I lost my head and became insensitive to the things happening around me.

Everyone was ordered out of the armored vehicles and made to lie down behind banks of earth that reminded me of dikes by the rice fields in the countryside. Thunderchiefs and Cobras took turns strafing the enemy. The radio beside me did not cease reporting the casualty situation of the infantry and Rangers.

There was a report of an officer and an American adviser lying on the ground wounded behind an APC that had backed up over them. It left us stunned and hurt. On the front, besides bombs and bullets, many kinds of death awaited the men. What was I to think of these things I had never before imagined?

Fifteen minutes later, the artillery and planes were ordered to cease fire. The communists were no longer in the forest but had retreated into trenches and tunnels close to the South Vietnamese soldiers. The sky-shaking noise of the enormous bombs suddenly stopped, giving way to the rattle of small arms fire.

By 9:00 p.m., the front was quiet. Courage, anger, and the exhortations of Gen. Tri and Lt. Col. Dong had altered the face of the battle. I could not get out of my mind the image of armored carriers turning to withdraw and wounded soldiers helping each other away from the fighting. Now those war chariots were still there. So, too, were those same soldiers. Under a command that was determined, daring, and unflappable, these men had fought unbelievably brave. They had fought ever harder despite growing casualties as if they did it for their fallen brothers-in-arms as well.

After giving final instructions to the various units, Gen. Tri signaled for us to return. On the way back to the landing zone, we had to keep our heads down to avoid being hit by bullets flying past. Again and again, I found myself tripping over wounded men lying around waiting for evacuation.

At the landing zone, the chopper ordered by Gen. Tri to evacuate the wounded had not yet returned. Those still alert told us that the landing zone had to be changed twice because of the enemy's B-40s. And two wounded soldiers lying nearby were killed at this place where they harbored their last hope.

I sat down on the ground. The physical exhaustion was nothing compared to the emotional drain I experienced. The wounded lay all around, their faces contorted in pain from all manner of injuries. The red glow of the flares did not diminish the pallor of the men's faces. Each time they heard the "fut-fut-fut" of a helicopter's rotors in the air they raised themselves and looked up expectantly. My heart trembled violently. I wanted to do something. Like, hold them and weep. Like, offer to take upon me some of their pain and suffering. But my shy, timid character kept me back.

Finally, in the last minutes of a day filled with bombs and gunfire, death and pain, in a night illuminated by the red-lighted flares amidst gun smoke, my mind suddenly opened up. I understood why soldiers, whose stories I had overheard at a coffee house in the city, could squabble over some little thing someone said would, here on the battlefield, be ready to give their lives for each other.

And it was then, too, that I realized why the Republic of Vietnam still had generals who, after giving decades of their lives to the military, yet earnestly gave their all to the battlefield, even to die on the front, throwing away all the glory and position they had earned.

Woman War Reporters

All this time I was very uncomfortable as a woman reporting the war. Always surrounded by men in an environment requiring toughness, bravery, and other so-called masculine traits, sometimes I feared I was losing my femininity.

To my good fortune, it was during my assignment with the general that I got an answer to my prayer.

One day, I came upon a woman stranded in the field who was hoping Gen. Tri would give her a lift back to Saigon in his helicopter.

Marie Joannidis was a Greek journalist born in the city of Alexandria, Egypt. A graduate of the University of Lausanne, Switzerland, with two degrees in political science and law, she went to work for the Agence France Presse (AFP). I had a few good female friends, but Marie became not only a close companion but also a big sister and mentor, who taught me much about Western professional journalism. Soon we were arranging to go out to the front together.

Marie Joannidis (1944-2013).
Photo: Agence France Press.

Six years older than I, Marie was tall, with a strong voice and a sharp mind. A talented reporter, she was assertive and straightforward in both her work and her ordinary life. She was never afraid to ask a question and could hold her own in a debate.

Meanwhile, I was petite, lacked confidence in a crowd, and new to journalism. And yet, in spite of our differences, Marie and I took to each other at once, though I had to learn to get used to the disapproving stares and irreverent quips of my male colleagues when they spotted the two of us together.

Perhaps no other relationship could have come at a better time and been more relevant to my needs than my friendship with Marie. She made it possible for me to turn a corner in my life that allowed me to realize my desire to be a more professional journalist. From then on, I concentrated on developing my skills as well as my femininity. Over time I transformed from a schoolgirl from a sheltered home, shy and embarrassed when faced with difficulty, into a woman who could speak with confidence and strength, and write with greater fervor.

For her part, Marie was happy to have a young friend to whom she could pass on her experiences, both in profession and life. In return, I helped explain Vietnamese culture and provided her with news and information.

Because of our friendship, I had a permanent invitation to her Tuesday-evening gatherings for journalists at her apartment on the top floor of the Tax Plaza. I was often the only Vietnamese in the crowd of foreigners. Sometimes, though, other Vietnamese would come, such as Senator Tran Van Don, Representative Ngo Cong Duc, or Press Secretary Hoang Duc Nha. Once in a while a general took part, most often Gen. Do Cao Tri.

One day when Marie and I were on Gen. Tri's helicopter about to leave Tay Ninh to return to Saigon, I noticed a young man running up, shouting amidst the noise of the rotors, asking if he could come on board. Gen. Tri's chief of staff indicated that the chopper was full and motioned for the pilot to take off. The young man on the ground looked up at me sitting in the open doorway, questioningly. I raised my eyebrows while pointing to the press tag on my shirt.

Marie looked at me and then at the young man and laughed. She predicted that the two of us had not seen the last of each other.

Later, I learned the young man's name was Duong Phuc, and he worked for Armed Forces Radio.

Oriana Fallaci:
"Wait... Til You're Older..."

One day in early 1971, I met the world-renowned Italian photojournalist Oriana Fallaci on assignment in Kampong Cham. On this occasion, my regular traveling companion, Marie Joannidis, had had to remain in Saigon at the last minute. In a cold, patronizing manner, Ms. Fallaci told me to let her know when we were leaving for Tay Ninh on Gen. Tri's helicopter.

I was both awed and pleased to meet her, as I had long been an admirer of this iconic reporter. To me she was the world's number one reporter in the technique of interviewing: one of a kind, tempestuous, never allowing her subject to dodge a question. I collected all her articles and read everything I could about her life. Oriana Fallaci had been known for a long time, but she really came into her own with her interview with Vo Nguyen Giap in 1969.[23] That was the first time a Western reporter had managed to gain an interview with the Communist Defense Minister, who previously had declined requests to meet with the press.

Her report on the interview, with its keen, meticulously ordered questions that brought out the essence of the replies, provided the reader with a true picture of the subject. From the article, the reader could see how Gen. Giap was cold, unfeeling, and brutal, "a real communist." The portrait was especially clear when he was asked about the slogan "Born in the North, Die in the South," a campaign that coerced hundreds of thousands of youthful soldiers from North Vietnam to march to their deaths in the South, casually he replied, "Such is war."

Oriana Fallaci (1929-2006). Photo: Epoca.

I admired Ms. Fallaci's unique talent. Nearly everyone among the international journalistic community in Vietnam had great respect for her.

When I met her, I was only twenty years old and therefore strove to put on a serious face to conceal my inexperience. Ms. Fallaci was twice my age but looked and acted as if she were thirty. In her professional life, she was a wary lion, unapproachable, famous for wanting to work alone, independent and arrogant.

Now, at midday, Ms. Fallaci and I were seated on an M113

---

[23]Gen. Vo Nguyen Giap was the commander of the Vietnamese Communist forces during the war with the French from 1946—1954, then Defense Minister for most of the war against South Vietnam and the Americans.

armored personnel carrier heading toward the front line. The APC was camouflaged with tree leaves, and the soldiers placed more cover on our equipment to hide us, they said, from the enemy's B-40 rockets.

All of a sudden, there was an enormous explosion. I was thrown back by the force of the blast; my tape recorder was knocked from my hands. When I looked to my right, I saw that the APC to that side was on fire. The soldiers who had just moments before been sitting around the vehicle smiling and waving at us were no more. Explosions rained down all around us.

Our APC roared and plunged forward. The soldiers who had been sitting on the outside next to me now stood inside, turning the gun and firing in the direction of the enemy. I realized then that I was the only one still sitting on the outside of the carrier.

Everything happened so fast I had no time to respond. I was surprised to find myself paralyzed but not frightened. A minute passed before I realized that Ms. Fallaci was not next to me. I looked around desperately.

"Oriana! Oriana!" I cried.

I was afraid she'd been thrown off by the blast and left behind. As I was about to shout again for her, I felt a hand on my foot and looked down to see the famed reporter poking her head up from inside the APC. Staring at her disheveled hair in disbelief, I asked myself, *how could a veteran war correspondent like Oriana Fallaci hide inside an armored vehicle?* As this thought went through my mind, I felt a burst of pride at my pluckiness.

That evening on the helicopter heading back to Tay Ninh, the cocky little girl that I had become decided to ask Ms. Fallaci the question that had been turning in my mind. I had to shout into her ear above the noise of the chopper's blades and the wind raging in the open doors.

Thuy in Kompong Cham, Cambodia, 1970.

"I didn't think you could be

frightened, so why did you hide inside the APC?"

She looked at me. In the graying light of the day's end, the bright glow of her eyes unsettled me, and I suddenly realized how foolish and childish I was. Then she answered me in French.

"Attends jusqu'à tu es plus âgée! Wait until you're older."

I've never forgotten that reply.

Every time that silly child in me comes up again—which it regularly does—I recall the light in Ms. Fallaci's eyes and the words she spoke. And I remind myself with all humility, "Wait until you're older!"

Unsung Heroes

I gradually became accustomed to life on the front. When I was free to go back and forth to the lines, I tried to talk to the soldiers. I also ran up to help those who were wounded.

There were men whose bodies were torn up, their faces bloodied, but who looked at me with a light in their eyes that told how much they missed their families. They looked at me as if looking at the mothers, wives, older sisters, or girlfriends they longed to see in this critical moment of their lives. They looked at me with a hope of surviving, of being able to return to a normal life.

It got to where I could recognize that light in their eyes. An earnest pleading for life, filled with hopefulness yet overlade with worry. A look of those who had no more illusions about life, of men who realized they were likely going to leave this world.

I often paused to gather my thoughts, to see how much my heart was stirred by this look in the eyes of men during their final moments. The realization that I was the last person a man would see as he lay dying was a horrible feeling, terrifying and yet overwhelming in its affirmation of life. It was this feeling that marked a significant turning point in my emotional growth, making the fact of living more precious than anything. At the same time, I saw how death could be nobler than living a meaningless or useless life.

When I was not standing beside the wounded, I was surrounded by soldiers full of vitality, fighting to defend their homeland. And I saw that the front line infused a person's brain with a keen perception of survival, a type of exhilaration that was stronger than any other feeling about life that I had experienced in my twenty years.

My senses became sharp and alert. My eyes captured every detail, my ears could distinguish the different types of gunfire, and when the shooting stopped, we waited anxiously, anticipating what would come next. I felt pity from the depth of my heart when I watched a soldier writhe in pain as medics removed his burned shirt, taking off the flesh with it.

I did not get a transition period leading to my maturity. From the very first day, I threw myself into the merciless realm of wartime death and experienced every feeling that people who spend years on the war front eventually come to know.

Each weekday morning I went up to Bien Hoa to catch the early helicopter flight, then spent the day on a different battle site in Cambodia, returning to Saigon at nine or ten at night. The next morning, the driver took me to my newspaper office so I could slip my report under the door.

I didn't bother to find out if the readers liked my articles or what my editor thought about them. I was focused only on the front, and I knew that I would never return to my old job. The editorial office in Saigon now seemed all too quiet and dull compared to the noise of guns and bombs and facing death on a daily basis.

I admired the men I encountered on the front. They were completely unlike the coarse, ill-mannered soldiers one might run into during their leave in the city. On the battlefield, they were sentimental, loyal, and considerate.

I was astonished by the contradictions in human feelings that I witnessed. In the midst of a brutal fight, the soldiers often displayed love and compassion, keeping an eye out for each other, always ready to sacrifice their own lives for their comrades without the slightest hesitation.

There was one soldier named Bao, 21 in years but an old man from the war. As he told me about a buddy of his named Phuoc, his face became twisted in pain and his eyes glazed over like one who had just returned from hell. His close friend had died right beside him.

As the most experienced man in the battalion, Bao had volunteered to take point when Phuoc stopped him.

"He grabbed my arm and pulled me back," Bao said, his face in his hands. "He said to me, 'your wife is about to have a baby.

Don't take any chances. Let me go instead.' Phuoc was just 18 and had never had a girlfriend. Up to this point he had been a joker, always kidding around and making us laugh. This time he was serious."

I heard countless stories like this, stories of one guy going out ahead of the others, or coming back to rescue someone, or slowing down to wait for a buddy who had fallen behind and then getting killed. I began to notice a pattern to the war front shown by the extraordinary actions of ordinary men.

No soldier was prepared to give his life because he wanted to be a hero. They placed themselves in life-and-death situations coolly, the way they had been trained. It was the way of a warrior who had self-respect and cared about his brothers-in-arms. It was in the eyes of outsiders that he became a hero.

I came to realize that fighting on the front was not about life and death but, rather, self-respect. Once he was in combat, a soldier did not care about big words like "patriotism" or phrases like "defending the fatherland" or "keeping the peace." It was all about protecting one another and living and dying with loyalty to your buddies, which civilians, living a peaceful life, would have a hard time to understand. It seemed to me that even the love between husband and wife or the feelings of parents for their children lack the potency and urgency of the relationship between fellow soldiers. It is their first duty.

War became a way of expressing human nature, maintaining justice and preserving love.

The soldiers I encountered showed me the same care and attentiveness they shared with one another.

Thuy with APC, Kamphong Cham, Cambodia, 1970.

Many asked, "Why are you out here? You should be living safely in the city, making yourself pretty and going out with your boyfriend. What are you doing in this place?"

Another might say, "All this smoke will ruin your skin, and all this dying will make you look old. The front is no place for a woman."

The way I saw it, the front was no place for anyone. But I answered, "I'm here because I want to see with my own eyes what you are doing on the front line so I can let the people back home know."

"What we're doing?" they'd holler. "We're just attacking the enemy or protecting ourselves, so the enemy doesn't kill us. If you don't get out of here, miss, you'll be killed too!"

Every day I thought about the possibility of being killed at any time. But this concern did not reduce my thirst to be out on the front. I found the front many times more exhilarating than life in the city especially for a woman, who was always supposed to worry about her looks and the way she dressed and had to deal with social pressures.

Over time I began to realize, and accept, that if I lost my life on the battlefield, I would die a meaningful death among the worthy company.

With this view of death held in common with actual soldiers, I came to understand why they were so rude and destructive when they visited the city. Since they had to fight to stay alive from one minute to the next and watch their buddies fall in battle, when they finally got leave, they saw how people in the rear had plenty to eat and drink, wore fine clothes, and enjoyed security and peace. Meanwhile, a soldier's pay was often not enough to support a family living in two places, and if the husband was unfortunately killed, the wife and kids were left without a future.

The contrast in lifestyles made the soldiers angry when the city people failed to respect the sacrifices of those who were protecting their country. This was particularly notable in the way they defended their buddies when city folk looked down on them for their dirty uniforms and emotional outbursts, consequences of their traumatic experiences in the field.

The Price of Glory

General Do Cao Tri particularly exemplified this spirit. Whenever one of his soldiers encountered some difficulty—whether it was an APC bogged down or a unit surrounded by the enemy—he was there to resolve the situation personally. I witnessed numerous times when he ordered his helicopter to descend in the midst of a firefight or climbed onto an armored car to direct the action, ignoring the warnings of his staff.

Once on our return to Bien Hoa, I asked the general why he never spoke up or tried to correct the rumors circulating about him. He just shrugged.

"I'm not a politician; I'm a general. If my soldiers understand me, that's enough. My soldiers don't have enough time to fight the enemy, so why should I waste time pandering to public opinion?"

I made bold to inquire further, "But why do people keep hurling bad reports about you?"

"Ask your colleagues in the press, Miss!" he replied angrily. "None of them comes out to the front to watch us risk our lives. All they care about is getting a hot story to sell newspapers. I don't pay any attention to them."

As I spent more time with Gen. Tri, talking with him during return flights from the front or over dinner with his friends at La Casita, his favorite restaurant in Saigon, I heard him talk about how he was thrown in jail after one coup then promoted after another. He said he hated politics because politics turns people into schemers with no conscience. Fame and power, he confided, made him many enemies, and he trusted no one.

A frank Southerner, Gen. Tri always spoke his mind.

"I love fighting on the front. I love being the hero. That's why I go out every day to be with my men."

He smiled bitterly.

"Those close to me think I would be better off staying in Bien Hoa where it's safe. But, strange to say, I trust the war."

Gen. Tri believed that out on the front, he knew who his friends were and who his enemies were. The war gave him the chance to live with honor, to spend his days in dignity. He then became thoughtful, paused for a while, then continued, sadly.

"In war, there is a clear line between friend and foe, whereas, in the city, people always step over that line and I never know if someone is going to stab me in the back when I'm not looking."

The more he talked, the more I came to understand and respect him. Quite often, I would listen to his discourse on "important matters" and ask myself why he was telling these things to someone as young and inexperienced as me, a novice news reporter who could have been his daughter. In time I came to see that what he called "the price of glory and power" had made him unable to trust anyone enough to share his thoughts. With me, on the other hand, he seemed to be talking to himself, because I was there to listen and sympathize, and I never talked back. He was like a teacher who knew too much and had much he wanted to say. Meanwhile, I was like his pupil, ignorant but eager to soak up his knowledge.

Looking back, I can see that these conversations about his life experiences completely altered my perspective on my own life. As a young woman with ambition and drive, I developed a higher regard for honor and power when I saw the price they demanded in return: the loss of one's peace and happiness. Especially, causing one to lose the ability to trust others, something I would never want to lose.

///

At the end of 1970, General Cao Van Vien, chief of the South Vietnamese Joint General Staff, signed an order awarding the Silver Star for Valor to four correspondents who had been on assignment in Cambodia. Three of the four worked for the foreign press: Le Minh of Time-Life, Nick Ut of the Associated Press, and Marie Joannidis of the French Press Agency. I was the fourth reporter, working for the Vietnamese press.

And so, in early January the next year, the four of us stood at attention before a large contingent of soldiers representing the various branches of service on the parade ground of III Corps Headquarters in Bien Hoa. Le Minh and I wore our press safari suits. Marie had on a conservative dress. Only Nick Ut was in the camouflage outfit he usually wore to the front.

After a parade with military flags while the band played rousing music, the master of ceremonies read off the order from the Joint General Staff which explained why the four reporters deserved this special honor usually reserved for fighting men who had shown exceptional bravery.

The Silver Star decoration ceremony, III Corps Headquarters, Bien Hoa, January 1971. From left: Marie Joannidis (AFP), Thuy (Su That), Lê Minh (Time-Life), and Nick Út (AP).

Gen. Tri came to each of us in turn to present the medal. When he reached me, he smiled as he pinned the award on my collar.

"You are the youngest woman to receive this award. Be careful."

Then he added a quote from the 16th-century philosopher Michel de Montaigne, "*Chaque médaille a son révers!*" Every medal has its reverse side.

Thuy and Gen. Tri at the Silver Star decoration ceremony.

A Hero Dies before His Time

In February 1971, I joined my family for a vacation on our tea farm in Bao Loc. Upon my return to Saigon, I took a bag of pineapples from the family garden to Gen. Tri's Saigon home, asking that they be sent to him at his private residence in Bien Hoa.

That night the general called to thank me for the gift and invited me to accompany him the next day out to the front. He hinted that there were significant changes in the works that I should know about. I accepted his invitation.

About an hour later as I was preparing my gear, I suddenly remembered that I had an appointment at the newspaper office for a new assignment. I called the general's staff and told them I'd have to postpone my trip to the front for another time.

The next morning I was at the office of *Than Phong* (Spirit Wind) newspaper to pick up some new material they had received from the Department of Defense regarding a current subject, a Navy doctor named Ha Thuc Nhon. Lt. Nhon, who was well known for his defiant condemnation of corruption in the government, had taken over the Nguyen Hue military hospital in Nha Trang. When the MPs came to arrest him, he fought back and was killed in a shootout. The doctor's death shook the public. After the investigation, *Than Phong* obtained the transcript of the report from the Defense Department and I was asked to write the story.

Around noon, a colleague from another newspaper bounded in shouting that Gen. Tri was dead. At first, I thought he was playing a cruel joke. To prove it, however, he turned on the radio, and I listened in shock as the Minister of Defense announced that Gen. Tri and his staff, along with American journalist Francois Sully, had perished when their helicopter exploded over Tay Ninh.

At once I called the general's home, and the person on the other end of the line confirmed the news. I began to shake, and my mind went blank. I could still hear his voice on the phone the day before, inviting me to join him on his mission. Now he was no more. And I... if I had not postponed going along with him...

Not only did III Corps fly the flag at half-mast while the soldiers wept, but all of Saigon went into mourning for the general. That evening his picture and the story of his career filled the front pages of newspapers all over the country. My paper asked me to write a piece about Gen. Tri.

My article, half biography and half eulogy, was something I had never wanted to write about anyone, much less Gen. Tri. Yet, in spite of my personal grief, it seemed that I was the one who should write about him since I had been privileged to get close to him. The managing editor, Tran Viet Son, titled the article "A Hero Dies before His Time" and said it was the best thing I had ever written.

Lt. Gen. Do Cao Tri was just 42 years old when he died on Feb. 23, 1971.

///

The day of Gen. Tri's funeral, I wore an airborne uniform as I accompanied Col. Nguyen Thanh Chuan, chief of the III Corps Rangers and one of the general's closest associates, to the military cemetery in Bien Hoa, which was to be his final resting place. Gen. Tri had declared that he was happiest when he was with his soldiers, in life as in death. Now his wish was being fulfilled. Gen. Do Cao Tri was the first general to be buried in the military cemetery, where he would lie beside thousands of other fighters from the South Vietnamese military.

In accordance with his wishes, the general's coffin was transported on an APC from the 3rd Cavalry under Col. Tran Quang Khoi, his most loyal officer and closest friend. His uniform, cap, gloves, sword, riding crop, and medals were placed on top of the casket.

Gen. Tri's coffin on an armored personnel carrier, Bien Hoa, Feb. 26, 1971.

We stood in the shade of a big tree and silently listened to President Thieu and other government and military leaders as they praised Gen. Tri. They all spoke of his accomplishments during the past two decades and his wholehearted dedication to the country, even to the point of giving his life.

As I watched the people who filled the cemetery to honor this leader, I was overcome by the deep love the members of the armed forces had for him. When I heard them refer to him as

President Nguyen Van Thieu at Gen. Tri's funerals, Bien Hoa, Feb. 26, 1971.

"the late colonel general," I started to choke up. No one wants to advance in rank amid the incense and candles of their funeral, their body wrapped in the flag, washed in the tears of their loved ones.

When the honor guard had fired the final salute, and the casket was lowered into the grave, I could no longer hold back my tears. I looked at Col. Chuan, a hardened Ranger for whom one might think death was a thing of no consequence; he, too, pulled out a handkerchief to wipe his eyes out of feeling for his dear friend.

How one lives, so one dies. Gen. Tri gave his all for his country and soldiers, and now his body was covered with the flag of a grateful fatherland and interred among thousands of his beloved fellow warriors. The nation had lost a hero. The army and the people of South Vietnam lost a courageous general, a talented man fully devoted to his homeland and his men.

For my part, I lost a rare teacher, one who showed me that rectitude and aptitude always earn respect, no matter at what age.

///

A few days later, Col. Chuan took me to the crash site in Tay Ninh, and I learned more about the crash that had killed Gen. Tri.[24] After meeting with Pres. Thieu at Independence Palace to discuss changes in command, Gen. Tri had flown to Tay Ninh for a briefing, and then took off for the Cambodian front to continue the operation there. A few minutes after takeoff, the helicopter lost control and crashed. All ten on board died. Most were people I had come to know during my eight months on the Cambodia assignment. Among the victims was Francois Sully, a veteran journalist of the Vietnam War.

Sully was born in France and spent 24 years in Southeast Asia, covering the French war for Time-Life, and then serving as a photojournalist for UPI before becoming bureau chief for *Newsweek*, his position at the time of his death. He was highly respected by his peers, who called him "a journalist's journalist" because of his ability to gain access to individuals from the highest ranks and stations in government and military to street children. So taken was he with the many orphans he encountered that Sully opened his residence to many of the homeless children he found on the streets. He had even made his life insurance payable to the orphans living in his house. On that fateful day, Sully was thrown out of the spinning helicopter and fell 75 feet to the ground. He died of his injuries shortly after.

The story troubled me greatly. I was supposed to have been on that flight, not Francois Sully. And while I thanked God for allowing me to survive, I was haunted by the bizarre thought that if I had been on that helicopter, no one would have died because my fate had not yet been fulfilled. Otherwise, I wouldn't be alive today!

After that, I was always on guard, ever watchful, fearful that something might happen when least expected. Obsessed with the idea that "it should have been me," I was determined to do as much as I

---

[24] Rumors abounded as to the cause of the crash, with many suggesting that it was not an accident but an assassination. Some said that Gen. Tri had been considering a request for support in staging a coup d'état against President Thieu (he would have been the key person for such a coup, given that he was the most powerful military man and had a large number of troops stationed near Saigon). Some said that other powerful men felt intimidated by Gen. Tri's skills and victories, especially when the international media wrote several positive reviews on him. Adding to this attention, President Thieu had publicly announced that he wanted Gen. Tri to take over the command of the Lam Son 719 operation from the current "failing" (Thieu's word) officers.

could each day because there might be no tomorrow.

I quit writing for newspapers and took a full-time job at Voice of Freedom radio, a station funded by the U.S. government that broadcast into North Vietnam. On weekends I worked for Radio Saigon, translating news from French for the hourly broadcasts. I worked without rest and yet I felt that I should be doing more. I didn't allow myself any time for personal relationships, nor did I want to be tied down to anything or anyone.

But just one year later, someone came along who pulled me back to myself.

Chapter 10

Fields of Blood

Love and the Battlefront

■ THUY

I actually met Phuc for the first time at Lai Khe airfield near the An Loc front in April 1972. There I recognized him as the young man who had asked for a lift on Gen. Tri's helicopter in Tay Ninh two years earlier, whom Marie Joannidis predicted I would see again. I also remembered him as the dauntless reporter who had asked Pres. Thieu a question that got everyone to stop and listen at Khe Sanh the previous year.

I'd known about him for some time. Whenever I heard the voice on Armed Forces Radio announce "This is Duong Phuc reporting from the front..." I knew the story would be hot, straightforward, and honest. Listeners favored his news reports because they were lively and so real they felt as if they were indeed part of the action.

Phuc was also known for the passion he put into his work heightened by his fearlessness in the face of death when he went out after a story. His colleagues often related how he might disappear on the front line during a firefight, then reappear with an extraordinary report. They said he was always on the move, so caught up in his work that he never had time for light conversation or relaxing with friends.

As I learned more about this professional associate, I began to pay more attention to him when we were together for media events. Especially after he swiped my hairclip on the way to An Loc.

The Siege of An Loc:
Chronicle of Meritorious Service

■ PHUC

In the Spring of 1972, the communist army stepped up its attacks on cities in the South as part of its "Easter Offensive," and the capital of Binh Long province was in dire straits.

Because An Loc lay just 90 kilometers north of Saigon, the South Vietnamese government was afraid that if this city fell, the way would be open for the communists to advance into the South. The enemy was determined to capture this base and had cut it off from neighboring cities since early April.

The North Vietnamese Army (NVA) had committed four full divisions to this front, supported by two armored battalions, artillery batteries, and anti-aircraft units. All told, the communists had 40,000 troops with tremendous firepower. Meanwhile, there were just 7,500 men from the 5th Infantry Division and local defense forces fended for An Loc.

Brig. Gen. Le Van Hung, commander of the 5th Infantry, and his staff were isolated in An Loc. Every day they faced a torrent of shelling. The city, reduced to a four-square-kilometer area, received an estimated 8,000 rounds in a single day. Nothing above ground was safe.

The NVA had cut all supply routes into the city, gradually tightening the noose around it. No one knew what was happening in An Loc as communications were sporadic and any news that reached the outside was not good. Everyone knew that the defenders were short on ammunition and supplies and suffered constant shelling. The communists rained artillery fire on the command station as our side attempted to drive back the enemy. All supplies had to be dropped by parachute; consequently, much of it fell into the hands of the attackers.

"While I Remain, An Loc Will Remain!"

Every war correspondent in Vietnam wanted to go to An Loc to get the inside story, but that was next to impossible. At first, the South Vietnamese command banned reporters from flying into the city, in part because it was so dangerous, but also to conceal how small the defending force was.

At one point I joined several other correspondents including Le Thiep of *Chinh Luan* daily, Nguyen Manh Tien of Radio Saigon, and Nguyen The Tuat Hai of Voice of Freedom, in taking a chance to reach An Loc through Chon Thanh on Route 13. But we only got as far as the Tau O River, also known as the River of the Spirit of the Dead as it was the site of countless violent deaths resulting from communist efforts to block the ARVN from opening the road during the past two months.

I was fortunate to escape death on this short road when I accompanied the 11/20 Armored Squadron trying to break through. We were with Capt. Duc Tai, the squadron commander, who had become famous for his actions during the Cambodia incursion the previous year.

The morning we were to set off, Le Thiep and I were preparing to climb on board an M113 APC with Capt. Duc Tai to lead dozens of M41 tanks into Binh Long when Nguyen Manh Tien called us back to ride in a Jeep with the rest of the press corps at the rear of the convoy. Five minutes later we heard shelling and steady machine gun fire. We all jumped from the Jeep and raced to where the sounds were coming. There we found a tank crewman wailing.

"A 122 rocket got Duc Tai's carrier!"

The convoy halted beside the road, and a rescue team took the bodies of Capt. Duc Tai and the others back to Lai Khe. The reporters returned solemnly to Chon Thanh while Le Thiep and I stared at each other in stunned silence, a shiver running through us as we realized how we had cheated death by just moments.

The next day we returned. The only way into An Loc now was by helicopter. The NVA's anti-aircraft fire was very effective; they had downed quite a few planes that tried to resupply the base. The newest and most potent weapon in their arsenal was the SA-7 heat-seeking missile provided by the Soviet Union.

By this time I was a familiar face on the battlefront and enjoyed the favor of commanders who supported me during my assignments. I made going to An Loc a priority and formed a team with other reporters from radio and the press. Now and then Thuy was in our group, still the only woman representing the media.

An Loc had been devastated by the shelling, and smoke from the fires could be seen for quite a distance. The world was anxiously following the battle and saw it as a decisive contest between the Republic of Vietnam and the Communist North. The foreign news services were pessimistic that An Loc would hold. Thus when Gen. Hung declared, "While I remain, An Loc will remain," few people believed him.

The most significant blow from the foreign media came on April 8, when the BBC broadcast a series of adverse reports about the battle, stating with certainty that An Loc would fall, followed by the collapse of the entire South Vietnamese military. This prediction by a major news service at the beginning of the battle created an atmosphere of pessimism and dread all through the South.

It was due to the adverse psychological effects of these broadcasts that the military commanders relented and decided to allow reporters into An Loc to report the actual situation. The aim was to boost morale, but also to bear witness to the heroic efforts of the South Vietnamese soldiers in the hope that once the world saw how hard the ARVN was fighting, they would support their effort.

From the middle of April, we sought every means to enter An Loc. But by then the communists had spread a web of deadly anti-aircraft fire over the city, covering every flight path in and out, making it virtually impossible for anyone to slip through. And so, we correspondents could do nothing but play the waiting game for days at the Lai Khe airfield, sleeping on the tarmac and putting up with chafing winds that kicked up the hot sands.

A Hairpin Falls Out of the Blue

■ PHUC

On April 29, 1972, reporters Nguyen Manh Tien, Tuat Hai, and I finally got approval to go to An Loc. Helicopters were to transport the news crew directly into the town amidst anti-aircraft fire and shelling of the base. If it were going to be hazardous getting in, it would be even more so getting out as it was uncertain the helicopters could land to pull us out.

As I was preparing to board the chopper, amid the clamor of voices I recognized that of Vu Thanh Thuy, the female reporter from Voice of Freedom I had seen back at Khe Sanh and had promised myself I would find a way to meet. Now, up close, I could see she was quite young and, besides her peculiar eyes, she had a smile that

DUONG PHUC - VU THANH THUY

224

set off a beauty mark on the side of her mouth that made her look both sweet and provocative at the same time.

At a time when women reporters were a rarity, the presence of a young female correspondent wearing a military uniform and going out to the front for news story was quite impressive. Just her being in a place where women were not likely to be found told me that she was a determined character.

While my colleagues were climbing on board, I hung back and turned around. When she came within arm's reach, I noticed a silver hair clasp glimmering in the late afternoon light in her shining black hair. Without taking time to think, I put out my hand and snatched the pin from her hair.

Taken by surprise, she was about to grab it back, but she caught my wrist instead.

"I'll give it back," I said, "if we're lucky enough to survive."

The press corps stood still, watching us. Thuy grew red in the face and let go of my wrist. The soldiers all laughed, and soon the other reporters were laughing too, a bit of comic relief before we set off on a perilous assignment.

Without thinking, I dropped the hair clasp into my shirt pocket where it might protect my heart. Then I climbed into the helicopter and immediately pushed aside the whole incident to focus on the danger ahead.

Dropped Behind the Lines

In 15 minutes, the helicopter transporting the news crew approached the rubber tree plantation close to An Loc. Just before landing, however, we were enveloped in a shower of anti-aircraft fire, and the landing zone was shelled, causing us to turn around and head back. The pilot took us at treetop level to avoid the missiles, but that left us vulnerable to the enemy's machine guns and AK-47s. We had gone only a short distance when a fierce volley of gunfire struck us. The chopper's nose was hit, smoke obscured the view, but the pilot, lieutenant Vo Van Co of 223 Squadron, maintained control of the aircraft despite being wounded in the right shoulder.

He flew us for several kilometers before making an emergency landing in an open field. The crew of four, plus three correspondents, jumped out and ran for our lives, chased by communist soldiers who had us in their sights. As had become second nature to me as a reporter, I turned on my tape recorder and began reporting the frightening developments as they unfolded and the peril that was about to befall us.

Just when things looked the worst, a Special Forces gunship roared in with guns blazing while a second helicopter dropped down to rescue us. As we scrambled aboard the aircraft, the landing area lit up with fire, and other choppers covered the forest. As we flew through the smoke, I held my breath while the helicopter pulled us away from danger.

The next day, the Armed Forces Radio broadcast my on-the-scene report. Radio Saigon aired a similar story by Nguyen Manh Tien. Listeners heard our frantic account of the action amid the chaos of gunfire, shells exploding, helicopter blades chopping the air, and soldiers shouting as we faced disaster with the enemy closing in. The tape stopped as I said farewell and turned off the machine when it appeared we were about to be caught. The listeners were left on the edge of their seats, not knowing the outcome of our hair-raising story. After a while, my voice returned to the airwaves as I continued my report, recounting our last-minute rescue.

This incident had a profound effect on me in my role as a journalist. I did not think that my survival was due to luck. Instead, I believed that it was a special gift from God to allow me to fulfill my mission of bringing the truth from the front to the people in the rear areas. From then on, I saw the task of communicating the truth as more important than any personal affair. And for now, my colleagues and I resolved to find a way back to An Loc.

As it turned out, my radio story played a part in my winning the heart of Thuy, who was in Saigon listening to the broadcast, weeping in fear when I bid the audience farewell. At that moment, she felt the fragility of human life, as she told me later, and decided to let go of her reservations and doubts due to the extreme differences in our characters.

I did not forget my promise to return Thuy's hair clip. At my request, a friend delivered an envelope to Thuy at the Voice of Freedom station. Inside the envelope were the hair clip and a note inviting her to dinner to thank her for the good luck the little accessory had brought me.

Later, I went to the VOF station to see Tuat Hai and find out if Thuy had accepted my letter. As it turned out, she was at the desk beside his, busy typing. When I greeted her, she looked up, eyes wide open, then nodded and went back to her work. Feeling awkward, I turned and began to talk to my friend.

Another visitor walked in, and Tuat Hai introduced him to me. But before he could address Thuy, I suddenly blurted out, "This is Duong Vu Thanh Thuy!"

The visitor looked at me confused while Tuat Hai burst out laughing. Meanwhile, Thuy glared at me with her haunting black eyes, then quickly looked back down and went on with her typing.

Embarrassed, I followed Tuat Hai and his friend outside. Before leaving the station, I walked back in, went straight to Thuy's desk and asked if she had read my letter. She nodded but did not raise her eyes to me.

"Thank you for returning my hair clip," she said.

"Well, how about dinner? Will you come?"

She blushed but still did not lift her eyes from her work.

"Thank you for the invitation, but I don't know...I have so much work to do...."

Swallowing my pride, I said quickly, "I'll be at La Pagode Friday at six. If you're not there, I'll be back Saturday at the same time and stay there until...you show up!"

I spun around and left, my heart throbbing, a pathetic mixture of pain and longing.

Thuy did not appear on Friday. As I had promised, I went back to La Pagode on Saturday and waited. Just when I was about to leave, she walked in.

We talked for hours.

Nguyen Ngoc Binh
and the Deadly Ground

Soon after that, the press team once again climbed on board a helicopter headed for An Loc, now in its fourth week under siege. With four infantry divisions and squadrons of Soviet tanks, the NVA took cover in the dense rubber tree forests from which their anti-aircraft guns, SA-7 missile launchers, and machine guns fired endlessly on the city.

During the first two weeks, it was nearly impossible for aircraft to land in An Loc. Hundreds of wounded lay on the airstrip and landing zones waiting for evacuation. But those sites became the primary targets of enemy shelling. As soon as a plane or helicopter was heard approaching, the barrage would begin. Only rarely did a brave pilot manage to bring his craft down, but just long enough for the reinforcements to spill out before he had to take it back up. There was virtually no time to pick up the wounded.

Still, there were a few times a helicopter was able to hover just above the ground while those men who had the strength ran to grab onto the skids and climb inside as enemy fire forced the craft to rise. Those who got there a little later grabbed onto their comrades' legs. It was a horrific scene: the helicopter rising with a chain of wounded men dangling in the air with machine guns and mortars firing, and rockets flying past above the landing zone covered with smoke.

Photojournalist Tuat Hai captured the incredible scene, and his photograph appeared in the *Stars and Stripes*. Looking down from a helicopter, he witnessed another chopper with soldiers clinging to the skids, then several more men hanging on to them. As the aircraft rose, the force of the wind coupled with the movement of the plane caused one man to lose his grip and fall to the ground.

Helicopters flying low to avoid anti-aircraft guns were susceptible to small arms fire and even B-40 rockets manned by soldiers who tied themselves to the top of the rubber trees. That was what had happened to us the previous time we'd tried to get in. And it was the reason one of our colleagues died the next day.

Our team that day included Nguyen Manh Tien, Do Van My (Elephant My), and myself. We split up to ride different helicopters carrying supplies to An Loc. We sat on the floor with doors open on both sides. I was next to the door hanging onto the metal leg of a bench to secure myself against the force of the wind blowing inside. Nguyen Ngoc Binh, a cameraman for the Armed Forces Film Bureau, sat in the doorway of a chopper flying parallel to mine to get shots of supply drops around the city.

As his helicopter passed mine, our eyes met. He grinned and gave a mock salute. All of a sudden his aircraft plummeted down, spinning round and round, and then falling into the smoke below. The chopper had been hit from the ground, inadvertently shielding my plane from the gunfire. All eleven on board were presumed dead, as their bodies were missing.

More than a month later, on June 11, Elephant My, one of Binh's colleagues, was with an infantry unit on action in Tan Khai trying to reach An Loc by foot. On the way, they came upon the wreck of a helicopter with 11 decomposing bodies, none wearing dog tags for identification. The communists usually took fallen enemies' dog tags as war prizes. Elephant My recognized Binh by a camera he wore. He packed his friend's remains in a pair of ammo cases and sent them back to Saigon on an evac helicopter while he continued on to An Loc.

///

Finally, on June 13, two months after my helicopter had been shot down; I made it into An Loc. The commanders wanted to limit the number of reporters allowed in because of the danger. Women especially were not allowed. So only four of us—Nguyen Manh Tien of Radio Saigon, Anh Thuan of *Tien Tuyen* (Front Line), Gerard Hebert of Radio Canada, and myself for Armed Forces Radio—were taken with Captain Quy and reporter Tam Phong of the 5th Division press office on a flight to An Loc.

Left behind, Tuat Hai, standing next to Thuy, waved goodbye and wished us luck. I looked over at Thuy, the worry in her eyes making her forced smile appear more like a grimace.

We were on five helicopters carrying reinforcements into the city. The enemy's firepower was not as formidable as it had been two months earlier, so it was not until we landed that we encountered opposition. The entire team jumped out of the chopper and ran for the rubber trees where we threw ourselves into foxholes beside the LZ (landing zone).

As I raced for cover, my tape recorder flew off my shoulder and disappeared. After much searching, I found my indispensable cassette, but the machine was broken and unusable. I then ran to our designated assembly point by the plantation's gate, late and out of breath. Sweat mixed with the red dirt characteristic of the Binh Long soil covered my face and body, startling Nguyen Manh Tien, who thought I'd been hit and was severely bleeding.

The last jog into An Loc was only a little more than a kilometer, but we had to slow down, running for cover whenever we heard the whistling of incoming rounds. Many burned-out Soviet T-54 tanks lay scattered by the road. We passed a rise called the Hill of the Spirit of Death after hundreds of wounded men, trying to make their way to an evacuation point the month before, were slaughtered there by NVA shelling.

Due to the heavy bombardment, it was sometimes weeks before the dead could be buried. A terrible stench permeated the area, the peculiar smell of human corpses exposed to the sun.

The closer we got to the town, the greater the scene of devastation. The shelling spared not a square foot of ground, not one house or building left intact. Lampposts fell, broken in pieces and scattering, and electric wires everywhere. Parachutes from previous helicopter supply drops covered the street. Ironically, the only thing still standing in the ruined city was a statue of a soldier, untouched, after some 200,000 rounds had fallen on An Loc.

General Le Van Hung (1933-1975)

■ PHUC

General Le Van Hung, An Loc, June 1972.

My first meeting with Gen. Le Van Hung left a deep impression on me. The armed forces journalists, including Elephant My with his huge camera, Nguyen Manh Tien of Radio Saigon and myself, were led down into his bunker, which also served as the forward command post. Before my eyes could adjust to the dim light, I saw a figure from among those seated around the bunker rise to approach. Although he wore an olive-green T-shirt and no symbol of rank, I recognized Gen. Le Van Hung at once from photographs I'd seen. I even kept a picture of him in my wallet because I admired him so much.

Before then, I had become acquainted with Gen. Hung through some interviews over the military telephone from Lai Khe. Later he would tell me he knew my name from my radio broadcasts, including the one describing my abortive attempt to enter An Loc. Now he stepped right up and put his arm around me before I even had a chance to salute. The general had a gentle smile, though his face was thin and pale from days living underground.

The interview in the bunker was quite unlike any I had conducted before. Gen. Hung sat in front of his "operations desk," which consisted of ammo crates stacked on top of each other. There was only one lamp in the bunker emitting a dim light. I stood next to the general holding a tape recorder borrowed from Nguyen Manh Tien.

Gen. Hung described the battle situation in a soft but deep voice. He praised the soldiers at An Loc for their bravery and endurance under extreme conditions. Most of all, he told the people in the rear to rest assured, An Loc was standing firm and would prevail.

"While I am alive," he declared, "An Loc cannot be lost!"

I concluded the interview with a question that perhaps caught him off guard.

Duong Phuc (center) during an interview with Gen. Le Van Hung (left), An Loc, June 1972.

"General, is there anything you want to say to your family? Your wife must surely be listening to this report."

He smiled, apparently moved, but spoke succinctly, saying that he hoped his wife and children in Saigon were well and they should know that he was doing fine.

Given the conditions during those days, I wasn't able to transmit my report directly to the station, so I asked Gen. Hung if I could use his hotline. Then I played the tape recording over the phone so the interview could be aired on the Armed Forces Radio immediately afterward. Nguyen Manh Tien used the line to send his report to Radio Saigon and, even though the sound quality suffered from the makeshift transmission, the interview raised the spirits of the people in the capital. It was the first time they heard the general's voice on the airwaves since the siege began.

After that, I asked the general if we could conduct a brief interview outside the bunker so it could be filmed in the sunlight. When Gen. Hung balked, I suggested that the sight of him on film would do much to heighten public morale. He finally agreed but made sure everyone wore protective gear since the bombardment was still going on. He wore a helmet and a flak vest over his T-shirt. I followed him outside, telling Elephant My to make it short and sweet.

The interview outside the bunker was later sent back and broadcast over Saigon Television and shown across the country. The picture was not clear, due to the smoke from the shelling, but it was aired over and over and treated as a significant event. All Saigon newspapers printed the interview and Gen. Hung's photo.

That night, in the command bunker, Gen. Hung treated me to a cup of hot tea. While there, I overheard him talking to his wife on the telephone. She had probably heard the radio broadcast, as the general said, "How did I sound?"

That was the first, and the last time I met Gen. Hung.

Those Who Fought to the End

During the desperate time at An Loc, Gen. Hung worked day and night. He kept in constant contact with all branches of the army to remain up to date on the military and civilian situations, as well as the enemy's position around the city. He and his officers moved like wraiths in the darkness of the bunkers.

It was quite hot underground, and most of the men wore only T-shirts or were stripped to the waist. But the weight of their task did not dull the courage in their faces, which had turned sallow from lack of sunlight. They were all on edge, ready for a protracted fight against attack or shelling by the NVA.

In a meeting with the press, Gen. Hung, in his ordinary and straightforward manner, expressed concern for both soldiers and civilians, agonizing about the adversity suffered by the people of An Loc caught in the middle of the battle. He was effusive in his praise for the fighting spirit of the soldiers, who day and night risked their lives to hold onto the city and boasted of the each of the units, from the local and popular forces to the airborne troops and Rangers that participated in the city's defense.

When asked about his personal situation or feelings, Gen. Hung brushed aside the question. He described instead the courage and extraordinary devotion his officers displayed in the most basic tasks, such as carrying water to their men or siphoning gas from a broken vehicle to operate a generator to keep contact between An Loc and the outside. To him, these small and undistinguished acts performed under constant bombardment could have cost lives but preserved the life of the city in its time of need.

Duong Phuc, left, and an unidentified soldier at an An Loc battlefield, June 1972.

During the several days we, reporters, were at An Loc, the general let us sleep in his private bunker, which he never seemed to use. When he finally needed rest, he caught a nap on the operations table or in a canvas chair.

I stuck next to Nguyen Manh Tien to use his tape recorder. When the shelling was too intense for us to leave the bunker, we would sit and chat with the soldiers. Once the fighting died down, we crawled to another shelter to see if we could get a story there.

Obtaining clean water was a challenge, so on those few days, we did not wash. Gen. Hung reminded us to not sweat over small things. Maybe bathing could wait, but not brushing our teeth or washing our faces. On the second day, I asked for a small cap-full of water, just enough for the three reporters to clean our teeth and scrub our faces.

Conditions regulated our actions. When the bombs started falling, we took shelter in the bunkers like ghosts. But when the shelling stopped, and the skies were eerily silent, everyone popped out of their holes like ants leaving their nest and ran from one trench to another. When the next shelling began, all activity ceased.

As soon as there was a lull, Tien and I immediately launched ourselves out of the bunker and ran to another one to talk to the soldiers. We only had a few seconds to change places before the air ripped with the whistle of incoming rounds. When that started, we dropped into the nearest hole.

Airborne Commandos: Dying for Their Country

Although Gen. Hung had ordered us to wear protective gear when we stepped outside for the interview, after that I realized that I could move faster if I weren't weighted down with a flak vest, helmet, or backpack.

In talking with the soldiers, I heard many stories of unbelievable cruelty that had occurred at An Loc. For example, the town's hospital and the church received the most bombardment from the communists. The enemy deliberately targeted places where people congregated to gain the maximum number of casualties and cause confusion and loss of morale among the civilians and soldiers.

I heard of how in the An Loc hospital hundreds were killed at one time. The victims were not just wounded soldiers but also people from the town who had come there for safety, trusting that international conventions would spare a place marked with a red cross. But rules and laws meant nothing to the communists, who disdained the values of the humanitarian world. Countless civilians died on April 15 when the NVA shelled the church where a thousand people had gone for protection and to pray for peace during the bombing.

President Thieu (right), Gen. Le Van Hung (center), and Gen. Cao Van Vien (left) during a visit to An Loc, 1972. Photo: ARVN archive.

While I was there, I had the opportunity to witness a different kind of event. The press corps came to the headquarters of the 8th Infantry regiment at a ruined house on the road called Twilight Highway. At that time, Col. Mach Van Truong, the regiment commander, promoted a lieutenant to the rank of captain for leading a battalion that raised the flag on a captured hill.

But the scene that most moved me at An Loc was that of the Red Beret Airborne Commandos going out under the raining artillery fire to collect bricks to build a wall for the Commando cemetery.

During the two months of fighting, the number of dead on both sides was so high there was no time to bury them all[25]. Corpses lay everywhere, and few were left in peace as continued bombing tore them up on the open road. Even the shallow graves that had been hastily dug were blasted apart. Still, the Commandos managed to construct a serviceable cemetery in which to bury their comrades right beside the ruined Binh Long market. In the surreal atmosphere of a dead city, amid the exploding bombs, the deep feeling of comrades-in-arms expressed by the living for the dead brought tears to my eyes as I read the handwritten lines on a placard planted at the graveyard:

A makeshift graveyard for ARVN's 81st Airborne Commando Battalion, An Loc. (1972)

At An Loc, History Records Their Brave Deeds,
Airborne Commandos Who Lay Down for Their Country

We later learned that these verses were from a Miss Pha, a young teacher of Binh Long who lost all her family to the battle. She suffered a piece of shrapnel to her leg and was rescued by the Commandos, who took her to the hospital for treatment. One day, as she watched the Red

---

[25] Casualties from both fighting sides at An Loc were estimated at 10,000 deaths with nearly 90 tanks destroyed and 30 aircrafts lost.

Berets going from grave to grave during the shelling to inscribe the names of their fallen comrades, touched, she composed these lines and offered them to the Commandos in gratitude for saving her life. After the battle, posters carried these verses circulated throughout South Vietnam. They became a source of pride for all Airborne Commandos.

Despite the devastation, the seemingly certain loss of An Loc turned to victory, thanks to the U.S. air support and the heroic perseverance of Gen. Le Van Hung and the 7,500 defenders, who had withstood 68 days of constant bombardment and nonstop attacks by 35,470 North Vietnamese troops.[26]

Summer Ablaze: Quang Tri, 1972

In June of 1972, I arrived at the front in Central Vietnam along with Thuy and some other reporters. We were on Highway 1, a major thoroughfare that runs the length of the country. In more peaceful times, this road, straddled by sand and dry grass like a desert, enjoyed bustling traffic since it connected Quang Tri city with Hue. It was on a nine-kilometer stretch there that occurred one of the most horrific incidents of the war.

This time the highway was covered not with busy commuters traveling by motorized vehicle, bicycle, and foot but with thousands of corpses rotting in the sun. They were primarily citizens of Quang Tri who had been fleeing the advance of the North Vietnamese Army during the massive spring offensive.

As at An Loc, the communists began their attack on Quang Tri at the end of March with ferocious artillery barrages and tank assaults aimed at isolating the ARVN in the city. They accomplished this with the unremitting bombing that lasted for days.

When it appeared Quang Tri was about to fall, local authorities ordered an evacuation of the citizenry to Hue, in the hope of sparing the city from being destroyed and lives saved. The fleeing of tens of thousands of people created a snake-like procession southward along

---

[26] Gen. Le Van Hung took his own life on April 30, 1975, after President Duong Van Minh surrendered to the Communists and the NVA was about to seize the IV Corps, where Gen. Hung was the Deputy Corps Commander.

Highway 1. Exposed and defenseless, they became an easy target for enemy artillery concealed less than 7 miles on the forested mountains to the west.

An essential component of traditional Vietnamese culture is the people's loyalty to the land of their ancestors, preserving their fields and farms and maintaining family graves. Before 1954, when the communists took control of the North, there was never a time in Vietnamese history when large numbers of people abandoned their native villages and towns. From that time on, wherever the communists went, the citizens of that place fled.

The communists were not hesitant to fire directly into refugees, even unarmed civilians. The soldiers among the mass of people fleeing Quang Tri were only a small number to guide the thousands of civilians—including women, children, the elderly, and the wounded—to safety.

Some 5,000 people died in the massacre; their bodies spread across the highway.

The Highway of Terror

By the time Thuy and I reached the area, the bodies had been exposed to the elements for nearly two months. Hot winds carried the overpowering reek all over. We were stunned, unable to comprehend how so many people could have died at one time in so large an area. Observing the victims, I noticed that most of the bodies were riddled with thousands of tiny pieces of steel. One exploding cluster bomb emitted sharp pellets in all directions with such force and speed that they could penetrate the wall of an armored vehicle. This type of weapon dropped everyone around so fast it caught them in whatever action they were performing at the time. We had never seen anything like it.

"Oh, God!" Thuy cried. "They never had a chance!"

I felt my heart suddenly seize. Thuy quickly made the sign of the cross, then turned her head and vomited. Near where I was standing I saw a mother still holding onto a baby at her breast. Both mother and child lay motionless beside the highway like a pair of gray puppets on a grotesque stage.

The scene was one of the unimaginable horrors. Bodies everywhere. Scraps of clothing and personal items. Cars, motor scooters, bicycles, even ox carts. Carrying poles, bags ripped apart, their contents strewn every which way. Every type of vehicle, from military personnel carriers, Jeeps, and medical service trucks to passenger buses and private cars, all riddled with holes.

We approached one ambulance and looked inside the back door blown open in the hot wind from the west. There we saw bodies still lying on stretchers. The dried and blackened corpses of the rescue workers sat slumped on either side of the vehicle, their armbands flapping in the breeze looking from a distance like hands waving to us.

The victims lay on the road in shreds of clothing. Some lay prone, others on their backs with their faces to the sky. Some bodies curled up as if trying to escape the bombing. Two children nestled in their mother's arms. A child lay across the back of its father sprawling face down on the ground, the child's arms still clinging to the father's neck. Most of the corpses were dried and purple, like something you'd see in a museum for Egyptian mummies.

There were sections of the highway so packed with bodies that there was no room to put one's foot. Wiping off her tears, Thuy gingerly made her way one step at a time. We used sticks to lift and gently push aside pieces of clothing to make sure we didn't trample on any corpses that had dried up after months in the sun. The prodding of our sticks stirred up flies and insects from the blackened bodies. Inside a bus wholly covered with holes from projectiles, the passengers sat sagging in their seats, apparently all killed instantly.

The still air brought a shiver to us. There was only the oppressive stench. Not a sound, not a bird singing or insect chirping. We unconsciously held our breaths as if our respiration might disturb the souls of the innocent victims. The only noise was that of tarp covers flapping in the hot wind, sounding like the background of a horror movie.

Although I was a seasoned war correspondent and had seen the full range of the effects of violent force, I still could not understand why the communists so ruthlessly fired into decent, ordinary people fleeing down the road. Surely they were aware these were only refugees. Yet they fired into them like madmen with their eyes closed. Even into women and children.

This was indeed more appalling than anything I had imagined the communists would do. Before this, I had harbored a ray a hope (albeit a fragile one) that one day the two sides would seek a way to resolve their differences and put an end to this terrible war. But after witnessing this scene, I recognized the brutal, undeniable truth that the communists were fanatics without a bit of conscience. How could anyone treat others like that? How could I accept that human beings could murder ordinary, innocent people so atrociously?

The terrifying thought came to me: *This war must end. There's been too much misery for too long. The communists must be wiped out.* As I saw it, my homeland and my people could no longer endure more horrible killing and dying caused by people who followed this thing they called "communism."

I looked over to Thuy, whose eyes brimmed with tears. She stood by each body for a long time, as if saying a prayer for the person's soul and straining to share with me her impression of the victim's story before his or her death.

As we walked this road the newspapers would dub the "Highway of Terror," we kept looking at each other as if to reassure ourselves that this was not some crazed nightmare and we were still alive. Even though Thuy and I did not know enough about each other to express intimacies, we both recognized the profound sorrow that we shared. And the temporary physical pain that turned into an intense emotion became a mission of the heart, urging us to throw ourselves harder into our work in the hope that somehow it might bring about an end to the cruel and senseless killing.

President Thieu (right) during a visit to Quang Tri front, 1972. From left, Gens. Ngo Quang Truong, Cao Van Vien, and Bui The Lan. Photo: ARVN archive.

In one way, this experience helped those in the media join together on a mission to expose the true face of the communists for our respective audiences. But that was just an external aspect. On a deeper level, each of us took in the profound sorrow differently. And these feelings continued to haunt those reporters of South Vietnam who were present on the Highway of Terror that summer in 1972.

War Correspondents:
Living and Dying in Their Profession

The responsibility of heading a team of journalists from television, radio, film, print, and photography under the military Psywar Department often fell on me. Although I was the senior-ranking officer, in reality, we were all on our own, only providing mutual support when necessary. Many of the foreign press corps joined us when traveling by themselves could be dangerous due to the fighting and road mines.

Among our group was 1st Sgt. Tran Van Nghia, a cameraman for Armed Forces Television and someone I held dear. He was older than me, married with eight children, but he loved to go out and film the front. With his cheerful, energetic personality, everyone liked him. He did have the drive to be the first person on the scene, and we often had to pull him back to stay with the pack. But soon he was off again, running out front to get the right spot to shoot his film.

Once we were on assignment when, suddenly, we heard a burst of AK fire. We all hit the dirt. I watched Nghia fall to the ground, his camera flung to the side. As our soldiers provided cover, we ran up to our friend. He laid face-up on the dry earth, his body marked with several gunshot wounds, his clothes covered with blood. His film camera was still rolling. Also killed were two correspondents for ABC Television: Terry Khoo and Sam Kai Faye. Faye had run up to help Nghia when he was shot down.

The day before, three correspondents, including one Vietnamese, were killed while accompanying the Marines in Phong Dien. Nguyen Thanh Liem of the Armed Forces Television was shot in the chest.

Another war casualty, who was a close friend of ours, was Gérard Hébert of the Canadian Broadcasting Company (CBC). He accompanied us to Quang Tri during the early days of the battle, following the Vietnamese Airborne troops, whom he much admired, declaring that they "always fought like lions."

Hébert was a university professor with the air of a philosopher, poised and gentle. He preferred to follow the Vietnamese reporters to gather accurate information about the Vietnamese armed forces to show the Western press that they were mistreating our soldiers. He liked to tease me by speaking about me in French to Thuy.

Gérard Hébert (1932-1972).

Then he left us and the Airborne to go with the Marines first into Quang Tri. On July 22 we heard the sad news that rocket fire had killed him.

I often wondered why so many of my colleagues died in the field, and I remained untouched. Many a time death came so near I could feel its breath on my face. Once, for instance, I was talking with a soldier when he suddenly collapsed with a bullet in him as I stood right beside him, stunned.

Even as I mourned the loss of my friends and colleagues, I firmly believed one day the war would end, and I was confident I would be alive to see it. The others laughed at what they considered my inordinate self-confidence, but I still held to my belief. As more and more war reporters died, the families of many of my colleagues begged them to remain in Saigon, where it was safe. But most interpreted their survival as a responsibility, a duty to keep working in place of their fallen comrades.

Once, a team of nine reporters, including Thuy and myself, were crowded into a Jeep I'd borrowed from an airborne commander. Coming off a short road, we found ourselves on a dirt lane strewn with debris and the carcasses of shattered vehicles. Everything suddenly became so still that even our boisterous conversations ceased. We all looked around warily.

We'd gone about 200 meters when Le Thiep of *Chinh Luan Daily* called, "Hey, look over there, you guys. That's a mine, isn't it?"

Nguyen Tuyen of Radio Saigon leaned out and gazed ahead, then cried out, "Mines! Stop the car, Phuc! The road is full of them!"

I slammed on the brakes, and the Jeep skidded to a stop, throwing everybody forward. Just then I saw the metal spikes of antitank mines planted in the road all around where we had stopped. Terrified, everyone sat perfectly still, afraid to set foot on the ground.

Our small group of Vietnamese war correspondents who shared life and death in the Summer of 1972 at An Loc and Quang Tri battlefields

Nguyen Tuyen
Radio Saigon

Vu Anh
Radio Saigon

Nguyen Manh Tien
Radio Saigon

Le Thiep
Chinh Luan Daily

Duong Phuc
Arm Force Radio

Vu Thanh Thuy
The Voice of Freedom

We were bold, experienced war correspondents, famous for our courage. Now, in only a brief moment, we'd become petrified with fear. Sweat pouring down my face, my heart pounding, my body stiff, I gripped the steering wheel tight in my hands, then slowly, carefully backed up, straining to follow in the tire tracks I had just made.

The others sat tensed, looking out and warning me with a shout if I edged off the tracks. From the corner of my eye, I saw Thuy make the sign of the cross and close her eyes in silent prayer, expecting that at any time there would come an explosion ending our lives. Although the distance I traveled was short, the time it took seemed an eternity.

Finally, thank God, I got us back on the main road. After I turned the Jeep around, I killed the engine, jumped out and stood gasping for breath. The others got out and sat down on the road. Thuy stood next to the vehicle, wiping tears from her face. None of us uttered a single word.

Death had passed by so very close, closer than ever, and the possibility was so real that I became even more convinced of the responsibility of those who survived to carry on for their fallen comrades. It was the reason we were still alive.

The Lost Child of Mai Linh Village

One time I followed the ARVN into a devastated hamlet in Mai Linh village. The village was totally abandoned, there was no one to be seen. I slipped inside some of the ruined houses to photograph villagers' personal belongings scattered among the ruins.

In one house whose roof had collapsed, I spied a bomb shelter in the corner, covered with an old board and a few dried palm fronds. I pushed the board aside and bent down to look inside.

Hearing a strange noise, I stood up, startled to see a girl of about six or seven sitting huddled at the bottom of the shelter. I was shocked at the sight of the frail little child, mere skin, and bones, her clothes in rags, her face and body covered with dirt, looking at first like a messy, broken puppet.

I approached her cautiously. She looked up at me with wide-open vacant eyes, all the while hugging her knees. She sat amidst bottles and filthy plastic bags that she had probably picked up somewhere. I noticed a small bunch of sweet potatoes with their roots still covered in dirt lying by her feet, one of them with teeth marks on it. I bent down to give her some dry rations. She didn't take them but only stared at me.

Suddenly she reached up and grabbed my ankle. I tried to sit down beside her, but she would not let go of my leg. I guessed she must have lost her parents in the assault, or else she'd become lost when the others ran away and had been wandering the village by herself. All during the constant shelling, this innocent child had been left frightfully alone in this place of devastation.

Overcome with pity, I reached down to pick her up. She put out her bony arms and held my neck tightly. Her head fell on my shoulder. A strange feeling flooded my heart as I tried to remain rational and figure out what I was going to do with this little girl, whom I called En, meaning Swallow.

As I carried her outside, a captain ran up and began to question her. She looked at him wordlessly and her grip on my neck tightened. I wondered if her ears had been damaged by the bombing or perhaps by lack of nutrition.

Just then Thuy appeared. I handed the girl to her and was surprised when Swallow reached out for her. It made me want to cry, and suddenly the thought occurred to me that I should take the girl and adopt her. I pictured Thuy as the perfect mother for this pitiful creature, to compensate for her loss and suffering.

I brought up the idea with Thuy. After thinking it over, with the little girl still in her arms nibbling at a biscuit, she gently brought me back to reality. Being single and always on the move, I was hardly able to take care of a little girl who had suffered emotional trauma and had gone so long without proper nourishment. She noted that the girl's parents or relatives were probably searching for her and the best thing would be to reunite Swallow with her family. I tried awkwardly to defend my position but came to see that my raw human emotions were no match for stark truth.

We told the captain we wanted to take the girl with us to Hue. There we'd deliver her to a social welfare office connected to a temporary camp for the refugees from Quang Tri. The captain insisted on handing her to someone from the village to help her find her family.

I was confused by my feeling. A child had so powerfully moved me. At the same time, I was disconcerted by the thought that this strange emotion could unexpectedly intrude on my job and my ability to reason.

Chapter 11

Love, War, and Reportage

The Power of Love

■ THUY

By the time Phuc and I started working together, accompanying the Airborne troops in the recapture of Quang Tri city in June of 1972, my complicated feelings for him were overwhelmed by what I had witnessed on the Highway of Terror. Before that, my reason had urged me to be wary of him because of the extreme differences in our personalities. At the same time, however, I found those same differences powerfully attractive.

The most significant difference between us was that Phuc acted from the gut whereas I thought things through. Once I watched as Phuc called the Psywar Department to report the death of cameraman Tran Van Nghia. I don't know what the person on the other end of the line said, but Phuc shouted into the phone, "Colonel, one of your boys dies, and you don't ask how, but you're worried about whether he broke the camera you just spent two million on?"

He slammed down the phone. I was frightened. I knew he cared about Sgt. Nghia and was hurt by his friend's death, but still, the man he was talking to was a colonel, his superior officer. I knew that in the military, insubordination could have unfortunate consequences. Luckily the colonel let it go.

On another occasion, Lieutenant Gen. Tran Van Trung, director general of Political Warfare Department, met with a dozen military correspondents including Phuc and me in Hue. The general gave Phuc

200,000 *dong* to "nourish you all." Phuc immediately divided the money among the ten others, taking nothing for him or me. Regardless, he followed the general's advice and treated us all to a big dinner that night at a restaurant in Hue. When he did not have enough money to pay the bill, he asked me to chip in.

Similar actions on his part, such as his impulsive interest in adopting little Swallow, performed in overzealous idealism, made me fear that a future relationship would be rocky. These very acts nevertheless moved me and made me admire his generosity and concern for others. And so I was pulled between the head and the heart. My head told me to keep my eyes open for the storms that awaited me in a relationship, but my heart left me extremely attracted to a man who could shut his eyes and follow what was inside him.

Another illogical aspect of our relationship arose from the horror of the Quang Tri front. I found myself gradually persuaded to let the emotion and peculiar romance of our love counterbalance the death and destruction that surrounded us. Thus, our feelings for each other increased at the same rate as our pain from the war and our passion for our work.

As a woman who was always on guard in my interactions with men, I could see that Phuc was impetuous, abrupt, and restless. He was charming yet self-centered, uninterested in

Phuc at the An Loc frontline, 1972.

others' opinions yet sensitive, hot-tempered yet romantic. Unlike most men who conduct themselves according to customs and social rules, Phuc was difficult to gauge. I often felt I was on an uncertain ground with him, like one in the presence of a tiger who was acting like a kitten.

Even though I was often cautious in the face of his unpredictability, I had to admit that I looked forward to being with him. It felt strange, even exciting, to have met someone who not only was unlike anyone I had known but who tried to break others' habits of thought. Many people scorned Phuc for being overly frank and having no use for social niceties. He talked straightforwardly and always said what was in his heart. I saw this as a positive trait in which I was lacking: I would give my opinion on a subject only after much thought and effort to avoid confronting others.

Phuc behaved differently from other men but not because he deliberately tried to be contrary. He expressed whatever was in his mind and didn't care what others thought about it or him. I found myself more and more drawn to his strange characteristics.

In the midst of the carnage littering the Highway of Terror, Phuc was still able to raise his voice and sing a soft, mournful song, as if sending off the souls of those who died unjustly and, too, to express the love for me that stirred inside him. While riding with a team of airborne troops, he disappeared into a field and returned holding an armful of yellow wildflowers. On another occasion, I returned to my room in Hue after a day of emotional interviews with survivors of the massacre when I discovered that the place had been invaded. There on the desk was a single yellow flower in a cup of water with a scrawled note, unsigned, that simply said, "Miss you badly!"

The Vietnamese War Correspondents Association

According to modern Vietnamese moral propriety, when a couple goes out on a date they are to be accompanied by chaperones from both sides. And so, some of our colleagues joined Phuc and me when we went to eat at a noodle soup restaurant on the Huong (Perfume) River in Hue. While Phuc and I could enjoy dinner in a romantic setting, our friends had an opportunity to relax and celebrate with us, and to discuss setting up a society of war journalists.

By the time we finished dinner, the Vietnamese War Correspondents Association had been formed, with Pham Huan of *Dieu Hau* as chairman. Among the other officers, Phuc became vice chair of external affairs, and I treasurer. The first members were all reporters who had been present on the Quang Tri front.

Phuc and I spent most of the time deepening our relationship without being too showy in front of our friends. Despite the awkwardness of the situation, our feelings for each other grew more refined, to the point that later on, upon entering a room we could sense each other's presence without actually seeing or hearing the other.

Before this, each did his or her own thing. We went out on assignments for our respective radio stations, and even though we followed the same missions and went after the same stories, there was still a bit of competition between us.

Phuc usually liked to work alone without any interference from others. Now he asked me to come along with him. We went back and forth across Highway 1 from Hue to Quang Tri so often that the road became a bridge connecting us with the war and with each other.

I never missed one of Phuc's reports, turning into a faithful listener and also a penetrating critic. For his part, he was not shy about sharing his professional opinions about my work. He felt I was too meek, too diplomatic when I should have been more direct. In time we influenced each other in how we performed our job. Listeners said that Phuc's reports were becoming gentler, less abrasive and hasty. Meanwhile, my stories were getting stronger, my observations sharper, and my positions more daring.

Thuy, during an interview with Gen. Bui The Lan, commander of the ARVN's Marines, at the front when the Marines retook the Citadel of Quang Tri, September 16, 1972. Photo: Bui The Lan's archive.

The Vietnamese Radio Stations

■ PHUC

In South Vietnam, the leading communication organizations were based in Saigon, and their offices were all located near one another.

Radio Saigon, founded in 1950, attracted many artists. During the 1960s and '70s radio was the primary means of popularizing new music, with performers coming to the studio to record their songs for later airplay. I learned much from the reporters and commentators during my years at Radio Saigon before I was called up for service.

The Psywar Bureau also drew in artists within the military for Armed Forces Radio. From 1964, one of its most beloved programs was "Da Lan, Little Sister on the Home Front," whose sweet voice comforted the soldiers far from their families. Other popular programs included "Songs for the Men at the Front Lines" by musician Manh Phat and "Melodies Old and New" by Duong Thieu Tuoc. The News Department, where I worked, included several well-known writers.

Then there were the Armed Forces Television and Film stations, and the Press Office. While not a military organ, the Press Office brought in reporters who specialized in covering the war. The Office of Arts and Letters, located next door to the radio station, served as a gathering place for famous artists of the South.

Also nearby was the editorial office of *Tien Tuyen* (Front Line) newspaper. Its staff included poets and novelists whose work constituted the foundation of the South's romantic literature up to 1975, a genre steeped in times of social disorder.

Around the corner from Radio Saigon and Armed Forces Radio was a building that few people in the South knew about. Known only as "Number 7," the mysterious location was home to four radio stations that broadcast across the 17th parallel into North Vietnam, including the Voice of Freedom (VOF).

I didn't work with any of the stations at Number 7, but on returning to Saigon after the Lower Laos operation, I frequented the friendly and conveniently located newsroom of the VOF to visit with some of my colleagues. The VOF held a special attraction for me since that was where someone with striking eyes could steal my heart with just a silent glance.

Journalists' Mission, Professional Competition

■ THUY

Inside Number 7, the largest of the four stations was the Voice of Freedom, directed by Lt. Col. Vu Quang Ninh from 1964 until the fall of South Vietnam. Col. Ninh was entirely devoted to his job and used to say, "Radio broadcasting has worked its way into my blood and become a public duty. Radio is my life; I can't do without it." As a refugee after the war, Vu Quang Ninh would create Little Saigon Radio in Orange County, California, the first Vietnamese broadcasting station in the U.S., where he served as president from 1993 until his death in 2013.

The VOF broadcast from its main station to a relay on the island of Con Te not far from Hue. From there, the radio waves beamed into North Vietnam where they could be heard clearly all the way to the border with China. Funded by the United States military, VOF was intended to reach the general population and soldiers of the North as part of the Psywar effort. In 1972, the South Vietnamese Army took over the VOF, which became a part of the Psywar Bureau.

The second station at Number 7 was Sacred Sword Patriot, first directed by Col. Nguyen Van Nam and funded through the U.S. embassy. It was a propaganda arm that employed former communist officers who rallied to the South. In coordination with Southern experts, it produced programs aimed at the cadres and people of the North. Most famous was its program "Born in the North, Died in the South," which announced the names of Northern soldiers who had perished or were wounded or imprisoned in the South. Communist authorities concealed this type of information from families to prevent unrest.

The third station was Red Flag. It used announcers with thick Northern accents, most of whom were cadres who had come over to our side and imitated an actual communist broadcast in phraseology and content. The aim was to convince the people of the North that it was a neutral station even as it described the freedom and rights enjoyed by the people of the South so listeners could compare this information to the oppression they faced under the communists.

The last station at Number 7 was Mother Vietnam, started by the Americans after the transfer of the VOF to the South Vietnamese. This station broadcast light artistic programs and pleasant stories. The most notable show was "Mai Lan," which broadcast directly to the people in the North.

I worked for Voice of Freedom. Its mission was to send messages of freedom and democracy to the people living under the communist regime whose only official source of information was government-generated propaganda, to help them see the differences between the way of life in the North and that of the South.

The North's propaganda machine consistently declared that the communists were "liberating the villagers of the South from foreign imperialist aggression." Meanwhile, the VOF presented stories of people who fled their homes and fields, risking death to escape areas captured by the communists, or of communist soldiers killing innocent people, as at An Loc and Quang Tri.

While the communists promised a "paradise" of freedom and plenty, we showed that the reality was completely different. We used the testimony of military cadres who rallied to the South describing the quality of life they found there as compared to the poverty and oppression they had left.

After being transferred to the Political Warfare Department, the VOF received complete support from Armed Forces Radio. Phuc and I strove to report the truth to both rear areas of the war; sometimes we broadcast a joint-report on both stations' airwaves.

While Phuc was embedded with the troops and took part as a soldier, without carrying a gun but a tape recorder and a microphone, I often flew to the front in helicopters with the commanders. By day I might ride an armored personnel carrier or leap from a helicopter into the battlefield, but at night I returned to Saigon to write my stories.

My goal was to bring the voice of the soldiers and people of the South to listeners in the North. In the arenas of politics and war, the line between us was clear; the enemy was despicable. But when you heard the voice of a wounded soldier, weak and shaking, any mother would weep, and any father would be moved, regardless of what side they were on.

That was the reaction we aimed for, and that shared purpose made us partners in idealism. Phuc told the facts, and I described the feelings of the subjects in our stories. In this way, we continued to strengthen our love through our professional relationship.

Since we were in the same profession, Phuc and I sometimes felt pressure from our superiors and colleagues to compete with each other. And, too, we were both passionate about our work and wanted to obtain the maximum results. As a woman, I sometimes enjoyed an advantage in gaining access to a story. On the other hand, my achievements were not given the same recognition in a male-dominated society and profession.

When I received the Silver Star for Valor in 1971, for instance, some of my Vietnamese colleagues protested, using the excuse that I was too young for such an honor.

In 1971, I submitted a story for the national award for best war reportage. The winner that year was Captain Phan Nhat Nam for his story "Tren Dinh Charlie" ("At the Top of Charlie") describing the battle for Charlie Hill. Second place went to marine captain Huynh Van Phu for "Tren Chien Truong Gioi Tuyen" ("On Different Sides of the Battlefield"). I received a third place for "Mot Ngay Cho Mat Tran" ("One Day for the Frontline") on the unsung heroes of the Cambodia operation. At the awards reception, one of the judges was surprised to find out that I was a woman. He'd thought the author of the story was a man who used a female name to get attention. "I didn't think a woman could know so much about the battlefield," he said.

In 1974, broadcast reporters were sent to a journalism training course, at the conclusion of which they had to write a report for class review. My story on "War Correspondents" earned praise but also ridicule from some of my colleagues, who said I had received help from Phuc. The unfair accusation stung.

The truth was that Phuc and I never discussed how to get stories, nor did we collaborate. We were both proud of our own ideas and methods. So while we might criticize each other's work, we didn't ask for help, especially in reporting or writing our individual pieces.

The 11th Airborne Battalion: Revived from the Dead

■ THUY

The first person to talk to Phuc and me about the 11th Airborne Battalion with fervor and pride was Col. Tran Quoc Lich, commander of the 2nd Brigade. We were seated in the airborne command bunker inside a ruined church by the My Chanh River. With shells exploding all around outside, the colonel spoke with us while simultaneously signing a stack of papers on his lap.

"After Col. Nguyen Dinh Bao died[27], the battalion nearly fell

---

[27] The story of the ARVN's 11th airborne battalion became well known in South Vietnam with its heroic commander, Colonel Nguyen Dinh Bao. The battalion went in with 451 paratroopers and after two weeks of ferocious battle, Col. Bao and his men had held on and all fought to their deaths, rather than surrender.

apart, and no one had confidence in it like before. But I'd like to tell you that I always had faith in the 11th and always put it at the head of the action. One way or another it would get back its old military bearing. That's because it's a unit with a solid tradition and it's made up of soldiers who are young, talented, and enthusiastic."

He repeated the word "young" for emphasis, going so far as to write it on Phuc's knee with his pen.

Later I asked Phuc about the colonel's surprising behavior.

"What is it about the 11th Battalion that makes him so excited?"

"Since the battle for Charlie Hill," he replied, "I haven't had a chance to keep up with this battalion. Before that, it was as famous as any other."

I recalled the face of Col. Bao on the large posters displayed at traffic circles in Saigon to honor him after the fatal battle and motivate the soldiers. His expression looked strangely sad as if foreshadowing his fate.

In the days that followed, I kept thinking about the 11th Airborne Battalion and the sorrowful face of Col. Bao, as well as Col. Lich's animated praise for the unit.

On July 5, 1972, we crossed a two-kilometer stretch of the Highway of Terror covered with burned-out vehicles and corpses lying in the sun before arriving at the base camp of the 11th. It was in a bombed-out hamlet some nine kilometers from Quang Tri city. Physically and mentally drained from the long trudge through the terrible scene of death and destruction, I forgot all about the battalion and Col. Lich's high praise.

After our interview with Major Le Van Me, the battalion chief, I searched among the rubble for a place to sit and rest. All at once the major blurted out, "Those foreigners are coming! I'd like to bar them from getting here."

I looked up in surprise. Here and there on the highway, I spotted maybe ten foreign correspondents—clumsy, hulking figures in helmets and flak vests, weighted down with photo and film cameras and dangling water cans—lumbering toward us.

"I really hate those guys," the major snorted. "When there's a battle I'd like to see those wise guys come and find out for themselves how our soldiers fight and maybe they'll stop talking nonsense."

I was shocked to hear such a rough talk from a young battalion chief. Major Me was tall and thin and looked more like a rebellious college student than a soldier with his unmarked cap turned sideways on his head. His face was indifferent even as his mouth spewed such vehement language.

Curious, I asked the battalion doctor about him. The doctor was a big man with an amiable face.

"It's because the foreign press gets it all wrong!" he laughed. "We're at one place and they'll report we're at another. They never go along with our men to see what we do, but they seem to specialize in making statements without verifying them. They don't think much of the ARVN."

I approached Major Me and related to him what Col. Lich had told us. He chuckled quietly. His gentle and unaffected smile contrasted sharply with his previous grouchy "rebellious" face. Then he introduced me to his men.

"That major over there who's so young and quiet—'cause he's shy—sitting daydreaming is my deputy commander, Maj. Thanh," Major Me said. "The captain with the ruddy pretty-boy face shouting into the radio is the operations officer, Capt. Tam. The lieutenant with the bristly hair and beard sitting there dozing is our gunny, who has a reputation as a hooligan. And the doctor with the big mouth and the fattest guy in the battalion needs no introduction, since everybody in Airborne, as well as the Medical Corps, knows To Pham Lieu."

After that, major Me sat down and chatted with us, as friendly and cultured as he could be. Here I saw two faces of the young battalion chief: witty and likable when relaxed, but when he bent over the map with his staff to discuss strategy, his face hardened, and his voice turned cold as ice.

In the days that followed, the 11th Airborne remained about one kilometer from Quang Tri to allow the 6th Battalion to enter the old city first. This must have hurt Major Me and the whole battalion, as they lost a chance to show the public that they had in fact "come back to life." The correspondents, however, enjoyed the break and the opportunity to gather the full story.

Since then, hardly a day went by when we did not stop by the battalion to inquire about the situation, drink cold tea from Major Me's canteen, listen to Capt. Tam's report or swap jokes with Dr. Lieu. Gradually, all rules of etiquette, posturing, and caution fell by the wayside, and the 11th Battalion became the best "lunch stop" for the Vietnamese media.

For us, the meals were a treat, especially on the days when the battalion received its supplies. After a morning of wearisome slogging, we joined the obstinate members of the unit to eat and shoot the breeze while shells exploded around us. We shared our candy and fruits, gave up our chairs, and tore newspapers into individual pages, so everyone had a chance to read. I offered them my little radio so they could get the news from the city.

One morning, as soon as he saw me, Major Me declared, "Every time you come it seems we don't get bombed, or at least not much. But once you leave, or if you don't come, we get pounded!"

His casual comment touched me deeply. I'm not one who easily falls for a man's flowery words, especially when they come from one as garrulous as Major Me. But in the midst of the "smoke and fire" of war, I couldn't help but be moved to see that I had become a lucky mascot to the heroic soldiers risking their lives here.

That afternoon, when we returned from the ruins of downtown Quang Tri, I was shocked to hear Capt. Tam shouting my name into his radio. Apparently, Major Me was giving me the most wonderful gift. Across the globe, it was common practice to use a woman's name when calling troops about to enter battle. The commanders of smaller units usually used the name of a wife, daughter, girlfriend, or well-known actress or singer. But was there ever a young woman who was right there at the front among the armored carriers and artillery, with guns firing and bombs falling, who heard her own name called by a unit that she could see with her own eyes as it fought a life-and-death struggle?

I was choked up and lost my tough exterior. Instead, I was a little girl flustered by this unexpected and charming act at the deadly war front. The soldiers seemed to pretend not to notice my discomfort.

"Oh poor me!" Capt. Tam teased. "I've been calling your name all day and night! What if I get used to it and start calling you all the time?"

"Look at that, Thuy!" Phuc chimed in. "Capt. Tam is a sharp-looking guy, and he's a hero, too!"

The others joined in as I became the butt of their jokes.

After that, I left for Saigon and did not have a chance to see this unit, of which I had become so fond. Later, when I read in the papers about the 11th winning an award for meritorious action, I swelled with pride, as though I were an actual member of their battalion.

One Day in Hanoi (1973)

■ PHUC

In early 1973, following the signing of the Paris Peace Agreement, I had an opportunity to realize my childhood dream of returning to the place, about which I felt I had to know more. I was going to Hanoi.

It happened quite unexpectedly. I received the assignment just the evening before. It would prove to be a historic trip, the first time since the country was divided in 1954 that an official delegation from South Vietnam went to the North.

The four parties to the Paris Agreement were the forces involved in the conflict: on one side the Republic of Vietnam (South Vietnam) and the United States, and on the other the Democratic Republic of Vietnam (North Vietnam) and the Front of the Race-Nation for the Liberation of the Southern Region of Vietnam (commonly known as the National Liberation Front or Viet Cong). As stipulated in the agreement, representatives of the four parties were to meet at Camp Davis located in Tan Son Nhat air base in a Joint Military Commission

Phuc, in Hanoi, 1973.

to finalize the release of prisoners on both sides. Each party designated three representatives, for a total of 12.

Our team consisted of Major Dinh Cong Chat, Major Pham Huan, and myself, then transferred to the Four Party Joint Military Commission. Our charge on the visit to Hanoi was to observe on behalf of the Republic of Vietnam the initial return of American prisoners being held at Hoa Lo.

At a time when the two Vietnams were at war, it was hard to imagine the scene: South Vietnamese officers in uniform and insignia strolling the streets of Hanoi 19 years after being forced to evacuate the region. Perhaps it was coincidental that all three representatives of South Vietnam were Northern exiles.

Later, once I got a real taste of the

communists' methods, I realized that I knew nothing about the techniques of propaganda.

///

On February 18, 1973, a huge U.S. military cargo plane landed at Gia Lam airport in Hanoi. On board were the delegations of the Four Party Joint Military Commission.

The Americans included a captain who spoke Vietnamese that was hard to understand and an Air Force colonel who did not say a word the entire flight. The remaining delegations, all Vietnamese, did not exchange words with one another.

By contrast, the committee representing the city of Hanoi welcomed the South Vietnamese warmly and was very attentive from the moment the delegates stepped off the plane. We were led to the airport's reception room where the head of the welcoming committee launched into a lengthy and earnest explanation of the rules for this inspection trip. His speech was translated into English by a North Vietnamese officer in a thick Central-region accent, of which we could barely make heads or tails.

My first impression of Hanoi was one of fear and apprehension because of all the flags and banners displayed everywhere. The airport was old and run-down but strung with brand-new flags and hanging slogans that covered the site with red, spotted with the yellow star. The similar decoration was even more striking in the city. Everywhere you looked there were portraits of Ho Chi Minh and boards with slogans and exhortations. I would eventually come to see that flags and pennants, slogans and loudspeakers were essential elements of a socialist society.

Once the bus had brought us across the Long Bien Bridge into the city, we had to take a ferry to reach the opposite side of the Hong (Red) River. As the rough-voiced translator explained, when the Americans bombed the bridge, one section had collapsed, so the citizens had built a pontoon bridge to connect the ends. He added that the wreck of a downed bomber was on display at the Hanoi Zoo, which we would be brought to "inspect" if time permitted. The Americans looked away, appearing uncomfortable.

The three members of the South Vietnamese delegation received the most attention. Separately, each of us had his own "host" standing close by. As head of our team, Major Chat was wary and wanted to avoid any complications. Pham Huan joked and playfully taunted his host, who tried to act nonchalantly. At one point he cajoled the young man to turn the bus so the delegation could pass by the Lake of the Restored Sword and tour this famous site. The cadre seemed to pretend to think it over. "Let us check the itinerary," he said. "We might just be able to make it happen."

The captain assigned to me was always cordial. Originally from the South, he told me his name was The and added, "I regrouped to the North. My wife and children are still down South. It's been a long time, and I really miss them, brother! How about you? Do you still have any family up here?"

I stammered some answer to satisfy him, but I was rather surprised by his gracious behavior and openness in personal matters.

They treated us courteously. We had lunch at the Independence Hotel, visited the Lake of the Restored Sword and Unity Garden, and drove around the streets of Hanoi before finally arriving at the Hoa Lo jail, the real purpose of our trip. According to the provisions of our agreement, we were allowed to inspect the cells and common areas where the Americans were kept and ask any questions regarding daily life in the prison, but we could not speak directly with the prisoners.

Hoa Lo Jail
and the American POWs

When we gathered in the conference room in the Hoa Lo jail, the warden, a captain with dark skin and a bristly haircut, gave a presentation on the prison's layout and activities. He paused after each sentence so the translator could provide his interpretation in English. The translations were long-winded and nearly drove the South Vietnamese up the wall. Meanwhile, to the Americans, it might as well have been Greek. When it came time for questions, no one had anything to ask, but the delegates from the National Liberation Front burst into applause.

The next item on the agenda was an appearance by representatives of the men who were to be released that day. We sat around a long table. Seven Americans were brought in and introduced as the leaders of the prison activity cells. The spokesman for this group was a pilot shot down during a bombing mission and incarcerated for some six years.

The prisoner's attitude and behavior left me in shock. Like a robot, he stepped forward and bowed from the waist, almost banging his head on the table. Then he stood straight up, spun to the left and bowed again, then up and to the right for a final deep bow. The other six men imitated his actions.

I was embarrassed and confused. What would make the American prisoners act this way? Each movement looked as though strings controlled it. Their faces were cold and expressionless. Only their eyes were indescribably sad, peering into space before them and not directed toward anyone, even when they addressed the visitors.

Each man stood at attention and gave his name, rank, military unit, serial number, and prisoner number. They looked haggard and pitiful in their striped prison garb. Only their lips moved while their bodies remained stiff and erect. The members of the South Vietnamese delegation were deeply troubled.

All of the visitors sat silently as the prisoners came forward. Only Pham Huan stood and saluted them. His face expressed his grief, and his eyes were red. Then the warden spoke up.

"The representatives of the Four Parties may ask questions."

Everyone was silent. Finally, the colonel in charge of the American delegation addressed the spokesman.

"How are you?"

"I'm fine, sir!"

I had never heard such a poignant exchange.

"Does anyone else have any questions?" the warden asked, and then quickly added, "If not, then it is time to visit the camp!"

The prisoners were led out of the room, and then we were taken to the jail.

In time I would come to know more about Hoa Lo from books by former prisoners. On that so-called inspection day, however, all I got to see were empty cells with sturdy bars, rows of sheetrock for beds, relatively clean and airy. The dining area was large, there was even a stage. The hallways and volleyball court had apparently been cleaned in preparation for the visit.

We were only permitted to "inspect" one row of typical cells, all empty, and not a prisoner in sight. By then it was around two o'clock, and I wondered, *where is everybody and what are they doing?*

I wanted to observe some activity of the prisoners. The others just looked at the empty cells without comment or question.

I turned to The, my cadre-host who had been shadowing me all along. "How come I don't see any American pilots?" I inquired.

The smiled pleasantly.

"Hoa Lo has many different sections. This one is for the men who are about to be released. They're probably getting ready to go to the airport soon."

Twenty prisoners were to be released in this round as a "present" to the United States after a secret visit by National Security Adviser Henry Kissinger the month before. The American delegation would receive a list of those to be sent home at the airport.[28]

We visited an exercise court with a basketball hoop and volleyball net.

"Miss Jane Fonda and Miss Joan Baez stood and performed right here!" cadre The informed me proudly.

Just then I spotted a group of Americans washing at an outdoor concrete cistern beside the exercise court. My jaw dropped. They were stark naked, silently pouring water on themselves. They did not speak. The only sound was the splashing water.

Everyone just stared at them. These men, once imposing in their flight suits sitting in the cockpits of powerful jet planes were now stripped bare, their bony frames bending over the tank to dip out water to bathe. No one knew how to react, so we all just walked by and averted our eyes.

For their part, the prisoners did not look up or acknowledge us, not even with a nod or a glance. Nor did they speak to one another. Dark and silent, they acted as if they did not see the delegation standing only a few feet away.

"They're getting cleaned up," Cadre The told me, laughing, "and putting on nice clothes to fly back to America."

---

[28] The first American POWs released from Hoa Lo were those who required immediate medical attention and had left Hanoi the previous week. After a secret visit to Hanoi by National Security Adviser and Chief Negotiator Henry Kissinger, the North Vietnamese offered him a "gift" of 20 prisoners to be released ahead of the others. He was asked to select the 20 men from a list of names provided by the North Vietnamese. According to some accounts, Kissinger, who knew none of the prisoners, circled 20 names at random. Unbeknownst to him, the POWs had decided among themselves that they would only accept release in the order of capture, the longest-held prisoners leaving first. When the POWs saw that different men were being prepared for departure, they refused to cooperate, causing a minor crisis, but were eventually ordered by their superior officer to accept release.

The three Air Force officers with us tried hard to remain stony-faced, but they were clearly affected by the scene. All of a sudden, Pham Huan broke from the group and hurried over to the prisoners. He stood next to them, straightened up and gave them a sharp military salute. He remained there at attention for some time, then turned and rushed for the lavatory. I followed behind and found him splashing water on his face—or more correctly, on his eyes, which were bloodshot. He just looked at me and shook his head.

I didn't know how much the American POWs had been mistreated physically and mentally during their years in captivity. But what I witnessed at Hoa Lo made me feel great sympathy for them and also made me angry.

We were approaching the final stage of the Hanoi mission. Twenty men in fresh, clean clothes boarded a bus that would take them from Hoa Lo jail to the airport. I watched as a crowd of Hanoi citizens, mostly women and children, surrounded the bus at the gate shouting curses at the "criminal marauders." Apparently, this scene was familiar to the POWs as they never looked up or displayed any emotion.

I noticed this same lack of expression on their faces as one-by-one their names were called out in the ceremony at Gia Lam. One couldn't really call it a ceremony, as it consisted only of reading a statement regarding the lenient policy of the communist government followed by the roll call of prisoners being sent home.

At the call of each man's name, a slim figure stepped out of line, stood before the colonel in charge of the American delegation, gave a salute, shook his hand, then went straight into the imposing cargo plane parked not far off. Through the open rear door, I saw rows of hospital beds with doctors and nurses waiting. The POWs were taken directly from Gia Lam to Clark Air Force Base in the Philippines for a medical check and processing for their return to the States.

The dramatic scene was over. The members of the Four Party Joint Military Commission flew back to Saigon. I looked around and spotted my host The standing with his colleagues. I went over and shook his hand.

His face changed completely, and he was no longer the amiable and considerate fellow he had been as my companion. He took my hand indifferently, like an actor who had just finished his performance, tired, waiting for this little drama to end so he could remove the mask he had worn all day and be his real self again.

Yellow Wildflowers on the Battlefield

■ PHUC

T he war was not only a scene of pain and tragedy, violence and heroism. It also provided the backdrop for a significant change in my life. For the first time, I was excited about something outside of my work. One day when I was riding with an armored unit, a thrill came over me. We were traveling through a field of yellow wildflowers dancing in the breeze that enlivened the otherwise desolate landscape. These flowers with their tall, thin stems bent under the advance of the APCs, then defiantly sprang back up, refusing to be crushed by the weight of the vehicles.

On that day Thuy was back in Hue writing her report for the VOF. I remembered that she had once told me how she loved this kind of yellow flower. If I guessed right, she would rather get a bunch of these daisies than some carefully arranged bouquet in a vase. Without another thought, I leaped from the armored car and ran out to gather an armful of wildflowers.

The APC had moved ahead, I had to run to catch up with it. In that unanticipated moment, I realized that life had changed right there on the war front. My love had blossomed like a wildflower with a delicate stem that could not be broken. I suddenly felt utterly at ease. In the midst of my obsession with work, I allowed myself to thoroughly enjoy the innocence and freedom of a first love thoroughly.

Some of the soldiers chewed me out for my outlandish, even risky, behavior. Others, however, were on my side. They were older and had experienced more of life, so they understood what I was doing. They knew I was a young man unable to fend off the urge to pick flowers for someone I loved. As they saw it, if I wanted to be romantic in the midst of the misery of war and express my heartfelt feelings, they weren't going to stand in my way.

That evening when I returned to Hue, I sneaked into the room Thuy was staying and placed the flowers in a large vase on her desk. The fresh blossoms brightened up the room. Unlike the previous time, I left no message except a note that said: "Picked on the front at Phong Dien." I figured that to do anything more would lessen the unique effect of the bunch of wildflowers that I had risked my life to gather on the battlefront for the woman I loved.

A Pledge Fulfilled

■ THUY

When Phuc and I decided to wed, it came as no surprise to any of our colleagues, who had seen us in the field, balls of energy that seemed never to rest. Phuc's brothers welcomed me with open arms, happy to see their baby brother settle down. My family was more hesitant at first, unsure that the bold reporter would surround me with the luxury and leisure they had hoped for me. I dispelled their doubts with a radiance that penetrated every bit of my being.

Our wedding ceremony, on January 6, 1974, was very different than others'. Instead of being married at Saigon Cathedral like my sister Kim Thuy's, our marriage Mass was held at a small chapel, Mai Khoi, where the Dominican priests ran a college dormitory on Tu Xuong St. This was the place where my parents had taken us for the daily Mass.

In lieu of a ten-course Chinese banquet at Dong Khanh Ballroom in Cholon, we had a simple but wonderful wedding reception by Western standards on the ninth floor of the Majestic hotel, looking over the River of Saigon. We did not deem a lavish wedding appropriate, but I gave in to my parent's wishes to go

Phuc and Thuy's wedding, Mai Khoi Chapel, Saigon, January 6, 1974.

through all the rites of a traditional ceremony, and Phuc gave in to his brothers' joy of showing off their love for their baby brother.

Our wedding photos show a young couple handsomely matched; the groom tidy and composed, arms around his beautiful and serene bride. In both our eyes, however, was a stoic, steady gaze, as if the day was really not for us but for our family and friends.

For us, the fields waited.

Thuy and Phuc, during their wedding reception, Hotel Majestic, Saigon, 1974.

PART IV

THE FUGITIVE
AND THE CAPTIVE

Chapter 12

The Long Giao Escape

Tracking the Prisoner

■ THUY

By 1977, with the help of Binh Minh, Tuong Vi, and Duyen, I was able to follow my husband's location each time he changed camps. Wherever he went, I tried to follow and visit, except when he was held on the Phu Quoc Island.

After he was transferred to Long Giao, I went there regularly. Friends took turns giving me a ride on their bicycles over the bumpy five-kilometer road from Long Giao camp to Cam Duong plantation, where we might find Phuc working in the forest. We got to know the vendors in the area, and from them, we gathered information about the prisoners' lives and work schedules. I made friends with some of the farmers who lived near the camp so I could stop at their homes for a meal or rest whenever I came to Long Giao.

Since I now received monthly support from my parents, I no longer worried about making ends meet and spent my time keeping in touch with Phuc. Eventually, I was able to see him regularly in the fields and figured out ways to contact him directly. I went to Long Giao twice a week, leaving at first light so I could return before dark. If I went alone, I'd set off as early as two in the morning and catch a coal-run bus (which was less expensive and went further), then take an auto rickshaw, or tut-tut, to Long Giao. Socialism had pulled Vietnam so far backward in time, and one of the consequences was gasoline scarcity and high prices. Thus transport outfits turned to old-style coal-run vehicles.

The "coal-car" was a truck with no windows or side door like a bus, just an opening in the rear by the stove that was kept fired up to provide power. The bed was closed off on the front and sides, so it was stifling inside. Add to that the heat from the stove, and passengers were kept in a constant sweat as if they were sitting in a sauna.

The first time I rode in one of these, I grabbed onto the stove to climb in and burned my hand so badly it took weeks to heal. The truck bed was just a wooden floor with no benches, so any passengers who didn't want to sit on the floor had to bring their own stool.

The passengers on a coal-car were typically women who made what money they could by selling odds and ends, coal, raw rice, tea, coffee, or whatever else they had. Under the communists, all economic activity belonged to the state; there was no private enterprise, so this kind of marketing was done without authorization. If the security police should stop and check them, their goods would be confiscated, and they'd be jailed. Despite the risk, people were so hard up they were willing to try to earn what little they could to keep their families from starving or being sent to the New Economic Zones.

The bus took us straight to Long Giao. From there it was only a short tut-tut ride to the re-education camp. Then I'd stop at a farmer's house and borrow their son's bicycle and make my way to Cam Duong plantation, which was better than walking. By dressing like a farmer and riding a bike, I would look less suspicious when I came in close to the fields where prisoners were working.

Sending Mail... Like Spies!

To send messages to Phuc, I devised a method of placing notes inside of cigarettes. Using a finely sharpened pencil, I wrote my letter on onion paper cut to size. I then removed the tobacco from the cigarette, rolled my note inside, then replaced the tobacco. It had to be done correctly to go unnoticed by the camp guards. After many practice tries, I became adept at the trick, and even my friends couldn't tell the difference between an untouched cigarette and one that I had tampered with.

In this way, I was able to compose one message a day for

Phuc, which I set aside for the time I could meet him. It was almost a game to me, brightening my existence a little and giving me some measure of hope.

As soon as I had twenty such cigarettes, I placed them in a package. Then I waited until my next trip to Long Giao so I could hand them directly to Phuc.

A week later I was riding the borrowed bicycle to Cam Duong plantation. Attached to the handlebars was a plastic bag in which I had put vitamins, common pain medications, some dried meat, pieces of sugar, a bunch of bananas, and two packs of cigarettes. When I reached the prisoners, by luck, I came first on Phuc's labor team on their way back to the camp carrying logs. I dismounted the bike and walked it alongside the prisoners. Then I removed one cigarette package from my bag and approached the guard.

After April 30, 1975, we had more contact with the communist cadres and discovered that most of them were addicted to smoking. They generally only smoked farmer's tobacco, since they couldn't afford regular cigarettes.

I held out the package to the guard.

"This pack of cigarettes is for you," I said. "Please let me pass on this bag of medicine to my relative, Brother Phuc."

Fortunately for me, on that day I had come upon an easy-going cadre who appeared to be craving for a smoke. He took the pack I offered him, then opened the plastic bag and inspected each item individually.

"You can give him the medicine," he said finally, "but you can't talk to him."

I hurried over to Phuc and handed him the bag, speaking as quickly as I could.

"In each cigarette, there's a little note. Take out the note before you smoke the cigarette, OK?"

Phuc nodded and immediately placed the pack in his pocket. Then he squeezed my hand, softly told me he loved me and continued on with his workmates. I stood and watched him go, my heart in knots.

In this way, I was able to communicate with Phuc and keep him informed as to what was going on outside the concentration camp. Over time, as more and more families came to see their loved ones in prison, the guards became used to these visits and allowed them to deliver medicine and small foodstuffs as long as there was no exchange of words.

Later I had only to walk by the area where prisoners were laboring and look for Phuc's gang. I'd stand by the barbed-wire fence staring at him until I was certain he noticed me, then drop a bag of medicine and cigarettes for him and walk away without looking back. His companions were used to my presence and let him know whenever I showed up at the Cam My-Cam Duong plantation areas where they frequently were sent to work that spring of 1977.

Other wives used this method to support their husbands, and before long the men were bringing things back to the camp, especially when they had cigarettes to bribe the guards. Because of this, I always included a second pack already opened for Phuc to give the guards while he kept the sealed pack with my little love notes for himself. There were times, though, when the guards inspected the bag and confiscated all the cigarettes while letting Phuc have only the medicines and food. He would have to watch with concealed pain as they lit up and puffed away all the messages I had worked so hard to compose and send to him.

A Plot to Steal Him from Prison

And so it went for the first half of 1977. I met Phuc a good number of times and brought him many cigarettes containing love notes to lift his spirits and bits of news from the outside. The latter made Phuc news source inside the camp and enlarged his circle of friends. Because of the effectiveness of our letter smuggling, I accepted other wives' requests to pass on information to their husbands through Phuc.

At a time when all over the South people were struggling to survive physically, such efforts as mine aimed at our spiritual and emotional well-being might seem impractical and a waste of energy. But in my mind, this kind of food for the spirit and the heart was more important than one's bodily needs when life was so hard.

As human beings, we can't control material conditions around us, but we can do so with our emotions and spirit. In our mind, we generate faith and will, things that are not influenced by our physical aspect. For Phuc and me, the nourishment of shared sentiments, the feeling of loving and of being loved, is the elixir that makes us strong, more potent than any other medicine.

As the days went by I took more risks. I'd wait for Phuc at the Cam Duong crossroads, where the Long Giao prisoners passed each day on their way to hard labor on the plantation. And I began to stand closer to the side of the road, so close that when Phuc walked by I could look him in the eye and convey the countless confidences I wanted to share with him.

Once I saw him move his lips as if mouthing the words "I love you." That alone was enough to light up my heart all during the 60-mile trip back to Saigon.

When An was a little older, and Binh Minh or Duyen came with me, I'd bring the girl along so Phuc could see his daughter and An might know who her daddy was.

Since the guards frequently changed the work sites, I might not get to see Phuc for a week at a time. One day the prisoners might be near the road, the next they could be taken deep into the forest while their wives and mothers were left standing beside the road in a fruitless vigil. Still, I kept writing letters, kept going to the camp to look for him. It was that action that nourished my love and sustained my heart's hope.

I was a 26-year-old woman, lonely and hurt, sensitive and weak in the face of life's difficulties. So I clung to my love for Phuc and An. It gave me the strength and faith to deal with the challenges thrown my way.

///

In April word was going around that the communist authorities had decided to deal more harshly with those reform prisoners who were deemed to have "a great blood debt with the people" and posed a threat to the security of their government. At the top of the list were politicians, writers, artists, intellectuals, and journalists, in short, all those who had played some part in the political struggle against them.

According to a rumor, these prisoners were to be transferred to the North. Northern Communists were in the process of extending their authority over the South by reducing the power of the National

Liberation Front, which had exhausted its purpose, and eliminating the positions of Southern cadres who had served them. They also planned to spread out the South Vietnamese prisoners in various Northern camps to avoid having too high a concentration of "reactionary" elements in the South, where they might collaborate with the local population should the latter become discontented.

I realized then that I had to help Phuc break out of prison. Or he would be taken away and lost to me forever. At the same time, one of my distant uncles was organizing an escape from the country. He said he could take my family along if we contributed some gold to the purchase of a boat and if Phuc could make it out in time.

My parents agreed to provide the gold. I set to work preparing what we needed: false identification papers, road passes (the communists required all people traveling from one city to another to have a pass), as well as a hiding place for Phuc until we could leave. I just had to find a way to "steal" him from the prison camp. I wrote down all the details of the plot on thin paper and planted the note in a cigarette that I planned to give him the following week.

My husband had no idea I was planning a "kidnapping" when he saw me one day in May 1977.

A Life-Changing Encounter

■ PHUC

I still recall the date of May 19, 1977, Ho Chi Minh's birthday. The entire camp was sent out to clear the fields of elephant grass, or, as they described it, "striving and motivating each other to celebrate Uncle's birthday." The grass grew head-high all the way to the main road. As we dug the earth, we watched people going back and forth and the auto rickshaws passing by on their route from Long Khanh to Cam My-Cam Duong.

I made my way toward the tall grass alongside the road, keeping an eye on the tut-tuts, knowing that Thuy was going to visit me that day. The week before we had communicated with each other using letters smuggled in the bags of friends who were visiting the camp.

Around noon, when the sun was bearing down, a bus from Long Khanh stopped at the crossing in front of a small stand selling drinks and snacks. Several people got off. Among them, I recognized Thuy in her brown peasant's shirt carrying a basket. Even though I'd been expecting her, the sight of my wife just then stopped me in my tracks.

She walked along the trench that separated the road from the elephant grass, her eyes searching the prisoners' faces. I knew she wouldn't be able to pick me out from all the men scattered across the field. I looked around to find the guards' location, I saw one soldier in a jungle helmet standing on a hill watching the whole work area. Dragging my hoe behind me, I crossed a clearing and headed toward Thuy, fully aware that I could not avoid being noticed by the guard on the hill. She saw me when there was just a small stretch of grass between us. She stopped short, and we gazed at each other, too emotional to react.

Her eyes darted behind me with a look of alarm. I turned to see the guard coming down the hill. Throwing aside my hoe, I rushed toward Thuy and leaped into the trench, hunkering down behind the cover of the grass. She sat down beside the road intending to speak. Then she looked past me, and the words finally came out.

"Here's a little food for you, Daddy."

She pushed a coarse bag down into the trench, and then pulled out a pack of cigarettes, drawing out one cigarette in particular.

"There's a very important note in this one," she said quickly. "Be careful, Daddy, OK?"

I took the cigarette and stuffed it into my pocket.

"How's little An?" I asked.

"Just fine."

I reached forward and patted her hand.

"How about Mama, are you all right? Try to keep going, OK?"

"Don't worry," she smiled. "Mother and daughter are doing well. We have what we need. Every month Papa and Mama send us things. We just need you to take care of yourself."

Just then there was a noise behind me, and someone from my labor unit gave a loud whisper.

"Quick! The guard's getting close!"

Thuy stood up.

"I'll be back this afternoon," she said, then hurried to the other side of the road and headed back toward the crossroads.

I grabbed the bag, intending to shove it into the grass when the guard appeared.

"Get up!" he screamed. "Bring that bag here!"

As I climbed out of the trench, the soldier snatched the bag from my hands, his eyes nearly popping out of his head.

"Who gave you permission, heh?"

He tipped the bag over and emptied the contents onto the ground: two small milk cans and some plastic bags of sugar and salt with sesame seeds.

I glanced around and saw that my workmates had ceased digging and were watching the proceedings closely. From far off the guard commander, Cadre But, stomped over and without any warning punched me in the face. I fell to the ground and received a kick in the ribs.

"Stand up! Remove your clothes and empty all your pockets!" Cadre But ordered, emphasizing each word.

Pretending to be in great pain, I slowly got to my hands and knees while I tried to think of a way to get rid of the cigarette Thuy had given me. I began to remove my pants, taking as much time as I could. Meanwhile, Cadre But turned to the guard.

"See if there's anything in there!" he ordered, indicating the items spilled on the ground.

The guard opened the cans and dumped out salted meat, then tore open the bag of salt and sesame. While they were busy inspecting these things, I brought my hand to my shirt pocket, found the cigarette, and tossed it behind me as far as I could.

An Unlucky Cigarette

I went on removing my clothes. Cadre But picked them up from the ground and inspected each piece thoroughly. He found the pack of Vam Co cigarettes in my pocket.

All of a sudden I heard a voice behind me.

"Brother But, look at this."

I turned around to see another guard bend down to pick up

the cigarette I had just tossed away, which broke under his footstep. He had removed a small piece of paper from it. But rushed over, took the paper and read it. I tensed up, wondering, *what did Thuy write in there?*

But turned and gaped at me, his lips trembling. He grabbed the soldier's rifle and pointed it at my chest, his face hard and red.

"You dare plot against the Revolution?"

The thought flashed through my head, *It wouldn't make sense for him to shoot me right here*, and I pulled back in a defensive position. Turning the rifle around, But lunged at me to drive it into my face. I dropped back, and the rifle slammed into my shoulder, knocking me to the ground.

"Tie him up!" But ordered, his voice shaking, "and take him back to the camp."

The guard picked me up by the hair, then pulled my arms behind my back and bound them with electrical wire.

"Move!" he shouted.

The two guards escorted me back to the camp just as the gong sounded ending the morning's labor shift. They shoved me onto the ground next to a Conex box, and then marched over to the tin building that served as the camp's headquarters.

A moment later, a cadre named Tuat, the unit's political commissar, stormed out of the office. He had beady eyes and dark skin, but now he was livid. Without a word he pulled me to my feet and untied my arms. Then he handcuffed me to a post next to the Conex box and stalked off.

The prisoners were returning from their morning shift. My old friends from the camp team—Ky, Nghia, Nguyen, Ta Anh and Luu Khuong—looked at me with fear in their eyes. Ta Anh paused uncertainly outside the barbed wire and waved to me.

Long after the lunch break, I was still standing there, hungry and weak. I was left alone. Perhaps they were trying to figure out the best way to deal with me. I struggled to remain calm, closing my eyes and trying not to think about anything, preparing myself for whatever lay ahead.

Suddenly I remembered that Thuy had promised she would return that afternoon. I felt a stab of pain in my stomach that soon spread to my whole body. I shook with fear. If she came back, they would surely catch her. I didn't know what she had written in that note, but it must have been serious for them to react like that. I was frantic, trying to think of a way to warn Thuy before she came.

As the afternoon labor shift approached But strode across the compound with Ta Anh, who was carrying a large backpack. I recognized the bag like mine, containing my sleeping gear and personal belongings. Since Ta Anh slept next to me in the barrack, they must have volunteered him to bring me my things for inspection. When they reached me But gave a command.

"Spread out the blanket and take everything out of the pack, one by one!"

My friend removed each object and laid it on the blanket in no particular order. Among the items were a photograph of Thuy and our daughter and a stack of notes Thuy had smuggled in to me over the past two years.

But stepped away to talk with Commissar Tuat. Without raising his eyes to look at me, Ta Anh continued to display my possessions while speaking softly to me.

"Out in the field, But called us all together and read your wife's letter. She told you to get ready to escape. She's made connections for an escape by boat next month with fake papers and a hiding place for you in Saigon."

He looked over at the two cadres still absorbed in their discussion, then turned back to me.

"You're in a tight spot," he said quickly. "Try to find a way out of here. They're planning to do to you what they did to Ngo Nghia."

"Just now, my wife told me she was going to meet me again this afternoon," I whispered as he stood up. "When you go out there, find some way to warn her so she can get away before they catch her!"

Ta Anh was stunned.

"If she comes back it'll be bad," he muttered. "I'll do what I can. You keep cool."

He turned back to the cadres and reported that my belongings were all out for viewing, and then he walked in silence to the camp.

But and Tuat carefully inspected everything on the blanket. When they were done, they took my photos and letters and returned to their office.

The Long Giao Tiger Cage

They left me with my hands cuffed behind my back around the post until evening. When the second labor shift was over, Commissar Tuat came and released me, then led me into the office. The camp warden was already there, sitting behind a desk on which lay my file from the time I first entered the prison system along with the stack of photos and letters that Tuat had taken from me.

Tuat began to question me about my past. I repeated the same story I used every time I had to declare my background: *I was a journalist who became a lieutenant war correspondent for the South Vietnamese military. I reported on the fighting in Laos and Cambodia, and I was a representative of the Four Party Joint Military Commission that went to the North to accept American prisoners of war released from Hoa Lo prison in Hanoi in 1973.*

I figured I didn't need to mention that I'd helped my colleague Pham Huan publish the book *One Day in Hanoi* about our mission to observe the POWs and the treatment they received. The book had rankled the authorities in the North. Anyway, a copy of it was in my prison file.

Finally, Tuat handed me some blank paper and a pencil.

"Write down your entire plot to escape from the camp," he ordered. "Be truthful, and your crime will be reduced. Try to deceive us, and the Revolution will judge you accordingly. Do you hear what I'm saying?"

After that, Tuat took me outside and threw me into the Conex box next to the fence by the food warehouse. The shipping container was old and rusty, left by the American army. Dubbed "tiger cages," the boxes were used by both sides for solitary confinement.

The box was only big enough for a man to lie down in. There was no lock on the door; instead, they threaded a stiff wire through two holes and twisted it outside into two rings secured by a metal lock. The floor of the cage was damp, filthy, and cold.

///

Early the first morning, the guard opened the door to let me use the latrine. I took the opportunity to familiarize myself with the layout of the camp and the barbed-wire fences surrounding it. I was determined to escape. Otherwise, they'd execute me the way they had Ngo Nghia in Trang Lon. The problem was how to get a piece of metal I could slip through the wire and twist until it broke. All I could find by the latrine were two nails, too short for my purpose. Still, I placed them in my pocket in case they might come in handy.

In the afternoon, Tuat came to collect my declaration; three pages of writing that went around and around, neither admitting to the crime of "opposing the Revolution" nor denying it.

The next day immediately after my trip to the latrine, Commissar Tuat pulled me into the office. This time there was a new cadre there who I assumed was of higher rank than the regular camp cadres. Tuat stood at attention, "Reporting, Comrade!" he announced, and then left the office.

The new cadre seemed to be a practiced hand at interrogation. He strode back and forth in front of me, and after each question, he slapped me in the face. I took the beating all morning, repeating my answers over and over as he tried to get me to identify my accomplices in the plot to escape, the organization that made false papers, and the address where I was to be kept hidden in Saigon.

"I don't know," I responded firmly, enduring the slaps. "I don't know anything at all."

Finally, he picked up an old board spiked on one end with rusty nails and beat me repeatedly on the back and shoulders. Before sending me back to the cage, he had a few last words.

"We arrested your wife yesterday afternoon. If you make an honest declaration, you and your wife will have your crimes reduced. If not, she will get the beating in your place."

This revelation struck me with more force than the drubbing I had just received. My head swam, I bowed low to avoid looking at the cadre, concealing my rage and refraining myself from jumping on the bastard.

Then Tuat came and led me back to the Conex box just as the sky was growing dim. I dropped to the floor and fell asleep. When I woke up, it was quite late. I remained awake until morning, hurting at the thought that Thuy was in jail somewhere and wondering who was taking care of little An.

I like to think of myself as a strong-willed man who can deal with any situation. This time, however, I felt utterly helpless.

Chapter 13

On The Run

Malicious Beatings

■ PHUC

Over the next several days the story repeated itself, with the same questions punctuated by beatings of various sorts. Once the interrogator became furious with me and smashed a hard farmer's pipe on my head. I rolled over, pretending to pass out to avoid further blows.

One day Commissar Tuat spoke to me.

"The Revolution has cracked harder nuts than you. Wait till we take you to the firing range, then you'll come groveling to us."

By then I knew that no matter what I declared, sooner or later the communists were going to take me to the firing range. They wanted to get to the bottom of the escape plot and the people forging papers, which they thought I knew all about.

In fact, I knew nothing, but sometimes I hinted that I might have information just so they would continue the interrogation. Once they realized they were not going to get any more out of me, they'd probably take me out and finish me off.

I hadn't been able to find the piece of metal I needed to work the wire on my cage, but I firmly believed I had to escape and felt my spirit and body were still fit enough for it. I pretended to be ill and weak and walked with one foot dragging. They supposed my leg had gone bad because of my cramped confinement in the cage.

At times when the interrogations became too intense, I pretended to blackout to avoid harder beatings. Once, however, the cadre dumped hot water from his farmer's pipe into my face and pulled me up by the hair so he could resume battering me.

On the eighth night, it poured rain, and my cage was flooded. I was drenched and lay huddled, shivering the whole night.

The following morning when I was let out to relieve myself, I caught sight of a short piece of metal that someone must have dropped right next to the fence by my Conex. On my way back from the latrine I asked the guard for permission to hang my wet clothes on the fence to dry. With his nod, I hurried there, removed my clothes and hung them right above the spot where the piece of metal lay. I was wearing only my undershorts when I reported to the cadre's office to receive my daily beating, this time with an electric cable.

In the afternoon I asked if I could gather back my clothes. With the guard standing away behind me, I pretended to drop my shirt. As I picked it up, I rolled the piece of metal in it and carried it back to my cage.

After the guard had locked me in and left, I unwrapped my shirt and examined my find. It was a sidebar from a bicycle's luggage rack, firm enough and the right size to slip into the twisted wire on the door. Elated, I began to think about escaping that very night before it was too late.

I also knew that if the plan were found out, they'd probably shoot me on the spot.

Escape and Flight

That night the rain fell in torrents, just as it had the night before. I worked the metal brace into the wire on my cage and, with my hands at both ends, began twisting. The door rattled against the metal box. Fortunately, the rain beat so loudly on the roof it covered the noise so I could put my best into the effort.

After an hour or so the wire finally began to twist with the brace. Encouraged, I turned it several more times, and the wire broke. I fell back into the cage exhausted. Despite the cold rain, my body was covered with sweat.

As morning approached, the rain stopped. I pushed the door open and stepped outside, then dropped to the ground and wormed my way past the camp headquarters meeting rooms. When I reached the manioc fields, I stood up and ran bent-over between rows of plants toward the path I usually took to enter the labor fields.

It was still dark out, but I was more than familiar with the way. I dashed over clear fields toward the stretches of elephant grass and continued running to the trench where I had met Thuy nine days before. Once there, I jumped inside and lay still, tired and anxious, my heart pounding.

I had made it out of the camp, but my ordeal was not yet over. The farther away I got the better. I knew that the people who lived in the vicinity of the camp were displaced Catholics from the North. I figured I should be able to get some help from them.

It was becoming light out, and I could hear the voices of people on the road. I got to my feet, climbed onto the highway, stood erect and headed for the Long Giao market, following behind some of the locals who were taking their wares to sell.

By the time I reached the market the sun had raised. A bit further on I spied a tut-tut stop near some of the vendors. Suddenly the tut-tut was surrounded by jungle helmets. Panicking, I turned and darted down the side of a house and circled around back to where I found a path that ran through the village.

I couldn't allow myself to be seen in the market in the light of day.

The soldiers who were waiting for the auto rickshaw heading for Long Khanh could have been from other camps and wouldn't recognize my face. But after nine days huddled in a cage, my beard grew out, my clothes dirty and torn; it wouldn't have been hard for them to figure out that I was an escaped prisoner.

I quickened my pace down the path behind the market to the adjacent hamlet. There I heard chanted prayers coming from one of the houses off the road. I barged inside to find a woman praying the rosary. She looked up at me, startled.

"Please, auntie," I said quickly, "I'm a re-education prisoner who just escaped from the camp."

She jumped to her feet.

"Jesus and Mary, oh my Lord! Well, where do you plan to go?"

"I don't know yet. Auntie, is there a road going straight to Saigon?"

"You'll have to take the main road and get a tut-tut to Long

Khanh. From there you can catch a bus to Saigon. You have to hurry. It's dangerous to stay around here!"

"Please, auntie, I don't have any money. Can you help me?"

"I can give you one *dong* so you can ride the tut-tut. Here, take it," she said. "Now, go in peace, all right? Poor thing. May the Lord protect you!"

I accepted the money and thanked her, then turned and looked for the way to the main road. There was no other way. I'd have to get to Long Khanh and decide what to do next.

I stood beside the road trying to appear inconspicuous and waved down a tut-tut. The three-wheeled motorized vehicle used as a mini-bus passed me and stopped a short distance away. I ran up and jumped on, then wedged myself on a bench beside a lady, not looking at anyone else. Just as the driver gunned the engine, I saw one of the camp guards sitting at the end of the same bench. Our eyes met, and he gaped, stammering.

"Huh? Huh? You..."

He lunged at me and grabbed me by the shoulders.

"Driver!" he shouted. "Stop! Stop!"

I jerked out of his grasp and, gathering my strength, socked him in the face and rolled out of the tut-tut.

My head hit the ground, and I heard the little bus brake sharply as the guard shouted. I bolted up and sprinted for all I was worth into the neighborhood off the road, clambered over a barbed-wire fence and slipped into someone's backyard garden.

A woman was sitting on a stool doing her laundry over a basin. As soon as she saw me, she jumped up and made the sign of the cross.

"Oh Lord!" she cried.

I ran past her into her house, saying, "Please, let me hide a bit. They're after me...."

I rushed to a low bed in the corner, got down on the floor and squeezed underneath, pressing myself against the wall. There I laid face down, listening to my breathing and the pounding of my heart.

Soon I heard footsteps and the guard's voice.

"Did you see a re-education prisoner go by?"

"No, no, I saw nothing...," the woman replied, her voice trembling.

The footsteps went off in another direction. A moment later, the woman whispered above my head, "Come out. Come out from there."

I squirmed out, stood, but before I could say thank you, the woman took my hand and said in a halting voice, "I feel very sorry for you re-education prisoners. But please pity me, too, you understand surely. I can't rescue you. It's too dangerous."

Her face was pale as she took my hands in her own, trembling hands.

"Yes," I answered, "I wouldn't dare bother you, auntie. If you have a man's clothes in the house, though, please let me change."

She looked at my old, tattered ARVN uniform and shook her head.

"You must leave now, right now!" she said, nearly crying.

She let go of me and stepped back. As I turned to leave, I could hear her voice behind me.

"May the Powers Above protect you! May God forgive me."

Confused, I didn't know where to go. I was sure the guard was somewhere nearby, and more soldiers were bound to come and surround the area. Suddenly I heard a church's bells. I ran back to the woman's house. Her eyes grew wide as she clasped her hands to her breast.

"Oh my Lord! Oh my Lord!"

"Auntie," I said, "please point me the way to the church."

"Go this way," she said, tremblingly pointing to the left. "When you come to the corner, turn right, then go straight to the clearing and you'll see the church from there."

"Thank you," I replied, patting her on the back. I turned through the gate and ran off in the direction she'd indicated.

Duyen Lang Church.
Photo taken in 1980

The Old Priest
of Duyen Lang Parish

I rushed into the church. Their prayers interrupted, the people in the back pews turned to look. I pressed forward, asking out loud, "Where is Father? Please tell me."

Stunned by this outburst, they merely

stared at me in silence. The ones up front also turned around, their prayers falling off.

Finally, a young man in the front row stood up and approached me.

"Father is in the parish rectory," he said. "Go this way."

I ran to the front, glancing at the statue of Christ on the wall, then sped out the side door and around to the back of the church. The rectory's door was ajar, so I pushed it open and walked in.

It was a rather large building with many rooms. I walked hurriedly to the last room, next to the bathroom. There was a small bed there, a table and chairs, and an armoire for the priest's vestments. Looking around, it seemed to me that the safest place to hide was still under the bed, so I slipped down and slid over against the wall.

A while later I heard slow footsteps enter the room. From where I lay I could see the hem of a black cassock. I debated whether I should come out of hiding right then or if my sudden appearance might be too much of a shock for the new arrival.

Then a dog padded inside and stuck its muzzle under the bed. Now it began to bark.

It was useless to hide anymore, so I crawled out and stood in front of the priest expectantly. He was only momentarily taken aback and quickly regained his composure.

"I'm an escapee from a re-education camp," I explained. "The guards were chasing me, so I ran in here. Please help me, Father. Let me hide somewhere for a little while, then I'll go somewhere else. Help me. If they catch me, they'll shoot me right away!"

"All right," he replied in a gravelly voice. "Stay here."

He was very old, likely in his late eighties, his face wrinkled, his voice weak. He said no more, asked nothing, but went to the armoire and selected one of the vestments. After pulling it on, he left to conduct Mass.

The Pastor of Duyen Lang Church. Photo taken from his tombstone in 1998

I thought that perhaps being so old, the priest had not grasped the seriousness of my situation. The guards must have surrounded the neighborhood by then and begun searching for me. Surely the church would be the first place they'd consider. So I felt I needed to find someplace safer to hide. I inspected the armoire. It was taller than me, the door was mostly glass with the bottom part made of wood, and it was filled with the priest's long religious robes.

I opened the wardrobe door and stepped inside, then sat down and made myself small so I couldn't be seen through the door's glass. I pulled my legs in close, hunched my shoulders, and dropped my head. In that position, I fell asleep.

I woke to the sound of the old priest coughing. I felt sure he didn't know where I was. I pushed open the armoire door and was about to step out but stopped short. Beside the old priest, there was a middle-aged woman in the room. She didn't seem surprised to see me; perhaps he had already informed her of my presence.

"How can you lie inside there?" Father said. "Come out and use the bed."

"Please, Father, let me stay in here," I pleaded. "I'm afraid they'll come and search the place."

He nodded and said they had already come looking for me. Soldiers had entered some houses along the street and checked out the church, but they hadn't entered the rectory. Then he asked his maid if there was anything for me to eat. The woman nodded.

"Follow Ms. Nhan inside and have dinner," he said to me.

The woman broke in.

"Wait, let me bring it here. There are too many people coming and going inside."

He agreed and retired to another room. The old priest never asked how long I might be staying or how I planned to leave.

Ms. Nhan brought me a large bowl of rice and another bowl of warm soup. After I had eaten my fill, I climbed back into the armoire, curled up in the bottom and tried to coax sleep.

When I woke up, it was dark outside. There was a conversation going on in the room between the old priest and another man. Quietly I raised my head up to peer through the glass. In the dim lamplight, I saw a young priest having dinner with the old pastor.

Given that the two clerics were discussing parish affairs, I concluded that the young man was the assistant pastor. He was about 40 with an intelligent, ruggedly handsome face. He spoke in a deep, precise voice, in contrast to the old priest who was slow and gentle. I thought that if I were to talk with this younger man, he would find a way to help me out of this dangerous place.

I never heard myself mentioned during the meal. It appeared that the young priest was unaware that I was in the rectory. Thus, I decided that the old pastor did not want anyone other than Ms. Nhan to know of my presence.

After dinner, the young priest left the room. His superior approached the armoire and called to me.

"Come out and eat supper."

Father had left me a few pieces of pork and some vegetable, which I ate using his bowl and chopsticks.

Ms. Nhan came in, and the three of us discussed how they might help me. Father suggested that the next morning I should take the earliest tut-tut to Long Khanh and from there catch a bus to Ho Nai where I'd be safer. He gave me money for the fare. Ms. Nhan advised me to slip some cash to the bus conductor so I could sneak on. But, she said, first I should bathe, shave and change my clothes.

Father gave me one of his outfits. It was tight, but I tried to make it fit. That night I had a good sleep on the old priest's bed while he slept on the parlor sofa.

Old Priest and Young Priest

The next morning I woke to the tolling of the church bell. I got up and quickly get ready to leave. The elderly priest was nowhere to be found; I guessed he was in the church for early Mass. Ms. Nhan wasn't there either for me to say goodbye. I opened the back door, went around to the front, and walked to the road.

A while later a tut-tut approached. Even at a distance, I noticed several jungle helmets bobbing inside, indicating the passengers were soldiers. I retreated and hid behind a tree until the vehicle passed. Waiting for an autorickshaw here seemed too risky— I could easily run into another guard who'd recognize me. Besides, the tut-tut would probably have to stop at any number of checkpoints along the way to Long Khanh.

I retraced my steps to the rectory, but the back door was locked. Hearing sounds in the bathroom, I swung myself up and looked inside the window. There was the young priest brushing his teeth. I called to him softly.

"Father, open the back door for me."

Then I dropped to the ground and went around back to wait. I heard a couple of clicks before the door opened just wide enough for the young priest to stick his head out.

"Who are you?" he asked, astonished. "What do you want?"

"I'm a prisoner who hid in the room since yesterday," I said as I slipped inside. The priest reached out and pushed me back outside. I stepped forward as I heard the lock click shut.

"The old Father let me hide in the wardrobe yesterday!" I called, pounding on the door. "He gave me money to take the bus, but I couldn't catch it and came back. Please open the door!"

There was no answer, only the sound of footsteps receding into the house.

I went around to the front and knocked on the door, but all was quiet inside. I didn't know where I might find Ms. Nhan, so I went to the church. As it was early, there were only a few parishioners seated in the front rows.

The old priest was hearing confessions. I entered the confessional and knelt down, then whispered into the screen.

"I couldn't go. Please let me back in your room."

Father got up and came around the confessional without looking at me. He casually left the church and walked toward the rectory with me following behind. Without a word, he opened the door and let me in. I heard the door being locked from the outside. Then I returned to the armoire and closed the door behind me.

After Mass, the old priest returned to his room. I could hear him talking calmly to someone. He said he was feeling tired and asked the other person to drive him the next morning to the hospital in Ho Nai.

I lay hidden until noon. Ms. Nhan knocked on the door and brought me a bowl of steamed sticky rice. She didn't ask what had happened, but her face expressed worry and fear. I remained in the armoire all day.

At night the young priest arrived to have supper with his pastor. Again they talked about the parish. Neither one mentioned me. In discussing the congregation, the young priest spoke earnestly, as he had the night before. He likely had no idea I was hiding just steps away from him.

After the young priest had left, the old pastor called me out to eat. He only said that the next morning a car was to take him to Ho Nai, that I was to come along and sit beside him, and that I was not to speak to the driver.

At daybreak the next morning, just as the old priest had said, there was a La Dalat model car waiting in front of the rectory. I went in and sat next to the priest in the back seat. Another man sat up front by the driver. We left Long Giao and arrived in Ho Nai without incident.

During the trip, the priest sat half asleep and said not a word to anyone. I, too, kept my mouth shut. Now and then the two men up front spoke to each other in whispers. Neither turned to address me, probably at the old priest's instruction.

The car stopped in front of Sao Mai hospital. When I got out, I wanted to bid the priest farewell but couldn't open my mouth to speak. He took my hand tenderly in his.

"There, go in peace, my son," he said in a tired, slow voice. "The Lord will watch over you."

I knew that if I tried to say anything I'd break down. So, I just nodded goodbye, turned and headed off toward the market area. I hadn't gone far when I suddenly stopped. I spun around and ran back to the car panting. The old priest waited patiently.

"Father," I said, "I don't know your name."

For the first time, I saw him smile.

"I'm Father Trac.[29] What's your name, my son?"

I told him and could not hold back tears.

---

[29] Much later I would discover that he was Fr. Tran Ngoc Trac, pastor of the Duyen Lang parish in North Vietnam until 1954 when he brought his entire congregation to the South. More than 2,000 parishioners followed him from settlement to settlement until they established a parish in Long Giao and built Duyen Lang church. He died in 1981 at the age of 94. He was already 90 when I encountered him after my escape from prison.

In Destiny's Hands

Ho Nai was only 70 kilometers from the prison and still within the jurisdiction of the soldiers searching for me. Although I was free of the camp, I was still in danger. I needed another plan. Fortunately, Thuy had a relative living in the town. I quickened my pace and headed for the market.

In broad daylight, I became self-conscious about my appearance. Father Trac's clothes were too tight for me and didn't resemble what the people here were wearing. I was afraid that anyone looking at me would guess right away that I was an escaped prisoner.

Everything seemed to have changed in the two years I was in prison. Now all the money had the face of Ho Chi Minh on it, and nearly everyone was dressed in the dark peasant clothes called *ao ba ba* like the Viet Cong wore.

Even the streets looked different, to say nothing of the way people behaved. It was as if my country was under the domination of a foreign power. Even the security police had on strange green and pink uniforms that I had never seen before. I felt as if I were on another planet.

Sister Phi lived in front of the market in the center of town. I'd been there once before. Her place was divided into two sections: the outside was a covered courtyard with a vending stall displaying a variety of goods, behind it was the family's living quarter.

The courtyard felt familiar, except for the giant red flag with a yellow star and the portrait of Ho Chi Minh on the wall.

Sister Phi was standing behind the counter talking with one of her customers. She stopped abruptly as she saw me, her eyes gaping in astonishment. She glanced quickly toward the door to the house, and then said something to her visitor in a low voice. Once we were alone, I approached and greeted her softly.

"Hello, sister Phi. How are you?"

Phi shook her head, confused. Instead of answering my question, she asked, "How about you? Are you well?"

Our conversation seemed banal, out of place in the odd situation we found ourselves in. I figured I should get straight to the point and told her my story.

"I need a place to hide here in Ho Nai," I concluded. "Can

you help me, sister?"

Without replying she led me into the house and set out some food. Pity filled her eyes as she watched me eat hungrily.

"I'm not worried about myself," she said, "but I don't think I can convince my family to accept the danger of helping you."

I understood her position and tried to think of any other place I could go. The truth is, her house right on the marketplace with people coming and going all the time was hardly a safe place to hide. I told her I needed to go somewhere farther from the prison camp, beyond where the soldiers would look for me. All I wanted was a way to get to Saigon to find Thuy. Phi figured that I should take the bus to Saigon, but I was concerned about the fact that I had no identification papers. From Thuy's letters, I had learned that now everyone was required to carry documents that could be checked at stops along the way.

Then I remembered that Thuy's Aunt Chi had moved here after the fall of Saigon. Her husband, Uncle Trac, had been head of the Vung Tau Social Services Office, and the family had moved to the countryside so that he could hide his identity and avoid re-education. Sister Phi brightened at the suggestion and said she knew where they lived. We agreed that I should stay there until I could get to Saigon and contact Thuy.

Sister Phi took me an hour's walk to the farm, which lay behind a thick forest. When we arrived, the family was about to have lunch. Once they got over the shock of seeing me, I related the story of my escape and asked if I could stay with them, as I could see no other alternative. They were an older couple and lived with their three children, so I sensed their apprehension.

"If I'm caught, they'll execute me," I said to bolster my argument. Aunt Chi had serious misgivings, but Uncle Trac was more disposed to help.

"You can stay here," he said, "but you have to understand that all of us are in an extremely dangerous position. You must be ready to flee whenever somebody comes. I'll show you where you can run to."

The family lived in a small hut with a roof of palm fronds. There was the only room in the house for two large bamboo beds and a small table. Uncle Trac made another bed for me by placing an old door on a few homemade bricks. At night we would move the table to a corner to make room for my bed.

The house sat in a vast field, with a single narrow trail leading from the road to the residence. Those inside the house could see if someone was approaching from a distance and thus warn me so I could slip out the back door. Uncle Trac took me out the back and across the field into a stretch of head-high elephant grass, then down into a densely wooded valley. He instructed me to flee there should anybody approach and wait for his signal to return when the road was clear.

Reluctant Farmer

For the next two months, I worked as a peasant farmer. The landscape was beautiful in summer with the green of young plants covering the paddy fields. I did what I could to help Uncle, though truth be told I was not a skilled farmer. But staying busy outdoors all day kept me from dwelling too much on Thuy and An.

The week after I arrived, Aunt Chi sent someone to check on Thuy in Saigon. The people there had lost touch with her since she'd gone to Long Giao. Meanwhile, little An was staying with Binh Minh. Later, Uncle Trac's daughter who lived in the city got hold of Binh Minh, who in turn told her that Thuy had been arrested when she went back to see me. My wife was accused of working for the CIA, plotting to break into the camp to rescue me.

The news struck me like a hammer to the head. The soldier who interrogated me had said they'd caught Thuy, but I'd hoped he was lying. Now I knew she was being held at the police station in Xuan Loc, more than sixty miles from Saigon, where I imagined her being harshly questioned.

My first impulse was to go at once and try to rescue her from the police. But how could I get around without identity papers, and where would I get a weapon? I didn't know what to do, but my head and my heart both told me I had to do something. I considered trying to contact my old friends in Saigon, especially those former soldiers who were on the run and still had guns, and maybe we could come up with a plan.

I didn't dare tell Uncle and Aunt of my idea for fear they would try to stop me. Instead, I merely said I wanted to go to the city for a day to check things out.

Uncle Trac listened patiently. He was suspicious of my intentions, though his eyes expressed sympathy.

"I think," he advised, "that you need to go to the church and pray for guidance."

The next morning I accompanied the family to church. It was a long walk across numerous rice fields. The dawn spread a rosy mist over the rice paddies. The pealing of the church bells in the fresh air eased my nerves along the way.

The small church was filled with the faithful. This was a tiny Catholic village, and everyone seemed to know everyone else, as they greeted each other and shook hands. I was a stranger in their midst and felt lost in the crowd. It was the first time I had appeared in public. I had the feeling that someone was watching me from behind and that soldiers were ready to arrest me and take me away at any time.

I went straight to the last pew and sat with my back against the wall. The fear of being spied on from behind followed me the entire time I was a fugitive in Vietnam. Wherever I went, I looked for a spot by a wall to eliminate one direction from which they might come for me unexpectedly. For years afterward—and perhaps for my entire life—that feeling of being watched from behind was an obsession, a part of my character, and I'd have to sit with my back against a wall before I felt relaxed.

Throughout the religious service that day, I felt a mixture of sweet comfort and pain, a sort of exhilaration of being free to come to Mass after two years in prison. In my ears were the prayers and responses of the congregation, but my thoughts constantly wandered to Thuy in jail where she was likely being mistreated. I knelt down and prayed for her, asking the Lord for a clear mind to make the right decision. I bowed my head, closed my eyes, buried my face in my hands and immersed myself in my thoughts until I noticed that my hands were drenched in tears.

After Mass, I didn't wait for Uncle Trac and his family but walked straight home. I picked up my hoe, went out to the rice field and began to work like a madman. I understood then that this was not the time to take risks to do anything about Thuy.

A few days later Binh Minh came up from Saigon to see me. I asked her to go to Long Giao in my stead and try to get in touch with Thuy, to bring her a little food as well as news about me. She made a good effort but was unable to reach my wife.

I lived from day to day, just waiting. Frustrated and depressed, I just didn't know where to turn. Binh Minh came to see me many times, she had no more idea of how to proceed than I did.

I would have to wait for a miracle.

///

One day in July I was up on the roof to repair a leak in the fronds. Focused on my task, I lifted my head to wipe the sweat from my eyes when I spied a woman's figure approaching through the rice fields. It looked like Thuy. It was too far away for me to be sure but at once my heart felt a twinge as if stabbed by a needle. A chill went up and down my spine, I became paralyzed in body and soul. I was afraid I was hallucinating.

The figure came closer, displaying the sprightly movements I so fondly recalled, and I could not suppress my emotions. I opened my mouth, whether to laugh or cry and nearly fell off the roof in my excitement.

She walked along the path dressed in a conical hat, black pants and a brown long-sleeved shirt that could have belonged to any countryside woman. But the way she held herself and her long, quick strides designed to reduce the distance between wife and husband were unmistakable.

I leaped from the roof but lost my footing and fell. Ignoring the pain, I got up and sprinted toward her. As I came closer, I saw that she was quite thin and pale. My heart pounded, my breaths came in gasps, and I was overwhelmed with a mix of pity and joy.

She must have felt the same as she halted in her tracks and stared at me. Our eyes met, then we examined each other from head to toe, saying nothing, not even a greeting.

Finally, I opened my arms and took her to me. She sank into my embrace like a fragile leaf. I wanted to hug her tightly but was afraid I might crush her.

The sound of hurried footsteps approaching woke me out of my dream.

Binh Minh had followed Thuy with our two-year-old daughter. Now she came up quickly and gestured for us to get inside the house.

Thuy stayed with me until the next day. We were up all night, sometimes talking in whispers, sometimes simply gazing at each other in silence, hardly believing we were together again. I wished that time might stand still and tomorrow never come. Neither of us slept that night, afraid of wasting one precious moment together. I told her about my flight from Long Giao prison, but I was anxious to hear her story.

A Trap Is Sprung

■ THUY

After leaving the bag of medicines in the trench beside the prison camp that morning, I left right away without looking back. Consequently, I didn't see the guard beat Phuc. Nor did I have any idea that they had discovered the note inside the cigarette or that Phuc was later thrown into a tiger cage and violently interrogated.

I'd given him many packs of cigarettes with messages inside, none of them had been found. But that last note was too important, so I'd kept the cigarette separate, and it caught their eye. In that letter, I described in detail my plan to help him escape, how I would ride a motorcycle to Long Giao and come right past the place he was working to spirit him away and hide him until a boat was ready to leave two weeks later.

That afternoon there was a sudden downpour. I was staying in the house of a local farmer along with several other women whose husbands were in the camp when I came down with a fever that racked my entire body. One of the women performed *cao gio*[30] (the traditional treatment for fever and chills), massaging my skin with oil and scraping down my back and sides with a coin. It got so cold, I had to borrow the host family's army jacket to cover the thin peasant shirt I had worn from Saigon.

My friends were concerned about my condition and advised me not to meet Phuc later that day as I had promised. But I couldn't

---

[30]cao gio /*cow zaw* or *cow yaw*/

give up on my plan. The future of my family rested on Phuc getting out of the camp so we could all leave together on a boat. I couldn't wait any longer since rumor had it many of the men in Long Giao were to be transferred to the North in the next month.

My friends and I walked the two-kilometer road toward the site where Phuc's labor gang had been that morning. Something felt different. The prisoners were wearing only their underclothes, despite the afternoon cold of the highlands after the rain. In my previous visits, I had never seen them in shorts when working in the tall, sharp grass. Their labor seemed more earnest as if they were under strict observation. They set to their work, with no one pausing to look up and wave as we came by, the way they usually did. This surprised and unnerved me.

When I reached the spot where I'd seen Phuc earlier, I saw a few familiar faces from his labor cell glance up, and then quickly look back down, their eyes darting side to side and gesturing with their hands incomprehensibly. Then some other men did the same. They seemed to be trying to tell me something.

There was a good distance between them and me with two barbed-wire fences in between. It looked as if there were more armed guards than usual, keeping an alert eye out with their weapons ready. I was afraid to stop and try to figure it out. To ease my growing fear, I searched for Phuc among the laborers. If I could just see him and know that he had gotten the message, then I could be assured and take the bus back to Saigon and make the preparations.

But Phuc was not among them.

The other wives and I stopped at a snack stand at the crossroads by the rubber plantation. The little shop sold iced tea, bananas, sweets, and cigarettes. The wives and mothers of re-education prisoners

The same refreshment hut at Cam My - Cam Duong, Long Giao, was still there in 1998.

often stopped under the shade of a tent outside to wait for their men to pass by on the way to work.

I sat down at a little table with Nghia, whose husband was in Phuc's labor team. I looked out across the barbed wire to the prison, wondering about the peculiar way the men were behaving and the reason for the extra security. I was becoming apprehensive and asked myself whether I should take the next ride out of Long Giao or stay and wait for Phuc to appear.

Just as I had decided to tell my friend that we should leave, I noticed Cadre But, the man in charge of Phuc's labor cell, heading toward the snack stand with a posse of armed soldiers. Within seconds I understood what was happening. I turned to my friend and pressed my small purse into her hand.

"If anything happens to me," I instructed her quickly, "take this back to Saigon and give it to Binh Minh. Inside are my house key and all my papers and money."

As she looked at me questioningly, I suddenly had another thought.

"Tell Binh Minh that I hid some money on the left side under the bookcase in my room. And tell her to take care of An for me."

Leaving my bewildered friend at the table, I stood up and walked to the counter. Before my friend could follow, Cadre But and his soldiers came and blocked the door.

"I ask that everyone here remain in your seats," he ordered. "Don't anyone move as we conduct our business."

After assigning two men to guard the door, he took four others inside the shop. He looked all around, and then walked straight up to me.

"Are you 'sister' Thuy?"

Looking at the cadre's angry expression and the frenzy in his threatening eyes, I felt a chill running down my spine. I silently nodded.

"Are you the wife of 'brother' Phuc who came this morning to visit him?" he barked.

I looked directly into his eyes, which shone like those of a mad dog, his malaria-affected dark lips pressed shut viciously.

My heart shattered, and my spirit died within me. Yet strangely I sensed pain but not fear. Being pushed into a corner had awakened my survival instincts. As there was no way out, I felt surprisingly at peace.

"Yes," I answered.

Cadre But removed his pistol from his side and pointed it at me.

"I have orders to arrest you as a spy for the CIA, opposing the Revolution, plotting to sabotage the re-education camp and release the inmates. If you put up any form of resistance, I have orders to shoot you on the spot!"

He wagged his gun to signal two guards to begin marching forward. I came next with Cadre But, who stood behind me keeping his pistol at my back. Two other soldiers brought up the rear.

As I stepped out of the shabby little shop, I threw a quick glance at Nghia, hoping that she would remember my instructions. She just sat quietly, her face pale, my small purse on the table in front of her.

Caught in the Net
of the Long Giao *Bo Doi*

As we marched down the road from the Cam Duong crossing back to the Long Giao camp, I walked under armed guards, my heart numb. Along the way, the local people I'd come to know talked among themselves. They grew quiet as I passed by. Some of them looked at me with pity.

I knew most of these folks. At one time or another, they had helped one of the other relatives of prison inmates in this camp or me. Nonetheless, I avoided looking at anyone for too long, afraid the guards would notice and give them trouble later on. I knew the cadres would immediately go out and arrest anybody they thought was connected to me as they investigated the grievous crimes I'd been charged with.

On the other side of the barbed-wire fence, the prisoners stopped their work to watch me pass. A profound, suffocating silence enveloped us in the crisp wind of that mountain afternoon. All I heard was the clop-clop of my wooden clogs on the asphalt road as I gazed at the stony faces of the men behind the fence. Among them were Phuc's mates from the labor cell, the ones who'd been signaling me earlier. Only too late did I realize they had been trying to warn me.

Now my heart was heavy for them. These were men who had shared the good and bad, the worst of times with my husband. I knew each one. I knew, too, their wives and children, their fathers and mothers, who had come to my house to prepare packages, not just for their own men but for the whole team because the labor cell's prisoners shared their food with each other. Now they stood watching me being led off by soldiers. Phuc wasn't with them. And perhaps I wouldn't see their families ever again.

Now I was learning what it meant to be arrested, to have my freedom taken away, and to lose my rights as a human being. I walked in the middle of my escort, my heart placid, unfeeling, but my mind filled with images of my former freedom.

The image of An, now two years old, wearing the white satin pants and pink shirt I'd just made for her, still fast asleep when I left her that morning. The image of Phuc standing inside the fence, his sorrowful eyes following after me when I left him a few hours ago.

My Papa and Mama, brother and sisters in the photograph I'd received the week before from the United States with their expressions of hope to see me again. And the boat waiting at Bac Lieu to take us out to sea and away from here.

That morning these pictures had been bright in my mind and given me the strength to live and faith in the future. Now they were only dim shadows in my memory. I felt the tears in my eyes. I wasn't afraid of dying. Nor did I fear jail. I was only afraid that those I loved would suffer now that our future was being wiped out.

Cadre But pointed me into a hut by the camp gate next to the sentry box. A female soldier around 30 years old was waiting there already. Her hair was bound in a single braid, her face pale and cold as ice, her beady eyes sharp as a knife. She ordered me to remove the military jacket I had borrowed from the villager, and then she searched me. Finding nothing, she addressed me in a perturbed voice.

"Where's your gun? Where's your grenade?"

"I have nothing," I said, shaking my head.

"Let down your hair!" she barked.

Ordinarily, I kept my hair free, but when I traveled, I rolled it in the back. Now I removed my hair clip and let it fall. The soldier ran both her hands through it searching for whatever might be hidden among the tresses. She felt around my ears, perhaps expecting to find some type of modern espionage technology appropriate for an agent of the CIA. She also checked inside my pockets, the cuffs of my pants, and down every seam of my clothes. Once again she came up empty-handed.

"Where is your purse?" she demanded.

I felt a twinge of glee that they hadn't seen me give my purse to my friend at the snack stall. I feigned ignorance.

"What purse? I didn't bring anything."

The cadre glared at me a long time, and then ordered me to sit down on a wooden chair in front of a long table in the middle of the room. She left with my borrowed jacket. I could hear her saying something in a soft voice to Cadre But and the guards outside.

I sat quietly, shivering from the cold in the thin pants and shirt I'd been wearing all day. The fever returned and made my head burn while my hands and feet were cold. I was wrenched with worry about Phuc. I had no idea where he was now and what they were doing to him. And I thought of my little girl waiting for her mommy to come home.

As dark began to settle, Cadre But entered with six armed guards who escorted me to a Jeep. When one of the soldiers brought out handcuffs, I grew alarmed.

"You're seven men with guns, and you have to handcuff a lady?" I asked, trying to conceal my fear.

Cadre But hesitated, and then motioned for the guards to get me in the Jeep without bothering with the cuffs. I sat in the back with soldiers all around me the entire ten-mile trip to the police station in Xuan Loc. I asked Cadre But if I could send a letter to let a friend know to take care of my daughter.

"With parents like you and your husband," he snapped, "your kid would be better off raised by the state so she can become something."

Then he added, "Your husband can still receive clemency, whereas you, sister, will never get to see your family again since the police won't treat you as decently as we do."

His words cut me like a knife.

Chapter 14

Taken Into Custody

Conflict Between
North and South

It was dark when we arrived at the police station. After I was formally transferred from the military to the police, they led me into a room, empty except for a table in the middle with a chair at each end. I looked around for any tools of torture as I'd heard were used by the Viet Cong, but there was only the dank cold.

A thin man in civilian clothes entered the room. Behind him came two more men dressed in security police uniforms of khaki and pink. While the latter two stood by the door, the thin man looked at me like a chef staring at a fish on a chopping board. His bony face bore the pale color of chronic malaria, and he stood stooped like one who'd spent years living in underground tunnels. In his hands was a folder containing the photographs and letters I'd sent to Phuc over the past two years.

He waved the folder in front of my face as if to show he knew all about me and my treacherous schemes. I remembered what Cadre But had told me about how the police treat suspects. Fear gripped my spine, my throat tightened. Then I forced myself to take a deep breath and face my terror head-on by speaking first.

"If you know all my crimes," I said without thinking, "do you still have to torture me?"

"What you talkin' about?" he asked in a thick Southern accent, apparently taken aback.

I answered as if in a single breath.

"The soldiers in the re-education camp said that you police aren't as decent as they were to me and I wouldn't survive here. I'm scared, so I want to know if you're going to torture me."

Controlling his anger, the police chief clenched his jaw and held his lips so tight he almost whistled through his teeth.

"The Revolutionary security police are not brutal like the secret police in your illegitimate government, sister!" he spat out.

He scowled at me, then turned and left the room.

I could hear him and another man speaking in raised voices. As I sat alone in the chilly room, I searched for a reason why the police chief might have responded so violently to my question about torture. I'd only asked because I was afraid and wanted to deal with the awful truth from the beginning. But the policeman's reaction reminded me of something I'd read once when I was assigned to write a series of articles about Southern revolutionaries who had "rallied" to the South Vietnamese government. Their changing sides were viewed by the North as a betrayal of "Uncle and the Communist Party."

This particular piece of intelligence mentioned a serious breach between the so-called National Liberation Front (NLF) of South Vietnam and the North Vietnamese Army (NVA) as they fought side-by-side against the ARVN and the United States. It studied the attitude of resentment on the part of the Southern cadres who followed the NLF in the idealistic goal known as "resist the Americans and save the country" but did not want to place themselves entirely under the authority of the Northern Communists.

I also thought of the times the former journalists got together at my friends' noodle soup stand and discussed current affairs in the South after April 30, 1975. We met with other Southern journalists, and some of them had heard from other Vietnam Press colleagues who had been Vietcong undercovers. These reporter spies then moved on working for Saigon Giai Phong Daily, the communist paper published right after April 30, 1975, who had access to top-level documents.

According to what I heard, once the war was over, the differences between the Hanoi Communists and the NLF became more pronounced. Instead of sharing power with the NLF as they had promised, the Northerners integrated the Southern revolutionaries into the communists' cumbersome administrative machine, thereby solving two problems at once: to dissolve the power of the Southern Liberation Forces and to appropriate two decades of fighting by the

Southern cadres as their own.

Following a series of internal disputes and intervention by their foreign allies, in the end, power was divided into two sectors: Hanoi took control of the People's Army and the large cities of the South. Meanwhile, the NLF controlled the security police in the South and managed smaller towns and the countryside. This unequal distribution of power created bitterness and resentment among the Southern cadres, feeling their NLF was phased out like a lemon being squeezed dry and discarded, resulting in a grudge war not only between the forces of the North and South but also between the army and the police.

It occurred to me that I had unconsciously understood the root of that war. An innocent question spoken out of fear had accidentally picked at the scab of a fresh wound on the flesh of the Southern Communists. I thought of the lesson from Vietnam's history and the slogan I'd seen everywhere during the war: United we stand, divided we fall. It seems the victory had brought with it a germ of division among the communists. I saw that I could use that division to my advantage to survive. Suddenly I wasn't so frightened, and my mind began to search for ways to deal with my situation.

When the police chief returned, he calmly proceeded to question me in the manner typical of prisoner interrogations, making me declare all the details of my life that led to my arrest. And I calmly answered all his questions, looking him in the eye to show my sincerity. I was relieved when he responded positively to my attitude. After a few minutes, he began looking at me, instead of down at my file or pacing back and forth. Perhaps he was seeing me as an individual, not simply another faceless enemy of the Revolution.

The Xuan Loc Women's Jail

That night, even as Phuc was confined in a tiger cage, I was taken to a jail cell no less miserable. The room was completely closed except for small holes drilled in the door to prevent the prisoners from suffocating. I counted about ten mosquito nets piled together in layers on the cold, damp floor. I hadn't been issued a sleeping mat and blanket, or a mosquito net to protect me from the pests who were famous for carrying malaria in that area.

As soon as the door closed behind me, I sat down right next to it, cold and hungry, with no idea how to fight off the mosquitoes that tormented me. All of a sudden, one of the nets opened up, and I heard a woman's voice.

"Come and lie down inside here before the bugs become the death of you."

Without giving it a thought, I crawled inside the mosquito net.

"Thanks," I said in a soft voice and lay down at a corner of a mat. I didn't sleep a wink all night, distressed about what was going to happen to me, worried about little An, and full of guilt for bringing suffering to my husband. With no idea what tomorrow would bring and feeling utterly despondent, I cried nonstop until morning.

When the gong sounded to mark the start of the day, sunlight was already making its way through the door's holes. Everyone got up and collected her mats and nets. There were a dozen women including me in the cell. My hostess for the night was a plump young woman of around 20, careful about her appearance, who seemed to live apart from the other prisoners.

Our morning meal was delivered to the cell door. The young woman who had shared her net brought me my portion of rice cooked with yellow manioc that smelled of mold. I shook my head, unable to eat.

"Suit you," she said with a shrug. "You can look down your nose at jail food, but you'll find out that if you don't eat, you won't have enough strength to get out of here."

I didn't answer, watching her eat heartily. I noticed that her mat and mosquito net were larger and cleaner than those of the other women. She had a lighter complexion and was more delicate looking than other cellmates, but her appearance was too stylish for a prison. Just a glimpse of her in the daylight told me who she was.

"Thanks for letting me share your net, Miss," I said, then moved closer to the door.

A big woman advanced toward me glaring.

"Go back to your whore Hue," she complained. "This spot's taken!"

I turned to look at Miss Hue. She smiled, unruffled, and continued eating. While I hesitated, undecided where to go, a small, severe-looking middle-aged woman scooted over on her mat.

"You can sit here, sister," she said.

I said a quiet thank you and sat down next to her. I hugged my legs and buried my face in my knees, trying to fight the fear that again threatened to overwhelm me.

After the meal we were all sent to perform tasks in the jail— all, that is, except for Miss Hue. She returned to her mat and lay there half asleep.

Most of the prisoners were sent to work in the kitchen. Along with several others, I was assigned to sanitary duty, cleaning the courtyard behind the jail under the watchful eyes of two guards with rifles. One of them came up to me.

"Don't be so foolish as to think you can steal any of these sweet potatoes in this garden!" he shouted. "You'll be hung from the post."

I nodded, but didn't dare ask what he meant by "hung from the post."

Upon my return to the cell that afternoon I was dizzy with hunger. I quickly ate my meal, ignoring the smell of rotten manioc in the rice.

Night fell. While I looked around to see where I should sleep, the middle-aged woman, whose name was Sister Khanh, brought me a mat that was worn around the edges and a torn net she had found. She arranged her mat so I could spread mine by the wall and helped me tie up the holes in the net with rubber bands. I had to hang the net really low to avoid leaving space where mosquitoes might enter.

Miss Hue looked at me and shrugged.

"You don't want it nice but would rather make things hard," she said coolly.

I didn't answer, mindful of how she had kept me from being attacked by mosquitoes on my first night in jail.

Political Prisoners vs. Criminals

During the first days, I nearly went crazy with despair. I thought about my daughter suddenly without her mommy and daddy. I grieved over my husband being mistreated in prison. And now here I was facing interrogation and threats from the police cadres. I couldn't eat or sleep, my mind constantly urging me to make a break for it. If I succeeded, I could reach my child and care for my husband; if I failed, that would put an end to a life of abuse and desperation.

But it was Sister Khanh, a nun from the order of the Lovers of the Holy Cross, who with her comforting voice patiently reminded me to keep hoping for that happy day when I would see my family again. She taught me to overcome my suffering by reciting the "Simple Prayer" of St. Francis of Assisi. I softly chanted this hymn to myself dozens of times each day, whenever I felt sad, homesick or depressed. And in this way, I was able to get through the seemingly interminable days in jail.

Half of the women in the cell were political prisoners. Among these was Sang, five months' pregnant, arrested in a house full of anti-communist leaflets and charged with taking part in "Restorationist" activities.

The nuns Khanh and Thiem were teachers at a local school. They were accused of "political activities contrary to the Revolution" for teaching religious dogma during class. Sister Khanh was the order's treasurer and had the added charge of "dispersing the order's property which should have come under the control of the Revolutionary government."

Two Buddhist nuns, Cuc and Muoi, were guilty of remaining at their temple to pray and not returning home as ordered when the state dissolved religious institutions.

And I was implicated in the crime of "sabotaging the re-education camp and plotting to kidnap a prisoner."

Among the civil lawbreakers was Miss Hue, arrested for violating Revolutionary morals, that is, prostitution. The remaining women, Thanh, Hoa, Tam, Lan, and Thai, were all in for robbery, murder, and assault with a deadly weapon.

Our living arrangement was disorderly, but with the presence of the religious women, who were quiet and proper in their behavior and went out of their way for others, there was less conflict and discord among us.

Sister Khanh was a tiny woman of indomitable will and exceptional strength. When we worked in the blazing sun, she sacrificed her drinking water to those who needed it more. She took on the more arduous tasks that no one else wanted to do and never complained. Her strength shone in her face. Whether enduring the insults of the police or hunger and deprivation, she appeared extraordinarily calm, her soul at peace in the hands of God.

She also had an admirable memory. Every Sunday she recited passages from the Bible and Gospels for me to write down. That night, the seven Catholic women would sit in a corner pretending to talk but actually have a sacred service. Simple as it was, it proved to be very moving.

The religious writings that I recorded were also smuggled to the three men's cells, where some 200 prisoners were crammed. The men were only allowed out of their quarters for a few minutes each morning to visit the latrine under guard. The rest of the day their sanitary needs had to be dealt with inside their oven-like cells.

Nearly all the men were in jail for "counter-revolutionary political activities" or had been captured in the forests as members of "Restorationist" armies. Although this jail was supposed to be a temporary holding place pending investigation, some of the men had been there for two years without benefit of a trial. Two-thirds of the men were Catholic. Because of the overcrowding, the men could not gather in groups as could the women but remained mixed, political prisoners with thieves and murderers, not to mention cadres planted among them to seek out anti-government sentiments.

The two sisters and I wrote our scriptures with fine pencil on toilet paper and passed these to the men. It was a perilous practice, but Sister Khanh was determined to bolster the prisoners' faith during their time of darkness and suffering.

///

One Sunday morning, the women prisoners were called out of their rest time to clean the Xuan Loc police station. The six common criminals were assigned to kitchen detail. That left the political prisoners the entire task of cleaning the front and back yards along with the police office and prisoner areas.

Sister Khanh and I were responsible for the outside. From there I was able to see the buses that ran on the highway on the other side of two barbed-wire fences. While I swept, I couldn't help but look up at the buses heading toward Saigon, where my little daughter lived without her parents. During the times I'd gone to visit Phuc in

Long Giao, I'd given An to one of my neighbors just for the time being, expecting to return and pick her up that afternoon. The food and clothing she had were only enough for that day. But now ten days had gone by. Being without her mommy for that long, how would she be getting on now?

Tears blurred my vision of the buses on the highway. I wanted to run out onto the road, jump on a bus and go home to hug my little girl. But I had enough presence of mind to know that if I tried such a thing, I'd be shot down in cold blood, just like a male prisoner who'd tried to escape not long before.

I looked over the whole prison grounds as a daring idea formed in my head. Lost in thought, I forgot what I was doing until Sister Khanh brought me back to reality.

"Thuy, do you remember what holiday this is?"

Still dazed, I shook my head.

"The Pentecost," Sister told me. "I thought you'd remember because it looked like the Holy Spirit just placed a fire inside your heart, heh?

"After we finish here," she went on, "I'll have you copy down the Gospel for today, OK? And tonight we'll ask the Holy Spirit for an answer for each of us."

I stared at her in surprise. How could she have known what was in my heart? Her eyes were gentle but shone with superior hidden wisdom, which came from her faith in the immense power of God. I surrendered to those eyes. Although my mind could not stop looking for a safe way to escape the jail, my heart was quiet and no longer burned madly.

The Raffle

That night our modest supper consisted of a bowl of moldy manioc with some rice and a teaspoon of salt. Although I was quite hungry, I just couldn't get myself to swallow. I was haunted by the thought of my little girl all alone. In the end, I pushed my bowl aside and ran to a corner to cry, so as not to disturb the others who were already red-eyed.

Afterward, as the guards were busy preparing their own meal, I sat down next to Sister Khanh and hurriedly recorded the day's

Scripture readings based on her dictation. Then she asked me to write down the seven graces of the Holy Spirit on seven small slips of paper: Wisdom, Understanding, Counsel, Fortitude, Knowledge, Piety, and Fear of the Lord. These were to be used following our Sunday service in a raffle in which each of the Catholic prisoners would select a special gift from the Holy Spirit. I hoped to receive the gift of Fortitude and prayed silently, *Dear Lord, if I pick this gift, I will see it as your acceptance of my decision, and I will place everything in your hands. Tonight I will flee from this jail.* Actually, I had stacked the odds by folding that piece of paper a little differently from the others.

By eight o'clock, the policewoman responsible for instructing us toward our rehabilitation had completed her task and locked us in. The Catholic inmates gathered in a corner as if to discuss the day's lesson, while we actually prepared our service for the Pentecost. I was assigned to read the Gospel passage, often stopping as the words caught in my throat. When I reached the part where it said, "In a room behind a locked door for fear of arrest, the Holy Spirit appeared and lit upon Mother Mary and the disciples..." I was struck by the similarity between that scene and our current position: we, too, were in a locked room, afraid and in despair. I started to cry, as did the others around me. Even Sister Khanh lowered her eyes.

After the service came the raffle. I was the second to take a chance. I looked at the six papers left, trying to find the one that said "Fortitude," the one thing I desperately needed to face the dangers I would encounter if I were to try to escape. I closed my eyes and prayed, then reached for my gift.

Anxiously, I opened my paper and was surprised to read the word "Wisdom" printed on it. Underneath, Sister Khanh had written, "Become like a little child, I will take care of everything." This was a familiar phrase attributed to St. Theresa of Lisieux, my patron saint. I was astonished by coincidence and suddenly felt strangely at peace. Being in prison with all its troubles and cares, what would be better than to "become like a little child" and let someone else take care of everything? I was usually stubborn and found it hard to trust others, but on this night my heart was calm, and I forgot the darkness of the prison cell. I no longer burned to try and escape, at least not that day.

It turned out that on that very night three inmates broke out, two male political prisoners and one female criminal. One of the men was shot and severely wounded as he scaled the barbed wire, while the other was captured the following day at the bus station. The woman, Miss Hoa, was caught three days later at a relative's house two miles from the jail.

When Miss Hoa was returned to Xuan Loc jail, her face and body were bruised and bloody. She did not come back to our cell but was placed in solitary confinement. Once I was given the task of taking her the single daily meal she was permitted. I found her on the filthy cement floor lying spread-eagle, her legs in a wooden stock and her arms chained to a pair of iron rings set near the floor. The stench of human waste and festering wounds was nauseating. She seemed to be starving and quickly raised herself up to eat from the bowl. The strain on her chained wrists cut into her flesh and opened up her bleeding wounds.

Her miserable appearance distressed me to tears. I sat next to her on the floor and scooped food into her mouth with my hands. She looked up at me, her eyes shining with gratitude, her cracked and bloodied lips forming a crooked smile as she greedily chewed the rice mixed with dry sorghum. I would have stayed until she was done, but the guard shouted for me to get out. As I backed away, I watched as Hoa licked the food from her bowl like a dog crazed with hunger.

That night I couldn't sleep. That is how I would have ended up had I persisted in my stubborn plan to escape that Pentecost night.

A Game of Wits

Thanks to the lessons I learned from Sister Khanh to pray and place my fate in God's hands, I felt stronger in dealing with those interrogations the communists referred to as "working." Sister showed me how to keep my mind relaxed and not worry about what to say but ask the One on High to speak through me what needed to be said.

I followed her instructions and felt less anxious and afraid when I faced the police cadre in the interrogation room. However, I still had to muster all my willpower to maintain my composure during political confrontations. Each meeting was like a battle between two competing ideologies. I refused to budge from my position.

"There was no conspiracy with the Americans and former government to help me plot to resist the Revolution or sabotage the re-education camp. I acted alone. I thought up the whole thing myself."

"No one gave me money to make papers or purchase a boat. It all came from friends of the family."

"It was I alone who wrote all those letters. I decided to help my husband escape from the labor camp. There was no organization involved."

"My sole objective was to have my husband with me."

I resolutely denied all the accusations and told the cadre over and over that Phuc and I were not CIA agents wanting to spring all the prisoners from the camp. I added that we had no connection to the Americans during the war.

Every day I stuck to the story that I was a lonely and desperate wife who just wanted to help her husband. I explained that I couldn't raise my child alone, so I took a chance to rescue Phuc so we could be together, and that was all.

The more he listened to this excuse, the more the cadre appeared to be uncomfortable with the "selfish" and "petit bourgeois" attitude not only on my part but on that of South Vietnamese women in general. He expounded on the ideals of communism held by those like him who had regrouped to join the Revolution. Once he angrily accused Southern women of being spoiled by the decadent materialistic lifestyle of the *My-Nguy*—the Americans and illegitimate South— and only thinking of themselves. I agreed with him, realizing that this made me look less guilty than being seen as a female war correspondent that plotted to spring her husband from prison.

His aim was to suppress my lousy attitude by lecturing me on the sacrifices made by those who'd fought for the Revolution. His voice grew in intensity as he described how the liberation cadres gave up their families, their wives, and children, for higher ideals, the opposite of selfish and degenerate people like me.

From his remarks, I realized that he had been a student at the University of Saigon active in the group run by Huynh Tan Mam, a medical student and member of the NLF who advocated a pro-communist, anti-war stance. I also heard his bitterness at how after the victory of the Revolution, the Southern cadres were forced to continue making sacrifices so that the South could "advance swiftly and forcefully into socialism."

As if to prove that the Southern cadres were more civilized than I had been led to believe by the Northern soldiers at Long Giao, the police chief treated me with a condescension that was at the same time polite. Apparently, he was upset that the Northern soldiers had maligned the Southern security police. And I thanked God for giving him a "petit bourgeois" pride such that he regularly boasted of how he lived for noble ideals of the country and Party.

After more than a month of questioning, the cadre was becoming dubious of my responses; although he seemed to believe that I had acted entirely alone. Indeed I had acted in the independent manner of one who has lived in a free and democratic society. He, too, had grown up and been educated in the South, and so, even though our points of view were entirely at odds, he still treated me with civility in the manner of an intellectual. I couldn't understand why someone like him would be a police chief in a small district city like Xuan Loc when he should have been working in a big city or a university.

The Bait

A week after Pentecost, Sister Khanh returned from the interrogation room and announced that she was being released. She told me that the authorities had agreed to let her go if the order turned over all its property to the state. Before she walked through the barred gate, she gave me a little advice.

"Remember to recite the Simple Prayer, Thuy."

I was happy for her but knew I was going to miss a very precious friend. Without her guidance and care in the dismal jail, especially all that she shared with me spiritually, I didn't know how I could go on. I always believed that I would survive. Thanks to her, not only had I defeated depression, but I understood more. In particular, I came to see that I could face life's difficulties through my own willpower.

One morning when I was called in for "work," a term used instead of interrogation. I entered the room to find some cigarettes and small pieces of papers lying on the table.

"If you have been telling the truth, 'sister,' about there being no *My-Nguy* organization behind you," the cadre said, "show us right here and now how you got those little notes inside the cigarettes."

At once I picked up a pencil and wrote a few tiny words on a slip of paper, then proceeded to demonstrate how I could deftly insert the sheet inside the cigarette without leaving a trace. Seeing that, the cadre seemed to believe me.

From then on I was never again called in for "work." The way I saw it, I had been dropped from the list of dangerous political prisoners and placed instead on the list of weak and selfish women of petit bourgeois South Vietnam.

By that time I'd gotten used to life in jail. I wasn't as depressed as before. I even made more friends among the 200 inmates. As Sister Khanh was smuggling copies of Scripture into the men's cells, we unwittingly created a mutual aid society between the wards. And I began to feel more at ease despite being behind bars and forced to perform labor every day.

After two months, I heard some of the guards say that some of the women prisoners—myself among them—were to relocate in the coming week, to a long-term prison. And then the police chief called me into the interrogation room and informed me that Phuc had escaped from the re-education camp.

At first, I didn't believe him and responded that the camp soldiers had probably executed my husband. But I began to wonder if it were true when he explained that Phuc had broken out ten days after my arrest and, now, two months later, the camp soldiers could find no trace of him.

He went on to say that the security police were willing to release me if I signed a pledge to inform them as soon as Phuc tried to get in touch with me. He encouraged me to turn in my husband because, as he put it, no one could escape for long the net of the Revolution. It would be better for Phuc if he turned himself in to the police instead.

I immediately signed everything he asked, including a paper stating that I was released on probation and must report to the local police in my area. Although this was like trading a small jail for a larger one in which I was required to report my activities, movements, and contacts, all I really cared now was the prospect of seeing my daughter again and searching for Phuc.

I said farewell to my friends in prison as I helped deliver meals to the different cells, and they chipped in enough money for me to take a bus back to Saigon. On the bus trip, I changed routes several times to throw any police off my trail. Then, instead of going straight to the local police station to report, I went to see Binh Minh at the embroidery shop where she worked.

My friend nearly jumped out of her skin when she saw me.

"*Troi dat oi!* Heaven and earth! Did you escape from jail too, my girl?"

Once I had reassured her that I was legally released, she filled me in on Phuc's situation. I asked her to take me to see An and Phuc before I reported for probation. She had me wait at a coffee shop while she ran to pick up An at Tuong Vi. Then she took both of us to Ho Nai. From that point on, wherever my friend went, she had to check carefully to make sure she wasn't being followed.

On the way to Ho Nai, Binh Minh told me what had happened after she learned of my arrest. The three journalists went straight to my house and searched for any letters we had smuggled during the two years Phuc was in prison and burned them all. Then Binh Minh and Vi took turns watching An.

///

Exhausted from telling Phuc my story, I sat holding his hand without letting go while I looked out at the rice fields. The sky was brightening with fresh rays of dawn spreading rosy light over the golden grains.

Aunt Chi came out of the kitchen and placed two steaming bowls of noodles in front of us on the stool that served as a table.

The Ability to Survive

■ PHUC

A ll night long as Thuy told her story, I sat looking at her to convince myself that I wasn't dreaming. The more she related, the more I came to see that this woman who I'd believed was so fragile had developed strength and fortitude in the crucible of adversity.

Thuy advised me not to tell An that I was her daddy. The security police liked to come up to children and casually inquire about the goings-on in the home. An had been only two months old when I was arrested, she would not know me now, two years later.

So Thuan An called me Uncle. This was particularly hard for me as I wasn't able to interact with my daughter as any father would, and we didn't like having to lie to her. Still, there was no other way to be safe.

Just seeing my family peaceful and free was a miracle. I wanted nothing more than to live with my wife and daughter. But I knew full well that under the communists Thuy and I would never have a tranquil family life like we had before.

I'd already been too much of an imposition on Uncle Trac and his wife. Plus, Ho Nai was too far from Saigon for Thuy and me to maintain communication. After talking it over, Thuy agreed to work on getting my identity papers and a place to hide out until we could prepare a boat for an attempt to leave the country.

The next day, Thuy returned to Saigon and got in touch with Father Hoang Kim, a Catholic priest and close family friend, who was a well-known Gospel composer. He knew a group that forged papers for individuals living in the anti-communist underground.

In 1977, everyone in Vietnam was required to carry a citizenship card or voter ID card and a travel pass if they went from one city to another. The police could stop a person at any time and demand to see these papers. There were checkpoints all along the roads. Without identification, I would not be able to enter Saigon.

A few weeks passed before Thuy could get the documents. The group asked for 300 *dongs*, the equivalent of a year's salary for a mid-level public worker, for one voter ID and one travel pass.

In keeping with a strict arrangement between the group and Father Hoang Kim, Thuy was not to know anything about the forgers and must not divulge anything about their existence. During the next two years, while I hid out, Thuy had to return to Father Kim many times as the government kept changing its identification and travel forms.

My new name was Le Van Bao. I disguised myself by wearing clear glasses and combing my hair differently. I didn't want to be recognized in Saigon, but this wasn't easy given that I had appeared on TV reporting war news and my voice was familiar from the radio. Whenever someone recognized me and approached, I had to pretend I didn't know what they were talking about.

It saddened us all when I had to part with Uncle Trac and Aunt Chi. Aunt gave me ten ears of cooked corn in a plastic bag. She choked up as she told me to be careful when I got back to Saigon. Uncle Trac remained composed. I knew he was a strong man who didn't want to show his feelings. As I stammered out a thank you for all their help, he interrupted me.

"Don't thank us. You must always remember that no one escapes the Lord's plan, no matter how strong or clever he is. Remember to pray regularly and listen to God's message."

I held in my emotions and bowed respectfully. They said I could use their farm as a hideout if things became difficult in Saigon. Even with false papers, they knew I would face many dangers in the city.

As far as I was concerned, my first wish had come true. I was back with my wife and child. Now we had only one more wish: to flee the country and find freedom.

PART V

EVASION ON LAND
ESCAPE BY SEA

Chapter 15

In The Hands of God
... And Good Friends

A Somber City

■ PHUC

B inh Minh took me on her motorcycle from Ho Nai through downtown Saigon to my hiding place in Cholon, the city's Chinatown. By traveling as a couple and wearing the nondescript *ao ba ba* we were less likely to attract attention, and indeed we encountered no difficulties during our trip.

Returning to Saigon for the first time after two years in prison, I was apprehensive, fearful of being exposed and arrested, despite having identity papers. I was also disconcerted to see that the city I loved had changed so dramatically. The site of South Vietnam's capital, a center of commerce and culture, was now the drab artifact of a socialist system that rejected the trade and allure of civilization.

The noisy, bustling Saigon of the recent past seemed to have vanished entirely—or more correctly, it had shut itself down to escape the watchful eye of the "Revolution." The buildings' facades were decked in blood-red flags, banners bearing fanatical slogans, and monotonous portraits of "benevolent Uncle Ho." The city's gay colors were, if not entirely wiped out, then covered over with the lifeless hues of a communist state.

Large homes were partitioned into living complexes for multiple families. Elegant villas were commandeered by high-ranking leaders from the North who were arriving in increasing numbers to claim their prizes. Beautiful gardens were dug up to grow sweet potatoes and vegetables. Swimming pools became enclosures for livestock. Markets and private stores now housed the offices of communist officials. The citizens no longer dressed in colorful, decent clothing, but all looked the same in the dull garb of lower-class workers struggling to make do in a public factory that encompassed the entire city.

All these changes brought filth and disorder to Saigon, destroying the vestiges of civility and culture. I now knew I would have to leave. My fool's dream of remaining in my homeland with my fellow Vietnamese under the communists had gone up in smoke. I saw not even a hint of a hope there could be peace and revival under such a system. If I was to do anything for my family or my country, I could never do it here.

A Garret in Cholon

I hid in a little crawl space of a small wooden house in District 1 of Cholon. The space, right under a tin roof, was dark and hot, with just enough room to spread a reed mat. There was no actual door; I gained access through a trapdoor in the ceiling of the room below.

High up was a tiny round window, but it was always kept shut. Only at night after all the lights were out did I dare open it to let in some fresh air. In all the months I lived there I never saw the light of day. Meals were brought to me by the owner of the house, Aunt Ri, a close friend of Thuy's mother.

During the two years when Thuy and I were looking for a way to flee the country, I was taken to a series of such safe houses. That was the most nerve-racking period of my time under the communists. I was afraid to go out, even with false identity papers. Still, I had to change hideouts frequently due to random raids conducted by the security police.

All across the South, the authorities applied this method to terrorize the population and surprise anyone who might be living in a home in which they were not registered. The police didn't need an official reason or a search warrant, but arbitrarily searched one area one week and another area the next. I lived in constant fear of discovery and always had to be ready to make a quick getaway in case the police should unexpectedly show up.

One time my host warned me that the police were in my neighborhood. I managed to slip away, but there wasn't time for Thuy's friends to find me another hideout. I roamed the streets aimlessly until late at night. When no one was around, I crawled underneath the steps of a small church. It was pouring rain, and I crouched on the cement foundation, wet and cold, scared and hopeless as I waited for the dawn.

In the morning, the church opened for Mass. I went inside and sat through each service. Afterward, I sneaked into a movie theater where I took advantage of the dark to get some sleep before making my way to the next hideout.

Precious Friendships

■ THUY

Meanwhile, Thuan An and I lived in our little house by the Hoa Hung market where we had stayed before Phuc's re-education incident. By the terms of my probation, I had to report to the police daily. Also, each week I turned in a log of all my activities, no matter how insignificant, such as crossing the street to the market or borrowing sugar from a neighbor.

Because I was closely watched, I had my three good friends serving as contacts and preparing the hideouts I arranged for Phuc. When a location was suddenly raided, and Phuc had to flee before the scheduled day, the homeowner contacted one of my friends to let me know, and we had to come up with a new hideout. After a while, they became familiar with the routine and were able to handle the situation by themselves in an emergency.

Phuc and I were able to meet regularly, but always in ways arranged by my friends. I couldn't visit him in his hiding place, and he couldn't come to the house. So, we'd get together clandestinely in the dark of a movie theater, in a deserted restaurant, or along a river where we felt no one would be watching us. The more our love and longing for each other were challenged, the stronger our feelings grew, and each time we met was a source of joy.

Once Phuc was nearly caught when we were in a small cafe beside the Saigon River. It was the first time the police stopped to check our papers.

We were meeting that day with some friends from the Vietnam Press Agency to discuss an escape plan. On this occasion, the security police suddenly surrounded the neighborhood, blocking the streets in and out. Not content with checking everyone's identity papers, they also had everyone empty their pockets or handbags. Carrying gold or dollars was considered a treasonable offense. I had on me 10 Liang of gold leaves, equivalent to 18 ounces, to pay the organizers of the escape, so we were further concerned. Since our table was on a balcony overlooking the river, I dropped the plastic bag with my gold down into the water.

Phuc began to panic, but there was nowhere to run. He had never before had to show his papers to the authorities, and since his ID had often been redone as circumstances changed, we weren't sure how he'd react. The officers looked at him and gruffly asked his name and address. Fortunately, he was prepared and had memorized his current information.

When they were finished with their inspection, the police made all customers sit for an hour while they harangued us on "Revolutionary morals." It so happened the communists were conducting a campaign to "wipe out all remnants of *My-Nguy* culture" by confiscating and burning books, newspapers and music tapes produced in the South before April 30, 1975. To further stir things up, they forbade couples, including husbands and wives, from displaying affection in public, even holding hands or sitting next to each other—such actions were a "violation of the tradition and morals of the Revolution."

Luckily for us, on that night we were not sitting as couples but as a mixed group, so we avoided being isolated by the police and asked to "work" with them.

I had been so worried about being caught with the gold that I hadn't thought much about dropping it into the river. Still, later that day, we all returned to the cafe after dark. For two hours we waded in the shallow waters under the balcony, groping here and there before finally retrieving my bag of gold leaves.

■ PHUC

T huy's band of women colleagues played a significant role in our survival. Before our country fell, I'd only met Binh Minh, Tuong Vi, and Duyen a few times at press conferences; we never became well acquainted. After they became close with Thuy, my wife told me all about them in her letters. So by the time I finally met the three in person, we seemed like old friends.

During my life on the run, I learned even more and came to admire the organizational skills and personal strength they and Thuy displayed. Now, as during the war, Vietnamese women often experienced periods of their lives when men were absent and couldn't participate in family affairs. As a result, the wives and mothers had to become self-reliant and resilient.

Thuy's friends were all female journalists, talented, confident, and respected by South Vietnamese society. They also enjoyed full lives materially and with their families. Now they showed they could efficiently respond to the present dire situation. I had the utmost respect and appreciation for their stamina and fighting spirit.

Papa or Uncle?

When I saw my daughter An, I was shocked by how much she'd grown during the two years I was away, and I regretted not having been present to observe the early stages of her life. I wasn't there when she learned to walk or began talking. I hated the communists even more for stealing my time and joy as a father and now tying my hands so that I couldn't take care of my wife and child.

I was saddened, too, to see my little one dressed in plain clothes like most people of the defeated South. If we hadn't lost the war, she'd

Thuan An, age 2, Saigon, 1977.

have worn pretty dresses and skipped and played like all carefree children in a prosperous, peaceful society.

Although Thuy had made her cute hats and sewn flower patterns on her clothes, my daughter did not look like a natural little girl from a decent family. She was a child of Communist Vietnam, and if we didn't get her out of there soon, she'd likely grow up to be gray and somber before her time, just like the little girls in the Soviet Union I'd seen in communist books who wound up resembling their grandmothers.

I tried not to feel offended when An didn't let me pick her up. When Thuy told her to give "Uncle" a hug, she'd run away and hide behind "Ma" Binh Minh. When our friend prodded An to come to me, I'd motion for her not to force the girl. I tried to act nonchalant even as my heart was breaking. In my head I understood. An was nearly three, and she was bright. Her eyes would go from her mother to me, sad and confused as if she was thinking, *where's Papa, and why doesn't Mama go visit Papa far away? And who is this Uncle that Mama seems to be so friendly with and she doesn't talk about Papa anymore?*

I felt terribly sorry that my daughter had become a victim of this world in which we had to lie to survive. And I pitied myself, too, for not having the right to call my daughter "Papa's little princess."

Each time I left my wife and child to return to my hideout, I'd lie awake all night thinking about my predicament. And I hurt inside for having to depend on others around me when I could do nothing to protect my family and be of use to them.

■ THUY

I did all I could for An, but living on the fringe of a communist society did not allow me to indulge my daughter as I would have liked. As long as my parents provided financial support from the United States, I didn't have to worry about making a living and providing for the two of us, and I could even help my friends a little. But I still had to live discreetly for our own safety.

In the eyes of my neighbors, I belonged to a family that followed the *My-Nguy*: I was the wife of a re-education prisoner, a person who "owed a blood debt to the people," an "unproductive element" and worthless to communist society.

In short, I was a "bad apple" and therefore unemployable. The local police kept track of An and me, and the April 30 cadres watched us every minute. They were always coming around and asking little An about what went on in her family.

They knew nothing of how I received money from my parents through a secret network of friends with relatives in the U.S. and Vietnam. For my family's security, I kept that information hidden.

I didn't dare dress An any better than the other children in the neighborhood. And I taught her the incorrect words for some of the better foods she ate, such as chicken and ice cream[31], so that if asked by prying police what she'd had recently she would innocently tell them the wrong thing and throw them off track.

In those days, everyone struggled with hunger and want, and many people starved or were homeless. Our food was rationed by the state so that no one had enough. In every house, people had to mix sorghum or tubers like sweet potato and manioc with their rice. Economic activity was sluggish, the future under the communists was so bleak and uncertain that we constantly pinched pennies. In Vietnam, the chicken was a luxury, not to mention ice cream, and could only be purchased at an inflated price on the black market.

I could see that Phuc pretended not to be hurt when An seemed distant and didn't run to him. And I understood how hard it was for him to be close to her when he had to act like an uncle rather than her loving Papa, whom I had always mentioned before this "Uncle" came along.

On the other hand, Phuc was pleased that I had a support group of former colleagues who helped me in many ways and now came to his aid as well. Receiving comfort and assistance from these women may have made him appreciate the difficulties we'd faced and the character we'd shown working in a field dominated by men.

His attitude changed. He became less harsh, more thoughtful and considerate, more circumspect in his behavior with my friends. In return, the women benefited from having a man in their lives after so long enduring the austerity and isolation of communist society.

---

[31] Ga (chicken) was the most expensive meat in Vietnam, so An would call it "Ca" (egg plant). Ice cream, a luxury treat, would be called "Cam" (orange).

Probation and Evasion

For the first six months, I was under strict surveillance by the security police in Hoa Hung district. Naturally, the policeman in my neighborhood was assigned as my probation officer.

The district station was located on the corner of the street where I lived. Anytime I needed to leave my house, I had to stop there first and ask for permission, even if just to cross the street to buy food at the market. If the officer wasn't there, I had to either wait until he returned or go back home, because if he happened to show up at my house when I wasn't there, he'd immediately report me for violating probation. Some days I waited hours to see him.

Each week I submitted a log of my activities for that period, including where I'd gone and what for, who I saw and what I said, and so on. The officer was a young man of around 20, a second-generation cadre more interested in going out and enjoying himself than in doing his job. As a result, my weekly report often mentioned in detail how I'd waited for hours before getting permission to go to the market.

After several weeks of reading the same reports over and over, the officer grew irritated.

"Why do you write so much like this? From now on, only write one page."

After a few months, he told me I no longer had to ask permission to make short trips, and soon he said that I only needed to ask when I wanted to leave the city. As for the reports, they eventually became monthly instead of weekly.

■ PHUC

As I continued hiding in the crawl space in a house in Cholon, I felt increasingly confined and alone until I thought I was going to lose my mind. After a while, I decided I needed to get out at night for some air and to relieve my stress.

Thuy was also concerned about my mental state, so she asked Binh Minh to visit me regularly. Her other two friends were saddled with responsibility for the practical aspects of the survival of their parents and younger siblings. Binh Minh, who lived with her parents, had less to worry about. She was also more suited to our lifestyle: it wasn't enough just to survive, we wanted to get the most out of whatever life we led. And so every few days Binh Minh rode to see me on her bicycle (instead of a conspicuous motor scooter requiring black market gas), bringing some roast duck and, since she loved a good drink, a little liquor to share with me.

I learned from her that after I broke out of prison, the camp authorities at Long Giao discovered a letter from Lt. Hoang among my effects. Suspected of abetting my escape, Hoang was investigated, stripped of his rank, and bounced from the service. When this happened, I was in hiding and Thuy was in jail. Before heading back to the North, Hoang visited Binh Minh to bid farewell and to relate his story. Out of sympathy for him, our three friends collected a little money to help him get started as a farmer in his village. On our behalf, Binh Minh gave him two small pieces of gold from the valuables she was holding for us so he could "buy a bit of peace" with the officials in his home area, and also in recognition of the humanity he shared with us.

Binh Minh was plain-spoken and had a sense of humor. When I seemed absolutely miserable in my little garret and wanted to get away for a while, she was ready to lecture me.

"Listen, my friend. Get used to living on the lam. You aren't able to beat this place because you're a dangerous criminal and they're on the lookout for you!"

"I've never been convicted of anything, and I haven't broken any laws!" I protested.

Then she looked me straight in the eye and laid it on the line.

"My friend, you ARE a criminal AND they're out looking for you. Anyone who's seen with you, whether it's Madame Thuy or one of us, will be arrested right along with you and become criminals, too. Got it, friend? You'd better accept the bitter reality!"

She had a big smile on her face as she emphasized each word. All arguments exhausted, I threw up my hands in surrender.

I no longer had power over my own destiny. My fate was appropriated by others as soon as I bowed my head and fell into the trap of "reporting for re-education." My pride had taken a beating in the face of this reality, but I was willing to place my life into the hands of Thuy's good-hearted friends.

The authorities were still in the midst of their campaign against "bourgeois compradors." They stepped up their security checks and regularly reviewed household registries. The area where I was hiding seemed to be particularly in their sights because of its many lanes leading in and out of Cholon, the commercial and residential quarter of the ethnic Chinese in Saigon.

Even after shutting down all private enterprises, the communists used the campaign to openly confiscate property and homes of business families. At the same time, the cadres had an excuse to search any house for gold or U.S. dollars that might still be hidden. Once found, the money was immediately "confiscated" and the owner charged with being a "bourgeois comprador," for whom else could possibly have such valuables?

Once a raid commenced, the other homes in the neighborhood were alerted, giving me a chance to slip out and hide in the market until it was over. One night, however, the first house the police came to was Aunt Ri's. I had no choice but to lie flat in the garret, my heart going a mile a minute and thinking it was all over. Fortunately, they only compared the number of residents to the registry, glanced around the house, never thinking about the attic space, then moved on. The experience gave cause for concern. I'd lived in that house too long; maybe it was time to find another hiding spot.

After that, I stayed in several places on the outskirts of the city with Thuy's relatives or people they knew. When Ta Anh was released from prison, he and his wife let me hide for a few weeks in an elementary school where she worked. Another time I returned to Ho Nai and hid in the house of a man named Chinh. The family was very religious and attended church services every morning. In time I became bolder and accompanied them. But Ho Nai was an hour's bus ride from Saigon, and it was hard for Thuy's friends to maintain contact, so I gave up and went back to Cholon.

The Press Village

One day as Thuy and her friends were discussing what to do with me, Binh Minh came up with an idea. She had a vacant house in the Press Village in Thu Duc where her family lived before the war's end. Since her husband, Tran Dai, was sent to a re-education camp, she had abandoned the place and moved in with her parents. Now she suggested taking me there for the time being. At least it would be closer to Saigon.

The house was part of a pilot project financed by the South Vietnamese government to expand the capital city and reduce crowding caused by the war. The homes were sold at a reasonable price to journalists; consequently, it was known as the Press Village, and the neighbors were all colleagues from the media. Like Binh Minh, many of the residents had gone to live with their extended families to save money, leaving their homes vacant. I shouldn't be noticed if I hid out in one of them.

Binh Minh took me there on her motorcycle and left me at her house with several days' provisions. Then either she or Tuong Vi came by every few days with more supplies. I had to stay indoors and not make a sound. I couldn't cook or open doors or windows, or do anything that might draw attention and let the neighbors know someone was living there.

For two weeks I lay staring at the ceiling or reading every book in the house. Although I had more freedom of movement than in the crawl space in Aunt Ri's home, I came to see that social isolation was harder to bear than physical discomfort. I searched for any cracks or openings in the walls through which I could view the street or other houses.

My hearing became acuter. I seemed to notice every sound around me, even those coming from far off. A neighbor was secretly teaching his child to play the violin, and I listened for hours as the inexperienced student drew the bow over the strings repeatedly until I had memorized the melodies myself.

My sense of smell grew sharper, too, maybe because I craved the fresh meals I'd had at Aunt Ri's house. Now, forced to eat canned or dried food all the time, my stomach churned whenever I caught the scent of cooking from the neighbors' kitchens. The two scents that drove me crazy were fried garlic and *pho*[32] noodle soup. Just the smell of either of these made me want to run out the door and find where they were coming from. The fragrance of garlic cooking in oil overpowered everything else. And I dreamed of enjoying a huge

---

[32] pho /*fuh*/

bowl of noodles drowning in broth with beef, peppers, cilantro, and basil, eating to my heart's content.

When my mind was not on food, it went to thoughts of getting into a boat to cross the sea, escaping with my wife and daughter and arriving on a foreign shore where we could build a life of peace and freedom. When the body is idle, the brain does double duty. I sat for hours visualizing the future (and fresh food).

Other times I fell into depression, convinced that living like a ghost, unseen and unheard, was becoming more than I could bear. Binh Minh and Tuong Vi came by sometimes with decent food good for a day or two, then left me with more canned fish, rice balls, dried fish, and other canned stuff. I was safe but still felt stifled, a prisoner in my ignorance of the outside world. With no time to talk or ask questions, I got little news of Thuy and An, aside from a whispered message as they handed me my provisions, much like a brief headline to a news story: "Thuy misses you badly." "An just learned a new song." "Mother and child are well." "We'll leave soon." "The plan is ruined." "Working on another idea." "Police still following Thuy." "More news on the escape next week."

After a month of this ordeal, I had lost weight, and my morale was low. I sent word to Thuy that I couldn't take much more of this "incarceration" and wanted to go back to Saigon.

So the women found me a new hiding place. While I waited, Tuong Vi moved in with her young son, Viet Anh, to cook for me. In that way, the house had an official resident, and I could walk about inside without worrying if the neighbors heard noises coming from the home.

Dang Thi Tuong Vi (1946—2006)

With Vi and her son around, my life became more relaxed and active. And I got to eat *pho*.

I also got to know Tuong Vi better. Of Thuy's journalist friends, she was the least talkative.

Dang Thi Tuong Vi was the niece of the well-known literary couple, poet Tran Da Tu and author Nha Ca. Before April 30, 1975, Vi was one of the stars of the Vietnamese Press Agency. Besides working for the government's news agency, she freelanced for private newspapers including *Hoa Binh* (Peace) and *Song* (Life). A sentimental and selfless woman, Vi had a son with journalist Nguyen Khac Nhan, born six months after the fall of South Vietnam. She and her son had been living with her parents and siblings since.

She cooked for me every day, but she and her son had their meal either before or after me, never at the same time. One might say she was the most traditional of the women journalists, always serious, tactful, discreet, and cautious in her behavior. However, after a few weeks together I had an opportunity to recognize the big heart she shared with her friends and was touched by her devotion to me. In particular, I saw how much she loved Thuy and was willing to do anything for her.

One day when Tuong Vi was gone with her son to Saigon to visit her parents and buy food, I suddenly heard loud footsteps outside. At first, I thought it was a bunch of kids planning to vandalize a vacant house. But then there was a loud voice.

"Search carefully in each room to see if anyone is hiding in these houses!"

I bolted upright, accidentally banging my head on a post. Looking around, I couldn't see any place to hide other than the ceiling. I clambered onto the beams and tried to swing higher.

Heavy footsteps thumped outside mingled with shouted commands. Finally, I climbed as high as I could and worked my way into a corner where I couldn't be seen from below. I lay there perfectly still while the police conducted their raid of the Press Village, a process that took several hours. For some reason, they did not search every house, skipping the one I was in. After they left, I waited another hour or so before coming down, half dead with exhaustion. I was utterly dejected and thought about turning myself in just to put an end to my running.

The next day Binh Minh and Tuong Vi came to the house and found me lying in apathy with no will to live. Then they told me about the new escape plan. Thuy had contacted some relatives who agreed to take me in temporarily. I wouldn't be staying anywhere for more than a few days, and I'd have a little more freedom of movement.

Meanwhile, Thuy was no longer subject to tight control in her activities, so she started working on our escape and once in a while would come to visit me.

I went from house to house. Although this involved frequent movement, it was more comfortable for me than being tied down to any one place. I also became more adventuresome and learned some of the tricks of going about on the streets and how things operated in the new society. This brought me into contact with those networks that supported people living in the underground, as well as organizations that helped those who wished to escape the country.

A Prisoner Visits a Prisoner

While I was hiding out in the garden shed of one of Thuy's relatives, my sister-in-law, brother Lan's wife, came to see me. As we talked, she mentioned that in the coming week she and her oldest son Khue would be going to Long Thanh to visit Lan in prison. When I heard that, my heart grew restless with the desire to see my oldest brother, who was like a second father to me. I asked if I could go in place of Khue.

I expected her to refuse and was surprised when she answered matter-of-factly, "If you want to see your brother, that's fine. But you'll have to have proper documents."

When I approached Thuy about obtaining the documents, I didn't explain what I needed them for. She was concerned about my propensity for risk-taking but knew that if I'd made up my mind to do something, she couldn't stop me. So she took it upon herself to get the ID and travel permit for me. Since these papers had to be authentic, she went to Fr. Hoang Kim, whose secret organization typically provided forged documents but could also get real ones, at a price, issued by the district office. They asked for 500 *dongs*, twice the cost of false papers.

With my documents in hand, I took my sister-in-law on a motorcycle for the two-hour ride from Saigon to Long Thanh. Once at the prison, I passed through two lines of security before I sat down across from my brother. Lan couldn't believe his eyes when he saw me. Soon we were both crying.

The visit lasted only 15 minutes. He asked me to take care of his wife and children, and if I had a chance to "visit Aunt Hai" (meaning get out of the country like his sister-in-law), he hoped I would take at least one of his four children with me.

That night, back in my hiding place, I felt miserable. I knew whatever the cost, I had to find a way out of Vietnam. At the same time, I knew that my natural impatience would make this task hard for me and perhaps endanger those who were helping me. I was uncomfortable sitting passively. For now, all I could do was pray for some light at the end of this tunnel.

The Underground Money Network

■ THUY

After Phuc had been going out for a year using false ID papers without incident, we began to feel less wary. I'd believed the communist apparatus was a tightly run machine, and the authorities followed my every footstep to observe what I was doing and locate the runaway prisoner, Phuc.

In fact, the security police were rather corrupt and incompetent, relying on their intelligence officers and local police. But these informants were becoming increasingly venal and used their positions to enrich themselves. Consequently, I took more risks and made more significant efforts to come up with a plan to leave the country. The more we probed, the more we encountered people working together to hide fugitives and develop escape strategies.

Despite this, for two years we experienced one failure after another. My parents sent us money any way they could. Without their financial support, we could never have survived in Vietnam. Everything required money and lots of it. For just to make do in Vietnam, we might not have needed much. But living on the run, purchasing false papers that had to be continuously changed, and the cost of buying a place on a boat at around five liang, or $1,250, a person, the expenses added up.

My entire family was living in the United States, except for sister Thanh in France. Phuc had two brothers living abroad: Hung, a former diplomat residing in Canada, and Bao, who fled in 1975 and lived in Kansas City.

After the war, the U.S. placed an economic embargo on Vietnam, so there was no legal way to send money into the country. My parents used a method based on trust commonly practiced by families of emigrants.

Having American dollars in Vietnam was considered a treasonous offense, and if caught, a person would spend time in jail. Meanwhile, the Vietnamese currency was mostly worthless and continuously changing anyway. The safest unit of payment was gold. And so, most significant transactions were based on that metal. Wealthy individuals in Vietnam needed to transfer their assets to relatives abroad before the communists seized them. To accomplish this, Vietnamese émigrés gave an amount of cash to someone living outside of Vietnam connected to one of these wealthy families. News of the transaction was wired (there was not yet direct phone service between America and Vietnam) to the wealthy person, who would then deliver an equivalent amount of cash or gold to the intended recipient.

In my case, the delivery person came to my house and, without saying a word, handed over the gold and left without a receipt, which would have been evidence of a crime. This affair would seem to be fraught with risk, but in fact, the Vietnamese established a secure financial network that benefited both sides. Each party trusted the other, and the system worked quite well.

Sea Flight and Dishonesty

It was because of the underground money-exchange network, which was based entirely on trust that we were able to survive in Communist Vietnam. The authorities must surely have known about it, but they were helpless to infiltrate and control it. Nor could they monitor the communication network, since the telegrams were sent in code. The only danger was in getting caught carrying gold on your person, which would lead to immediate arrest with direct evidence of treachery.

Although the communists had won the war and held all the power, the Northerners were much poorer and less educated than the people of the South. After April 30, 1975, the soldiers and their families from the North saw for themselves the reality of life in South Vietnam and realized that the justification for all their sacrifices during the past two decades—namely, to "liberate" the South from poverty and exploitation—was a sham. Feeling duped, they became greedy and unprincipled, easy to buy off. It was in this environment that the movement to flee the country blossomed, not only in the South and Central regions but also in the North. Everywhere along the seacoast people looked out longingly for a chance to escape the poverty and oppression of communist society.

Everywhere you went you'd hear people talking about escape attempts: who got out, who failed, which organizers were legitimate and which ones phony. Many attempts failed right offshore, while others reached the shuttle boats before having to turn back. Few made it out to the larger fishing boats. The exception was the forced evacuation of Chinese residents as the government tried to purge the population of ethnic Han in the late 1970s, especially during the military conflict between Vietnam and China. From January of 1979, the Vietnamese government allowed the "official" sale of places on escape boats to these residents (at an inflated price), benefiting from both the expulsion of unwanted "foreigners" and the appropriation of gold and property from the evacuees.

For two years, we were involved in 20 proposals, but only two of them resulted in an actual boat and neither eventually worked out. Time after time we said farewell to family and friends, hoping that finally, they wouldn't need to worry about us anymore. Then, after the plan came to naught, we returned home physically weary and emotionally defeated, our money gone, and our future uncertain.

Not a few hopefuls gave up after four or five such failed attempts. After more than 10 tries we, too, were worn out and discouraged, but we couldn't quit. Given our situation, if Phuc and I didn't get out of Vietnam, we would end up being shot or rotting in prison. For this reason, our friends didn't let us abandon our goal.

Early in our attempts to escape, we lost all our investment to deception and fraud. As the family of a fugitive, we had to flee at any price, so we were easily victimized by unscrupulous characters. Some organizers cheated us outright, taking our payment and then disappearing. Another time our plan failed and when we demanded our money back, the organizer threatened to expose Phuc and turn us in. After losing our money and watching helplessly while better-organized boats made it out to sea without us, we began looking for ways to deal with the con men.

Demanding Money Back

■ PHUC

T huy and her friends did a little investigating of the person in charge of the failed escape plan. I went to the man's house and demanded our money back.

When he threatened to report me to the authorities and have me arrested, I stood in his doorway and shouted at the top of my lungs, accusing him of organizing escapes and cheating people. I then told him that if he didn't give us back our payment, I'd be back with a gun and get down to serious business.

Of course, I had to run away before the police came looking for me. But the owner of the house couldn't escape his home and neighbors, so he was forced to deal with me and either refund the payment or come up with another escape boat pretty soon. Although my violent reaction had an immediate effect, I knew it was incredibly risky. There was, I felt, no other choice since we couldn't afford to be cheated all the time. And whereas others who failed to escape could always return to their homes, we had to continue trying to flee until we succeeded.

■ THUY

A lthough Phuc's method of restoring our money was effective at that time, it was fraught with danger. Our friends advised more prudence in the future, reminding him that it was better to lose money than people. Still, there were legitimate escape trips that we'd missed because we didn't have the money at the right time, so my women friends and I got more involved.

We came up with several strategies for demanding refunds that worked quite well with people of bad character. Such individuals were generally cowards and conscious of their guilt, so we needed to be brave and make ourselves masters of the situation rather than victims. One method was for two of us to go to the person's home and wait for him to return. We'd spend the day in his parlor, making ourselves at home, sitting in the middle of his living room and reading. If someone showed up, we told them why we were there. This went on until the man came and discussed the matter with us. It usually took two times before he returned the payment, since he didn't want to draw attention to himself and what he was up to.

If the person lived too far away, we'd go once and obtain his address, then send him telegrams. In those days, telegrams were only used by people living abroad to contact their families or send money. Postal workers made a fuss whenever one came in; soon the whole neighborhood knew, and the recipient would have to pay them to keep quiet. The security police also took notice. In our case, we sent daily messages the likes of "Return our money" or "Still owe five liang gold." The swindler would contact us quickly and take care of the matter to get us off his back.

We had other methods, some mild, some severe, depending on the circumstances. Often we simply had to turn their threats back on them, since they were usually weak in the knees and didn't have a just complaint. Through these efforts, we managed to retain much of our investment and thus could keep on trying to escape. It also showed that with a functional support group we could do just about anything.

Entrusting Our Lives to Strangers

■ PHUC

D uring my two years as a fugitive, Thuy and I frequently traveled back and forth between Saigon and Vung Tau as well as other coastal cities seeking some way to leave the country. Although we paid our way, came to the shore, and even got to the small boats many times, we only boarded the big boats twice.

We bid adieu to family and friends far too many times, ate far too many *bon voyage* dinners, and accepted far too many farewell gifts, including handkerchiefs "to wipe our tears" and scissors to "cut our ties," traditional symbols of parting. Eventually, it became embarrassing. After a time, Thuy and I only said goodbye to our closest friends before quietly slipping away.

Before each trip, we paid the boat owner or trip organizer in gold, and after each failure, we waited and waited for them to organize another attempt. The organizers would generally not refund our money but would reserve us a place on the next boat, thus keeping us from working with someone else.

Each time was the same: I had to trust the organizers, hand over the payment, and, if things didn't work out, wait for them to come up with a new attempt. A few days before departure, we were given a brief outline of the plan. The day of, we took a bus to the gathering place and waited in a safe house for the time to set out.

The period I feared most was when we stayed among strangers, putting our lives and belongings entirely in the hands of the organizers. Then we were divided into small groups to follow the local guides to the rowboats, which took us to the shuttle boats before we finally reached the big boat. The entire time we had to maintain silence and obey our guides completely.

There were times, too, when we walked all night to the taxi boat only to be suddenly warned that the trip was canceled and we had to go back. Our investment would be lost. Other times we might be robbed on the road and have all our money taken. When that happened, we didn't know if the trip had been real and we'd just been unlucky or if it had all been a scam from the beginning.

■ THUY

There were a few actual boat escapes but we did not have enough money to pay for the whole family. I then tried to convince Phuc to leave by himself. I analyzed that his situation was in greater danger so he needed to flee first, and we would not have to worry about him. It then would be much easier for An and I to make arrangements to follow him later.

Once there was a boat escape leaving from Phan Thiet, but we had only five langs of gold left, just enough to pay for one person. After many days persuading and pressuring, I finally got Phuc to reluctantly agree to leave by himself. Binh Minh took him to the train station for the early departure to Phan Thiet, thinking that without seeing and saying goodbye to little An and me would make it easier for Phuc to leave.

In the afternoon, I visited Binh Minh at her broidery shop. The two of us were sadly talking and guessing that at this time, Phuc would have been getting ready to embark the escape boat. Suddenly, I looked out of the window and saw Phuc standing right there looking in. Binh Minh hurriedly came to him and took him to a coffee shop nearby. After watching around to make sure that no one was following any of us, I joined them at the shop. Binh Minh and I then found out that halfway to Phan Thiet, Phuc got off the train and took the return train back to Saigon. He decisively said, "We either survive together or die together, I am not going to leave by myself."

Fortunately for us, that boat escape got canceled, so the organizers refunded half of the payment I made for Phuc.

Chapter 16

Gambling With Destiny

Vu Thi Binh Minh
(1944—1978)

Of my three companions, Vu Thi Binh Minh became our tightest friend. Being less encumbered by family matters than Tuong Vi and Duyen, she could spend more time with us. Her personality was very congenial, and our relationship was closer than family.

Binh Minh had a degree in law, but rather than practice in that field, she became a reporter for the Vietnamese Press Agency. Her husband, Tran Van Dai, was an assistant to the Minister of Labor and a professor at Dalat University. As she said, "The good thing about being a woman is that you have choices. Why should I sweat and slave as a law drudge when I have a husband to support me so I can do whatever I like? As a journalist, I can combine work and pleasure. So that's what I'm going to do!"

She was utterly candid and spoke her mind, regardless of whom she was talking to. But she also had a comical streak and left us in stitches when she mimicked her old boss and colleagues in the press room. Everything seemed to amuse her, and she even made fun of herself.

After Tran Dai was released from re-education camp, our two families considered leaving together, but that never came off. Then in late 1978, Binh Minh's aunt set up a boat escape for her extended family. Tran Dai, Binh Minh, and their daughter were slated to go. Our friend begged to let us come along and even offered to give up her own family's spot to let us leave first, but her aunt refused, insisting this was for relatives only. It was with a heavy heart that we bid farewell to our friend and savior, our daughter's godmother, and one who had shared the bad and the good with us the last few years. She and I had become exceptionally close. No matter how hard the times were or how low I got, she was there to lift my spirits and give me hope. While I was glad for her family that they had a chance to flee, I was deeply saddened.

A second blow came a few months later when Tuong Vi fled the country. The owner of a boat at Rach Gia let Vi and her child take the place of Binh Minh's family, who had already been paid for. After only a week at sea, their boat landed safely at the Leamsing refugee camp in Thailand. Phuc and I shed tears of joy when we heard the news.

Meanwhile, Binh Minh had disappeared without a trace. None of her relatives still in Vietnam heard anything from the more than 100 people on that boat, which left the country on Oct. 2, 1978. It was years later that we found out her family's boat had been stranded on a coral island in the Philippines. After half the passengers slowly perished, others broke up the boat and used the planks to try and float out to sea in the hope of being rescued. Only two survivors were picked up by a Japanese merchant vessel after days of drifting. The refugees said that Binh Minh's family had stayed behind on the boat.

///

After losing two of my closest friends who'd stood by me during the past four years, I fell into a deep depression. Meanwhile, Phuc was having trouble living apart from us. So I decided to give up my house and skip probation to live with him on the run.

Taking advantage of the corruption of local officials, we arranged for my cousin Huyen Nga, the daughter of Uncle and Aunt Trac, to take over the house so it wouldn't fall into the hands of the state.

Thus we began a new phase of our life together. But now, being with Phuc and experiencing what it was like to live as a fugitive family, I realized what a nightmare it was. The sound of footsteps at night terrified us. Any noise could rattle our nerves. Phuc was always ready to climb up into the ceiling whereas I had to find a place to hide in the armoire. Thuan An slept with the house owner's children in case Phuc and I were forced to make a run for it and couldn't take care of her. An still called Phuc Uncle, and if anyone asked where her daddy was, she answered that he was in a re-education camp.

Each night we prayed for the safety of Binh Minh's family. As for us, I only prayed that we would make it through to the next day. I didn't dare to ask for more.

We lived like this in constant fear until brother Lan's wife let us stay with her. She'd heard I was carrying my second child and felt I shouldn't be living in such an unstable situation. It was a dangerous move for her since she would be in deep trouble if we were caught in her house. But what else could we do?

Besides, Phuc had promised to take one of Lan's children with him if he escaped. It was common for families to send some of their children with a relative when they didn't have the resources to leave as an intact family. Also, the wife often had to remain behind to wait for her husband in prison and to hold onto the house in case the escape failed, and the children came back.

15 Days Adrift

■ THUY

I n February of 1979 we set out on a serious escape attempt. Earlier, after brother Kien had gotten out of the country successfully, he introduced us to the group that organized his escape. Now it was our turn. I was six months pregnant at the time.

After nearly 20 failed attempts, our network contacts had dried up. Phuc's outlook was dim, so we jumped at this latest opportunity. We came up with the gold demanded by the boat owner—a small fortune of 10 liang, or about $2,500 US in 1979—and, trusting in Kien's connection, paid in advance. This gave us priority on the upcoming trip, despite my condition. Boatmen typically refused to take a pregnant woman on board as they believed it brought bad luck. I remember hearing stories of boats caught in storms where the passengers wanted to throw a pregnant woman overboard as an offering to the Sea God.

Phuc and I were aware of the physical dangers to our second child and me, but we were desperate. So it was that we set out, bringing along dry crackers to help with seasickness, our hopes high.

There were five in our family group: besides Phuc, me and An, we brought along two of brother Lan's children, Khue and Mai. In all our attempts, this was the first time we actually made it to the "big boat" that would take us out to sea. The boat was called "big" to distinguish it from the skiffs that taxied us from the tree-covered shoreline to the fishing vessel that was our ride to freedom. Our "big boat" was 10 meters long and three meters wide, barely large enough to hold the 38 refugees crammed on board.

As soon as we reached international waters, we gave a cry of joy and congratulated one another on what we believed was the start of a bright future. Phuc took a bag of salted prunes

A typical fragile escape boat. Photo: United Nations, 1979.

from a hidden pocket sewn into his shirt and handed it to me. That was the fruit I craved most during my pregnancy. As we celebrated our first success, Phuc patted my swollen belly and spoke to the baby inside.

"You'll be born in the promised land of freedom!"

That night, however, a storm broke out, and the rising waves battered our boat, threatening to send us to the bottom of the ocean. We crouched down and clung to each other throughout the ordeal. By morning the weather had calmed, but that same day the engine died. It was then our "mechanic" reluctantly admitted that he knew nothing about machinery but had lied to gain free passage on the boat.

And so we drifted aimlessly for 15 days.

I lay on the deck exhausted. My worries now were not only

for the baby inside me and my four-year-old daughter, who squirmed and cried from hunger, but also brother Lan's children, whom Phuc and I had promised to take care of as if they were our own.

Love in the Hardest of Times

The boat rocked and pitched on the endless ocean. Waves rose and crashed all about us, keeping us always drenched. The able-bodied passengers took turns bailing water and sheltering the children.

One morning—I can't remember which day it was since by then each day was like all the others— we woke up to an agonized cry.

"Oh, God! The water's gone! What happened to it?"

An inspection of the fresh water tank revealed that it had taken a beating and the water had run out. Meanwhile, the food container had been drenched by the waves, and the supplies were ruined.

"We're all going to die!"

There wasn't a single drop of clean drinking water on the boat. The sun beat down on us relentlessly. The little dry food some of the passengers had brought proved useless, as eating it just made them thirstier. It did appear that we were all going to die.

After discussion, some of the men decided to boil ocean water and collect the steam. They rigged up a device from a can and pipes, wrapping clothes around the pipes to prevent the steam from evaporating before the water dripped into a pot. In this way, they were able to generate about a pint of water per person each day. In all my life I never tasted anything so wonderful.

Although I knew each of us was given one pint a day, there were some days when Phuc gave me a half-pint extra. As I eagerly drank it down, I asked him why I got more, to which he merely replied that it was for the baby inside me. But then one night I overheard one of the others at the steamer talking to Phuc.

"You'd better drink your ration if you want to stay alive to take care of your wife and kids. If you keep giving it to her, you'll die first."

Since then I refused to drink more than my share and waited

to see with my own eyes that Phuc drank his ration.

When the engine stopped working, so did the pump and bailing had to be done by hand. Phuc took responsibility for mustering the passengers when their time came to bail or to boil water. But he often had to take over for someone who was too weak to complete his shift.

After a few days, the fuel for boiling water was used up. We all contributed clothes or other burnable items to keep the fire going. When those ran out, too, men started removing nonessential pieces of wood from the boat to stoke the fire. But that didn't last long either. Finally, when there was nothing left to burn, we gave up.

In that state, we drifted for days. Our flesh burned, our lips cracked and bled. We lay listless and starving.

I was racked by hunger. My throat burned and my body screamed for water. The baby inside me had not moved in several days. I lay on the deck barely breathing, obsessed with images of fresh, sweet water. I dreamed of the showers I used to take at home, the clear streams flowing from my head to my feet, then down the drain. Why had I been so wasteful? Why hadn't I held out my tongue to catch the precious drops then? And here I was dying for just a little water to wet my parched lips.

Every once in a while Phuc came to me with a spoonful of water he got somewhere, I savored each drop. It seemed to awaken my senses and revitalize every organ in my body.

Little An remained beside me, weak from crying for something to eat and drink. Once, when she crawled to the side of the boat to relieve herself, a man sitting nearby handed her a jar. He asked for her urine, explaining that a child's urine was potable. At first, she cried out in fear, but then she quieted and asked for the jar for herself. I was too tired to see what she did with it.

It was only when we spotted a ship at sea that we came alive. We scrambled to our feet and shouted, waved, even wrote "SOS" with charcoal on a white cloth that we spread on top of the boat for them to see. But every ship passed by.

Once we were so desperate, we set the boat on fire to force a ship to rescue us. We knew that maritime law required vessels sailing in international waters to come to the aid of anyone in distress. But the vessel lumbered on, and we had to douse the fire to keep from destroying our boat.

Compassion Fatigue

Twenty-two ships from around the world came into view, but not one stopped to rescue us. Some came so close we're sure the crew saw women and children desperately clasping their hands begging for help, but at each time the ship turned and pulled away. Later we would learn that by 1979 it was common practice for international ships to ignore the Vietnamese boat people. Their governments ordered them not to pick up refugees because once they did, the captain became responsible for them, and the nation that had commissioned the ship was required to accept the refugees for resettlement. For that reason, they just stopped saving people.

Vietnamese refugees using a river boat for sea escape. Photo: United Nations, 1979.

Ignorant of this policy, we were incensed and frantic whenever a ship sailed away, leaving a refugee boat to serve as a floating coffin for the dozens of people awaiting a slow death.

Nothing left us more pained and disappointed than watching people of the civilized world turn their backs on us. Phuc and I promised ourselves that if we made it to a free country, we would use all our communicative resources to share with the world the hurt and sorrow of the boat people abandoned on the sea. I had my own powerful dream to one day return to these waters on a ship to rescue more refugees. Unbeknownst to me, Phuc had the very same idea.

Burial at Sea

■ PHUC

After 12 days at sea, even I, young and active and enthusiastic at the beginning of the trip, felt so hopeless that I lost all motivation. I couldn't stand watching my wife and daughter languishing on the deck while I was powerless to do anything about it. Thuy and An hadn't spoken in two days, too weak to make a sound.

One woman's face was swollen from the heat, her puffed lips purple and formless except when her cracked, white tongue stuck out as she tried to breathe. A man stripped naked, thinking that would keep him from being burned by the sun; in just one day, however, his flesh stretched and peeled as he cried out frantically. Another man's nose grew so swollen it shut his nostrils, he had to breathe with difficulty through his mouth, which became swollen, too.

Most of us were so overcome with exhaustion we couldn't look at each other or try to help. Our eyes glazed in despair and reflected only death.

After about two weeks one young man, driven mad by thirst, leaned overboard and gulped up the sea water. I pulled him back and asked those nearby to keep him from trying again. But we were all too weak and dispirited to maintain watch over him. He ended up sneaking to the side and scooping water with his hand, gorging on the ocean. We found him rolling on the deck delirious. Within two days he was dead.

Now everyone noticed. We wrapped his body in a blanket and said a prayer, then tossed it into the sea. The corpse floated alongside us for a long time. We all prayed for his soul to be at peace. I asked that his spirit watch over the rest of us and help us make it through this ordeal. An hour later his body had moved far away and disappeared in the waves.

The deceased was a younger cousin of a colleague of mine, Nguyen Duc Nhuan, business manager of *Song Than* newspaper and the man who organized this boat trip. Nhuan helped many people escape to freedom. However, on one trip, as the refugees were about to be rescued by a commercial ship, they rushed in a frenzy to one side of the boat, causing it to capsize, killing many still inside, including his own wife and child.

With the passing of this young man, the other passengers abandoned all hope. No one had the strength to continue bailing, though we knew that in only a day or two the boat would fill up and we'd sink. We seemed to be on the ferry taking us to the underworld.

But the ocean wasn't finished with us yet. The waves pushed and rocked us side to side. The current pulled us forward, then backward. We continued to drift, bobbing on the broad sea for one more day. On the evening of the very day we said goodbye to the unfortunate young man who only wanted to slake his thirst, we found ourselves closing in on land.

We were back at Vietnam.

Arrest... and Escape

On the fifteenth day, as I lay in the boat half conscious, I heard voices that seemed to come from another world. Struggling to sit up, I saw a group of people standing in a higher boat looking down at us as if observing a pile of corpses. Then I noticed the communist flag and froze with the realization that we'd been captured. At the same time, I was relieved that my family would not die forlorn on the ocean.

I crawled over to Thuy, An, and my nephew and niece lying in the cabin. I hugged my wife and daughter, speaking to them as if to myself.

"We're going to shore. Soon we'll have all the water we want. Don't worry about being arrested. At least we're alive!"

I was sure that I'd be returned to the prison system and likely face execution, but I didn't care. The main thing was that my family would be safe.

Some of the border guards laughed, saying that fate must be on our side to let them find us before we perished at sea. They towed our boat to a fishing village called Vinh Chau in Bac Lieu province. There they forced the men at gunpoint to get out and pull our boat onto the beach, then help everyone off. Once we were all on shore, they herded us to an old temple nearby.

I was shocked that after two weeks of thirst and starvation we still had the strength to heave the boat full of people and assist the women and children off. Then again, the guards were armed, so we had no other choice.

At the temple, they ordered us to sit down on the floor. Then they proceeded to search everyone, taking any money, gold, jewelry or other valuables, as well as our papers. I slipped off my wedding ring and tried to hide it beside me, but in my weakened state I was too slow, and a guard snatched it right away.

When they'd taken everything they could find, they handed out forms on which we recorded our names and addresses. To avoid being discovered, Thuy and I used fake names. I was Tran Ngoc Tuan, while she became Vu Nga Dung, the name of Binh Minh's younger sister who had already escaped Vietnam and whose papers Thuy was using.

By then night had fallen. The villagers brought us drinks made with sugarcane, and some kind-hearted folk even gave us thin rice gruel to regain our strength.

Once we had eaten, the guards lined us up to march to the police station. Women, children, and those too feeble to walk were allowed to ride in an ox cart. The night was pitching black; you could barely see the person next to you. We stumbled down a path between two rows of growing rice like ghosts traversing the mantle of darkness, accompanied by the creaking of the cartwheels. I slipped through the line and pulled myself onto the cart to talk to Thuy, keeping my face low so I wouldn't be noticed. As soon as she saw me, she whispered.

"You need to get away before we reach the jail. They'll find out you escaped prison and kill you!"

"I can't leave you and An!" I protested.

She took my hand and motioned for me to go.

"If you stay," she said, "there's nothing you can do for us. They'll kill you, and then they'll kill us all. The only way you can help us is to run."

I felt guilty about leaving a pregnant wife and small child, plus two young relatives. But Thuy urged me to be realistic. She reached into her hair bun and removed a ring.

"I kept this hidden," she said, slipping the ring onto my little finger. "You can use it in an emergency."

The cart halted in front of the police station, where the sentry opened the gate. The refugees in the ox cart waited for those on foot to enter first. That's when Thuy squeezed my hand goodbye and pushed me out. I dropped from the cart and ran into the bushes beside the road, hoping the darkness would cover my movements from the guards.

Once everyone was inside the gate, I crawled out and started to walk down the road toward a light in the distance. The area was unfamiliar to me. I had no idea what to do or where I was headed. Plus, after 15 days on the sea without food or water, I was still unsteady on my feet. Gathering my strength, I dragged myself forward, step by step. I wondered how I'd be able to get away if I were stopped. After a stretch, I came upon a marketplace with empty stalls. There, completely spent, I dropped to the ground and fell into a deep sleep.

///

I woke to someone pulling on my leg. It was the market's security guard. He looked me over in the dim light of the lamps hanging from the stalls. I didn't know how long I'd been asleep, but it was still dark. As far as I could tell, this was it.

"You're a boat refugee," the guard said, helping me to my feet. He kept a grip on my arm when he saw I was unable to stand by myself. "You should be at the police station with the others. So what are you doing here?"

As I berated myself for not using the cover of night to get farther away, the guard seemed to be looking me over.

"Did they take everything from you?" he asked suddenly.

I understood his meaning at once and displayed the ring Thuy had just given me. His eyes lit up. As I removed the ring and handed it to him, I said silent thanks to Thuy.

He dropped the ring in his pocket and told me I wouldn't be safe unless I got out of the district. I figured he wanted me far from his village, the sooner, the better so he couldn't be implicated. Now he had to help me.

When I told him I didn't know the roads in that area, he guided me to a bus station, where he handed me 10 *dongs* for a ticket.

"If you're caught for whatever reason," he advised me, "don't say you ever saw me, you hear? Do you understand what I'm saying? It's for your own good."

He tried to sound threatening, but I could tell he was scared of being found out. Right now he just wanted me out of his life.

And with that, he turned and left.

I waited for the bus in a state of high anxiety. The sky was beginning to lighten. I was barefoot and wore a black shirt I'd borrowed from Thuy, having burned my own in the fire on the boat. My flesh was charred by the sun and my face marked by the smoke from days collecting steam from the boiler. My hair, filthy and matted, stank of fire. I hadn't shaved in weeks. It didn't take much for someone to guess I was a boat refugee. I tried to make myself small in the back of the bus, but some of the passengers kept turning to glance at me.

The bus stopped in Can Tho. I remembered that Mai Hoa, a friend and military journalist, lived there, so I got out to looking him up. He wasn't home, but his younger sister, Nguyen Nhung, gave me a change of clothes and a little money. I washed up and dressed, then went for a shave and haircut before boarding a bus to Saigon and my sister-in-law's house.

The next week, sister Lan went with me to Vinh Chau to get An out of jail and deliver food and money to Thuy and Lan's children. She also inquired into ways to "facilitate" Thuy's release.

Reality and Loyalty

■ THUY

I was seven months' pregnant by then. When another refugee woman gave birth in jail and was sent to a clinic, I volunteered to accompany her as an aide. Seeing my condition, the police agreed to let me attend to the woman during the day.

That gave me an opportunity to go out in the street each day to visit the clinic, as long as I returned to jail at night. I had some money from my sister-in-law, so, after assisting the new mother with her various needs in the morning, I strolled around the nearby market, supplementing my diet to revive the baby still quiet inside of me. I also bought something for my niece and nephew and some others in jail.

Each day that I passed the bus station, I had to fight the urge to get on a bus and head to Saigon, where my husband was waiting for me. I knew I should see a doctor to find out about my pregnancy. And I needed to work on another attempt to escape. Plenty of reasons to break jail and go home.

But I still had my niece and nephew to worry about. The obligation to sister Lan, who relied on us and was now protecting us, outweighed my personal interests. I struggled with this—responsibility versus personal need—each time I watched a bus leave Vinh Chau.

In any case, my brief foray into freedom ended the next week when the new mother was sent back to jail with her infant. My opportunity to slip away was gone. I reflected sadly on my experience and how it was sometimes harder to fight oneself than contend with another.

A couple of months later, after more groups of failed boat people were brought in, the facility became too crowded. At that point, the Vinh Chau police decided to release all the women and children from the earlier arrests.

On June 26, 1979, our second daughter was born in Tan Dinh medical clinic. Since I wasn't named in the household registry for sister Lan's house, I was technically not eligible to

Thuy, Phuc, and Thuan An at Baby Su's baptism. Saigon, 1979.

have my child in that clinic. However, thanks to a nurse who knew sister Lan and a doctor on probation after having been released from a re-education camp, baby Su came into the world without any record, and mother and child received the care they needed.

Phuc and I named the girl Duong Vu Chau Giao to commemorate the two places Phuc had just escaped from, Vinh Chau and Long Giao, and to give those names a positive connotation in our lives. Sister Lan and her children affectionately called the baby "Su" after the French pastry *chouchou* (in Vietnamese *su su*) because of the girl's tiny size, the result of malnutrition from our escape attempt and jail.

D Day

■ PHUC

Sister Lan's house was located on Tran Khanh Du Boulevard, a residential street along the large Tan Dinh market that covered 10 city blocks. On the other side of the market was Hai Ba Trung Street, the main road into downtown Saigon.

For the first few months, I didn't dare leave the house. Should visitors arrive, one of the children was sent to warn me. Then I'd climb over the wall in back and disappear. The market, which was about four kilometers from the heart of Saigon, proved to be an excellent place to evade detection. The crowded stalls with people going here and there created a cover and distraction for anyone trying not to be noticed.

Also, the busy market attracted peasants from the countryside. Although they couldn't afford the fees or deal with the burdensome regulations of operating a kiosk or stall, they eked out a living selling on the street. Extolled by the communists who declared "The people are masters, the proletariat is the ruler," the peasants could come and do much as they pleased. Any actions taken against these poor people were condemned as "petit bourgeois" and thus anti-communist. Thus, residents along the marketplace could do nothing but ignore the vendors who took over their street to conduct business.

This made it easy for me to blend in with the poorest

elements of society. Amid the hubbub of the market, new faces were hardly noticed, even in a society based on vigilance and suspicion.

So I'd wander around, waiting for the all-clear signal—perhaps one of the kids would give a whistle—and go back to hiding in the house.

"We have to stay one step ahead of the communists," sister Lan used to say each time I came back.

///

When the morning of October 19 arrived, the sounds of street vendors calling out their wares and the noise of people coming and going resounded into the yards of the French-style villas along Tran Khanh Du Street.

On the other side of an iron gate, behind a house with a milk fruit tree heavy with fruit, nestled in the corner of the maid's quarters, my family was still asleep. I was on a mat spread on the brick floor, my back against the small bed where Thuy and the two children lay. My wife was restless, while the baby on her stomach slipped gently down to rest on top of her older sister, who was clutching a doll.

The room was always dark with the windows kept closed, since they faced the back wall that separated the building from the alley.

In the main house, sister Lan's family was already awake and busy with their daily routines: making breakfast, sweeping the front yard, and getting the kids up and dressed. I heard my sister-in-law tell the others not to wake us in the back.

"Today Aunt and Uncle need their rest."

It suddenly struck me what day this was. I jumped up and opened the door on my way to the main house. At once I ran into the old nanny. She had stayed on with sister Lan in exchange for a place to live during the hard times under the new government. Instead of greeting me as usual, she thrust a small piece of paper into my hand.

"There's news," I whispered to Thuy when I came back into the room. She quietly sat up and shifted the sleeping children to the side as I opened the slip of paper.

"Mrs. Hai is ill. Please come to see her this afternoon," I read.

We looked at each other wordlessly, feeling both excited and anxious.

I gave Thuy's shoulder a light squeeze as I slid past her and made my way to the main house. There was much to discuss with sister Lan, my oldest brother's wife. Although the household had been making preparations for some time now, I knew that today there were last-minute issues that needed to be resolved and arrangements prepared for any unforeseen events that might arise. With my brother still in a re-education camp, I wanted to be sure his wife was ready to make it on her own.

After the aborted attempt with us, their oldest son Khue had escaped with my brother Kien and was living in Norway. Now, sister Lan wanted to send her other son Hoa with us. The daughters, Mai and Diem, were to remain at home with her to wait for their father. Although sister Lan wasn't the only woman in Saigon forced to manage a family without a male to help out, I was worried about her and wanted to talk things over carefully. And I wanted to show my gratitude to her for saving our lives.

■ THUY

Phuc was gone making final preparations with sister Lan, and my niece Diem went to Kien's house to get his second son, Khoa, who was coming with us. Meanwhile, I started packing. I got out the vitamins and energy pills that would be essential once we were out at sea. These items were in such high demand that they were sold as soon as they showed up on the black market.

Then I went outside to check on my lemon-sugar mix drying in the sun. Lemon-sugar was said to be good for thirst and boosting energy, besides being inexpensive and easy to carry. Thuan An got some cans of condensed milk for Su, who at four months of age needed this to supplement my breast milk.

"Mommy, do I wear my special clothes today?" An asked.

"Yes," I replied as I dressed her little sister. An went to the dresser and pulled out three shirts which she proceeded to put on, one over the other. By now she was used to the routine of getting ready for the "border crossing." She carefully buttoned the shirts herself, but she needed help putting on an extra pair of pants. Then I smoothed her clothes so they wouldn't look bulky.

"Today you go with Uncle," I told her. "Mommy wants you to be good and do whatever Uncle tells you, OK?"

"I must be quiet and always go with Uncle," she said as though reciting a lesson.

"You're so good! Now, if someone asks you anything, what do you say?"

"I don't say anything."

"That's right. Now go up to the house. Have some bread and drink all your milk, hear?"

"Yes, Mommy."

She jumped off the bed and ran from the room, her arms hanging at her sides. By this time the little girl had gotten used to hiding her feelings, knowing how to stand at attention and choose her words carefully.

A few seconds later I heard her footsteps returning. An ran to the bed and searched under the blanket.

"I'm bringing my baby along, OK, Mommy?"

She took out a cloth doll that "Ma" Binh Minh had made for her before leaving.

I patted my daughter on the shoulder.

"An, if you eat a good breakfast, yes you can. You have to be strong today."

She hugged her doll and left.

I shook my head sadly. *Why not let her take her toy?* I thought. *Maybe it'll bring her luck.*

I remembered my close friend, whom I hadn't heard from since she left. But before my eyes got teary, I pushed the memory aside and concentrated on my packing.

After counting my gold rings, I placed them in the secret pockets I'd sewn into our clothes. All my gold leaves had been changed to rings and chains, which were easier to carry and conceal. I could not forget the time a necklace had been yanked from my neck when we were robbed.

I tucked some money into my pocket for bus fare and the few things we'd need along the way. Since that time I'd converted my jewelry into cash, I'd learned how useless it was to save communist money, which had no lasting value. The people involved in escape attempts wouldn't accept cash.

Once I was satisfied with my preparations, I nursed Su, and then went to the main house to join the others. Sister Lan advised me to eat so I wouldn't get hungry, then feed the baby milk with watery gruel to fill her stomach for a while.

I followed her inside and worked on my sewing, hiding one more gold chain inside the waist of Su's pants and more in the peaks of the little wool bonnet I'd made her. Then Mai reminded us that the bus was about to leave. I put away my work and stood up to leave.

At the gate I gave a farewell hug to sister Lan, then Mai and Diem. I waited patiently as Hoa said goodbye to his family. He'd never been away from them before, so his mother offered some advice. The 12-year-old understood that this trip was somehow crucial and assumed he was going out of the country to be with his brother in some faraway place called Norway. He had no way of knowing that a boat trip of this kind we were about to embark had no predictable destination.

Phuc gave instructions on how we were to leave.

"Khoa and An will go first and sit with me. Hoa will follow and sit with Thuy and baby Su."

We nodded in understanding that the family needed to break up so we wouldn't attract attention to ourselves.

"Is everyone ready?"

"Yes," the children chorused.

Our farewells were quiet and grave with no sign of emotion. Phuc turned and walked out with Khoa and An. Before disappearing through the gate, An turned back and waved.

I handed Hoa the bag and started to lead the way out. Soon, however, he was ahead of me, excited to be part of a daring adventure.

Like An, I turned to look back and raised my hand to wave goodbye to sister Lan, Mai, and Diem.

Chapter 17

Adversity at Sea

Ngoc Ha Village

■ THUY

O ur first rendezvous point was the village of Ngoc Ha, some 90 kilometers from Saigon. We rode, however, for another hour and a half before I got out with Su and Hoa. Then we stood in the road as the old vehicle roared away, blasting foul black smoke in our faces.

I heaved a sigh of relief, glad to get off the crowded bus filled with the odors of passengers trapped inside in the sweltering midday. I also wanted to escape the onlookers who seemed to be sizing us up, trying to decide if we might be on our way to flee the country.

As we walked toward the village, Hoa ran ahead, curious to see the world outside his home for the first time. There was a single route that led from the main road to the village, bordered on both sides by green fields. I gazed at the familiar little yellow wildflowers on either side. Everything looked just as it had the several times before when I'd been here. I knew I would soon encounter the same tight-lipped souls in hut number 1 that I'd met before.

The peasants in the halfway house appeared detached from their guests, but the food they provided was warm and delicious. The residents of Ngoc Ha were clearly expecting many arrivals before nightfall.

This was one of the many Catholic villages that sprang up in the Mekong Delta region when Northern Vietnamese fled to the South after the 1954 Geneva Accord. Here were the homes of those country people who disdained city living and wanted to maintain their association with each other in a village setting, preserving their own parishes and settling along the canals and waterways convenient for rice farming.

Ngoc Ha was composed of families from the Hanoi region who built their homes amid the fertile lands of the South. Its location was advantageous in another way. It lay among the channels that led to the sea, making it ideal for organizing trips out of the country. Both because of their hatred of the communists and to make a little extra money, the people of Ngoc Ha cooperated with the escape organizers by allowing their homes to be used as meeting places and way stations for refugees before they headed out to the larger boats offshore.

///

Phuc and I had been here a half dozen times during the past year, but all our escape attempts so far had failed. Sometimes we had to walk a considerable distance before reaching a "taxi" skiff that would take us to the "big" boat. The only time we actually made it out to sea was the one where we ended up drifting for two weeks only to end up back in Vietnam.

I recalled my first visit to the village. At the advice of the locals, I'd worn the coarse clothes and rubber sandals of a peasant to blend in. I also tied my hair in a tight scarf like the women who lived there. Before leaving, the refugees were coaxed into handing over to their hosts what was left of their Vietnamese currency. Just before reaching the taxi boat, however, our guides abruptly informed us that our plan had been compromised and we had to disperse. Still in shock, we made our way back to the village, where we looked up the hosts who had taken our money.

Recalling this, I counted the money I'd brought along. After 20 escape attempts, I no longer trusted anyone, so I set aside a certain amount as a gift for the host family and kept the rest for myself, not enough to worry about wasting if we should finally be successful in getting out.

When we reached hut number 1, I stepped inside and bowed to greet the six people already there. They were almost finished with their lunch. I sat down and ladled a bowl of soup to ease my stomach and keep up my strength.

By an unspoken rule, refugees meeting in Ngoc Ha were not to get to know each other or engage in any actual conversation. This was for our own safety in case the trip went awry, and we were arrested: the less we knew the better for everyone involved.

After a quick lunch, I found Phuc a few doors down, taking a nap with Thuan An. As more people arrived, it became evident we would be going on a large boat. This made me nervous, but I did my best to calm myself. Then it began to rain, the drumming of raindrops on the roof made me drowsy.

Shortly before dusk we were aroused and told to get ready to leave. The organizers gave us final instructions. We'd heard all this before and knew the rules by heart: *No talking. Keep your footing and don't fall into the paddy fields. Parents with young children must give them cough medicine or tranquilizers to make them sleep, so they don't start crying and betray the escape. If you drop anything along the way, leave it and keep moving so you don't get left behind. Avoid all noise. Watch out for communist security patrols...*

Seated beside the four children, I closed my eyes and said a prayer. Meanwhile, Phuc seemed to be deep in thought. The rain was getting harder, I heard him sigh anxiously. We knew we had to leave in the dark of night, when there were no moon and stars, with as little visibility as possible. But I still asked Mother Nature to have pity on us and not have us go out in a storm that made our passage more difficult.

Superstition and Burial Ground

Night fell quickly once the sun had set. Phuc and I were separated into two groups to increase our chances of at least some of us making it safely.

When it was totally dark, our guides arrived on bicycles, then dismounted to lead us on foot. Phuc was in the first group. Since I had a baby, I was taken out of the village by myself on a bicycle. I was used to this treatment and no longer asked to be kept with my whole family. Although the organizers planned the most efficient ways of moving their crowd, I knew that sometimes they made decisions based solely on superstition and misogyny. It was because of this kind of thinking that some pregnant women got threatened to be thrown overboard as their pregnancy was blamed for a boat engine failing. Many Vietnamese going out to sea retained these weird ideas even in this modern time.

The men who organized the escapes discriminated against women. Sometimes they refused entirely to take mothers with small children, the reason being, understandably, that a young child might start crying and give them away on the road. Thus, women in my position had to know the boat owner or organizer or be ready to pay extra for the privilege of leaving the country.

I realized I was fortunate to be included in this group, so I followed the guide's instructions to the letter. I held Su tight in the infant harness strung to my front and said not a word as we marched out of the village and into a large cemetery. The guide dropped us off behind a big grave mound.

"Wait right here for me to come back and get you," he whispered.

He climbed back on his bicycle and disappeared into the darkness. Now I was alone in a dark field surrounded by fireflies that flickered and darted about like ghosts. Although I knew I was only a short ride from the village, the quiet and dismal surroundings made me feel like I was at the edge of the world. I looked up at the starless sky and tried to keep from thinking grim thoughts.

The Vietnamese are afraid of ghosts and cemeteries. I'd already dealt with my fears in the house in Hoa Hung, but I felt Hoa shivering as he gripped my hand. My skin began to crawl. In the pale blinking of the fireflies, the graves seemed eerie, even threatening. I closed my eyes to block them out and repeated the prayer to the ghosts Mama had taught me.

Our guide was gone for a long time. Hoa started slapping at the tombstones to chase away the bugs.

"Don't make a sound!" I scolded between my teeth. "The police will hear you!"

Su squirmed in my arms. I'd given An and the baby cough medicine to make them sleep, but it didn't seem to be working on Su, who was probably restless from hunger. Once in a while, she uttered a short cry; panicking, I quickly placed my hand over her mouth.

Hours later I finally heard a voice cut through the night. Hoa and I followed the sound and discovered our guide had returned, this time without his bicycle. He held out a rope for us to grab onto. We walked behind him along the narrow dikes through the rice fields. By then the medicine was working on Su, I was relieved to hear her regular breathing in the carrier hanging in front of me.

I gripped the rope hard to stay on track and keep my footing on the muddy ground. When I did slip, my foot would sink into the wet earth, and it took some effort to pull it out and shake off the muck.

It was slow going through the field. Then I felt the rope grow slack. I heard whispering. Someone coughed.

The Taxi Boat

■ PHUC

I carried little An on my shoulders from the bus stop to the village. After a good meal at the way station house, I told her to take a nap. It was hot out and the mat she rested on was rough and uncomfortable, but eventually, she fell asleep.

She was still asleep when we started down the path. I carried her again, patting her back as I walked. More than once she slipped in my arms so that I had to heft her gently to keep her from waking up too soon.

My group was the first to arrive at the little rowboat that would take us out to a larger fishing vessel. I placed An on the floor under the seat, then helped the others climb in. Once we had about ten people on board, the boat was heavily weighed down. I reached out to touch the surface of the water and found that the waves came right to the edge. So I held my breath and sat still, afraid that any movement might tip the boat and sink us.

Two men rowed us offshore. They moved very slowly, sometimes drawing us under the overhanging trees to conceal our presence. When I heard the oars of another boat, I knew we were approaching a "taxi" boat. Soon the passengers were transferred from the rowboat to the shuttle.

As I stood up with An in my arms, I nearly fell. An arm reached out to help me regain my balance. I took a deep breath and cleared my head. That was the second time that night I'd nearly fallen. In this endeavor every minute counted; if I slowed things down the opportunity to escape would be gone.

More rowboats arrived and deposited their passengers in the taxi, which was equipped with an outboard motor. I searched for Thuy, and then overheard someone say the boat with her group had gotten lost and would be left behind. I almost died. The previous afternoon's heavy rain had flooded the channels, making it harder to find one's way. Shaking all negative thoughts from my mind, I had to believe that my wife and child were going to make it. If not, I would abandon the trip and stay with them.

To our mutual relief, we were reunited on the taxi boat.

Thuy came up beside me, drained and panting. The six of us sat against the side of the boat, huddled together to make room for others.

When the boat was full, the motor was started, and we set off on what was considered the most dangerous leg of the journey. The ride to the big boat took us across waters patrolled by communist guards, so we had to stop and hide more often than we had in the rowboat. Sometimes the pilot would cut the motor and slide us under cover of trees until a patrol boat passed. We breathed easier each time the engine was restarted, and we continued on.

At one point Thuy was resting her head on my shoulder about to fall asleep when she suddenly jerked up to the sound of two men whispering.

"That's the tree," one said, "the one with the branch leaning to the right."

I was close enough to see the pilot pointing to a tree extending over the water, its twisted roots lying both above and below the surface. I couldn't help but notice that the branches pointed to the left.

"We need to go a little farther to be sure," the other man said hesitantly. "If there's no other tree like this we'll turn back."

The boat sailed on. I closed my eyes and prayed that God would show them the right way to take us to the big boat. At a fork in the channels, we encountered another boat. There was a tree reaching over the water that had a trunk split in a large "V." Thuy and I looked at each other. The two men expressed satisfaction, and we went on.

The fact was that the lives of our family and many others were in the hands of amateurs. I was about to give them a piece of my mind, but Thuy clapped her hand over my mouth and shook her head.

Our lives were at the mercy of others' incompetence.

"It's just like our last trip," Thuy whispered. "Just pray it doesn't end the same way."

Lying flat on one's back in a small boat with no cover in the murky night, unable to see anything and not allowed to make a sound, was a frightening experience. For Thuy and me, who had become accustomed to being masters of our own fate, the greatest challenge we faced was placing our lives in the hands of others.

The organizers generally paid off patrol boat captains to ignore any unusual activity on the escape routes. But the communists didn't always keep their end of the bargain and might stop a boat and arrest the refugees anyway. In the mixed-up dire circumstances of post-war Communist Vietnam, trust sometimes exacted a very high price.

International Waters, the South China Sea

■ THUY

This was our twentieth escape attempt. Even when we reached international waters, I didn't dare believe we'd actually broken away from the scourge of Vietnam. Sitting with my husband and the four children, I remained wary and alert.

During the last four years, our lives had followed many twists and turns and confronted us with complex challenges. All we had left to rely on were ourselves, our friends, and the love we

An escape boat similar to our boat of 81 people leaving Ngoc Ha in 1979. Photo: UNHCR.

shared. Now, on a fragile boat sailing on the open sea, I sat with my back against Phuc, my children in my arms, and reflected sadly on my homeland. I pictured Tuong Vi waiting for us in a refugee camp and remembered Duyen, who had sent us off with the words, "Now you two can go out in public holding hands and not be afraid of being watched by the police."

At the same time, looking out at the black waves extending far into the distance, I thought of Binh Minh and hoped that our friendship would be strong enough to let me feel her presence when we passed the area where she had disappeared.

I considered myself lucky to have found a level place to sit in the crowd of women and children, unlike the last trip where I'd balanced awkwardly on the uneven bottom of the boat. The current boat was 39 feet long and 13 feet wide, just big enough for the 81 refugees aboard to sit or lie down and still have a little freedom of movement. However, the cramped quarters caused frequent conflicts regarding space and hygiene.

It took us about 10 hours to reach international waters. Fortunately, we had set out on schedule and reached our goal before dawn. This was important because no matter how generously they were bribed, the patrols couldn't pretend to not see anyone out at sea during the daylight hours, and we had to sail beyond the patrol area before the day-shift crews appeared.

After a few hours out we'd been caught in a torrential downpour, large raindrops battering the boat like gunfire. Many of the passengers became seasick, their vomiting turning the boat into a fetid mess. An and Su began crying from restlessness and hunger, but neither Phuc nor I could do anything to comfort them. Even mixing formula for the baby was difficult with the rocking and pitching of the boat.

Our arrival in international waters elicited cheers from the passengers. They hugged each other, overjoyed. Not only were we safe from communist patrols, but now some of us could come to the upper level, allowing those below to stretch and ease themselves. As for me, I restrained my feelings. The best way to protect me against disappointment was to remain impassive in the face of change. I'd have liked to go on the deck with the others, but since the children were asleep, I stayed in the foul-smelling cabin among the pale and groaning passengers sprawling around us.

It was still raining, and the wind was gaining strength,

whipping up massive waves and frightening the passengers. The pilot noted that if we were near shore, we'd be heading for shelter.

Phuc came below to where I sat huddled in the cold.

"Do you think we'll make it through the storm?" a woman asked.

He didn't answer. We were starting to worry, too. All around us families were holding hands and praying. The mournful tone of their incantations sounded like a funeral prayer.

I was getting uncomfortable. I'd had plenty of experience on boats, so I didn't get seasick, but with so many others retching around me, I couldn't stop my stomach from heaving. Unable to stand it any longer, I woke up the girls and followed Phuc to the upper deck. With Hoa and Khoa, we sat in silence, numb inside, wondering if we would see tomorrow.

Winds, Waves, and Conflict

We were two days out of Vietnamese waters, and still the storm did not let up. Powerful winds and surging waves rocked the boat violently. Through the mantle of rain, we could dimly make out land in the distance. Some of the families asked the pilot to turn back.

"Better risk arrest as escapees than all die on the sea in such a storm!" declared one woman through tears as she comforted the child clinging to her.

Several others voiced their agreement. Phuc stood up to counter them.

"We've already come this far," he shouted. "Why do you want to turn back? Others made it, so can we. We have to. Whether we live or die is up to fate. We just have to be determined, and God will help us!"

The passengers were divided in opinion. Although inside I agreed with Phuc, I could see that returning was a realistic choice. The storm had gone on for days without letup, the women and children were sick to the point of dying. If we turned back, we'd probably end up in jail, but at least we'd still be alive.

As the argument mounted, the pilot began to turn the boat around. Just then we encountered another vessel. With the poor visibility, it was impossible to tell if it was a police patrol or a fishing boat. While we considered our options, we heard a gunshot.

People started screaming, those who had been arguing before now came to help the pilot steer the boat out of range of the other vessel. Everyone was frightened out of their wits; no one brought up the idea of returning to Vietnam any longer. I sighed softly and said to myself, *it's a sign from God that we should go on.*

Phuc's face showed his satisfaction with the turn of events. He, too, believed that God had intervened and made the decision for us.

The following day we sighted land. Some of the men offered to help the pilot row toward shore. From a distance, it appeared a long strip of land on the horizon. There was speculation that it might be Malaysia or the Philippines—even, suggested someone, Hawaii! These were all fantasies since we had hardly sailed far enough to reach those shores. But dreaming helped them forget their hunger and despair.

As we sailed closer, someone shouted, "That's Con Son Island, my friends."

Others protested, but a few men who looked like they'd been in the military concurred.

"Turn around! That's Con Son. Quick! We need to get away from here!"

Con Son was a prison island belonged to Vietnam. Now everyone urged the pilot to head the other way.

That night the storm calmed down, and the waves subsided. We went below and fell into sleep.

A Faulty System

The next day the engine, which had been running smoothly up until then, sputtered and died. The boat began drifting.

Surprisingly, I found myself unruffled and unafraid. It seemed that whether floating aimlessly on the ocean or fleeing arrest in Saigon, it was all the same. At least on the sea, I didn't have to lie to survive and still harbored a bit of hope for the future. Living or dying on the sea was preferable to the slow death of the soul that came from hiding from the communists.

As we sat holding our children, we were relieved that, unlike last time, the current wasn't taking us back to Vietnam. Instead, we were heading into the Gulf of Thailand.

We bobbed and rocked on the waves. Meanwhile, the passengers tried to get the boat's mechanic to take a look and see if the motor could be repaired. It was then we discovered that, once again, the "mechanic" knew absolutely nothing about engines. Phuc wanted to jump up and teach the man a lesson, but after seeing the imposter's gaunt face as he lay sick on the boat's deck, he was forced to accept how living with the communists had brought a man to the point of lying to save his life.

There was general agreement that the entire escape system was rife with incompetence and neglect. Most organizers were solely concerned with making money and gave no thought to the consequences their decisions had for so many people. The escape vessels were usually just rickety old fishing boats not intended for travel on the open sea. The entire coastline of Vietnam was populated with fishermen, so there were many boats available for a price. Boats changed hands often and were hard for officials to keep track of, and besides, many officials could be bought off.

The smugglers bought small motors (the authorities had "nationalized" all the large engines) that they kept hidden from the police. Fuel, too, belonged to the state, so boatmen had to buy it in small quantities that they stored, concealed until they had enough to run an engine for several days.

It was the same with the crew: catch as catch can. Declare that you can sail a boat and you become a captain. Claim to be an expert in machinery—even if you only know how to fix a motor scooter—and you're a mechanic. There was no time to check a person's qualifications or judge their honesty.

Shortly before the departure date, the organizers brought the motor to the boat, often without testing to see whether it actually worked. Around that time, too, someone brought the cans of fuel that had been buried somewhere and now had to be kept hidden in the boat.

In most cases, once the refugee boat made it past territorial waters, the motor either died or ran out of fuel, or else there was no more food or water. The frightening thing was that the lives of scores, even hundreds, of refugees, leaving with all their lives' possessions, would perish innocently due to the shortcomings or irresponsibility of others.

One might ask why so many people accepted such a flawed system. It was simply their need to leave the country at any price, and the desire exceeded the means. The people felt that death at sea was preferable to a slow death with the communists.

I have deep faith in God's protection and believe that everything happens for a reason, even if we don't always know what that reason is. I just could never agree to live under the communists, especially with children. If necessary, I'd sacrifice my life so that my children might know what it is to be free.

I got a chill down my spine the first day An came home from kindergarten singing, *"I asked my Mommy if she could tell/ How many American airplanes fell. I dared her on her fingers to count: One, two, three, four..."* and *"Last night I dreamed of Uncle Ho...."*

It was horrifying to think that arithmetic homework was used to brainwash such an innocent mind using the *My-Nguy* to teach numbers: "Yesterday, Uncle *Bo Doi* killed two American soldiers. Today he shot three puppet soldiers more. How many *My-Nguy* did he eliminate altogether?"

153. TRÂU CŨNG ĐÁNH MỸ

Hồi ấy, giặc Mỹ còn chiếm miền Nam nước ta. Một buổi trưa tháng bảy, trời nắng như đổ lửa. Bầy trâu đầm mình ở vũng nước cạnh đường. Một toán lính Mỹ đi càn về, mặt đỏ gay, mồ hôi nhễ nhại. Chúng ào xuống lầy súng đẩy trâu đi, giành chỗ nằm cho đỡ nóng. Bầy trâu vùng dậy, mắt đỏ hoe. Những cặp sừng cong, nhọn hoắt, chém vun vút. Một tên Mỹ bị trâu chém chết ngay trên vũng bùn. Nhiều tên khác bị thương, khiếp hồn kéo nhau tháo chạy.

Nực cười trâu biết xung phong,
Đuổi quân giặc Mỹ, góp công diệt thù.

A sample lesson for second grade pupils, excerpt from a communist textbook after 1975, titled "Even A Water Buffalo Fights Against the Americans."

153. Even Water Buffalo Fights against the Americans

(Excerpt from a communist 2nd-grade textbook)

At that time, the American marauders seized the South of our country. One midday in July the weather was hot like fire. A herd of buffalo was wallowing in the water beside a road. A platoon of American soldiers passed by, their faces flushed, their sweat flowing. They charged down using their guns to drive the buffalo away to gain the water for them to cool off. The buffalo rose up, their faces are red with fury. Their sharp curved horns slashed this way and that. One American was gored and died in the mud. Many others were wounded and ran for their lives.

How funny that buffalo know how to fight, Chase off foreign raiders and wipe out our foe!

Everyone Bailing Water

■ PHUC

There were a total of 11 children aboard the boat. Su was the youngest at four months. Some four or five were around An's age, four to six. None of the kids seemed to suffer from seasickness, although they were tired and hungry and sat close to their parents for protection from the weather. The ordeal overpowered their usual restlessness and quieted them.

We'd brought along packages of ramen noodles, but they were salty and made a person thirstier. Su was content with her milk. And while An at first made a face and refused the lemon-sugar, which she thought was too sour, she later found it quelled her hunger some.

Without a working pump, our boat was taking on water. The men took turns bailing, day and night, using small bowls and empty containers. I was one of the few hardy persons on board. Most of the passengers were from the city and unused to being on the sea, and now they lay on the deck in considerable discomfort. Although I was tired, I was able to supervise tasks. We organized a three-man chain: the first scooped water with rice cup and poured it into a basin held by a second man who passed this to a third who dumped it over the side. The water flowed back in.

When not on the bailing shift, I took the initiative to manage other necessary activities. I made sure people were awake for the night shift, as we could not afford to cease clearing out water at any time. Naturally, there was some resentment, but I think most of the passengers welcomed my taking charge to prevent things from getting out of control.

In the days that followed the weather were clear and the sea relatively calm. We drifted on. There was no map. The boat had no mast to attach a sail to nor oars to enable us to keep moving.

Everyone was hungry and weak. One of our two freshwater tanks had been smashed by waves the very first day, and now the second was almost empty. A few younger guys began swiping food and drinking water, sparking discontent among the passengers.

One morning, the captain group decided to distribute all the food on board. They determined that the supplies they had bought for the trip now belonged to their families, and only shared a little bit with the others. The rest of us were unhappy with this arrangement but too exhausted to fight about it or speak up.

But this time I'd had enough. I marched over to the food supply and announced that from now on it was to be distributed equally. The captain group made a move to jump me but held back when they saw that the majority was behind me. Before I could speak again, someone gave a shout.

"There's a ship, friends! A big foreign ship!"

Everyone raced to look out at a huge cargo ship on the horizon. The refugees cried out of joy. Many of those who had lain helpless below deck now came up to see for themselves. Some of the men removed their shirts and waved them at the ship. Soon everyone was calling out and waving whatever cloth they could find to signal the passing vessel.

"Save us! Please save us! Help! Help! Please!"

The ship approached close enough that the crew on board must have seen us. One of the women burst into tears.

"We're saved!" she cried. "God bless us, we're saved!"

The ship approached cautiously, then continued on until it disappeared over the horizon.

Some of the refugees failed to understand what was happening and continued shouting and calling for it to rescue us. Others slumped to the deck, hugging their families and weeping in despair.

All I could do was hold my wife and children while remaining calm and placing our lives in God's hands.

Praying for Rescue

At night I went up to the captain's deck to join some others taking turns steering. Even without a working motor, we needed to keep the boat as steady as possible. On the open sea in the dark, the small vessel carrying 81 desperate souls was little more than an aimlessly drifting leaf.

We tried using a big blanket attached to a stick as a sail, but that didn't help us move any faster. Some men suggested using planks as oars, but we had completely lost our bearings and didn't know which direction to go. Then, after our blanket-sail was torn by the wind, we replaced it with clothes bound together.

On day seven the current rose, lifting our boat to the crests of tall waves then dropping us down into the troughs. The sea tossed us back and forth and side to side as if attempting to throw us off.

The night was terrifying. Towering waves crashed down upon us. The boat rose and fell, each time threatening to send us to the bottom of the sea. It was a miracle we remained afloat in the storm.

Thuy and I held An and Su tight, using our bodies to shield them from the sheets of water that lashed at us. Hoa and Khoa, who up until then had tried to behave like young men by helping me with the various tasks on the boat, now huddled against us shivering and afraid, as much in need of comfort as anyone.

Families gathered together to hold hands and pray, according to their beliefs. Some called on God, others Buddha, and not a few petitioned the gods of the ocean. Loved ones clung to each other in tearful farewells, certain that this day was to be their last. Frightened children begged their parents for reassurance.

Meanwhile, the boat continued to flounder, careening and rolling in the monstrous waves.

Then a child's voice was heard.

"Mommy, is that a big ship?"

The sounds of praying stopped as everyone paused to look in the direction the child pointed. A cry rose up.

"It is a ship! A big one!"

Forgetting their recent painful experience, the refugees moved to the side to look out at a large commercial ship whose image grew more distinct as it came closer. One man waved his shirt hopefully.

"If they don't rescue us this time, the sea will drown us. We have to make sure they know we're here!"

We quickly made a pile of clothes and, as a giant wave lifted the boat, someone lit the clothes on fire. Folks jumped up and down, waving their arms and making noise, while others fanned the flames so the fire would be seen in the dark night.

On and on the boat dipped low and then rose high up with the sea's surge. The grand and striking ship slowly sailed on until it was lost in the distance.

We quickly put out the fire before it destroyed our boat. Some of the refugees howled in anger while others quietly wept, their hopes and energy spent.

The next day the seas were quiet, everything was as it had been before: we bailed water from the lower deck, we encountered more cargo ships and lit signal fires, and we watched bitterly as the vessels passed by without stopping.

Little An made a game out of counting the ships that went by.

"Mommy, what comes after 20?" she asked Thuy one day.

Her mother traced the numerals on her palm: 2, 1.

"Ah, two-one, right?"

The little girl didn't expect that her innocent question would make a woman sitting nearby burst into tears. Thuy nodded, and our daughter counted on: two-two, two-three...

Then Thuy turned to me.

"If we survive this trip, I promise never to forget these days. And I hope that someday I can return here on a ship to rescue people."

She spoke with soft determination as if making a personal vow. I nodded, numbly watching as another ship passed by and vanished on the horizon.

Again... Drifting and Being Ignored

■ THUY

I f I were asked to choose which experience the boat people found the most painful when they were on the ocean, I'd say it was when foreign ships deliberately turned away and left them to die, something the refugees would never have imagined.

About 30 foreign ships passed by, but, as in our previous time at sea, not one stopped to pick us up. I grieved for the boat people who had no homeland and no nationality and found themselves at the mercy of people willing to do unconscionable things.

In the days that followed, the weather was very calm. We were trapped in the same spot, an enormous prison surrounded by waves reaching to the horizon. By now we were becoming stir-crazy, confined day and night on a small, crowded boat with no way out and no idea of the future.

Phuc and I maintained our sanity by finding tasks to keep us busy or sitting to talk to each other. Phuc was often occupied with business related to the boat. I tended to the children. Su was teething, which made her fussy. Hoa and Khoa joined other boys swimming in the ocean or trying to catch fish. Some adults went in the water as well, not to play but to get clean.

A blue tarp had been laid out near the boat's bow to capture rainwater and funnel it into an empty tank. Some of the boys came up from swimming and scooped up a handful of water to drink, only to spit it out in disgust.

"Yuk. It tastes like gasoline!"

The others laughed, but no one else tried any water.

I sat most of the time quietly, not talking to anyone and trying not to overthink. Every morning when I awoke, and every night before I slept I made the sign of the cross, offering my day or night to God, preferring not to ask the entire family to pray like other families. I'd gotten used to hiding and keeping my thoughts private, and this made it easier for me to conceal my feelings from others.

I sat all day with Su on my lap, staring blankly in front of me so as not to invite conversation with anyone. However, one woman was not deterred. Thu was around forty and tried to befriend me. She'd come alone, hoping to be reunited with her husband who had already resettled in Australia. Once she saw Phuc take an active role in managing the boat, she moved to get close to us. Since I was 11 years younger, Thu became the big sister, carrying Su for me and helping watch over An. She was bright and liked to talk, and I soon found myself grateful for her company.

With Thu coaxing me out of my shell, I began opening up with other women onboard. We shared stories about our children and talked about our plans for the future. We talked to kill time, to drive out unwanted negative thoughts, to stave off the depression that bore down on us.

Those were the relatively good days.

There were times, though, when despair so overwhelmed us we didn't feel like talking. Even my two little ones remained silent. An didn't speak at all and Su didn't bother to cry. No one cared to say it out loud, but we all knew that at any time the boat could turn into a floating coffin.

Fragile Existence

I love the sea. From the time I was little I was familiar with the Vung Tau seacoast where my parents had a vacation house that we visited on weekends. When I got older, if I felt tired or stressed I would leave Saigon and spend a few days by the sea, sitting for hours gazing at the ocean and contemplating the immensity of nature and people's ability to tame the wind and waves.

But with the arrival of the second week drifting on the endless waters, the ocean lost its charm. Especially at night.

Each massive dark wave that fell on the helpless little boat was a nightmare. I tried to keep Su from getting wet, but that proved impossible as the entire boat was drenched by the onslaught.

By day I was parched and dry beneath the sun, the breath from my nostrils was the only living sign.

By night the darkness was suffocating, every wave that struck the side of the boat terrified me. I felt as if a grim shroud were dropping tighter over me to take me to the abode of the dead.

But there were nights when the sea was calm, the moon bright, and I forgot about being hungry and tired and lay on deck gazing at the stars. As I looked at the points of light twinkling up in the vast sky, it seemed the endless ocean all around me, and even human life was nothing but a dream. And it struck me how fragile we all were. For no matter how talented or wealthy or happy or famous any of us was in life, just one wave could wipe us away without a trace.

The more nights I spent at sea, the more I began to fear sleep. Even when fatigue overtook me, I slept only a few hours at a time, terrified that I might disappear into the darkness.

Each morning as I woke to find the dawn shining on the immense ocean, my heart was filled with gladness that the sea had granted me another day.

And another...and another...

And so it went until the refugee boat encountered a menace more horrible than ocean and waves. It was then I realized that people can be more terrifying than the powers of nature.

PART VI

THE SHORES OF HELL

Chapter 16

Ruthless Rescue

Thai Fishermen and Baby Su
October 28, 1979

■ THUY

Early in the morning of October 28, we encountered a fishing boat. It was quite large—three times the size of our boat—and the half-naked men on board, swarthy and well-muscled, stood in a line scrutinizing us.

We waved to them and signaled for help.

They pulled up alongside, a few of the fishermen climbed down to our boat. One of our men spoke to them in Vietnamese, but they didn't respond. When asked if they spoke English, they again didn't answer. We determined they must be Thai, though none of us knew that language.

They did, however, understand when we pointed to our motor and indicated we needed help. The fishermen went over to inspect it and, after making some adjustments, started it up. We cheered and bowed to our Thai benefactors gratefully with clasped hands. The fishermen smiled and returned the gesture.

Then someone suggested we chip in and offer them a token of our thanks. A hat was passed, and we contributed some of our watches and rings.

The fishermen accepted the gift with nods of approval, then

turned and climbed back on their boat.

A moment later they returned, this time with their entire crew. They were no longer smiling but strode among us menacingly carrying rifles and machetes.

They rounded us into one portion of the boat then split into two groups. One group stood guard over us while the other conducted a thorough search of the boat and seized anything they could find.

I watched this scene with trepidation. Back in Vietnam, I'd heard talk of Thai pirates, but I never really expected to have to face them myself.

When one of the pirates approached where I was standing with Su, the baby suddenly screamed. As I rocked her to quiet her down, the pirate became irritated. Without bothering to search me, he passed on to the next victim.

The baby's outburst caught the attention of the pirate chief. He walked briskly toward us, looking steadily at Su, and began to tickle her. She stopped crying at once. Then he held out one finger, and she reached her little hand to grasp it, gurgling happily.

The chief burst out laughing. He spoke to me in Thai while pointing toward Su. I shook my head uncomprehendingly. Then he pointed to Su then over to his boat. I didn't want to believe what I suspected he wanted.

When he repeated the gesture, I no longer had any doubt. He wanted to take Su with him. Panicking, I tried to indicate that she was too young. This time the chief pointed to Su, then to An standing beside me, and then to me before motioning toward his boat. I froze in terror.

Oh God, help me! I prayed. I clasped my hands and begged, pointing to An, Hoa, Khoa and Phuc to show we were all together.

The chief said nothing but just stood a long while looking at us. Meanwhile, his men moved around us as they continued to search the other boat people.

Finally, the chief stopped one of the pirates who was carrying a conical hat filled with jewelry taken from the captives. He reached into the hat and removed two gold chains, one with a cross and the other with a Buddha figure. Holding up these items in front of me, he again pointed to Su. I indicated the one with the cross. The pirate chief placed the chain around the baby's neck.

All I could do was nod my thanks, then watch in fear and astonishment as the chief returned to his boat.

He came back again, this time with a can of fresh water, which he handed to me. Pointing to Su's empty milk bottle with flicks of rust from our old water tank, he motioned that I should use the good water for her formula, rubbing his stomach as if to say that it was better for her. Once again bewildered, I nodded my understanding.

After the pirates had completed their search, the chief ordered them onto their boat. Two of the men came back toting a large sack of rice and some dried fish. The chief exchanged his small nautical compass for our larger, but nonfunctional, one. With gestures and a string of words we didn't understand, he seemed to be telling us that now our motor was fixed and we should be able to reach the mainland.

He pointed out the direction we should take, then scanned the entire boat before returning to his vessel and giving the order to shove off.

Still reeling from the encounter, a number of the refugees remarked that we were lucky to be alive and unharmed. At least they'd given us rice and some food and shown us the way to reach Thailand.

I removed the cross from around Su's neck and returned it to its owner. The encounter left me quite shaken, I wondered how the pirate chief could have let us go so easily. If I hadn't seen it with my own eyes, I would never have believed that the leader of a pirate band, in the midst of robbing a boat full of helpless people, would behave so kindly to a four-month-old baby.

We sailed in the direction the pirate had indicated. By afternoon we passed some islands in the Gulf of Thailand. The scenery was idyllic, with sandy beaches, snow-white coral, and clear blue water.

Once we realized that these were all uninhabited islands, we turned away intending to go on. We hoped to come to a city or large port so we could get help from the United Nations refugee assistance organization.

I also wanted to get in touch with some friends from foreign news services who were stationed in Bangkok after the war. Among them were my dear friend Marie Joannidis from the French Press Agency, Jean-Claude Pomonti, the bureau chief from *Le Monde*, and Francois Nivolon of the French daily *Le Figaro*.

Pirates on the Gulf of Thailand

After ten days of aimless drifting, we were finally backed on course. All of us were energized and optimistic about setting foot on a free shore and being resettled in a Western country.

Everyone, old and young, was in high spirits, believing that by evening we would no longer have to live on a small boat on the open sea. As Phuc and I gazed at the rosy sunset washing over the gulf, we remarked that this would be the last time we'd witness the close of day as boat people.

Suddenly, racing through the dazzling glow of the sunlight on the water came a Thai fishing boat. It was painted blood red. The men on board were dark and brawny, wearing only the wrap-around sarong pants typical of members of the Thai lower class. Some held machetes and knives at the ready.

Even before they tied up to our boat, some of the men leaped aboard, as many of the refugees scrambled to get out of their way. The pirates immediately seized several people and began searching them for valuables. Unlike the men we'd encountered that morning, these thieves moved violently, snatching away scarves and pulling at shirts to look for booty. Before long, however, they cried out angrily, apparently signaling to their comrades that there was nothing of any value on our boat. When one of our men tried to speak up, he was struck in the face. Others were kicked and beaten as the pirates rushed about on their greedy hunt.

I clutched Su tightly to my chest, fear growing inside as I realized that these were not ordinary fishermen who supplemented their trade by robbing refugees at random but, rather, professional pirates who pursued their crime unrestrained. Their boat had no fishing nets or other gear to indicate they made their living on the water.

They raged and fumed, livid to find that we had nothing for them.

Phuc leaned toward me and whispered.

"If they touch us, we'll fight to the end, right, Thuy?"

A shiver went down my spine. We both knew that if anything should happen to us, we could not stand idly by, though we risked our lives if we offered resistance. But what then of the children? I didn't want to think about it. As I nodded in response to Phuc, I silently made a desperate prayer: *Oh God, if we must die, I entrust my family into your hands.*

Afraid that Phuc might react too quickly to the pirates' threatening behavior, I threw him a warning glance. After the Thais finished searching the boat and our possessions with little to show for it, they returned in outrage to their boat. We gave a collective sigh of relief when they gunned their engine and drove off.

"Animals!" one woman muttered as she looked after them. She raised her fist to curse them, then suddenly brought her hand back down as she watched the pirate boat stop a ways off and turn around.

Now it was barreling down on us.

As the distance between the two boats grew smaller, the roar of the pirates' engine clashed with the screams of the refugees.

"*Troi oi!* Oh, God! They want to sink us!"

The red boat plowed on, bobbing up and down and chopping the waves as it approached. As it was about to strike, it was caught by a big wave that carried it high even as our boat dipped down so that the bow of the pirate vessel crashed into the roof of our cabin, spilling pieces of wood in all directions.

The red boat turned around and pulled away, preparing for a second try.

Escaping Death by a Hair's Breadth

Everyone poured onto the deck. Many were on their knees begging the pirates to spare their lives. All were filled with terror. Their cries and shrieks mingled with entreaties and final prayers before impending death.

Phuc took the two girls and me in his arms. Hoa and Khoa clung to us, weeping in fright.

For some time I'd noticed a green fishing boat following us at a distance. The men on board that boat had stood watching while we were being robbed just now. It was smaller than the red pirate vessel, appearing to be a real fishing boat with nets hanging from its sides. The first time the red boat moved away to ram us, the green one sailed closer but did not give the impression of trying to intervene.

In my utter despair, I silently hoped the green boat would find a way to save us. All of a sudden, Su began to wail. I looked down at the tiny girl poised to endure a terrible death. The mother inside me screamed, *my child is too young, she cannot die!*

Without thinking, I struggled to my feet. Gathering my strength, I held baby Su as high as I could, hoping against hope that the pirates in the red boat would see this innocent child and be unwilling to kill her. At the same time, I prayed that the green boat would come and rescue us.

Seeing what I was trying to do, Phuc took the baby from my arms and went to the side of the boat, raising her up so the pirates could clearly see her. Su cried louder, her arms wiggling in agitation.

The men on the red boat paid no attention as they turned around and bore down on us again. Phuc stood his ground, his arms shaking as he held up the girl.

At that moment the green boat accelerated and closed on us. With its smaller size and less resistance, it moved faster than the red boat.

Once the green boat reached us, an old man jumped onto our boat and grabbed Su from her father. Going to the bow, he held the baby in one hand while raising the other to signal the red boat, shouting something in his language.

The pirates observed this in astonishment. One man gestured for his boat to slow down and move alongside us. The pirates shouted at the old man in anger. He shook his head and called back to them. Dissatisfied, the pirates aimed their rifles threateningly at both the refugee boat and the green boat.

The old man handed Su back to me and held up his hands as he called out something in Thai. His men brought out their weapons for a showdown. The two sides argued for a while. All this time the refugees waited with clasped hands, pale and trembling.

After a loud verbal exchange, the two Thai boats moved closer together, and the leaders continued their discussion. The old man pointed to Su. Then the pirate captain turned away and ordered his boat to leave.

The old man stood in the middle of the boat and, using his hands, indicated that he was going to tow us someplace where the police would come and find us. He kept repeating the word "police, police."

We remained in shock. This close encounter with death left us numb.

The crew of the green boat brought a long cable which they proceeded to tie to the bow of our boat. They then began to pull us away, with the red boat sailing ahead as if to guide them.

I was still anxious and confused, not at all certain we could trust the old man. Although he'd just saved our lives, we'd been traumatized by the incident and couldn't decide if we ought to be grateful or wary of what might happen next.

The Vietnamese discussed the predicament among us. There was a grave concern for the women, whom we assumed would be the next target. On board, our boat consisted of 20 women, along with 50 men and 11 children. What could the men do to protect the women without inciting the pirates to kill us all? The decision was made to conceal the women as soon as we landed at whatever place they took us. For their part, some women cut each other's hair short, put on baseball caps and smeared charcoal on their faces to disguise their gender.

"Now it's your turn to hide," Phuc said to me. "You need to find a really safe place and stay there, and I'll do whatever it takes to protect you. Don't worry about the kids. I'll take good care of them. Just protect yourself."

We were towed to a deserted island, called -- we later learned -- Koh Kra, or Kra Island. It was the largest of a group of three islands in the Gulf of Thailand, 180 miles south of Bangkok.

And it was to be hell on earth for the Vietnamese refugees.

The deserted island, Kra, in the Gulf of Thailand. Photo: VTT, 2017.

Kra Island
October 30, 1979

■ PHUC

As twilight fell we arrived at a rocky island. The refugees were all exhausted, hungry, and frightened.

The fishermen drew us to a coral reef where our boat ran aground. Our men were too weak to stand, but the Thai waved their rifles and forced us to get up anyway. They tied a rope from the boat to the beach and ordered the men to get off and stand in the water along the rope as a human chain to assist the others in reaching shore.

Once everyone was off the boat and had climbed onto the slope, we collapsed to the ground, gasping for breath. The crew of the green boat removed the rope, then boarded their vessel and sailed away from the island, anchoring far off. Some of the fishermen came back in rowboats and sat on the high rocks looking down on the refugees and the pirates in the red boat.

About half the red-boat pirates immediately jumped into our boat. Using axes and machetes they hacked away at our boat, breaking it apart to search for gold or cash hidden in the planks. The

Remains of refugee boats destroyed by pirates searching for valuables, Koh Kra. Photo: United Nations, 1979.

other pirates roughly examined the refugees themselves one more time in case there were any items we had concealed on ourselves since the first time. After they were all finished, they returned to their boat clutching the valuables they had found. Then they sailed away.

When we were sure the red boat was gone, we began to investigate our surroundings. Although it was night, there was some moonlight, enabling us to inspect the place. The whole island was composed of large rocks fused with chunks of dead coral covering the beach, which stuck up like stakes.

The slope was too narrow and slippery for us to remain there, so some of the men climbed higher to look for a better spot. They soon returned, informing us that they'd seen a large cave filled with algae and calcium deposits that could provide shelter. It smelled fishy but was high enough to receive some fresh air.

They led us on the difficult climb up the steep, slick mountainside. Some of the green-boat fishermen helped us bring food, water, and other provisions to the cave. It was slow going, but we finally made it. Though frightened and apprehensive about tomorrow, we were grateful that despite all we had gone through our group of 81 refugees was still intact.

The cave where boat people took refuge on Koh Kra. Photo: UNHCR, 1979.

Once we were settled in the cave, the fishermen brought water and fish they'd cooked for us. The old man took a last look around and nodded. Then they left for their boat.

I didn't know what was going to happen after that, only that we were alive and on dry ground. Totally spent, I just didn't want to think about it anymore.

Our first night's sleep on land was a fitful one. Thuy and I had to search all over for a relatively flat place on the coral for the kids to lie down. Thuy covered An and Su from the cold and damp. All night we moved them here and there to avoid the water dripping from the ceiling.

Fishermen and Pirates

When dawn broke the next day, I was more relaxed, despite the troubled sleep.

Looking out from our cave I was startled to find scores of Thai fishing boats surrounding the island. Some had nets out to catch fish. Others were anchored near the beach.

The first Thai fishermen who came ashore treated us in a friendly manner. They seemed to sympathize with our plight, understanding as some of our members tried to show by gestures what we'd been through. They even brought us rice and food.

A number of the fishermen paid particular attention to baby Su. They gave me sugar and signed for me to mix it with water for her to drink. One older man brought a can of condensed milk, a precious gift in this remote spot on the ocean. He sat and played with her for quite some time.

All day long the Thai fishermen stopped by to visit with us. We developed a crude form of sign language to communicate with each other.

I was able to distinguish three types of Thai fishermen. The actual fishermen, whose sole occupation was laboring on the sea, had no interest in robbery or assault against refugees. Although they spent their days working outdoors, their skin was a lighter shade than the others, suggesting generations of racial mixing as opposed to the darker Thais. These were the ones who visited us early in the day bringing rice, fish, and water.

The second type was those whose primary profession was fishing, but who turned to robbery when they encountered refugees. They found in piracy an opportunity to reap big gains by stealing from the boat people, mainly because the victims had no nation to protect them. Such was the first Thai boat we'd met. The crew robbed us but didn't harm anyone. Then they fixed our motor, pointed us to a safe place, and gave us food to continue our voyage.

The third type was the one to which the red boat belonged. These men gave up fishing entirely to rob and rape. They were savages who thought nothing of killing their victims, just like the red boat ramming us merely because they were upset at not finding anything to steal.

I tried to sign one boat captain who seemed decent: "Can you take us to the mainland?"

He laughed out loud and shook his head, though whether because he didn't understand, was confused, or had to refuse I can't say. In any case, it showed the difficulty we faced in communicating.

Later that day another group of fishermen brought us a sack of rice and a tray of dried fish. Among this band, there was one fellow who seemed particularly fond of children. He gave the kids sweets. Afterward, he sat and played with Su. This man had a kind face and wore the pink-colored sarong pants, so we liked to call him the "pink-pants fisherman."

Thuy approached him and gestured that she would like something to write with. He understood at once and returned to his boat for a pencil and a small notepad. The thin paper reminded me of the kind Thuy had used to send me love notes inside of cigarettes when I was in prison.

This time she wrote in French:

À mes amis de la presse de l'Ouest,

Je suis Vu Thanh Thuy, une journaliste Vietnamienne, capturée ici par les pirates Thailandais sur une ile déserte du Golfe de Siam, avec mon mari et nos petites filles. Nous sommes en tout 81 personnes, avec beaucoup de femmes et d'enfants. S'il vous plaît, informez immédiatement le Représentant de la Haute Commission des Réfugiés des Nations Unies pour qu'il vienne nous sauver immédiate-ment. C'est très dangereux pour nous ici.

En gratitude,
Vu Thanh Thuy

To my friends in the Western press:

I am Vu Thanh Thuy, a Vietnamese journalist, who with my husband and children is being kept on a deserted island in the Gulf of Thailand. There are altogether 81 people here, with many women and children.

Please alert at once the United Nations High Commissioner for Refugees to come and rescue us. It is very dangerous for us.

With sincere gratitude,

Vu Thanh Thuy

Although it was a slim chance, we hoped the good-hearted fishermen would take the letter to the mainland whereby some miracle it would end up in the hands of one of her colleagues now working in Bangkok. We believed that the note only needed to reach a Western news agency or editorial office and we would be rescued.

Thuy folded the page and handed it to the fisherman, gesturing for him to mail it for her. He nodded vigorously, but we weren't sure that he truly understood.

The refugees felt reassured at meeting these decent fishermen and had more hope for the general goodness of humanity. Not all Thai fishermen were pirates. And at least there was still good in the world along with evil.

After being rammed by the red boat on the sea, we were glad to at least be on land instead of drifting helplessly. Even if it was a deserted island, at least we could do something to survive instead of enduring hardship at the mercy of the ocean.

The fishermen who came that day sincerely helped us. Some of them went back and forth to their boat to get things for us. But every time we asked them to take us to the mainland, they just shook their heads.

Climbing the Mountain for Water
October 31, 1979

For the time being, we seemed to have sufficient food, but there wasn't enough drinking water. We could bathe in the ocean but had to seriously ration our clean water.

The good Thai fishermen indicated they couldn't share their

water with us. However, they pointed to the mountaintop, prattling in their language with one word, *nam*, repeating over and over. I just listened to them in confusion, but one of the children explained to me.

"Uncle, there's water up on the mountain. They're saying we can go up there and get water to drink. *Nam* means 'water'."

The kids had been playing with the Thais and picked up some of the language.

"That's great, friends," I said to the others. "Tomorrow morning we'll climb the mountain to get water."

The next day we rose early and collected various containers, then divided us into teams. Since there was no easy way up and down the slope, the task required forming a human chain to bring the water to our cave. Some of the younger men complained, arguing that everyone should be responsible for their own needs, but I insisted.

"We have to pool our energies if we're going to make it," I declared. "What I say is the best way, since we don't know how long we're going to be here and how long some of the fishermen will help us. We have to rely on ourselves. Does anyone have a problem with that?"

I looked straight at the gripers. When they didn't respond, I continued.

"All right then, it looks like we've all agreed. So let's work together on this."

We formed a chain that ran from the beach to the top of the mountain. As the lead team got close to the summit, we heard gurgling water. Looking in the direction of the sound I discovered a creek running into a natural reservoir the size of a well. We all ran up and dipped our faces into the fresh water to slake our thirst.

After we'd had our fill, we scooped water into the small containers we'd brought with us and transferred them down the line to a ledge. There another team poured the water into larger containers that were brought down to the beach for the people below. Once everyone was satisfied, we poured the rest of our first haul into an old oil tank from our boat that we'd lined with a sheet of plastic and buried in the sand.

The remainder of the day was spent carrying more water down to the tank. The teams developed a rhythm, and in just a few hours our supply tank was full. It was a rough workout, but we felt better now that we had enough water for the whole group to last several days.

Even with a water source now available, the act of collecting water and bringing it down the mountainside was difficult, and the women and children were unable to do it by themselves. Therefore we asked everyone to use water sparingly, just as we did during our boat trip. Meanwhile, we wrote SOS on a white cloth, attached it to a long branch and set it between the rocks at the mountainside where it might be seen by passing ships.

The men decided that each morning we would bring down water to replenish our supply for the day. Once we had settled in to rest, we noticed that the phony mechanics had slipped away so they wouldn't have to work with the rest of us.

Boat people raised an SOS flag on the cliffs of Koh Kra. Photo: UNHCR, 1979.

The Lighthouse Storage

While collecting water, we stumbled upon a little storage obscured by trees and boulders. It was the only human-made structure on the entire island.

The building looked like a small storage house constructed of bricks with a low flat roof. Thick red bougainvillea plants covered the walls and roof, their long, sharp thorns sticking out in all directions. The structure was so thoroughly camouflaged that you couldn't see it until you came right up to it.

I had to stoop to enter through the low, rotting door. In the dark interior, my eyes were struck by a dim light coming from the lamp. Once my eyes adjusted to the contrast, I found the round opening in the wall facing the ocean, just large enough to see the light from the lighthouse tower on top of the mountain shining through to signal ships. The pale light was not strong enough to illuminate the coral and rocky shore and crashing waves below.

On the green mold-covered walls we saw lines of words that had been scrawled in what looked like charcoal or brick, and even something dark red that appeared to be dried blood.

"*Troi oi!*" one of the men cried. "Look at this! It's Vietnamese!"

We ran to the walls and tried to make out the crooked words that seemed to have been written hastily in terror. Tracing the smeared letters with his hand, one man read the message out loud.

"Women... must cut their hair... stain their faces... disguise as men..."

Another man read, "Women... have to hide... or pirates will murder you..."

I strained to read a line that was barely legible.

"Pirates search... kill... rape... kidnap... please hide..."

The misgivings I'd felt on the boat when the pirates were checking the women to rob them returned more forcefully now as we read the messages on the walls. I grew horrified thinking of the fate about to befall the women of our group. Twenty women, including Thuy.

The frightening words continued to underscore the awful truth.

"Women beware of the pirates. Even the ones who are nice in the daytime will come back at night to harm you..."

As I read, I tried to control my emotions. The words seemed to come alive, dancing before my eyes. I was sure the writers had been trembling in rage and terror.

The man standing next to me dropped to the floor.

"Oh, God!"

We looked at each other and shuddered as we thought of our wives, daughters, and sisters.

The words on the storage walls haunted us all the way down to the beach. My insides grew tight with the anticipation that the very thing the boat people feared most on their journey was about to become a reality.

Before leaving Vietnam, Thuy and I had heard stories about pirates and the refugees. But in the closed-off world of the communists, where news of the outside world was scarce, we had nothing but rumors that we couldn't check out. Besides, in our desperation to get out of the country, we dismissed the seriousness of the problem and assumed that these pirates must be robbers like we'd encountered during our previous failed attempts to escape.

And this was the 20th century, undoubtedly piracy was something for the movies, not a real threat in this civilized time. Nonetheless, Thuy and I promised each other that should something arise, we would fight to the end to defend ourselves.

But here we were faced with the terrible fact of it, and I wondered just how we would be able to defend ourselves when we had no weapons. Also, most of us men had brought our wives and children. The worry and pain were devastating.

■ THUY

L istening to Phuc and the others describe what they'd found at the lighthouse storage, I was gripped with dread. My body froze, and I couldn't speak, but my mind searched frantically for any way to help survive the coming ordeal. I looked around as if a ray of light might appear to guide me past my terror.

Phuc gazed at me intently, alarmed at my silence. I maintained my composure. My method for dealing with a situation like this was to look for some way to confront it head-on rather than avoid it. After the initial agitation, I got hold of myself and began to consider how best to hide.

I felt Phuc's hand on my shoulder. I turned and looked at him. Husband and wife, we gazed at each other, countless thoughts passing between us that we could not express in words but felt in our hearts.

I paused a moment to collect myself, then rose and left. Walking beyond the others, I searched for a place with a higher vantage point from which I could better observe the layout. I scanned the island seeking a solution for myself.

Thai Navy Ship #15

That afternoon a Thai naval ship appeared in the Gulf. The refugee women rushed to the beach crying out, "There's a ship! A ship is coming!"

They scattered across the island to spread the news. I grabbed Su and ran after them to the beach.

"A big ship has come!" one woman shouted. "It's come to save us, friends!"

Indeed, a large gray ship was slowly advancing toward the island, looming over the small fishing boats around Kra. As it approached, we could see the Thai flag flapping in the wind. It seemed to be a coastguard patrol boat.

The number 15 was painted on its prow. I repeated it in my head, trying to believe that this was not a dream. Phuc ran up to join us. He, too, mumbled the number again and again as if etching it in his memory, for here was the boat that was going to rescue us.

We all hugged each other, happy to the point of tears.

When it reached the coral reefs, the ship dropped anchor, and a rubber raft was thrown down. Once on shore, several uniformed men climbed the rocky cliff to our cave where they were immediately surrounded by excited refugees.

"Anyone speaks English?" said a man we presumed was the commander.

A middle-aged man named Lu Phuc Ba stepped forward to speak with the sailors on our behalf. At first, the rest of us stood back to allow them to converse, but as soon as Mr. Ba translated for us that the Navy had come to rescue us, joy erupted, and everyone began talking at once, using broken English mixed with Vietnamese.

One woman grabbed the officer by the arm and tugged it vigorously, pleading to be allowed on the ship.

"I woman...sick...no medicine...," she stammered

Others broke in, all asking to be taken away on the ship. The officer raised his voice.

"Everyone quiet, please!"

Mr. Ba helped get them to settle down and explained that the Thai captain promised they would be rescued. Our interpreter also related our story to the sailors, concluding with the warning messages we had seen in the lighthouse.

We begged the captain to at least take the women and children with him so they would be safe while the rest of us waited for a boat. He tried to reassure us in a firm voice.

"Don't worry. No one is going to harm you. But this is a patrol boat, and I can't take civilians on board. I'll have to call another ship to come for you."

Despite his promise, worry gnawed at my insides. I held Su in front of his face.

"Please take my baby on your boat. She's only four months old, and I have no more milk for her."

He repeated his statement that he couldn't take anyone on board.

"I can't let you and your baby on my boat," he said, looking at Su in my arms. "But so you won't worry, I'll have my boat remain anchored here for the night until a rescue ship comes."

When this was translated, the refugees cheered and hugged one another. They shook his hand and bowed their gratitude for his help. We wanted to laugh and cry from joy at the reassurance of this representative of the Thai Navy.

Dreams... of the Future

That night after putting the kids to sleep, Phuc and I went outside to join the other adults. There were many still awake, and now they were enjoying the warmth of the fire. Some happily sang the popular song "Vietnam, Vietnam!" and clapped their hands in time. We ate all the food given us by the Thai sailors as well as whatever was left of our supply to celebrate as we shared our past stories and talked about the future.

Later, when the food was gone, and the fire was going out, we stood up and wished each other pleasant dreams and a good sleep in this last night in the cave of a deserted island before we were rescued, as the sailors had promised.

Beyond by the excitement, I didn't feel sleepy. Instead, I invited Phuc to go sit on the rocks and talk for a while.

The refugees gathered in front of the cave of Koh Kra. Photo: UNHCR, 1979.

We climbed up a high ridge overlooking the cave. It was flat and big enough for the two of us to sit side-by-side.

"I can't believe we're about to go to America," I murmured in his ear. "I'll see my family again."

Phuc put his arm around me and nodded. He seemed to be still under the spell of our farewell party by the fire.

"Finally we'll reach a safe place."

I dropped my head onto his shoulder and whispered as if talking to myself.

"I always knew there would come a day we'd reach the shore of freedom."

We sat like that for hours, softly sharing thoughts and dreams of the future and of life in a land that afforded freedom, security, and peace. Phuc reminded me of what Tuong Vi and Binh Minh had said to us.

"From now on we can go out holding hands and not be afraid of the police. We won't have to hide or use fake identities, no more plotting and scheming. And from now on you can say to An, 'This is your real daddy, not your uncle!'"

He seemed to be in a daze, thinking of how things would be.

"Then we'll have to put our lives back together. I don't know if I can find a job to support a family. I'm ready to do anything. I have to pay you back for all the hard times you've put up with."

"No," I replied. "In my parents' letters, they say we have to go back to school first. That way we'll have a more stable future. As long as we're close to Papa and Mama, right? The whole family has given so much to us."

Phuc nodded.

"You can make whatever you want of your future, Thuy! I never thought I'd live through all this."

"Thank the Lord," I sighed, "for protecting us and giving us each other during the hard times."

"Yes," he said. "Thank God for watching over our family."

It was quite late, and we needed to sleep, but I didn't want to stop fantasizing.

"I wonder if they have tamarind trees along the streets like in Saigon."

My mind wandered, I turned my sleepy eyes to the ocean. The moonlight reflected on the waves, rolling our present spectacle into a beautiful dream world.

"The ocean is so beautiful tonight," I whispered.

Phuc squeezed my shoulder.

"The days to come will be just as beautiful," he promised.

I suddenly picked my head up from his shoulder.

"Do you realize that tonight is the first night in four years that we can sleep in peace and not be afraid of anything?"

He put my head back on his shoulder and held me tighter.

"Our future will surely be bright," he whispered. "For sure. It has to be."

We sat there a while longer on the rock ledge above a cave where 79 of our fellow travelers were fast asleep.

Joy flooded our hearts. As I imagined the future, I felt strong enough to conquer the world.

That night, in the crowded cave on a floor of coral, where water dripped from cracks in the ceiling and ran down dampening us all, Phuc and I experienced a peaceful and comforting sleep for the first time in years.

Dreams... Shattered

November 1, 1979

■ PHUC

"Hey, everybody, wake up! The ship is leaving!"

A voice called into the cave. The people inside got up and shook off the sleep to see what was happening.

It was still quite early, but the sun was beginning to rise above the horizon, aiming bright rays into the cave still chilly from the night's dew. We gathered outside and saw the Thai patrol boat slowly sailed away.

"Where's it going?" one woman asked frantically.

A cold gust of wind accentuated the dread that descended upon us. Some of the men had already climbed down to the coral slope. With one hand holding the rocks for support, they waved a white cloth back and forth to call the ship back. The rest of us cried out and gestured to get the ship's attention.

"Come back! Come back!" we shouted.

Several of the sailors waved to us. The ship receded into the distance, and then disappeared. Someone cried, "But they promised!"

We could not believe that an officer of the Royal Thai Navy would break his word. Especially after remaining here all night to guard the refugees against attack by pirates. Utterly dejected, we slumped down beside the ashes of last night's festive fire. One man spoke up confidently.

"Surely they left because there a rescue ship on the way."

"Yes, that's right," said another. "That would make sense."

Added a third, "They couldn't just abandon us like that."

And then a fourth said, "That's right. They're navy officers. They had promised us. As a patrol boat, they must have other assignments. They must have radioed for someone to come and get us."

The talk continued in this vein until finally everyone was convinced that a rescue ship was headed for the island. A group of men volunteered to stand lookout.

Thuy and I exchanged glances and tried to maintain a positive attitude. We'd spent much of the night sitting on a rock gazing at the sea, talking excitedly about the promising future that awaited us.

I turned to the men.

"There'll probably be a ship here in a few hours. But we're out of the water. We'd better go and get some more."

A group of men stood up reluctantly. They probably figured there was plenty of water on the ship. But they followed me anyway if only to pass the time and keep their minds off the possibility that maybe things would not turn out as we'd hoped.

///

Just after noon with the sun burning overhead, the lookouts noticed something peculiar on the water.

It wasn't a naval ship as we had hoped, but a flotilla of small boats similar to the fishing boats we'd seen earlier. When one of the boats anchored offshore, and some men climbed into rowboats to approach the island, the refugees quickly gathered to discuss this turn of events. The visitors beached their boat and started to look around.

We could tell these were not navy sailors. Like the fishermen we'd seen earlier, they were stripped to the waist and wore wrap-around pants. But these men were younger, darker, and more aggressive. The refugee women were petrified with fear.

"They look really mean," whispered one woman as we considered the writings on the lighthouse walls.

The new arrivals spotted us and stalked over. They didn't display care or sympathy but seemed to be checking us out. Nor did they offer us any food or water, like the men we'd encountered before. Instead, they strode around the cave then climbed up the mountain.

"They're scouting the island," one man concluded.

When night approached, the fishermen returned to their boat. We watched in silence as they sailed away and the beach was once again deserted.

The night before, Thuy and I had banished all fear from our hearts, but now it returned with a vengeance.

Later, the refugees sat around the fire in front of the cave. There was no brilliant blaze fed by cheerful talk and laughter as the day before. Instead, the feeble flames created dark shadows on our faces, sullen, flickering in the sea breeze.

Thuy and I discussed our predicament.

"I have an awful feeling about this," she said.

I agreed.

"You have to find a hiding place, the sooner, the better."

I racked my brains to recall every place I'd visited on the island to see if anything suggested itself. Meanwhile, someone stood up and asked for quiet.

"I say all the men should make a circle around the women to protect them."

Another tried to reassure us by adding, "I agree. Those boats usually have seven to ten men on board. Some are old, and there are kids, too. That way only a few of them would attack the women."

Others protested.

"But they have weapons, and we have nothing."

"There are more of us," he countered. "If we fight them as a group we have a hope of saving the women."

In the end, the men agree to surround the women with a human shield.

Searching for Hiding Places

■ THUY

While the others talked I slipped away to search by the cave for a crevice in the rocks big enough to squeeze into. Whatever the merits of the others' plans, I intended to depend on myself first. I didn't expect anybody to protect me, nor did I feel comfortable placing my life in another's hands. But I couldn't find a space suitable for my plan.

After our dinner of thin rice gruel with dried fish that we'd been given the first day, everyone retired into the cave. The women were arranged deep inside while the men were positioned toward the outside to protect them.

It grew late. Everyone was fast asleep. I lay beside the children, too troubled to sleep. Finally, I sat up and looked outside. Moonbeams lit the night sky, dancing over the waves. I could hear the waves lapping at the rocks and coral on the beach. Everything was still.

All at once I heard a noise. At first, it was like someone calling, soft and low like an owl's hoot. Then it rose to a wolf's howl. Finally, the sound became louder, fearsome, like the roar of a wild animal.

The horrible cry woke everyone with a jolt. The refugees sat up in terror, groping in the dark, bumping into one another, crawling and scrambling on the floor. Some cried out in fear, looking for their loved ones.

The noise grew louder, coming up the cliff and heading in our direction. It was savage, crazed, and hungry.

Soon it was right in front of the cave, accompanied by dark specters whose shadows flickered on the walls from the light of torches. We saw faces painted in black and white, awful like ghosts. More figures screamed and clambered up the rocks, the frightening sound echoing all around the hapless refugees.

The first pirates to enter held guns. Those that followed had machetes. In their other hand, each held a torch. They waved their weapons illuminated by the flames. The two with guns blocked the entrance so no one could leave. Other pirates stepped inside.

The men's strategy of forming a protective circle around the women dissolved at once. The women looked down to avoid the glaring eyes of the pirates as they passed.

They pulled one girl up by the neck, and she screamed. One of the attackers put his hand on her throat, and then ran it down her chest. A second pirate let his hands slide along her arms. They laughed when the poor girl shivered in fright. Then they released her roughly.

They proceeded to examine us one by one, looking for jewelry and taking the opportunity to fondle the girls and women. When they realized that no one had anything worth stealing, they left.

We all sat in silence, anxious and worn out from the experience. Outside, there was absolute silence. No flickering torches. No beastly howls.

I softly called my husband.

"Phuc?"

He reached out and pulled me close.

"I'm right here."

I moved back to talk.

"Phuc, I'm really worried."

He was quiet for a long time. Finally, he answered.

"You should be. There's no reason they would leave us that easily."

"I'm going outside to look for a place to hide," I said. "If they come back..."

He helped me up and accompanied me outside.

Some of the others joined us and gathered around. The men discussed how they might fight back if the pirates returned. They lit a fire and sat around it.

"About how many of them were there?" one man asked.

"What does it matter?" a woman replied. "They have guns."

Another woman spoke in a trembling voice.

"So what do we do if they come again?"

As if in reply, a howl rose in the night, echoing throughout the craggy mountain. A series of howls followed.

We jumped to our feet. Some ran back into the cave.

My foot bumped against a stone that lay across a hollow in the rocks. Earlier I'd seen one of the refugees sitting awkwardly on it and guessed there was a crevice that went down between the boulders. With the stone out of the way, I saw a deep crack. I crouched beside it, and then pulled myself inside. My heart pounded, but I relaxed when I found there was enough space for me to fit in without being seen.

Night of Terror

■ PHUC

I set the rock in place over the crack that Thuy had squeezed into and sat down on it. And I didn't move when two gunshots rang out to signal the return of the pirates.

They climbed to our ledge and ordered everyone into the cave. I pretended to lose my footing and knelt down to whisper into the rocks.

"Stay there and don't come out no matter what!"

The attackers followed us in and split the refugees into two groups, pulling the women away from their men and pushing children from their mothers. The pirates who were armed with guns herded our men against one wall while they searched for anyone who might be hiding further inside.

Once they were done hunting, the pirates spoke rapidly among themselves. Each, in turn, leaned out to survey the refugee women, who huddled together in terror. The pirates laughed and pointed, apparently choosing their victims.

As the armed men stood guard, one of their bands approached a girl and dragged her outside.

Soon an earsplitting cry tore through the night. The refugee men pulled the children to them and covered their eyes to keep them from seeing what was going on. With Su in one arm and holding An tight against me with the other, I listened to the heart-piercing screams of the victim. One by one the women were pulled from the cave.

Some were assaulted on the rocks, others in the bushes. Some women were even violated right in front of the cave. The worst thing was that most were molested within sight of their husbands and fathers, who were going mad in their pain and desperation. One man wept out loud, calling his wife over and over.

"*Em oi!* My dear! I'm so sorry! There's nothing I can do, I can't save you! I'm sorry! Please forgive me!"

Others pressed their foreheads against the wall and moaned.

"*Troi oi!* Where are you, God? Where are you, Buddha? Mother Mary, please save us!"

Some men pounded their fists on the craggy wall until they bled, then pounded those bloody fists into their heads, sobbing.

Throughout the night, cries and screams filled the darkness. The sounds of clothes being torn, women pleading or trying to defend themselves, slappings and beatings, weeping, moans, sobs, all mingled with the savage roars and gleeful laughter of the demon pirates—hell's tumult echoing in the land of the living.

When one of the victims was brought back, the men rushed to take up her ravaged body as she swooned.

The guards ignored the men who ran to assist the returning women. Meanwhile, they were relieved from their post by those who had satisfied their animal desires. Others just sat outside the cave waiting for their comrades to finish their cruel game. They sat around the fire killing time. Some leaned against the rocks with their faces turned toward the sky, their eyes half closed in sleep.

The assailants talked casually among themselves, paying no heed to the sounds of grief and pain around them.

I grew nervous when the pirates went to sit on the rocks by Thuy's hiding place. And my heart tightened when one dropped directly down on the stone that lay right by her head.

■ THUY

A fraid of making a sound, I tried not to breathe too loudly. To keep from suffocating, I pursed my lips and let the air in and out in slow, deep breaths through my nose.

Along with the conversations of the Thai pirates above me and the terrible cries of the poor women nearby, I heard An calling.

"Mommy! Where's Mommy? Mommy!"

Just then something made of metal fell down the crack, rolled onto my shoulder and dropped into the darkness by my feet.

My body tightened in terror. My head began to spin, and my heart stopped beating.

■ PHUC

I crouched by the cave entrance holding Su and An, all the while keeping an eye on Thuy's hiding place. A pirate was sitting on the rock covering the crevice. At one point he took out his knife and began to clean it. He spat on the blade and wiped it on the waist of his sarong pants. His hands fumbled, and the knife dropped right into the crack between the rocks.

The pirate muttered something in Thai, then stood up and motioned for one of his friends to bring over a torch. The other guy was lounging on the boulders with the torch beside him. He ignored his friend and turned away. So the first pirate had to move the stone away and look inside the crack. He groped around, reaching in as far as he could. Suddenly he stopped and pulled back with a shout.

The others burst out laughing and came to see what had startled him. Even the man lying on the boulders was interested and this time he brought over the torch.

I became instantly alert. Holding Su tight, I brought myself to a kneeling position, ready to spring into action to save Thuy if they discovered her.

On the Verge of Death

■ THUY

I prayed over and over like one possessed, saying the only thing that came to mind. *Oh God, please save me! Save me... save me... Lord!*

Lifting my eyes, I saw the torch. All at once many sinewy arms reached down to grab my head and shoulders and pull me out.

I squirmed and kicked with all my might, screaming, "AAAAAAAHHHHHHH! Oh God! Oh God! Save me!"

The pirates gaped in surprise. Some laughed, amused, and pointed at me mockingly. One reached out and crudely fumbled around my clothes. Finding no valuables, he waved me off to his friends. Two of them stepped forward and took me by the arms.

I cried out with all my breath and struggled against them with the strength of a maniac, "AHHH... Oh, God... Oh, God!

■ PHUC

While the pirates standing guard at the cave's entrance were preoccupied watching the scene unfolding outside, I rushed past them with Su in my arm. Plowing headlong into the men around my wife, I nearly knocked one of them off his feet.

Then I pushed the baby into Thuy's arms. Confused by the sudden appearance of an infant in their midst, the pirates stopped pulling and stepped back.

At that point, shots rang out. The guards had come out of their shock and were running toward us. They cornered Thuy and me and pointed their weapons directly at us, their eyes full of murderous intent. I balled my fists, prepared to fight to the death.

Just then a voice arose, clear and confident. At the sound, the pirates let go and waited.

The man with the deep voice stepped forward. Taking Thuy by the arm, he drew her and baby Su outside the circle. As he pushed them into the cave, he spoke to the pirates in Thai.

I recognized him at once. He was older than the other pirates, and his voice had the ring of authority. He was the man from the green boat who had held up Su and saved us from being sunk by the red boat pirates several days before.

Why he should have appeared at these two critical moments was a mystery to me, one who was skeptical of miracles.

I stepped back but kept my fists clenched as I listened to the old man talk, trying to ascertain the drift of his words through his voice and gestures. Whatever he was saying, the pirates were apparently paying attention. Most of them had by then had their fill, while others were returning from the rocks and bushes. A few of the pirates argued with the old man, but finally, they shrugged and lowered their weapons.

The guards pushed me back into the cave as the others collected the crew's belongings. After bringing back the remaining victims, the pirates left the cave and disappeared down the mountain.

Children and women hiding inside a small cave. Photo: UNHCR, 1979.

Although the night was almost over and everyone was thoroughly exhausted, no one tried to sleep. We all sat quietly in the dismal darkness, the silence broken only by the sobs and painful moans of the women and the weeping of their loved ones.

I held my wife and children, paralyzed by hurt and shame which clawed at my insides, scars of my impotence in the face of the horrible violence perpetrated by the Thai pirates on the Vietnamese refugees.

Chapter 19

Days of Hell

The Coexistence of Good and Evil
November 2, 1979

■ PHUC

When we awoke the next morning we found many more Thai fishing boats gathered on the island. A band of Thai came into the cave and motioned for us to get up and come outside.

The women shrank from them and lowered their eyes, unwilling to look at the strangers. After the shame and hurt of the previous night, the refugees couldn't say for sure whether the fishermen approaching them now were the same as the ones who had assaulted them. Some of the Thai seemed rather familiar with us, so we assumed they were. But to the Vietnamese, all the Thai had the same dark complexion and crude manner, so it was hard to tell these fishermen from the pirates.

Now the visitors had us gather all our belongings and follow them to the other side of the island. After we'd walked a while, a young fisherman pointed to the beach below and repeated the word, "*Hat, hat.*"

He indicated that we were being moved from the cave we had occupied for the last few days to this area of the island where there was a beach with forest on level ground. They had us line up single-file, and with some pirates in front and others bringing up the rear, they guided us down to our new residence. The youngest ones among them, who looked like teenagers, ran alongside.

The boys seemed to enjoy baby Su and hung close to Thuy. From a bag, one boy pulled out a piece of netting that resembled a hammock and gestured for Thuy to put Su in it so he and another boy could carry her. Thuy looked at me questioningly, and then back at the boys, who were skipping along, singing and making faces to amuse the baby. When I didn't say anything, she placed Su in the hammock. The boys clapped and cheered.

Another boy ran up carrying a large banana tree frond. Then they took turns shooing away flies and shading the baby from the sun. They sang soothing songs to her and broke into laughter when she grabbed the finger one of them held in front of her face. The boys carried on like this all the way to the new location.

I didn't know if these teenagers had anything to do with the atrocities the pirates had performed the night before. If they had, I just could not understand how they could be so playful and gay like ordinary boys when they lived among a pack of swine. The Thai fishermen seemed utterly contradictory—one minute they were like normal human beings, the next they turned demons—and I couldn't comprehend their unexpected behavior.

When we reached the intended spot, the fishermen signaled for us to stop. We sat on the beach and looked around. It was a total contrast to the dangerous, rocky cliff and the cave where we'd come from. It was, in fact, quite beautiful and peaceful.

The beach side of Koh Kra, where the refugees were kept by Thai pirates. Photo: United Nations, November 1979.

The white coral beach glistened, and the clear blue water looked deceitfully good enough to drink. Tall trees lined the shore, offering cool shade. It resembled a scene from a postcard of a vacation spot. When the wind blew, the trees swayed like graceful dancers.

The Thais let us set up camp in a clearing beside the beach close to the water and in front of the shady forest.

From there we could see how close we were to the lighthouse we'd discovered. From the direction of the rocky beach on the other side of the mountain, we'd only seen that the lighthouse up against the high slope. We hadn't known that on this side it was a flat, smooth beach.

Still, in shock and fear from the night's terrors, we gathered fronds to make beds and families picked their own resting places. Meanwhile, some gathered to talk in hushed voices under the trees. The men arranged the cooking items around where everyone sat. We also strung up a blue tarp to act as a roof for our cooking area.

That night the men built a big fire and used an oil container cut in two as a cooking pot. Taking rice supplied by the fishermen, they cooked enough gruel for all of us. Besides the raw rice and dried fish, the fishermen had left us some cans of water and a few packs of Thai cigarettes.

A Pirate Macabre Party

About the time we finished cooking we noticed that the Thai fishermen who had moved us from the mountainside to the beach were returning to the island. They swooped down and sat near us with their own food, inviting us to join them.

We hesitated, but we were somewhat less apprehensive because we'd discovered that, unlike our previous location, this area had several places where we could hide. There were about half a dozen Thai men, and they seemed open and friendly. That, plus our stabbing hunger, made us decide we were better off accepting their invitation.

After supper, the fishermen rolled their own cigarettes and offered some to us. They began to sing, and several of them danced in their traditional style. Then they opened their arms and waved us in. They taught us some Thai songs and their local dances. They even gave the kids some language lessons.

"*Nam*," one man said pointing to a container of water.

One of the refugees made a wide arc with his hand to ask what this island was called.

"Koh Kra," the pirates chimed in.

Koh Kra. We repeated the name over and over slowly, focusing on each word. Such a short and simple name, yet so laden with meaning that fear caught in our throats. Those two words held tremendous power as if speaking them aloud might stir up a fearsome monster.

As we talked to the pirates, we also discussed among ourselves how to keep the previous day's nightmare from being repeated. We thought we ought to go along with those fishermen who were friendlier, hoping that by easing relations with them they might not mistreat us.

The party atmosphere wound down as night drew on. The refugees were growing weary, but the Thai seemed to be increasingly whipped up.

Then all of a sudden, the singing, dancing, and merry-making came to a halt, as if at the sign of an unseen master of ceremonies.

The pirates stood up and looked around. Then they each approached a Vietnamese girl and took her by the hand, leading her into the bushes. The girls all struggled and kicked, but the other pirates picked them up and carried them off.

The refugee men surrounded the pirates and tried to pull the girls away. That's when the pirates with guns drew their weapons and fired into the air. Others took out knives and machetes and threw the men on the ground. They took turns guarding the refugee men while their friends took their chosen victims into the woods.

There were fewer pirates than on previous night, but it was clear they were among those who'd participated in that atrocity and had come back to pick their favorites while leaving the others alone.

■ THUY

All that night I separated myself from the others and didn't participate in any of the conversation or dancing. Instead, with Su in my arms, I found a place to sit far off by the ocean and watched. Phuc brought me some rice and fish.

"You need to keep up your strength to deal with whatever might happen tonight," he said.

I knew what he meant. Neither of us saw anything in the pirates' goodwill and relaxed attitude that made us trust them.

"Are they using drugs?" I asked.

He looked at the fishermen who were laughing uproariously and putting their arms around the boat people, having quite a good time, and nodded.

"Looks like it. The stuff they're smoking has a funny smell. They're in a good mood now, but when it wears off, they'll be different people."

I shuddered. There was a macabre sense to the scene, like executioners dancing with their prisoners before beheading them. When the pirates settled down, we looked at each other. Su was sleeping peacefully in my arms.

"I'm taking Su with me," I said quickly.

Phuc agreed.

"There's only a few of them, and they look pretty groggy. I have a feeling they won't be as violent as last night."

Then I took Su and ran into the trees just as the pirates on the beach started taking away their chosen girls.

I spent the night huddled in the bushes. Su slept peacefully. My heart pounded so hard I could hear the pulsing in my head.

After a while, I started to feel myself being attacked by insects. I pressed the baby tighter to my chest, covering her sensitive skin with my body and the flaps of my blouse. When morning approached, I heard Phuc's whispering call.

"Thuy! Thuy!"

I saw his form in the morning twilight cautiously making his way across the coral that ran along the foliage.

"Where are you?" he called a little louder. "They're gone, you can come out."

In the dim light, he couldn't figure out where I was hidden. The bushes were thick and difficult to find one's way through.

When I was sure he was alone, I called out softly. He ran up and, carefully pushing aside the branches, helped me out and took Su from my arms.

I pulled up my pants legs to inspect my calves. In just a few hours my legs had been eaten up by centipedes, mosquitoes, and other pests. There were open sores and scabs sensitive to the touch.

"Oh Lord," Phuc moaned as he wiped my legs with his hands.

I winced and pushed his hands away as he was inadvertently irritating the wounds.

"It's all right," I whispered wearily. "I'm still lucky."

I rolled up my pants to air out the skin.

That morning the same fishermen came by and dropped off more rice and dried fish for us. Some even brought cooked food and cigarettes. Then they went fishing.

That evening they were back. After resting and having supper, they took the girls out to the bushes.

Hiding on the Mountainside
November 3, 1979

My pants legs were sticking to open sores that were becoming infected. I dreaded the prospect of going back into the vermin-infested bushes another night.

Phuc spent the day scouring the island for a new hiding place. When he returned, he told me he'd found a spot high on the mountain where he didn't think the pirates would bother to climb. I agreed to go there at once.

"Any place has to be better than where the bugs will get me," I said.

A woman sitting nearby overheard our conversation. Now she approached with clasped hands.

"I'm all by myself with no one to help me. Please, let me hide with you. You're the lucky one. Help me, too!"

I looked at her and wanted to cry in pity. This was sister Thu, the woman who had befriended me on the boat and whose husband was already in another country. Since coming to the island, she'd associated with the other women without families, so I hadn't seen her. She was one of those taken by the pirates the first night.

I looked over at Phuc to let him know I'd already made up my mind.

"All right," I told her, "come with me."

When I took her hand, she hugged me tightly for a long time, sobbing on my shoulder.

We decided it would be better to leave Su with the other children since trying to carry her up the mountain would be dangerous.

Of the 11 children in our group, all but the smallest were pretty much left alone on the beach to do as they pleased. Some hunted for anything edible or asked the fishermen for something to assuage their hunger. Hoa and Khoa hung out with some kids aged 10 to 12, while An was in a group of younger children. The older kids promised to keep an eye on Su. So we left the baby on the beach on a bed of palm leaves covered with clothing in the shade of a tall tree.

On the way to our hiding place, Phuc kept giving me a look to say that having an extra person along made it more likely we'd be discovered. But neither of us had the heart to refuse Thu's request.

Phuc led us up the side of the mountain. The climbing was tricky and precarious. He brought us as high as we could go to a place with large boulders that blocked the view from below.

"You two stay right here," he warned us. "Be careful and watch out to see if they try to climb up. Under no circumstances should you leave this spot until I come to get you."

Then he left us and went back down to stay with the children.

Sister Thu and I didn't speak to each other, too afraid to open our mouths. Every time our eyes met, we recognized the terror in the other and turned away quickly.

We were on the highest point of the island, sitting back against the boulders. From our vantage point, the people below looked like ants moving about on a game board. With a clear view down the mountain slope, we would be able to see if anyone was coming up in our direction. I hoped that the pirates would see how dangerous the area was and assume no women would have dared climb here to hide.

On the other hand, if they did find us, I came up with two strategies to preserve our honor. If it was only one pirate, the two of us could combine our strength and push him off the slope. If more than one, with just a single step to the side we would fall to our deaths on the rocks below. The second scenario was more likely, as the pirates rarely went hunting for women alone.

Around midnight it began to rain hard. After a while, I gave up trying to keep the rain out of my face. The wind whistled as it passed among the rocks and howled along the slope on the other side of the island. It seemed to be trying to push me out of my hiding place. I clung to the boulder to keep from being blown off the mountain.

The freezing storm cut me to the bone. I turned to Thu, whose teeth were chattering. We moved closer to share body heat. Our backs against each other, we used the rocks for support against the storm. I shut my eyes and tried not to think of the present, but pain and fear pierced me to my very core.

The night was dimly lit by pale moonlight shining on the waves. To my horror, the rock before me seemed to come alive. Bands of tiny creatures crawled over its surface like leeches. Black creeping things slithered on the moss-covered stone.

My left leg itched. I quickly reached down and found something biting my ankle. I caught it and pulled it from my wound. It stuck to my hand, and I had to use my other hand to tear it off and throw it away.

There was nothing I could do to protect myself from getting bitten. Then something like a rat went past my head. I heard the sound of scurrying, then clawing at the rock. I shuddered and said to myself, *Troi oi! Now a family of wild rats...!*

In the midst of all this, I recalled a Vietnamese proverb: "Bear small pains to avoid big disaster." I comforted myself with the thought that at least I was safe in hiding rather than subject to the misfortunes of those on the beach.

I looked down from my perch. The rain enveloped the scene in a gray mantle of gloom.

The Game of the Chase
November 4-6, 1979

■ PHUC

D ay returned and everything continued as before.
The food. The pirates. The hunt for women. The paralyzing fear.

The boat people had turned into puppets, going through the motions as if manipulated by strings without any feelings.

Especially the women. Many endured the repeated nights of their descent into hell then came back with the glazed-over look of those who were alive physically but had lost their souls.

Only the children were still having fun, exploring the island and playing games with the innocence of youth.

■ THUY

After several days I could no longer endure the ordeal of hiding on the mountain. To me, it was as terrifying as cowering in the bushes. There my body was eaten up by insects and burned by the cold. On the mountain, besides the fierce weather and assault by crawling pests, I was gripped by guilt as I witnessed the atrocities occurring on the beach below me.

"I have to find a new hiding place," I told Phuc one day.

I offered no explanation, and anyway, I figured he could never

A cave on Koh Kra where the women hid in 1979.
Photo: VTT, 2017

imagine what I'd seen during the night when the sky wasn't shrouded in rain and the moon shone on the island. Thu had also given up hiding in the high boulders and rejoined the other unaccompanied women.

While on the mountain I'd noticed the roof of the lighthouse storage surrounded by a large bougainvillea plant with red flowers. I decided to find a hiding place there. Climbing up I found some gaps in the thorny plant that covered the flat roof. I gritted my teeth and crawled in among the vicious sharp branches to a space high enough for me to sit up and wide enough to lie down and not be seen from the outside. Even if someone climbed onto the roof, they wouldn't know I was there.

Ironically, the pirates happened to follow the same route and built a fire below the lighthouse storage, not far from my spot.

The children were drawn to the fire. Khoa, Hoa, and An were there with Su. After a while, they lay down to sleep there. For hours I sat huddled in the bougainvillea, clenching my teeth while my daughter An called for me and Su cried all night.

■ PHUC

After a week on the island, the boat people had become familiar with the pirates' routine. During the day the Thai men went fishing. At night they anchored their boats nearby, then rowed to the island in small skiffs and began their violent activities. Late at night, they returned to their boats offshore.

Each morning the refugee men went to retrieve those women who had fled so they could have something to eat and be back with their families. Sometimes boats stopped by the island by day, and the fishermen came ashore. But these men were usually decent and just wanted to find out about us or share their food.

One morning while we were cooking rice gruel, one of the pirates approached Thuy, who was sitting by the cooking fire. He had a kind-looking face and polite manner. He gestured toward Thuy, then to the bushes, and then to Su. Another man came forward and nodded, making a cradling motion with his arms.

Thuy forced a smile and nodded, showing that she understood they were telling her she didn't need to hide in the bushes but could stay and care for the baby.

That evening, the same two pirates pulled me out and gestured that message again. Speaking Thai, they made me understand that I shouldn't worry, nothing was going to happen to Thuy, that she would be safe on the beach and didn't need to run away. I also pretended to agree with them, but inside I asked myself, *why should I trust these pirates?*

Ever since I saw the writing on the lighthouse storage walls, I advised all the women to flee. Better to put up with insect bites and the freezing rain than being the victims of these heartless men.

The Complexity of the Human Heart

All this time I'd noticed that the pirates seemed to be paying particular attention to the children, especially Su. They appeared to be fond of children and treated ours well. The pirates brought the children food, taught them to speak Thai, showed them games, and protected them from the dangers of an uninhabited island.

I was quite surprised when one pirate brought Thuy a can of condensed milk to prepare for Su, who was always crying. When they noticed Su's milk bottle was dirty, they took it away to wash in fresh water, and then scoured it with coconut pulp.

I saw all the traces of human character in them, good mixed with evil in each person. There would be good people in a bad crowd and vice versa. Some Thai fishermen were kind and generous; they didn't abuse the refugees but gave us food and water.

At the same time, there were some among the refugees who refused to share the life of the community but were concerned only for their own welfare. Still, despite any negatives, the refugees helped each other wholeheartedly and advised one another not to trust any pirate. Even if they behaved well, it could be a trick or merely a momentary action.

Every day as evening fell I reminded Thuy that it was time for her to get away. The pirates' daily return to their chosen women had become the norm, so much so that some of our numbers no longer paid any attention to it. A few of the other women even stopped hiding but remained with their families for comfort and support.

But not Thuy. She insisted on leaving the group as the day declined to sneak away to her hiding place at the lighthouse storage. She circled around to the rear along the mountain and climbed onto the roof to lie down among the thorny branches of the bougainvillea, suffering multiple scratches and tears in the process. She returned to us only when she knew the pirates had left the island before daybreak.

When the pirates saw Su by herself on the beach at night, they sought me out and suggested I persuade Thuy to come back and take care of the baby. I pretended not to understand them.

One morning, when Thuy and I were talking with a group of refugees from our boat of 81, among them was author Nhat Tien, a number of fishing boats came to the island. One of the crews was particularly kind and soft-spoken and displayed goodwill toward the refugees. Holding Su, Thuy approached them and gestured that she wanted paper and pencil. They smiled and provided these for her. She sat down and wrote a letter similar to the one she'd written in French on the first day of our arrival on the island, requesting the foreign press to intervene and rescue the boat people. This time, the letter was co-signed by author Nhat Tien, a member of the P.E.N. Club International, and Vice President of the Vietnam PEN Club in 1975. We were hoping that together with the media, the International Pen Club would lobby for our rescue.

She addressed it to the French Press Agency in Bangkok and handed it to the man who seemed to be the crew's chief. He accepted the letter, confused at first, then nodded his understanding of her wish. Then she pointed to the ocean and using gestures, asked them to take us off the island. They appeared to understand but shook their heads.

The Red Boat Devils

November 6, 1979

On the ninth day of our captivity on Kra, a steady rain fell. It seemed that a big storm was coming. The fishing boats—I counted more than 40—anchored all around the island. This meant that more than the usual number of fishermen visited the refugees. Some of them brought us rice and fish.

After a few hours, a strange boat arrived. Its frame was painted blood red, and there were maybe 25 men on board, about three times as many as on a typical fishing boat. The men climbed into two rowboats and quickly made their way to the island. As soon as they beached their skiffs, they pulled out their weapons and started waving them in the air.

The pirates charged over to the refugees, and, using machetes and axes, knocked over our water and food containers, smashing everything in sight. During the attack, they threw children to the ground and yanked little ones out of the arms of their mothers. And, most atrocious of all, they raped women right there on the beach.

Thuy was among those sitting in a hollow of the mountain to escape the rain when the shouting arose. I ran to warn her. Others were fleeing the violence, describing the scene between gasping breaths.

"The red boat savages! They're wrecking everything!"

"Friends, get away fast!"

I grabbed my wife, and with the other women, we ran as fast as we could. Thuy headed straight for the lighthouse storage's roof and dove into the thorny branches.

For a whole week we'd taken for granted that we would be left alone during the day so now we were caught off guard. Some, slow to react, just went into the bushes to hide.

The red boat pirates snatched those who remained on the beach and searched them most brutally, hitting or kicking them for the slightest provocation. A few of the pirates went to the boys like Hoa and Khoa and grabbed their genitals to see if they were indeed males. Satisfied with what they found, they let the boys go.

Two of the attackers held machetes in front of my face. Pointing to a limp figure lying on the beach after being raped, they wanted me to show them where the other women had gone. I played dumb and avoided their eyes. They shoved me into the sand and gave me a beating. When I remained unresponsive, they stomped off.

Nearby another refugee man was begging.

"*Troi oi!* I don't know where the girls are!"

He was kneeling on the ground with his arms yanked behind his back. His face was flooded with tears.

I buried my face in the sand, listening in anguish while they beat the poor man. They laughed and mocked him, seeming to derive pleasure from torturing a defenseless human being. And I felt I was going mad as I witnessed this scene, utterly powerless to do anything.

The Crew of Thom's Boat
November 7—8, 1979

The pirate crew that had regularly been coming that week was captained by a man named Thom. There were seven members and, except for one old man and a boy of about 14, all including Thom were among the pirates who raped refugee women on the first night.

Ever since they came to Kra each day and each night and only sought out the girls they had abused the first time. When they arrived by day, they brought food and supplies, sometimes sharing candy and cigarettes, and treated the girls solicitously.

At night, when Thom and his crew returned from fishing, they called out a greeting from afar, and the refugees greeted them back, acknowledging each by name. The pirates did not disturb the other women but looked only for those they'd already chosen for themselves.

These women had no safe place to hide or family to support them. Once the damage had been done and they realized it was useless to struggle against their attackers, the girls seemed to accept their fate. Numbing themselves against further shame, they took on the role of hostages in exchange for the protection afforded by Thom's crew, not only for themselves but for our whole group of 81 boat people.

The day the red boat pirates came to the island, Thom's crew raced in to find their girls and take them to their own boat for safety. They probably realized that they lacked the strength to fight off the other pirates if the girls remained on shore.

The following morning, two of Thom's crew sought me out and indicated that they were willing to take Thuy and Su on their boat with their girls. Bewildered, I wasn't sure how to respond.

Meanwhile, the red boat devils continued spreading terror across the island.

That night, a vicious rainstorm thrashed with icy winds, making the island even more dismal.

I sat with Su and An under a plastic sheet by a tall tree not far from the lighthouse storage. Now and then I glanced in the direction of the building surrounded by twisting bougainvillea branches where my wife was hiding. My heart broke to think of her there, dealing with the rain and wind for the past two days without cover, food or water. The space was barely large enough for her to lie still; if she moved, her flesh would be torn by knife-like thorns.

The night was dark, and the storm raged. It was so cold. I dressed Su and An in all their clothes but they still shivered. I was anxious for Thuy, wondering how she would stand the weather in her situation. Along with my pity for her, I was filled with shame at how all the men were powerless to help the women they loved.

I was so overcome with cold and hurt that I thought I was going to pass out. It seemed to me that there was no way Thuy could survive like this any longer. While she may have evaded the pirates, exposure to the harsh weather would surely kill her.

When the red boat pirates left the island in the morning, I placed Su down next to Hoa and Khoa, who were still asleep, and climbed up to the lighthouse storage's roof. With much effort, I reached Thuy and brought her down, her body stiff with cold. Our arms and legs were scratched bloody from the thorns.

"You have to go at once!" I told her anxiously.

She couldn't walk, her lips were cracked and bleeding, and her teeth chattered. She looked at me blankly.

"The red boat crew... are they gone?"

"Thom and his men have taken some of the girls on board their boat to keep them out of the hands of the red boat pirates. They came looking for me today."

She gave me an absent stare as if she hadn't heard what I said. I had to take her by the shoulders and press my face against hers until she came to. She struggled to focus, and only when I saw her eyes fall on my lips did I speak, slowly and forcefully.

"Thom and his crew will take you and Su on their boat with the others."

I shook her by the shoulders then rubbed her face and arms hard to get the blood circulating. Only after I repeated the sentence twice did she show signs of alertness. She leaned against me for warmth and was quiet for a long time.

Finally, she asked, "Can we trust them?"

I continued rubbing her arms and shoulders.

"I honestly don't know. But we've known them for a week. At least they're not as violent as the red boat crew. Those guys are totally evil and out of control."

When she seemed to waver, I went on.

"Thuy, I may be wrong. But I believe it's best for you and our daughter. You know Thom's crew loves Su and treats her well, and they've said many times you don't need to run from them."

With that, she seemed to come around. In the end, we agreed this appeared to be the best solution to a horrible situation.

On Board Thom's Boat

■ THUY

It stormed all day and night. More fishing boats came to Kra Island to escape the rain and wind. There were more than 50 boats. I knew it would be difficult to avoid so many men— close to 500—hunting for women, especially such brutal men as the red boat crew.

It looked like there was no other choice but to go with the girls onto Thom's boat. I made a quick sign of the cross and said a prayer placing my life in the hands of God, and followed Phuc with Su down to the beach.

When we arrived, Thom's crew was helping the girls onto their skiffs. Seeing Su and me, Thom motioned for me to join one of his men and two girls on a second rowboat.

As we set off from the island, I saw Phuc and An standing on the beach, two vague figures slowly becoming lost in the curtain of rain that darkened the sky.

All that day I sat on Thom's fishing boat, trying hard not to think of my husband and daughter back on the island. And I labored to convince myself that this was a wise decision to ensure my survival.

Everyone on Thom's boat treated me courteously. Besides Thom and his crew and the five refugee girls, there was an old man who usually remained on the boat with a boy helping to take care of things. Also, there was another refugee family, including a man named Tan and his wife and their young son. Tan was the younger brother of Kim, the girl who had become Thom's "hostage." Due to Kim's acquiescence in this unfortunate business, Tan's family received protection and care.

All in all, there were 17 people on board the craft. On the sides of the boat were two skiffs that the fishermen used to sail further out to cast their nets, then to bring in their haul at day's end. The old man and boy took charge of dividing the catch, either throwing the fish into the icebox or cleaning and drying them on deck. The refugee women stayed with the old man and boy while the others went to work. When the crew returned, we all ate together.

At night, Thom and the men took the girls in the rowboats back to the beach and brought them back later. The fishermen believed it was bad luck to engage in sex on their boat.

While the others were gone, the old man tried to talk to me, but I didn't understand anything he said. He brought out a can of milk for Su and played with her. Sensing my fear and suspicion despite his efforts to be friendly, he went below deck and returned with some photographs. He pointed to a picture of himself with an elderly woman and a group of children, a gentle expression on his face. He looked at Su and smiled and showed me a picture of his youngest son, who was about Hoa and Khoa's age.

I smiled politely, but I was still unsettled and didn't want to talk to him. I remained sitting at the side of the boat watching the waves rise in the storm as if gathering up the whole ocean and crashing into Kra Island like a black hole in the swirl of water.

The next morning, I learned that at least one other Thai boat, captained by one Chada, a friend of Thom, had picked up some of the refugee women to protect them from the red boat pirates while the rest remained on Kra.

A Promised Land turns out to be Hell
November 8—13, 1979

■ PHUC

The first night without my wife and baby daughter I was uneasy, worried especially about Thuy.

When I saw Thom's rowboat return to the beach, I ran to take a look and find out about her. But the crew took the girls with them into the woods. Reluctantly, I walked back to the other refugees and sat hugging my knees staring at Thom's boat off in the distance. I thought I saw Thuy holding Su and looking back at the island.

Suddenly there were chaotic shouts, and everyone ran to one side of the beach. I followed them and strained to see what they were pointing at. There was a small boat drifting towards the island.

It was too small to be a Thai fishing boat. It had no sail or navigation equipment, and it rocked wildly as the surf pushed it to shore.

"A refugee boat!" someone cried. "It's a refugee boat, my friends!"

His voice was a mixture of joy and distress. Then he sighed.

"Those poor people! When they saw land, they probably thought this was the Promised Land. They never knew it was really hell...."

At last the boat washed up on shore.

There were 21 people on board. We eventually learned that the group of 16 men, four women, and one child had left Rach Gia on October 29 in a sampan seven meters long powered by an outboard motor. They had been attacked by pirates ten times. One young man, Huynh Phi Long, had been thrown overboard while the pirates were searching for booty. He didn't know how to swim and drowned in front of his boat mates.

Some of the women were raped by the red boat pirates as soon as they staggered ashore.

Lamenting One's Fate

■ THUY

All during the time I was sitting on the boat with Su gazing back at the island, I was utterly despondent. I wanted to go back and be with Phuc and An, even though that meant confining myself to a terrible hiding place. But the horrible screams resounding from the island forced me to face reality and see the practical wisdom, even blessing, of my being on Thom's boat with my baby.

The captive girls bonded as they discussed their uncertain fate as "hostages" and confided in each other during the periods the crew was out fishing. At times they jumped into the water to swim and splash each other playfully, grabbing a few moments of innocence out of their days of misfortune. They were earnest in their dedication to one another, making sure the other ate enough to keep up her strength, though all we had was rice and fish with fish sauce.

One night, Su cried for milk, and as I reached for the bottle I had prepared for her, it slipped from my hand and fell onto the deck. I crawled along holding Su in one arm to keep her from waking the others as I groped for the bottle in the dark. Suddenly a dim light glowed in front of me, and I saw one of the pirates holding an oil lamp. Seeing the bottle in a corner, he picked it up and brought it to me. With a smile, he opened the cap and placed the bottle in Su's mouth. He stayed to help feed the baby, stroking her head gently as she devoured the milk.

I quickly took over the bottle-feeding and nodded polite thanks. Before the lamp went out, I saw the girl lying next to the pirate looking at me. She gave me a soft smile as if to say it was she who had asked the man to look for the bottle. I nodded to her appreciatively, to which she replied with a crooked smile, bespeaking her sadness and meek resignation regarding her pitiful situation.

All night I couldn't sleep, my heart breaking with the vision of those sad eyes and the bitter smile that marked the face of a Vietnamese girl who had fallen into the hands of pirates.

Once again I felt the sting of survivor's guilt, of being "luckier" than the other women and girls of our refugee group. This made me uncomfortable with the victims who suffered so much more than I did, and I felt a heavy responsibility toward life. I often encountered the pained and quizzical looks in the eyes of the other women. They seemed to be asking the same thing I asked myself throughout this ordeal, *why am I luckier than these women? Why have I escaped the pirates?*

I had no answer, but could only humble myself, bow my head and give thanks to God. I knew this question would follow me all the rest of my life with the mysterious debt I took on during those days.

Hiding in a Hidden Cave

One morning I heard Thom and his crew having an animated discussion. I didn't know what they were talking about, but from the urgency in their tone, I surmised their situation was dire and they were looking for a way to cope with it.

Thom called all the refugees together. Through his words and gestures, we realized that he had to sail back to the mainland to bring in his catch. He also indicated that they had come up with a way to ensure our safety while they were gone.

Near Kra, there were two smaller islands with sparse foliage that looked like giant boulders topped with trees thrusting out of the sea. There was no life on these, so they were unnamed and known as part of the Kra Island group.

Early the next morning Thom dropped us on the smaller of the two islands. Walking along the rocky edge by the water we came upon a small cave hidden underneath layers of hanging rock that formed a sort of roof. From far off, one would see only rocks and not suspect there was a cave behind them. The grotto was rather deep with a smooth sandy floor. Thom seemed to say this would be a safe place for us as no boats ever stopped by there.

He left us with some cooked rice mixed with fish and salt rolled into balls so they would last longer. He also gave us some dried fish and containers of fresh water.

Thom's "hostage" Kim, who had learned some Thai, translated for him.

"We're not to light a fire since that would expose our hiding place. We must stay in the cave and not go wandering about. They'll return in three to four days."

After giving us these words of advice, Thom and his crew returned to their boat and sailed off, leaving ten refugees in a cavern with just enough room for us to lie down. We immediately picked our spots.

Kra Island lay off the other side of our island, so that, although it wasn't distant from us, we were unable to see it from the cave. I chose a place by the opening and sat there with Su looking out at the vast and endless rolling waves.

All day long the ten of us sat in the cave watching the sea and not speaking to one another. At first, I was afraid for us being left by ourselves, but after checking out the spot carefully, I was reassured that the cave was blocked from view by the boulders. Ships out at sea would never suspect there was anything there.

Nonetheless, after all we'd been through, we couldn't help

being apprehensive. For me, I just sat nervously praying to myself that we wouldn't be discovered and asking God to protect my husband and child as well as all the others on Kra.

We had nothing to do except share our meals three times a day. After eating, we sat quietly casting our eyes out to sea, each troubled by our own private thoughts.

The Silent War of Resistance

My attention was especially taken with a girl I'll call Mai. She was beautiful, the most beautiful girl on the boat. Tall and slender, she had an oval face, big sad black eyes, a delicate nose, and full red lips that were always silent. Her beauty was natural, genteel, and perfect like a statue. She had come from Vietnam alone and was not acquainted with anyone on the boat.

Ever since that first night she was assaulted she never said a word to anyone. All day long she kept mum, her hands gripping shut her torn blouse that had lost all buttons. A woman from our group felt pity for her and offered to close the shirt with safety pins. Mai sat still and let her do as she wished, her face expressionless.

I didn't know how she managed in the nights that followed, but when we were on Thom's boat, I saw her huddled on the deck tight-lipped and staring into space. At night when the pirates took the girls back to the island, she followed mechanically, a strange cold look on her face as though the spirit had gone out of her.

Inside the cave, Mai always sat near the entrance hugging her knees and staring out at sea. At dinnertime, she held out her hand to take the rice but refused to eat the fish. When Kim noticed that the girl was growing thin and urged her to eat more, Mai just looked straight through her without responding. She ate by raising one grain of rice at a time into her mouth slowly, robotically. One of the other girls told me that all this time, even when they were on the island, Mai steadfastly refused to eat anything the pirates gave her.

I could see the bitterness and rage that she hid behind her stolid expression and sensed the lonely, improbable war she was silently waging. Weak, vulnerable, and starving, she patiently pursued her passive struggle, a tragic yet heroic figure, a Vietnamese woman against a Thai pirate.

November 10, 1979

In two days all the rice balls were consumed, and Thom had not returned. We bore our hunger, afraid to light a fire to cook the raw rice the pirates had left us in case we needed it.

But on the third day, many of us couldn't stand it any longer. We held a meeting and decided to make a small fire and cook rice gruel. We took turns sitting around the fire to conceal it and fanning the smoke so it would dissipate before rising beyond the cave.

About halfway through, however, we spied a ship sailing past in the distance. In a panic we quickly doused the fire, our hearts pounding in fright.

With that, we shared the half-cooked gruel along with dried fish, chewing slowly to trick our hunger and to stretch out the time it took to perform the only activity we had.

In our anxiety and fear, the hours waiting seemed to last forever. I spent the day sitting on a rock holding Su, feeling the tension and trying to be ready for whatever should happen next.

Pursuit and Torture
November 8-13, 1979

■ PHUC

While Thuy was away I took care of Thuan An and my nephews Hoa and Khoa. Hundreds of pirates swarmed over the island, hunting for women and terrorizing the refugees.

The women who were still on Kra scattered to find hiding places. But the number of pirates arriving to escape the storm kept growing. Together they scoured the island until nearly everyone had been discovered. Heart-rending screams and shouts could be heard all day and night.

The men were not free of the pirates' abuse. One man was beaten in an attempt to make him disclose where the women were hiding. When he refused to talk, they hung him by his neck from a tree. The branch was dry and broke under his weight, sending him down the slope.

They took another man and held a machete to his throat, forcing him to take them to the women. After leading them nowhere, he came to a rocky place where he pretended to slip so that he fell into the ocean to escape further torture.

There was an old man with three gold teeth that the pirates tried to twist out of his mouth. He begged them to stop, saying the teeth were only plated, not real gold. But they held him down and used pliers to remove them. His mouth full of blood, the man fainted while the pirates laughed, dropped the bloody teeth in their pockets and moved on.

In late afternoon the following day, during the storm, another refugee boat arrived at Kra carrying 37 people: 24 men, eight women, and five children. They had departed from Rach Gia on November 9 and been attacked by pirates six times at sea.

The boat people, now numbering more than a hundred, felt utterly hopeless and abandoned by the outside world. It seemed that no one in the free world, which valued human virtue, had any idea what was happening on the island called Kra in the Gulf of Thailand. No one could help us because only the pirates and the patrol boat number 15 knew of the existence of this deserted island or of our presence in this hell. This thought more than anything else drove us mad with despair.

Meanwhile, the pirates continued to use Kra as their personal torture chamber and amusement park. They supplied us with enough food to keep us alive, so they had victims for their abusive enjoyment.

A Boat People Massacre

The next day I was eating lunch with the children by our "kitchen" when I heard some young people calling everyone to come out to the coral reef. There we saw a small boat rocking in the water not far away. It was another refugee boat.

I climbed a boulder to get a better look. It appeared the boat people were struggling to steer their craft to the island, but the red boat pirates were deliberately blocking their way.

Then the pirates jumped onto the little boat and herded the refugees onto their larger vessel. After that, the pirates rammed and sank the refugee boat. Observing this, I supposed they planned to treat the newcomers the same way they'd treated the rest of us before: first, they'd search for valuables, and then they'd get down to their violent business.

But what I saw next surpassed my worst expectation.

The red boat pirates began throwing people off the boat.

In horror I watched my poor compatriots struggling wildly against the surf. Many were pulled under the green water of the gulf.

I recalled once swimming with my nephew Hoa around that area. I tried to keep up with him, but the rip currents kept pulling me back. I choked and swallowed water and feared I wasn't going to make it until Hoa lent a hand.

Now, as I witnessed these people fighting helplessly to stay above the surface far out in the gulf, my heart was filled with anger and resentment. These were feelings I had suppressed for days as I worried about getting Thuy to safety and acted as an unwilling spectator of the cruelty the pirates showed toward the others. I couldn't stand to see the things I was seeing, but neither could I turn away while my people were being thrown one at a time into the choppy sea. Unable to contain my emotions any longer, I fell to my knees and wept with everything that was in me, feeling my chest and throat tighten and squeeze as though I were drowning, too.

That day only 18 of the boat people survived and made it to shore. The group told us when they'd left Vietnam, there were 34 aboard. Since leaving Rach Gia, they'd been attacked ten times by pirates, the last time just off the island of Kra.

After sinking the refugee boat, the pirates had started tossing the passengers overboard, striking them on the head with their machetes if they resisted. Frightened by the spectacle, some of the refugees had jumped into the water trying to save themselves.

Those who were too weak went down at once. Others were smashed against the rocks. Their bodies littered the water and reefs between the boat and the island. In all, sixteen people died in the space of less than half a mile from shore.

One Day at a Time
November 14, 1979

■ THUY

B y the fourth day on the tiny island, I couldn't stand it any longer. Under nervous strain and hunger, not to mention having to deal with the uncertainty of how long we would all be waiting, I became obsessed with foolish thoughts of swimming back to Kra Island to be reunited with my husband and daughter, whose unknown fate haunted me.

I felt as though I'd been on this patch of rock for a very long time. I stopped talking to anyone. Crazy ideas filled my head. I gathered the strength of my rational mind to suppress the urge to do something reckless. So I kept to myself and spoke to no one, sitting frozen behind a rock with Su in my arms staring out to sea.

I'm sure the other women suffered just like me. Each time our eyes met, we turned quickly away, shuddering at having seen the despair in each other's face.

The next day around noon Thom's boat appeared before the mouth of the cave. We rushed to greet them as saviors. The truth is they'd returned just when we were at the end of our rope.

When we got back onto the boat, I startled the old man by smiling in reply to his greeting. He reached out to take Su while I climbed aboard and I willingly handed the baby over.

Thom sailed in by the island and anchored among the other fishing boats—46 of them by my count.

The weather suddenly started acting up as the wind raged and sheets of rain covered the island. What bothered me most was that the bad weather meant the pirates would be staying on Kra longer.

I sat on the deck all day and night, looking out at the island and wondering how Phuc and An were doing. One of the crew noticed me sitting there dejectedly and rushed over with a piece of paper and pencil, telling me with signs that I ought to write a note that he would take to Phuc.

Surprised by this act of thoughtfulness, I jumped at the unanticipated opportunity to communicate with my husband. I wrote a few quick lines before the man changed his mind.

Daddy,

Every day I pray that you and An, Hoa, and Khoa are safe. Mother and child here are all right. We've all come back from the small island. Write a little to let me know what's happening on the island and if I should come back.

Love and miss you. May the Lord preserve us!

Thuy

I watched as the pirates rowed to the island with my letter. My heart pounded in anticipation.

■ PHUC

I was sitting with An in my lap. For the past few days, she'd been feverish, sweating profusely despite the cold storm. I had no medicine for her, and there was no place on the beach to find refuge from the rain other than under the blue tarp that hung over our cooking area.

I sat there with my back to the rain, protecting my daughter from as much of the storm as I could. That's how I remained all day, peering out at sea, praying that Thuy and Su were safe and sound.

Worry plagued me. It had been days since Thuy and the other women had gone away on Thom's boat, and I hadn't heard a word about them. Then one of the men ran up, saying curtly that a pirate was looking for me.

I picked up An and followed him. Along the way, the other refugee and I didn't speak. Those last several days none of us talked with each other the way we had before. Fear and depression had deadened us physically as well as mentally, and no one really felt like engaging in normal social relations.

When we reached the beach, he said, "That one there, standing over there."

He pointed to a man I recognized from Thom's crew.

The pirate handed me a piece of paper folded in four, then pointed toward Thom's boat and said something in Thai. Nodding my understanding, I took the paper and hurried to get under an overhanging rock by the water's edge. There I carefully opened the paper, leaning forward to shield it from the rain.

After reading the note, I slumped back against the rock and clutched my throat to keep from shouting.

"Thank you, Lord! My wife and child are safe!"

Storm Again... and Pirates Again
November 14-16, 1979

■ THUY

T he storm grew in intensity, the wind howled, and the seas rose. It almost seemed to be trying to swallow the island in the sea.

That day was the worst weather in nearly three weeks. The rain pummeled the area with a roar, battering the trees and breaking anchor lines for many a pirate boat.

Thom's crew could not go out to fish that day. It was not only the refugees who became seasick, but even these veteran Thai fishermen also succumbed to the heaving ocean as the boat rose and fell with the monstrous waves.

My many weeks on the ocean had not affected me like this single day. Everything inside me seemed to have been thrown out. The other passengers fared no better. We lay sick and yellow on the deck, virtual corpses in a floating coffin.

■ PHUC

O n the island, the refugees hoped that the violent storm would diminish the bloodthirsty wickedness of the pirates. But the sad prey of those vicious hunters was not that lucky.

The storm seemed to have even stimulated these pirates. Armed with machetes and knives, they stepped up their search for victims, visiting every corner of the island, leaving no stone unturned as they uncovered each hiding place and ravaged its inhabitants. In bushes and trees, in caves and crevasse, in gaps in the coral from the sandy beach to the summit of the mountain, they found what they wanted.

All that day and night we heard no screams, no cries of fear and pain, from the women. All sounds were drowned out in the clamor of the storm.

■ THUY

T he following day Thom and his crew made their way to the island to escape the rough sea. The other women and I remained on the boat, entirely debilitated by sickness and drained of all energy. Only Su was alert as she lay crying for milk. I crawled unsteadily to the water tank to splash my face and clean my hair matted with vomit from the filthy deck. Then I prepared a bottle for my baby.

Anytime I felt a little more myself, I looked out toward the island. What was happening there now? Were Phuc and An, Hoa and Khoa safe? This would last only a few minutes, then the waves would swell, and I'd crumple to the deck, sick and feeling like I was going to die if I stayed on the boat much longer.

That night the pirates went to the island. I'd scribbled some lines in a note for Phuc to be delivered by the same pirate who'd brought him my last note. I wrote that I wanted to come back and escape the stomach-churning sickness.

The next morning when the pirates returned, one handed me a letter from Phuc:

> *Thuy,*
> *The situation here is very dangerous. A new boat has arrived. The pirates are insane and crueler than you can imagine. They tortured H. and hanged B. because they wouldn't tell where the women were hiding. The pirates set fire to the bushes. Whoever ran out fell into their hands right away. Miss N. refused to leave and so her whole back was burned.*
> *I know you're sick, but you can't come to the island now. It's hell. You will not escape it.*
> *Be patient. A helicopter flew over us. The pilot saw the pirates hurting us. We risked our lives to make the letters "S.O.S." with rocks in the sand. I hope we'll be rescued soon. Many pirates' boats have left already.*

There was no more room for him to write.

Chapter 20

On The Threshold of Life

A Savior Appears
November 17, 1979

The next morning as Thom and his crew prepared to row back to Kra Island, I asked them to let me and Su go with them. Phuc's mention of a helicopter and hope of rescue made me decide to take a chance, come what may. I couldn't stand another day of sickness. The storm had let up, the rain stopped, and the waves were not as high, I had thrown up everything that was inside me, but still, the rocking boat continued to make me heave. I was afraid I'd choke to death.

I no longer had the energy to think and act like a normal person. Meeting Phuc and the children again, I felt no pleasure. I was just too weak and found it hard to move and remain on my unsteady feet for any length of time.

Just as I set foot on the beach, there was a noise coming from the sky. A bright orange helicopter approached and circled the island.

Through its open door, we saw four people inside. One of them held out a banner bearing the letters "UNHCR," the initials of the United Nations High Commissioner for Refugees. The chopper came down low as if about to land on the beach. The refugees ran to the landing site.

Desperate hands reached up signaling a plea for help. Some of the people below tried to grab onto the landing gear of the little craft. The pilot immediately took the chopper up to avoid hitting people in the crowd or letting them storm the ship.

UN officials drop supplies from helicopter to the refugees on Koh Kra. November 17, 1979. Photo: UNHCR.

Someone called from the helicopter what sounded like instructions to remain calm as a police boat was on the way. But this was hard to hear against the noise of the helicopter blades, so the refugees continued to swarm onto the beach. The plane circled high as the men inside let down supplies including powdered milk, dried food, and medicine.

After 20 days of desperation, fear, and hunger, the refugees charged forward. I sat on the beach with Su besides An, watching in stunned silence as they fought over the supplies. The UN representatives called out again, this time more clearly: "Be calm... Be patient... A police boat is coming...to rescue all of you...."

They made several more passes over the island, taking pictures and surveying the layout with binoculars. Then they set off and disappeared over the horizon.

"Can you stand up?" Phuc asked me.

I nodded and struggled to my feet. Holding onto Phuc's arm, I took several shaky steps.

"That's good," he said. "You have to hide right now."

Taken from a helicopter on November 17, 1979,
the photo shows little Thuan An (third from left) among the group in back,
next to Thuy, in a black blouse and kneeling on sand. Photo: UNHCR.

Despite what we had just seen, Phuc retained his apprehension regarding my safety while pirates still roamed the island. He led me back to the lighthouse where I'd hidden among the bougainvillea. During the entire three weeks as hundreds of pirates had searched the island, this was the only place not far from our living area that they had not discovered.

So I hid all that day among the thorny branches. As I lay on the lighthouse roof, I could hear the activities and conversations of the other refugees. Looking through the flowery branches, I saw pirate boats anchored by the island. Some were already setting off. Most of the other crews were heading back in their skiffs to return to their fishing boats.

The ones who remained were apparently unnerved by the appearance of the UN helicopter. They ceased attacking the refugees and watched the island to see what would happen next.

Phuc and I agreed that I needed to remain in hiding. We weren't about to take any chances in what looked like our final hours on the island.

Gift from the Sea

■ PHUC

I returned to the beach to keep an eye on the Thai fishermen and pirates still on the island. All at once a group of refugees raced to the water shouting and cheering. I ran up to see what the commotion was about. The fishermen-pirates came, too, laughing and slapping each other on the back.

A giant sea turtle similar to the one that climbed onto Koh Kra beach in November 1979.

A giant sea turtle was making its way up the beach. Some of the refugees climbed on its back to try and stop it, calling on others to join them. The colossal creature just kept moving slowly and deliberately forward. It was enormous, about a meter and a half long and weighing perhaps over 200 pounds. It took ten men with sturdy branches to turn it on its back. Even then, the turtle continued to move its massive legs back and forth in the air as if it was still walking.

"Look at this turtle!" a man shouted happily, pointing to its swollen belly. "It's a female about to lay eggs, and she's coming on shore to bury them."

"That's no turtle," another countered. "It's what we people who live by the sea called a sea cow. It looks like a turtle, but the meat tasted more like beef."

A young man spoke up in excitement.

"If it's like beef, that's great! With this much meat, we can eat for weeks!"

With that, he took a large rock and tried to smash the creature's belly, but it made not a dent in the animal's tough flesh.

An older man clasped his hands as if in thanks to heaven.

"The sea cow only lays its eggs a few times a year. This is indeed a sign that God is going to save us, providing food to restore our strength after three weeks of want!"

After considerable debate and several attempts to work on the animal, we realized that we were unable to kill it and penetrate its flesh.

That's when a few Thai fishermen-pirates stepped forward. The refugees signaled that this catch belonged to us, but the pirates raised their swords threateningly, and we stepped back.

Using machetes, swords and axes they deftly slaughtered the sea cow. One man split the belly with his ax, and a pile of eggs spilled out. Some were as big as goose eggs, others small like chicken eggs. A young man rushed over and scooped some up in his hands.

"There're hundreds of them, friends!" he cried.

"The sea cow lays hundreds of eggs each time," the old man stated knowingly.

"That's what I said," the young fellow replied, "a hundred of them!"

He pulled out one the size of a tennis ball. While he was admiring it, one of the pirates stepped up, snatched the egg from him and smacked the youth's hand. The refugee retreated.

"They're going to take them all and not let us have even one?" he cried.

"Are you surprised?" said one man as the pirates sliced the meat expertly then set the pieces aside. "This is just another way they torment us, by making us watch as they have their fill."

But this time he was mistaken. The pirates only took the eggs and left the meat for the refugees. They even cut it into smaller pieces so it would be easier to cook. Before leaving, for some reason, they also left several dozen eggs.

The meat that was given to us was more than we had dreamed of, especially after a whole month without meat.

By nightfall, most of the pirates had left the island.

The storm was over, the UNHCR was aware of our presence on Kra Island, and the pirates were departing. There were only a few Thai fishing boats in sight, but these were not pirates. As if waiting to see what would happen, they sailed back and forth and did not trouble the refugees.

Many of the women came out of their hiding places to join their families. Thuy, however, insisted on remaining at the lighthouse storage covered by the thorny plant. The men went around the island calling out to the rest.

"Come back and feast, friends! Tonight we celebrate!"

Some carried the sea animal's meat to the beach while others got a fire going. That night, to celebrate the promise of the UN officers to come and rescue us, we ate and drank our fill. There was no energy left for dancing or horsing around, but we all joined in familiar happy songs. Our voices were weak, but they were full of joy and hope.

Now that I was confident the pirates were gone, I felt safe in getting Thuy to come out and mark this occasion with the rest of us.

■ THUY

This time when Phuc climbed up to my hiding place on top of the lighthouse storage, he didn't squeeze himself inside the bushy plant but called me to come out instead. As soon as I slipped out from under the sharp branches, he pushed under my nose a piece of savory meat wrapped in a big leaf. I couldn't contain my joy.

"Troi oi! Oh, God!"

From the first bite, I felt as if I'd never tasted anything so wonderful. I didn't dare to wolf it down but took small bits and enjoyed the full flavor. The juicy meat melted in my mouth, erasing my hunger and the pains accrued over days of seasickness.

After taking part in the feast and the excitement of knowing we were really going to be rescued, I told Phuc I wanted to return to my hiding place just to be sure. He agreed.

We stood up, and he led me back to the lighthouse storage where I crawled once more under the bougainvillea. There, for the first time in three weeks, I had a good sleep, after praying that tomorrow would give us new hope and a bright future.

Waking from a Nightmare
November 18, 1979

■ THUY

When morning arrived on the 21st day of captivity for the 81 boat people who had first been brought to Koh Kra by Thai pirates, a fresh, gentle breeze blew over the island. It was like a gust of new energy that dispelled the atmosphere of anxiety and terror we had known for the past three weeks.

Although I wanted to leave my hiding place and return to the beach, I was still weak. Now I lay on top of the lighthouse storage with my eyes shut to try and enjoy a little more sleep in the warming tropical sun. Then I heard someone yell from below.

"There's a rescue ship! A police boat's here, friends! We're saved!"

I got up quickly and scrambled through the branches that had protected me during the nights of horror. The needle-like thorns that scratched my skin no longer hurt. Rather, I felt light, as if the hand of God had come down to guide me back into the world.

I ran into Phuc who was coming up to the lighthouse to fetch me. He had Su in one arm and was holding onto An with his other hand. We hugged each other in joy.

"Is it true, *anh*?" I asked giddily while wiping away tears. "Is it true we're rescued?"

He only nodded, too overcome for words.

■ PHUC

As soon as the UN officials stepped from their skiff they tended to the refugees. A French doctor, Claude Bordes of the humanitarian organization Medecins Sans Frontieres (Doctors without Borders), immediately went to work caring for the injured and ill.

Meanwhile, the other representatives were taken around the island to where the women were hiding. The UNHCR field officer, Theodore Schweitzer III, personally approached the women to bring them from their hiding places. He wept when he saw the deplorable conditions in which they'd been living on precarious slopes, high up in a tree, in insect-ridden bushes, in spaces among the rocks carved out by the ocean where women had been forced to submerge their feet for days. Some of the refugees were too weak to walk by themselves, so he lifted them in his arms and carried them to the patrol boat, tears washing over his face.

The submerged cave on Kra, where the young woman hid in November 1979. Photo: VTT, 2017

One girl's survival was nothing less than a miracle. She had thrown herself into the ocean on the first night the pirates attacked. We all thought she was dead and were shocked to discover that the current had swept her into a cavern. There she'd lived half submerged in seawater for three weeks. She was nearly delirious when Mr. Schweitzer pulled her out. He could not disguise his horror at seeing her legs eaten away by crabs.

The women were found suffering from mental and physical deterioration. Some were barely conscious. Others showed signs of various degrees of shock and trauma.

The officers were all deeply moved by what they found. They made no secret of their respect and admiration for the Vietnamese women who, despite their vulnerability, displayed incredible courage and perseverance in the face of such atrocities. One cried out, "Oh my God! Oh my God!" as he picked up one emaciated young girl from the rocks.

Another remarked, "I never thought people could treat others like this."

UN official Ted Schweitzer tends to refugees on Koh Kra. Photo: UNHCR, 1979

Theodore Schweitzer III

■ THUY

Theodore Schweitzer III

"**S**ister Thuy, come quickly!" a woman called as she tugged at my arm.

I followed her, caught up in the exhilaration of seeing the police boat bearing UN officers to the island. The woman led me to a tall American with dark brown hair and bright eyes. Although dressed in shorts and a T-shirt, he had a commanding demeanor. It was clear at once that he was moved by what he had witnessed on Kra. Extending his hand, he introduced himself in French.

"*Hello, Madame. Vous parlez Francais? Mon nom est Ted Schweitzer et je suis le representative pour le Commissionaire des Refugiés des Nations Unies en Thailand.*"

I shook the hand of the man who had saved our lives and held it tightly. My voice cracked as I replied in French.

"Hello, Mr. Schweitzer. I am Thuy, a journalist and one of the boat people."

He smiled kindly.

"Please call me Ted. Can you tell me what happened here?"

I felt my emotions rising inside but swallowed hard and answered.

"We left Vietnam to find freedom and were attacked by Thai pirates. They took us to this island, and then abused us, raping the women all this time. I don't know exactly how long it's been, but my boat came here on October 29. I don't know what day this...."

I choked up and couldn't go on. He patted my arm comfortingly. To ease the moment, he changed the subject.

"Madame speaks French quite well."

At that point, I couldn't contain myself any longer. The emotions of the past month spilled out, and I cried and cried. Phuc ran up and put his arm around my shoulders.

Mr. Schweitzer gazed at the two of us. We were so small and thin we must have looked like children. He closed his eyes to hold back his emotion but tears streamed down his cheeks.

Then a Thai officer approached.

"Sir, there's not enough room on the boat for everyone. There are 157 people, but we can only take 70 or 80."

"Take the skiffs to the fishing boats anchored over there," Schweitzer ordered, "and see if you can hire them to transport as many as they can to the mainland."

He peered at the fishing boats sitting at some distance from the island and added, "I don't know if any of them were among the damn pirates who did this to the boat people. But it's the only way to get everyone off this hell hole as soon as possible."

The Thai officer replied, "Yes, sir," and went off to carry out the command.

///

Unlike the other pirates, Thom and his crew remained near the island. Perhaps they felt they had established a relationship with the boat people over the past three weeks and wanted to watch us leave. There were a few fishing boats nearby as well, but no pirates.

Observing from their position, Thom's crew could see that the police boat wasn't big enough to carry all the refugees, so they jumped at the offer by the UN to transport people to the mainland. Two more boats were hired to complete the task.

The police patrol boat led the three fishing boats from the island. My family was among 70 boat people on the lead cruiser with Mr. Schweitzer.

As we turned to leave, Phuc took me to the side for one last look at Kra Island. I could still see the blue tarp hanging from the two trees over our cooking area on the beach. Koh Kra looked calm and peaceful without pirates and refugees. Trees were rustling in the wind, white coral glistening in the sunlight, turquoise-color waters so clear one could see the sandy bottom, palm trees lined up the beach—an earthly paradise that had witnessed the most horrific atrocities ever occurred on its soil.

Mr. Schweitzer came up beside us. Staring at the island, he said the very thing we were thinking.

"It looks so heavenly," he sighed, "who'd think it could be a hell on earth?"

During the trip, he invited us to the command deck and asked us to relate all that had happened. Phuc and I told him the horrible details regarding what the pirates had done over the course of three weeks. We often had to pause to wipe away our tears.

A veteran UN officer, Mr. Schweitzer was no stranger to calamities ranging from war to natural disasters. Yet he was deeply affected by what he heard. He listened attentively, his face revealing sadness or anger as we described the cruelty of the pirates.

When we finished our account, I begged him to do something to stop the atrocities.

"I promise," he replied.

Then I asked for a favor.

"Ask, Madame. If it's within my power, I will do it," he said at once.

"Please give me a pencil and something to write on."

He laughed, then handed me his personal pen with the letters of the UNHCR and a small child's notepad with a picture of Thai dancing girls in sarongs.

The First Piracy Lawsuit
November 19, 1979

Later that day the small fleet arrived at Pak Panang, Thailand. By the time the UN officers took the refugees from the dock to the local police station, it was past midnight.

Tired and hungry but elated and happy, the boat people remained awake to answer questions from the police. Afterward, we were taken to an empty building behind the station where we ate rice gruel that the UN representatives had Thai vendors prepare for us. Then each of us was given a bamboo mat and blanket to spend the rest of the night sleeping on the floor.

Phuc and I didn't sleep. Instead, we stayed awake going over everything that had happened from day to day, writing down all the details from the time we left Ngoc Ha until that night. We ended with the words: "Now in the Pak Panang police station. Related whole story to Mr. Ted Schweitzer, the American who rescued us from the hell of Koh Kra."

The next day Mr. Schweitzer came to interview the boat

people. He made a file on each surviving refugee using their own words.

He asked the women who were victims of the pirates, "Do you recall the face of the pirate who assaulted you?"

Some nodded, pressing their eyes shut to hold back tears. Others wrung their hands and could not speak. Then there were those who nodded and pointed outside the police station gate. They were implicating Thom's crew, who were still there, visiting with the Vietnamese refugees.

It was Thom and his crew who brought us from the island to the Thai police station. At first, they'd been wary of the UN officers, but after they were hired to transport us to the mainland, especially when the refugees they knew interacted with them in a friendly manner, they continued to associate with them. At night they slept nearby, and the next day they were back, checking on the women they had abused. They were not sophisticated enough to see that now the women wanted nothing to do with them. They didn't realize that it was these women, whom they had forced to be their "wives" and serve as hostages, who identified them to the police as the first ones to rape them when they reached Kra Island.

The police recorded these pirates' names and photos, but they did not yet have all the evidence they needed to warrant their arrest. Nevertheless, words spread that these men had perpetrated crimes against the refugees.

Mr. Schweitzer wrote a report for the UN. It was also a legally binding indictment on behalf of the victims, publicly charging Thom and his crew with harming the refugees and asking the Thai court to bring them to justice. He asked the boat people to sign the petition with the victims as witnesses before a UN lawyer could file it with the authorities and the local court.

Pressure to Withdraw the Lawsuit
November 20, 1979

■ PHUC

The refugees had been kept at the police station for two days. During this time the local authorities provided us with food and water. Most of the officers appeared sympathetic and friendly with us. But we caught some of them talking to the pirates gathered at the gate.

As soon as word got around that the refugees had signed a legal petition against the pirates, the attitude of the police changed completely. Now they were irritated and treated us gruffly. Their conversations with the pirates left them anxious.

One afternoon some officers in civilian clothes came to see us. They spoke in unpracticed English as they tried to dissuade us from pursuing legal action. Making a complaint, they declared, would cause many problems for us. The accused would come after us to do us harm. Here in Thailand, we were safe, so why don't we just apply to resettle in another country to have a better life and drop this matter?

The language barrier made it difficult for the two sides to communicate, but their message was clear enough: Give up the lawsuit, or you and your people will be in danger.

All day the threats came in different forms and messages.

"Any refugees who accuse pirates will stay here forever. Eventually, the pirates will be released."

"If you don't drop the lawsuit, from now on the pirates will kill any boat people they come across on the sea."

"They'll come and murder all the witnesses and kidnap the Vietnamese girls to sell all over Southeast Asia."

Before we left Vietnam, thousands of others had crossed the Gulf of Thailand. Many had gone through the same things the 157 in our group had experienced. But up until then, no pirates had been prosecuted in a court of law because the witnesses who filed charges through the UNHCR were confined in the refugee camps indefinitely; eventually, they simply gave up so they could resettle abroad. As a result, no court had officially convicted anyone of the crimes.

Despite the sense that we were being threatened, Mr. Schweitzer was unable to transfer us out of Pak Panang since the police claimed they were not yet finished with their investigation.

Another morning, we were visited by a delegation of Thai men who said they had come from Bangkok. In particular, they wanted to talk to those who had accused the pirates. Thuy and I were not direct victims, therefore we were not allowed to act as witnesses. Still, the women who had been abused asked us to come along for the interview. Some members of the delegation appeared to be attorneys, while others were relatives of the pirates from Thom's boat.

They began by offering us gifts of food and asking questions of a humanitarian nature. Then they came straight to the point and asked the victims to withdraw their suit. One of them pointed directly to Thuy and said she was not harmed, and in fact, Thom's crew had saved her and her baby. Thuy responded that while she was grateful for that favor, she couldn't speak for those who had been abused.

When their efforts to convince the witnesses proved unsuccessful, they offered to negotiate a price for dropping the legal proceedings. After that, their voices changed and they became threatening, declaring that the trial would go on for years while the victims were forced to remain in Thailand, during which time their lives would be in danger.

With that, our group's representative, Lu Phuc Ba, ran out to find Dr. Claude Bordes and Mr. Schweitzer to report the meeting. When Mr. Schweitzer appeared, the visitors changed their tune and denied having made such threats.

The meeting troubled Mr. Schweitzer. He told us he would get us transferred to Songkhla refugee camp as soon as possible for our own safety. Specifically, he was afraid the pirates would try to murder the witnesses. He advised us to be careful and never go anywhere alone, but always stick to the group. At night we slept in a circle with the witnesses on the inside to protect them against intruders.

That same night Mr. Schweitzer and Dr. Bordes stayed up contacting the UN, the media and government authorities in Bangkok to report the threats and fears of the Vietnamese boat people in Pak Panang.

Songkhla Refugee Camp
November 21, 1979

■ THUY

The next morning there was a crowd of foreign journalists waiting at the police station asking to interview the refugees. Among them were some old acquaintances, such as Francois Nivolon of *Le Figaro* and Henry Kamm, a veteran correspondent and Pulitzer Prize winner from the *New York Times* Saigon bureau, now in Thailand. They assured us that once the international press reported on the story, there would be no retaliation against the witnesses.

By noon a special police team from Bangkok had arrived at Pak Panang to protect the refugees. Urged on by Mr. Schweitzer, the local police had no choice but to release us into the care of the UNHCR and process the transfer to Songkhla refugee camp.

On November 23, our group of 157 boat people took a bus from Pak Panang to Songkhla. There we joined more than 6,000 other refugees and heard countless tragic stories of escape and atrocity, some even worse than ours. Some boats had been entirely lost, while others were left with few survivors to tell the tragic tale. Some refugees trapped at sea without food or water resorted to cannibalism.

Vietnamese residents at the Songkhla refugee camp raised the flag of the former Republic of Vietnam to guide refugee boats to safety, 1980. Photo: Songkhla camp archives.

We also learned that many Vietnamese women, especially young girls, were abducted at sea. Investigations by the UN and other agencies would reveal that most were sold into prostitution across Southeast Asia or became sex slaves on pirate vessels.

The vast majority of Vietnamese refugee boats that sailed in the Gulf of Thailand were victimized by pirates. More than half of those that arrived had fewer passengers than when they departed from Vietnam.

The 81 people from our boat might be counted as lucky in that we did not lose a single one of our number.

And, despite the many adversities, our family's trip could be called a success when, in the end, all four of us reached the shore of a safe and free land.

Our first family photo as refugees on safe shores. Songkhla Refugee Camp, Thailand, December 1979.

Chapter 21

Vows, Dreams & Closure

The Effect of the Piracy Charges
November 24, 1979

The charges brought against the Thai fishermen-turned-pirates had led to the creation of the Committee Against Piracy by the United Nations High Commission on Refugees (UNHCR). The Committee's official task was to assess and develop plans to protect Vietnamese boat people against sea pirates.

A police station was set up on Koh Kra to prevent pirates' abuse and to assist in the transfer of refugees to the mainland. Schweitzer frequently came back to Kra to pick up refugees stranded there. In the following six months, Schweitzer had rescued a total of 1.250 boat people from Kra, before he moved on to a new post in Switzerland at the end of May 1980.

Without Schweitzer's compassion and hard work, the UNHCR's anti-piracy program eventually lost its effectiveness, followed by the termination of the police station on Koh Kra.

My family stayed in the Songkhla refugee camp for over ten months. In 1980, refugees with immediate family abroad usually got resettled within two months, but the Thai Court requested our group of 157 people to stay until those charged went on trial.

The harsh living conditions of the refugee camp and the prospect of staying there for an extended period discouraged many people in our group. Quite a few of them wanted the women witnesses to withdraw their charges so the group could get resettled.

Schweitzer spent a lot of time in reassuring and persuading the witnesses not to give up due to the lengthy court procedure. He said this was the very first charge brought against the pirates, and the international media was watching it closely; our giving up now would make it very hard for future victims to get any action against the pirates.

Facing the refugees' impatience, Schweitzer worked hard, pulling any UN connections he had to speed up the trial and to release immigration hold on our group of 157 Koh Kra survivors.

Thanks to his efforts, when the trial began, and the witnesses had given their testaments, our group of 157 was allowed to leave the camp for resettlement in a third country.

When our family left Thailand in September 1980, the defendant-pirates were not yet sentenced. We later learned that the Thai Court finally sentenced each of the defendants to eight months in jail. The sentence came a year after the charges were filed, meaning the accused got released right after the sentencing due to their time served while awaiting the trial.

The Unforgettable Vows
September 9, 1980

Upon our resettlement in September 1980, we joined and became active members of the Boat People SOS Committee (BPSOS). The committee came into existence

Duong Phuc and Vu Thanh Thuy during a speaking engagement in Minneapolis, Minnesota, November 1980. The event aimed at raising public awereness about the boat people's plight.

when its founders, UCSD Professor Nguyen Huu Xuong and writer Phan Lac Tiep, received a copy of our open letter to the international press, detailing our ordeal at seas and the 21 days of terror on Koh Kra. The group's mission was to alert the public about the piracy and to lobby for protection of boat people. Together with author Nhat Tien, we co-wrote *The Pirates in the Gulf of Thailand*, translated by James Banerian and published by BPSOS in 1980, documenting witness testaments by the victims of Thai pirates.

Besides the hours spent in English classes at San Diego colleges and tending to our family, we used the rest of our time for BPSOS work. Throughout the 1980s and half of the 1990s, we arranged our schedule and asked our family and friends to babysit our children so we could travel to conferences to speak and testify.

We also lobbied Vietnamese overseas communities to lend their hands to the BPSOS in its mission of rescuing boat people.

The BPSOS then joined forces with the French group Medecins du Monde (Physicians of the World) and the German's Cap Anamur to send ships to the South China Sea to search for and rescue boat people. Vietnamese communities from all over the world contributed millions of dollars to fund these rescue missions.

Thuy spoke in front of the UN headquarters at a gathering to request help in rescuing boat people, New York, 1989. Photo: Boat People SOS Committee.

Thanks to these joint efforts, a total of over 3,000 Vietnamese boat people had been picked up by the group's ships, including the Jean Charcot, Mary Kingstown, and Cap Anamur I and II. Also, the French Navy helicopter carrier Jeanne d'Arc lent a hand when it sailed across the South China Sea.

Pledge Fulfilled

During that time, from 1984 to 1988, we welcomed our third and fourth daughters, Binh Minh and Trang Thu. Phuc was working as a counselor for refugees at the Union of Pan Asian Communities and Indochinese Mutual Management Agency, while Thuy worked as an editorial assistant at *The San Diego Union*. We had our hands full, indeed; however, we could not forget our vows while at sea on a tiny refugee boat, dehydrated, thirsty, and hungry, desperately watching big ships pass by without lending a hand. We had vowed to ourselves that if we survived, we would someday come back on board a vessel that would stop to rescue the boat people.

So, we went back to the South China Sea on rescue ships searching for and picking up boat people, in 1986 and 1988.

Phuc volunteered for two months on the German ship Cap Anamur II in 1986, rescuing 13 refugee boats carrying 888 boat people.

From left, Dr.Nguyen Huu Xuong, BPSOS president; Dr. Rupert Neudeck, Cap Anamur president; and Dr. Alain Deloche, head of Medecins du Monde. San Diego, 1985. Photo: BPSOS.

Thuy aboard the Jeanne d'Arc helicopter during a search for refugee boats near the Philippines, April 1988. Photo: Jeanne d'Arc.

Thuy spent two weeks on a French Navy ship, the Jeanne d'Arc, in 1988, flying by helicopter over the South China Sea in search of refugee boats. The rescue mission also had a few guests, ABC News' "20/20" team and three European journalists. A "20/20" piece entitled "A Mission of Mercy" was broadcast nationwide on November 29, 1989, hosted by Barbara Walters and Hugh Downs. In total, those missions picked up 928 Vietnamese boat people.

At the beginning of 1990, the world's compassion fatigue had helped close doors on Vietnamese refugees. Hundreds of thousands of boat people got stuck for years, as long as a dozen years, in refugee camps across Southeast Asia. Many committed suicide when the United Nations'

Phuc on the deck of Cap Anamur II, preparing to help rescue a refugee boat in distress, September 1986. Photo: Nguyen Huu Huan/Cap Anamur.

repatriation program began. They would rather die than be sent back to Vietnam.

"Freedom or Death" was the motto across refugee camps. Remembering our experience at the Songkhla refugee camp, we took turn to visit refugee camps in Hong Kong, Thailand, Indonesia, Malaysia, Philippines, and Singapore to report on the tragedy of the boat people while lobbying for solutions to help these desperate refugees.

To this day, we continued to work with BPSOS and other refugee advocate groups to do whatever we could to help late-coming refugees, who were still fleeing the totalitarian communist regime in Vietnam, by crossing the Thai and Cambodian borders.

Phuc (sixth from left in standing row) and a group of refugees, among the 888 boat people rescued by the German ship Cap Anamur II, 1986. Germany granted resettlement to all rescued. Photo: Cap Anamur

In the Promised Land

We were both broadcasters from Saigon, with a passion for journalism not just as a profession but also a mission. The Fall of

Saigon in 1975 had cut us off from our trade. We never thought we could ever work again as journalists.

Thuy, center, with 40 refugees rescued by the Jeanne d'Arc, April 3, 1988.
All refugees were offered asylum in France. Photo: Stone Phillips

Resettled in America, we were willing to take any job to survive. We never dared to dream of working in the media field. Then, after five years in the United States, Thuy landed a job as an editorial assistant at *The San Diego Union*.

In 1997, we relocated to Houston when an opportunity for broadcasting work presented itself. We founded two radio stations, Radio Saigon

Thuy and Phuc at the Asian American Journalists Association's Lifetime Achievement Award Ceremony, Hawaii, June 23, 2006.
Photo: Mimi Duong

Houston 900AM and Radio Saigon Dallas 1600AM, *Saigon Weekly News, Saigon Houston Directory*, and Saigon Network TV 51.3. All are still functioning. We have been able to work side by side, managing our own company, Mass Media Inc.

As ethnic media journalists, we never expected a day when our mainstream media's colleagues from the Asian American Journalists Association would honor both of us with a Lifetime Achievement Award in 2006.

We have been so blessed for having been able to fulfill our seemingly impossible vows made at sea and to realize our wildest dreams. We even were able to go back to Koh Kra, not once but twice, to do something we had secretly dreamed of in the last 38 years, which is to pay our tribute to those perished in search of freedom.

Since 1979 after the nightmarish experience on Koh Kra, we have enjoyed peace and success in the U.S. However, we have not forgotten our fellow boat people who died on Koh Kra, buried in shallow graves, covered by rock. We could not forget the bodies of our fellow refugees drifting in the South China Sea and along the coasts of Southeast Asia.[33]

Phuc and Thuy on their return to Koh Kra 38 years after the UNHCR rescue. Thailand, 2017. Photo: Mai Tram Nguyen

[33] According to the United Nations High Commission on Refugees (UNHCR), 200,000 to 250,000 boat people died at sea from murder, storms or hunger and thirst in the 1970s-1980s. Over 1.6 million boat people have been resettled across the world. (Source: *The San Diego Union*, July 20, 1986).

A Sweet Closure

A few of the sixty-four tombstones with 204 names of perished boat people, Koh Kra, Thailand, 2017. Photo: VTT.

Therefore, when the opportunity came in April 2017, we gladly joined a group of ex-refugees returning to Koh Kra. Our dream was to help turn this former "hell on earth" into a memorial site for those who perished. Unfortunately, our mission was cut short by a sudden storm on Koh Kra that sent us back to the mainland.

Four months later, in September 2017, we returned to complete what was left unfinished. With our leader Le Hung from Canada and three companions, Ken Nguyen of Orange County, Thanh from Australia and Nhan from Malaysia, we accomplished our mission: setting up a memorial site with 64 tombstones, marking the names and dates of the 204 boat people who had perished in the South China Sea.

The Buddhist monks from Wat Samphreak Temple in Thasala, Nakhon Si Thammarat, helped build the memorial site and would help maintain it. The monks also vowed to come to Kra on a monthly basis to pray, as they had been doing in the last ten years, after learning of the tragedies the Vietnamese boat people had endured on that island and how those buried there had died.

The establishment of the Koh Kra memorial gave us a sense of closure. Despite the hardships and terrors, which at times seemed

---

UNHCR statistics showed in the year of 1981 alone, three-quarters of the 452 boats that arrived in Thailand were attacked by pirates an average of three times each. In addition, 578 women had been raped, 228 abducted and 881 were dead or missing. UNHCR statistics for 1975 to 1997 indicate that 839,228 Vietnamese arrived in UNHCR-operated camps in Southeast Asia and Hong Kong.

almost to destroy us, we realized the challenges reinforced our faith in each and everyone's resilience. All we needed to do was to try our very best; then God would send all the good people to help us along our life journey.

A multi-faith prayer service on Koh Kra, Thailand, April 2017. Front row from right, Buddhist Rev. Thich Huyen Viet, Catholic Revs. Pham Huu Tam, Nguyen Hung, and Le Hong. Back row from right, Duong Phuc, Le Hung, and Thuy. Photo: MT Nguyen

The cemetery and memorial for boat people perished in search of freedom, Koh Kra, 2017. Photo: VTT.

These challenges also strengthened our trust in humankind and our love for each other. Our faith in God was deepened, along with our determination to never give up, no matter what.

Looking at the water of Koh Kra, Thailand, 2017.
Photos: MT Nguyen

Phuc and Thuy walking on the Koh Kra beach, Thailand, 2017.

AFTERWORD

O ur story began with a romance in wartime Vietnam. The ending of the Vietnam War started a new war for us. First was the struggle to survive communist prisons, small and big. After escaping from them, we faced another battle against Thai pirates. Arriving at the Songkhla refugee camp, followed by our resettlement in America, we encountered more struggles, but we also received even more help from many kind-hearted people from all over the world for which we can never express our gratitude enough.

We wrote these last words of this memoir by the window of a beach house looking out to a Galveston beach, where we had set up a makeshift studio for Radio Saigon Houston so we could directly broadcast to Houston. Looking out to the vast ocean and listening to the slapping waves often brought tears to our eyes. We felt as if we got a glimpse of the drifting body of a starved-to-death refugee that was pushed into the ocean during a sea escape years ago.

When we looked down to the deep waters in stormy nights, sometimes we felt as if we saw shadows of multiple innocent Vietnamese souls rising from the ocean, trying to speak up, wanting to share their tragic fate from the depth of the South China Sea.

This memoir wishes to bring to the readers the heroic drama of *our* Vietnam, The Republic of Vietnam, where

Phuc and Thuy's first year in the U.S. San Diego, 1981.

countless unsung heroes shed their blood and sacrificed their lives for democracy. When the country fell under communist rule, many more continued to risk death at sea in search of freedom and human dignity. Once they survived death, they sprung from their sorrow to succeed in America and elsewhere.

Years ago, Binh Minh, Tuong Vi, and Duyen, the dear friends who helped us survive while hiding in Saigon, had wished for us that, *"... there will be a day, the two of you could hold hands walking on the street without any fear... "*

Now the two of us have held hands throughout our life journey, and we long for our friends who are no longer on earth.

Binh Minh perished at sea when her escape boat got stuck in a coral reef in the South China Sea in 1978.

Tuong Vi passed away of cancer in 2006 in San Diego.

Tran Thi Duyen survived cancer and lives in Saigon, Vietnam, with her three daughters and grandchildren.

///

We reunited with Thuy's parents in Dallas, Texas, on September 8, 1980, and then moved to San Diego, California, to be near Tuong Vi in April 1981. In August 1997, we relocated to Houston, Texas to resume our career in broadcasting radio.

We now live in Houston, Texas. At 73 and 68, we still broadcast full time on Radio Saigon Houston KREH 900 AM and continue to participate in missions helping refugees from Vietnam and members in our local community.

Our five children: Duong Vu Thuan An, 43, now a lawyer/entrepreneur, lives in Austin, Texas, with her husband and three children; Duong Vu Chau Giao (baby Su), 39, an accountant/businesswoman, resides in Austin, Texas, with husband and three children; Duong Vu Binh Minh, 33, a curate content producer for Apple Music, lives in San Francisco, California, with husband and two children; Duong Vu Trang Thu, 31, a Returned Peace Corps Volunteer (RPCV)/clinical social worker, resides in Houston, Texas; and Duong Vu Mai Kim, 28, an entrepreneur, manages the French Café Crème in Austin, Texas.

Phuc - Thuy at their 43th Anniversary. From left, Chau Giao (baby Su), Mai Kim, Phuc, Trang Thu, Thuy, Thuan An, Binh Minh. Houston, Jan. 6, 2017.

The Duong-Vu family at 2017 Christmas: Phuc and Thuy (center) surrounded by their five daughters, three sons-in-law, and seven grand children.

ACTIVISM RECOGNITIONS

The San Diego Union's Vu Thanh Thuy named Woman of the 21st Century by the National Organization for Women

National Organization of Woman's 21st Century Woman Award. Photo: NOW, Nov. 10, 1987

Vu Thanh Thuy and 21st Century Woman Award's Judges. From left, Faye Wattleton, Thuy, Gloria Steinem, Dr. Ruth Westheimer, Jane Byrne, Mathilde Krim. The sixth judge, Peter Jennings, was not available for the picture. Photo: NOW, 1987.

USA Today featuring the National Organization of Woman's 21st Century Woman Award, on Nov. 10, 1987

San Diego Tribune's story on the 21st Century Woman Award. Nov. 11, 1987

The Joseph Prize Award, May 1989

New York City Tribune, May 1989

The San Diego Union Story, 1989

San Diego Press Club Award, 1988

Honorary Doctor of Human Letters,
Marist College, May 1989

Commencement Speech at
Marist College, May 1989

VU THANH THUY

- Journalist/War Correspondent, The Voice of Freedom, Vietnam (69-75)
- Radio Broadcaster, Songkhla Refugee Camp, Thailand (1979-1980)
- Instructional Aide, San Diego City College, CA (1981-1982)
- Psycho-Social Counselor, Linda Vista Center, San Diego, CA (82-85)
- Editorial Assistant & TV Listing Editor, San Diego Union, CA (85-97)
- Founder/CEO: Radio Saigon Houston & Dallas, Saigon Weekly, Saigon Directory, Saigon Network Television, Houston, TX (1999 - current)

Social Activities:
- Speaker, BPSOS Committee, San Diego, CA (1980-1989)
- Rescue Mission, French Helicopter carrier Jeanne d'Arc (1988)
- "A Mission of Mercy" profile on ABC News "20/20,"USA (1989)
- Board Member, American Red Cross, Houston, TX (2001-2012)
- Thought Leader, Images & Voices of Hope, New York, TX (2006-present)
- Senior Fellow, American Leadership Forum, Houston, TX (2006-present)
- Board Member, New American Media, San Francisco, CA (2008-2015)
- Board Member, International Management District, Houston, TX (2008-present)
- Mission Trips: Haiti Earthquake (2006), Japan Tsunami (2010), Thailand Tsunami (2012), Philippines Yolanda Typhoon (2014) Cambodia child-sex (2015).

Awards:
- "1971 Silver Star," Army of the Republic of Vietnam
- "1972 Best War Report," Psycho War, Saigon, VN
- "1985 Poster Woman," San Diego City Schools, CA
- "1987 21st Century Woman Award," National Organization for Women, NY
- "1988 Médaille of Honor," Freedom Foundation, Valley Forge, PA
- "1988 Woman of the Year & Headliner", San Diego Press Club, CA
- "Honorary Doctor of Humane Letters," Marist College, NY (1988)
- "1989 Joseph Prize," Human Rights Award, Hebrew Union College, Israel-NY
- "1993 Woman of Achievement," June Burnett Institute, SDSU, CA
- "1996 Woman of Honor," Women Together Foundation, San Diego, CA
- "1997 Person of Quality," San Diego Union, San Diego, CA
- "25 Vietnamese Americans of 25 Years," New Horizon, UCLA, CA (2000)
- "2002 Woman in Media Award," Asian Houston Network, Houston. TX
- "2002 Entrepreneur of the Year," Asian Chamber of Commerce, Houston
- "2004 Asian Entrepreneur," Asian Entrepreneur Magazine, Las Vegas, Nevada
- "2006 We the People's Vision Award," International Channel, TX
- "2006 Asian Business Leadership," U. S. Pan Asian Chamber of Commerce, D.C.
- "2006 Lifetime Achievement," Asian-American Journalists Association, Hawaii
- "2008 Houston Women's Hall of Fame Induction," Women's Chamber of Commerce, Houston, TX

DUONG PHUC

- War Correspondent, The Voice of Saigon, Saigon (1968 – 1969)
- News Editor, Voice of the Army, Saigon (1969-1973)
- Member of the Four-sided Military Committee and the delegation to witness the release of first American POWs, Hanoi, North Vietnam (1973)
- Presidential Correspondent, The Voice of the Army (1974-1975)
- Political Prisoner at Trang Lon, Phu Quoc, Long Giao communist concentration camps, Vietnam (1975-1977)
- Prison Escapee and Fugitive, Saigon, South Vietnam (1977-1979)
- Radio Broadcaster, Songkhla Refugee Camp, Thailand (1979-1980)
- Staff Research Associate, University of California, San Diego, (1981-1985)
- Youth Delinquent Counselor, Refugee Service, San Diego, California (1986-1997)
- Founder/President, Mass Media Inc. - Radio Saigon Houston 900 AM, Houston, Texas (1997-current)
- Founder/Board of Directors, Saigon Network Television, Houston. Texas (2011-current)

Social Activities:
- Speaker, BPSOS Committee, San Diego, California (1980-1989)
- Rescue Mission, Mary Kingstown ship, Philippines (1986)
- Rescue Mission II, Cap Anamur ship II, Singapore (1988)
- Mission Trips: Katrina Hurricane (2005) Haiti Earthquake (2006), Japan Tsunami (2010), Thailand Tsunami (2012), Philippines Yolanda Typhoon (2014) Cambodia child sex mission.

Awards:
- "1972 Best Soldier," Psycho War, Saigon, South Vietnam
- "Bronze Star of Valor," Lam Son 719 battlefield, Laos, Army of the Republic of Vietnam (1971)
- "Silver Star," An Lộc Battlefield, Army of the Republic of Vietnam (1972)
- "1987 Sigma delta Chi Award for Excellence in Journalism," Society of Professional Journalists, California
- "2002 Entrepreneur Award," Asian Chamber of Commerce, Houston, TX
- "2002 Community Service Award," Houston Police Department, Texas
- "2002 Media Service Award," Houston City College, Texas
- "2004 Asian Business Leadership Award," U.S. Pan Asian Chamber of Commerce, Washington D.C.
- "2004 Asian Entrepreneur of the Year," Asian Entrepreneur Magazine, Las Vegas, Nevada
- "2004 We the People's Vision Award," International Channel, TX
- "2006 Lifetime Achievement," Asian American Journalists Association, Hawaii

The Value of Belief

By Vu Thanh Thuy

I believe in many things.

I believe in dreams, in hopes and in people. Even in the darkest moments of my life – and there have been many – I always believe that somehow the darkness will end. When there seems nothing to believe in, I have faith in achieving what seems like the impossible. Perhaps it's because I believe in destiny, but I know that if my time on earth is not up, anything is possible. The infinite possibilities make believing in the impossible easy for me to do.

In Vietnam, I was jailed twice as a political prisoner for violating the Communist laws. I faced starvation and death on a boat in the South China Sea while trying to escape from Vietnam, three different times. Once at sea, pirates held me captive on a deserted island in the Gulf of Thailand for three weeks of hell.

In all those horrible moments, the only thing I could believe in was overcoming the impossible and fleeing to safety. That kind of desperate, blind faith was able to keep me from giving up, knowing that that would be my only weapon to defend myself, my only means to survive, and my only way out of terrible situations. Ironically and mysteriously, my faith was reinforced again and again in many circumstances. Furthermore, I was ultimately rewarded beyond my wildest dreams.

When I was at my lowest, waiting for death from starvation and thirst in the South China Sea, we were ignored by passing ships that would not even stop to help us, much less rescue us, I vowed to myself that if I survived, I would come back on a ship that would not ignore people in need.

When I ran for my life as prey to be hunted down by the sea pirates, I swore that if I survived, I would tell the world the story of my people's tragic history. And I kept reminding myself and repeating those promises aloud to anyone who would listen.

At first, some people laughed at me, and sometimes, I laughed at myself. Who was I to dream the impossible?

I was just a new refugee who lived off the mercy of the United Nations and who was granted a visa to the United States. I barely spoke English, had neither money nor connections, and was just a poor and helpless Vietnamese refugee. But I kept believing and joined any organization that could help make my vows possible.

Believe it or not, people not only heard me but they helped me. France's Medecins du Monde (Physicians of the World) and Germany's Cap Anamur were two of the first organizations that joined with the Vietnamese overseas community to send ships to rescue 3,000 boat people.

It was eight years after my ordeal that I had the opportunity to return to the South China Sea. I didn't return on a regular ship but a French Navy helicopter carrier. We didn't just rescue the boat people who drifted by but actively went searching for them by helicopters. This impossible dream of mine became possible and was even documented by an ABC News crew and aired in 1989 on 20/20, hosted by Barbara Walters and Hugh Downs. The impossible wasn't just possible but so much more!

During my revitalized life, I have had a long list of mysterious "impossibles" made possible by my belief. They range from the day-to-day challenge of arguing with five teenage daughters to the unexpected success of our Houston radio station despite having no business management or marketing training. In partnership with my husband – a fellow journalist and business partner – we have weathered the work conflicts and trials of running a business. Now we continue to serve our fellow countrymen by being a voice and information source for the Vietnamese American community. Even to this day, after two decades of expanding into more media outlets, we still rely on our journalistic skills more than our marketing ability to keep the company running.

More than 30 years ago, we missed the opportunity to tell our story in a book and movie deal because we couldn't meet the deadline while working two jobs and raising five young children. Now we have finished writing our own book.

If our story is meant to be shared with others, I know it will happen. If our story can help others, I hope it will.

I have that faith because I truly believe.

Vu Thanh Thuy's piece is from a series of essays on Voices & Values of Journalism that has been created by Images & Voices of Hope with the generous support of the Fetzer Institute and the Janet Prindle Institute for Ethics at DePauw University. Our collective intention is to make these essays widely available to journalists, aspiring journalists and anyone interested in the field as part of an emergent curriculum to explore the deep foundation of values that support the important work that journalists do.

Transcript and Photos from

ABC News' Magazine "20/20"

broadcast on November 29, 1989

MISSION OF MERCY

Hosts Barbara Walters and Hugh Downs introducing ABC News' "20/20" program

▶ **Barbara Walters:**

Tonight, we bring you the story of a young woman who can never forget she was once a boat person. And through her eyes, you'll witness an actual encounter with a refugee boat, adrift hundreds of miles from land, and you'll hear pirates and tortures on the high seas. Stone Phillips takes her to where all of these happening and bring us an extraordinary account of a woman's mission of mercy.

///

▶ Stone Philips:

We have been at sea for six days, aboard a French helicopter carrier Joan of Arc. It's Easter Sunday, a beginning of another day of search and rescue, looking for refugees off the coast of Vietnam.

The view from our helicopter is one of the most beautiful sights on earth. Sunrise over the South China Sea. But this stretch of ocean is also the world's biggest graveyard. The lives and stories of more than 250,000 people who have died here are forever being erased by the waves. Today's Easter service in the ship chapel is dedicated to those nameless victims known to the world only as boat people. Leading the prayer is a Vietnamese woman named Vu Thanh Thuy, a boat person who survived.

▶ Thuy:

"Dear Lord, we are here today trying with all our heart to help our brothers and sisters, who are risking their lives on the ocean to find freedom... And for those who have died at sea, we pray to you, my Lord, to save their souls and give them eternal peace."

▶ Stone:

Thuy and her husband, Duong Phuc, are now American citizens. Two of their four daughters were born in the United States. They've been living in San Diego for eight years, and for eight years, Thuy has waited for the opportunity to go back to the South China Sea to help refugees.

Thuy receiving a South Vietnamese flag from Dr. Xuong Huu Nguyen, BPSOS President – Photo: Le Dinh Dieu

Before Thuy left San Diego, her fellow Vietnamese gave her a South Vietnamese flag to hold off as a signal to refugee boats that they've reached safety. When Thuy herself reached safety nine years ago, she and her husband published a diary of their escape to tell the world that Vietnamese like themselves were dying in the South China Sea. It was Thuy's own story of escape and torture at the hands of Thai pirates that caused these Vietnamese to organize and raise money to help the boat people. They call themselves the Boat People SOS Committee. And this year, they're sending Thuy.

▶ **Thuy:**

"We feel a great debt to other people because we survived while a lot of our people died. Even my best friend died at sea. So, I... I... made a vow to myself that if I could survive, I have to do something about that. My life,... our life, wouldn't belong just to us, but we'll try to do something... anything... to pay that debt."

▶ **Stone:**

Thuy boarded the Joan of Arc in Manila. In French, she's called the Jeanne d'Arc and she's the pride of the French Navy. Her specialty is anti-submarine warfare. In peace time, she's used for officers training and goodwill missions like this one. The Jeanne d'Arc has been assigned for one week by the French government to help a small ship called the Mary on a three-month rescue mission looking for refugees in the South China Sea. The Mary is funded by Medecins du Monde, an international organization of doctors, and by Thuy's Boat People SOS Committee.

Christian Ruyere, the Jeanne d'Arc's captain, showed us where his radar and helicopters would be searching. "So, presently, at this very moment, we are here, at sea, and we are searching southwest, this way,...

The Jeanne d'Arc helicopters would search 18,000 square miles a day for five days, just south of Vietnam, where the boat people try to cross to Thailand or Malaysia, a distant of 600 miles. The United Nations estimates that more than 2,000 boat people leave the Vietnamese coast each month.

On the first day of the search, we began to find out how difficult it is to spot a tiny refugee boat adrift in this immense sea covering nearly a million square miles, four times the size of Texas. We saw nothing. And if we didn't find them, their only hope would to be picked up by commercial ships. But Thuy said when she fled, no one stopped.

▶ **Thuy:**

"There were 36 international ships passed us by, but none stopped to even help us, not talking about rescue us, even help us..."

▶ **Stone:**

Thuy and her family were fleeing Vietnam to save their lives. She had been a war correspondent in South Vietnam, at age 20, she won the Silver Star for Courage reporting from the frontlines. In 1972, on a battlefield covered with corpses, she met and fell in love with Phuc, who was chief of the South Vietnamese Army's radio station newsroom. In 1975, as Saigon fell, Thuy was in the hospital giving birth to their first child. Within weeks, Phuc was arrested and sent to hard labor in a re-education camp. After two years, Thuy helped him escape and for the next two years, they lived in hiding, knowing they'd be shot on sight if they were found. Their crime: associating with the fallen regime of South Vietnam... and the Americans.

On day Two, closer to Vietnam, Thuy and I went up on our

Thuy (center) and Stone Phillips (behind Thuy) on a Jeanne d'Arc helicopter in search for the refugee boats. On the left was Scott, ABC News "20/20" cameraman and the French pilot, Dominique Deblon.

first helicopter search. Our pilot, Dominique Debblon, has shown us how to search with our eyes, starting from the horizon and working backward to keep our focus changing, our vision sharp. It was amazing to me to think that Thuy and her family had survived a total of 25 days drifting on this water. On one unsuccessful escape attempt, their boat, much like this one, was just 7-feet wide, 35 feet long, jammed with 81 people. Lost, their engine broken, no food or water to drink, they boiled sea water and drank the condensed steam to stay alive.

▶ **Thuy:**

"One the 15th day, a 25-year-old man in our group died of thirst,... he had his skin torn... broken... We just wrapped him up in a piece of blanket and... then... just dumped him overboard... From that point on, we all got very desperate,... we just stopped trying... we... we stopped trying to wave at the ships passing by, we... we stopped bailing the water out of the boat... we just laid down there and waiting to die."

▶ **Stone:**

Day Two of our search passed, and the sea was empty, except for an occasional cargo ship. The search from the bridge went on 24 hours a day. Thuy tried to escape 20 times, before she made it.

▶ **Thuy:**

"Night is the most terrifying part of the times, because at night, we couldn't see anything. Everything could happen at night, a big wave can turn the... can turn the boat upside down, and then, and then... that's it!"

▶ **Stone:**

The next day, as always, we waited for the helicopters to return to find out if they spotted any refugee boat. "Did you see anything?... No boat people..."

But a few hours later, we did see something in the water. Something unusual... It was a fleet of fishing boats from Thailand, but there were no nets in the water, no fish hanging out to dry. And the boats were all tied together, the men doing nothing. Thuy's, watching from the bridge, looking increasingly upset. She was convinced that these Thai fishermen were pirates, waiting for a more lucrative catch: boat people. In fact, she thought she even recognized one of the boats, the red one.

▶ **Thuy:**

- "We met hundreds of boats, and there was only one red one. So I just have the feeling that,..."

▶ **Stone:**

- "maybe this is the boat?"

▶ **Thuy:**

- "Yah..."

▶ **Stone:**

- "Nine years later?"

▶ **Thuy:**

"Yah...!" "They came, they got the women on their boat... they destroyed whatever they could...Uhm..."

▶ **Stone:**

The boat Thuy and her family escaped on was attacked three times by pirates and eventually towed to a small island called Koh Kra, off the coast of Thailand, where the pirates tortured them every night for 21 days.

▶ **Thuy:**

"At night, the pirates came back on the island... and they separated the men from the women,... they took the children away from their mothers... and then they... watched the men at gun point, and... Uhm... and each of them started taking one,... you know... one at a time... taking the women away from us... from the rest of us..."

► **Stone:**

And when some of the women hid, these pirates, often drunk, made a cruel game of hunting them down, often setting fire to the bushes to smoke them out. Thuy said that only she and a few other women were not raped, but they saw and heard much of what happened. They were finally rescued by a United Nations helicopter. These photographs taken the day of the rescue. Thuy and her husband wrote an open letter to the international press, recounting their ordeal on Koh Kra, hoping there would be a crack down on the piracy in these waters. But today, the pirate attacks continue: men thrown overboard to drown and young women raped and sold into prostitution in Thailand.

On day Four of the search, our sixth day at sea, Easter Sunday, we happened on a real fishing boat, this one Vietnamese. It was a chance for Thuy to meet some Vietnamese and perhaps for us to gather some intelligence.

By noon the following day, the Jeanne d'Arc's time was up. Its part of the search ended. The Mary, patrolling a few miles away, would continue, but without radar and helicopters. As we set course for Singapore, everyone on board felt, not only disappointment, but grief, that in the face of so much sufferings in these waters, the Jeanne d'Arc has been unable to make even a little difference.

Then, like a mirage, on a perfectly still sea, they appeared. 40 people, crowded onto a tiny little boat, barely sea worthy. As the boat drew closer, we could see they were scorched by the sun, dried lips and dazed, waving at us, disbelieving that we would really help them.

Minutes later, Thuy was on her way to make contact with the boat people. She had with her the Vietnamese flag she brought from San Diego. As she unfolded for the refugees to see, she fulfilled the promise she had made to herself nine years before, that she would return to the China Sea to help save others, that she would be on a ship that would not pass boat people by.

▶ **Thuy:**

"They have been at sea for ten days, drifting without food and water. For the last few days, the children had to drink their urine and... they... were about to die because they said that they couldn't get help from other ships passing by. They all expected to die."

▶ **Thuy:**

"Only those of us who stayed behind after 1975 would understand why did we leave, why do we have to leave. Over there where we belonged, over there were our home, our friends... Something's haunting me, something forced me to come back here,... to do something... to try... to make a little difference on others' lives."

▶ **Hugh Downs:**

Oh, she is determined to help others! It's moving!

▶ **Stone:**

She is.

▶ **Hugh:**

Stone, what happened to those people after they left the boat?

▶ **Stone:**

Of the 40, 25 were resettled immediately in France, the other 15 were taken onboard the Mary to the Philippines to await resettlement. Since our trip, the Mary has been back to the South China Sea twice and has picked up 454 more refugees.

▶ **Hugh:**

Now, people were in desperation to try these boat routes. They must have suffered...

▶ **Stone:**

Thuy and her husband are writing a book recounting these stories.

Vu Thanh Thuy (center) and the ABC News' "20/20" crew. Next to Thuy are producer Ene Riisna and correspondent Stone Phillips (kneeling).

ABC News "20/20" Senior Producer Ene Riisna and Vu Thanh Thuy on the French Navy's helicopter carrier Jeanne d'Arc (4-1988). Photo: Stone Phillips.

INDEX

A

B

Fay, Sam Kai 240
Fonda, Jane 72, 260
Four-Party Joint Military Commision 256-257, 261, 277

G

Geneva Accord 1954 359
Graham Martin 36

H

Hanoi 37, 72, 102-103, 120-122, 124-125, 129, 155-157, 166, 190, 256-258, 261, 277, 302-303, 360
Hanoi Hilton 72
Ha Thuc Nhon 216
Hebert, Gerald 229, 240-241
Highway of Terror 237, 239-240, 245, 247, 253
Ho Chi Minh 11, 68, 107, 121, 133, 140, 150, 257, 272, 289
Ho Chi Minh Trail 133, 140, 150
Ho Ngoc Nhuận 178
Hoa Hung 76, 80, 321, 326, 362
Hoa Lo Prison/Hanoi Hilton 72, 120, 256, 258-261, 277
Hoa, Xuan Loc prisoner 306, 310
Hoang Duc Nha 151-152, 178, 206
Hoang Hoa Tham 127
Hoang Thi Thinh 155
Hoang Xuan Lam 141, 153
Hoc Mon 128
Hong Son Đong 178
Hue 25, 64, 89, 117-118, 133-134, 136, 138, 146, 149-150, 179-182, 236, 244-248, 250, 262
Hue, Xuan Loc prisoner 304-306
Hung, Phu Quoc prisoner 98
Huy Cuong 53
Huynh Phi Long 426
Huynh Tan Mam 311
Huynh Van Phu 252

I

Independence Palace 37, 75, 150, 219

J

Jesuits 41, 44
Joannidis, Marie 154, 205-206, 214, 221, 381

K

Kamm, Henry 451
Kennedy, Jacqueline 170
Khe Sanh 140-141, 151, 153-154, 221, 224
Khoo, Terry 240
Kissinger, Henry 260
Koh Kra 17, 385-386, 395, 412, 420, 422, 424-425, 428-433, 437, 441, 443, 445-448, 453-455, 459-462
Kontum 25
Ky, Long Giao prisoner 108-110, 275

L

La Qui Trang 136
Lam Son 719 140, 149, 151-152
Lan, Xuan Loc prisoner 306
Le Duy Hoang 169
Le Hung 460
Le Minh 214
Le Phu Nhuan 127, 135, 138
Le Thi Phung 169-170
Le Thiep 223, 241-242
Le Trung Hien 150
Le Van Bao 315
Le Van Hung 222, 224, 230-234, 236
Le Van Me 253-255
Little Saigon Radio 250
Long An 25
Long Giao 73, 95, 103-105, 108, 111, 267-269, 271, 277, 281, 288, 291-292, 294-297, 308, 312, 327, 354

M

N

O

P

Radio-Voice of Freedom (VOF) 23, 83, 141, 154, 220, 226, 242, 249-251
Radio-Voice of Saigon 46, 125-127, 129, 133, 135, 141, 146, 150, 178, 216, 220, 223, 226, 229-231, 241-242, 248-249
Rangers 127-128, 194-197, 201-203, 217-218, 233
River- Ben Hai 133
River-Hong (Red) 257
River-Huong (Perfume) 117, 247
River-My Chanh 252
River-Saigon 264, 322
River-Tau O 223
River-Tchepone 142

S

Saigon 15, 23-26, 29, 31-34, 36-38, 41, 45-47, 49, 52, 54, 59-64, 66, 70, 76, 78, 81-82, 87, 92, 96, 101-103, 112, 122-127, 129, 135, 139-141, 146, 150-154, 157, 160-162, 165-166, 169, 172-173, 175, 177-180, 184, 191, 205-206, 210, 213, 216-217, 220, 222-223, 226, 229-232, 241-242, 248-251, 253, 255, 261, 263-264, 271, 276, 278, 281-282, 290-292, 294-296, 302, 307, 311, 314-316, 319-320, 322, 328-332, 337, 339, 352-354, 356, 359, 368, 376, 398, 451, 459, 463-464
Sang, Xuan Loc prisoner 306
School-Fraternite 166
School-Ho Ngoc Can 156-157
School-Marie Curie 166
School-Nguyen Ba Tong 173
School-Pasteur 166, 169, 172
School-Trung Vuong 158
Schweitzer, Theodore III 17, 445-453, 455-456
Sgt. Ly 127-128
Silver Star 214, 251
Sis Duong Lan 17-18, 35, 46, 50, 352-356, 358, 399, 411, 413, 424-428, 430-431
Sis Khanh, Xuan Loc prisoner 305-310, 312-313
Sister Phi 349-351
Sis Thiem, Xuan Loc prisoner 306
Sis Thu, boatmate 375, 414-416, 418
Son, Armored Major 196, 198
Southeast Asia 185, 219, 451, 454, 459, 462
South China Sea 365, 458-459, 462, 466
South Laos 133, 140, 142, 149, 151-152, 249, 277
Special Forces 138-189, 226

Sully, Francois 216, 219-220

T

Ta Anh 97-98, 104, 108, 275-276, 328
Tam, Airborne captain 254-255
Tam, Xuan Loc prison 306
Tan 97, 104, 108
Tan Dinh 353-354
Tchepone 142, 151
Television-Saigon 151, 232, 332
Television&Film-Armed Forces 142, 228, 240, 249
Tet Offensive 125, 145, 149, 179-181
Thai, Xuan Loc prisoner 306
Thai Binh 102, 155-157, 161
Thai Thuy 129
Thailand 17, 342, 369, 381-382, 385, 390, 432, 447, 449, 451-454, 456-457, 459
Thanh Hoa 117-118, 134
Thanh Tam Tuyen 124
Thanh, Airborne Major 254
Thanh, Xuan Loc prisoner 306
The Frequent Wind Operation 36
The, Communist Cadre 258, 260-262
Thom, pirate 422-430, 434-437, 439, 448, 450, 452
Thu Duc 158, 329
Thu Duc Military Academy 129
To Pham Lieu 254
Tran Da Tu-Nha Ca 330
Tran Dai 329, 341
Tran Luc 123-124
Tran Minh Hoang 101-103, 327
Tran Quang Khoi 192-193, 199, 217
Tran Quoc Lich 252-254
Tran Thi Duyen 19, 88-91, 100, 102, 267, 271, 323, 341, 366, 466
Tran Thien Khiem 35
Tran Thien Thanh 143
Tran Van Don 206
Tran Van Hai 127-128
Tran Van Huong 35-36, 151, 252-253
Tran Van Nghia 240, 245

X

SH PUBLISHING

10613 BELLAIRE BLVD, STE 900
HOUSTON, TX 77072
Phone: (713) 917-0050
Fax: (713) 917-0213
Email: vnmemoir@survivingvn.com
Website: www.survivingvn.com

Made in the USA
Coppell, TX
09 April 2021